The Taste of Ashes

The Taste of Ashes

The Afterlife of Totalitarianism
in Eastern Europe

Marci Shore

WILLIAM HEINEMANN: LONDON

First published in Great Britain in 2013 by
William Heinemann
Random House, 20 Vauxhall Bridge Road,
London SW1V 2SA

www.randomhouse.co.uk

Addresses for companies within The Random House Group Limited can be found at:
www.randomhouse.co.uk/offices.htm

The Random House Group Limited Reg. No. 954009

A CIP catalogue record for this book
is available from the British Library

ISBN 9780434022304

The Random House Group Limited supports The Forest Stewardship Council (FSC˚), the leading international forest certification organisation. Our books carrying the FSC label are printed on FSC˚ certified paper. FSC is the only forest certification scheme endorsed by the leading environmental organisations, including Greenpeace. Our paper procurement policy can be found at:
www.randomhouse.co.uk/environment

Printed and bound in Great Britain by Clays Ltd, St Ives Plc

Timuszkowi

CONTENTS

AUTHOR'S NOTE

This is a work of nonfiction. I have, however, changed the names (and in a single case an identifying profession) of many of the book's protagonists who are not public figures, in an effort to protect their privacy. A further note: because this book includes many citations from a variety of spoken and written sources, in the interest of clarity I have put quotations from oral sources in quotation marks and quotations from written sources in italics.

PREFACE

Eastern Europe is special. It is Europe, only more so. It is a place where people live and die, only more so. In these lands between the West and Russia, the past is palpable, and heavy. The past is also merciless: by history's caprice, here the Second World War and communism were inseparable historical traumas, one bleeding into the other, as Nazi power gave way to Soviet domination.

I came to Eastern Europe for the first time in 1993, knowing almost nothing. The previous summer, at the carnivalesque parking lot of a Grateful Dead concert in Northern California, I had sat on the grass amid the Deadheads, who were braiding hair, selling bagels, and smoking marijuana, and read Václav Havel's essays, the essays that had originally been published secretly, in *samizdat* editions. I was mesmerized by the romance of the Velvet Revolution, seemingly so untainted, and by the imprisoned playwright who became a philosopher-president, who went to live in a magnificent castle, and who made Frank Zappa one of his advisers. Havel seemed so generous, so loving toward the world, so *good*.

I came to Eastern Europe because I wanted to hear a story that ended happily. I wanted to learn how the philosophers came to power and the people were liberated. I wanted to understand the anticommunist dissidents of the 1970s and 1980s, who had been unafraid to "speak truth to power." Yet I found myself drawn into an ever more distant past: to understand the dissidents I needed

to understand the Marxist revisionists calling for a more democratic socialism who preceded them; to understand the Marxist revisionists of the 1960s I needed to understand the Stalinists of the
1950s; to understand Stalinism I needed to understand the Second
World War and the Holocaust; to understand the war I needed to
understand the depression and fascism of the 1930s and the un-
hinging, the dizzying possibilities, of the 1920s. And so while this
book moves forward in time from the early 1990s through the second postcommunist decade, it also moves backward in time, from
the 1980s to the years immediately following the First World War.
The pivot is the revolutions of 1989, which ended communism and
brought me to Europe.

All historical drama is acted through the lives of individuals.
The postcommunist moment that followed the revolutions of 1989
was a moment of disorienting freedom: spaces suddenly opened
for people to play new roles. They could find themselves inadver-
tently, as if by accident, in positions of power. The postcommunist
moment was also one of generational estrangement: in 1989 age
suddenly mattered very much. From its nineteenth-century beginning, communism had always been a generational history, a Freud-
ian family romance, each generation killing the fathers in its turn.
The fall of communism did not end the silences of one's parents or
resolve the feelings of guilt by contiguity with the crimes of earlier generations; it rather heightened demands for accounting with
the past. This desire for accounting raised disquieting questions:
Could the boundary between public and private, nearly effaced by
totalitarianism, be restored? Could the intimate and the political
be disentangled? The eclipsing of private space was among totalitarianism's deepest violations. In this way the totalitarian state was
unlike its merely authoritarian or monarchical predecessors: it distinguished itself—*it made itself*—by caring what lovers said in bed.
Was it possible to restore human dignity through truth, if arriving
at truth involved gazing anew through old peepholes?

Shortly after his defection to the West in 1951, the Polish poet
Czesław Miłosz wrote, "The man of the East cannot take Americans

seriously because they have never undergone the experiences that teach men how relative their judgments and thinking habits are." For half a century, on the eastern half of the European continent, people made decisions, often in extreme moments, most never believing that communism would end in their lifetimes, many never imagining that they would have to account for their choices in a world where all the rules had changed. This book tells a story about the darker side of the fall of communism, about the lingering presence of the past. After 1989 the ability to reinvent oneself was circumscribed: no one, after all, could change his previous life. Freedom meant being liberated, but also exposed. Openness was a key to both a treasure chest of knowledge about the past and a Pandora's box of unanswerable questions. This is a story, too, about the inescapable interplay between historical fate and individual choice. There were historical situations in which no decisions were innocent ones, in which all significant action was a betrayal of someone or something, in which all possible choices caused suffering. Nonetheless one had to choose. In twentieth-century Eastern Europe tragedy was endemic.

The lives of East Europeans after communism reveal the necessity of choice, the omnipresence of guilt, and the impossibility of closure. In the pages that follow these dilemmas are illuminated in large measure through an extreme case: Stalinists and the lives of their children and grandchildren. They are illuminated, too, through the lives of other former dissidents and former Stalinists, poets and politicians, Jews and Gentiles, Zionists and communists, old people and young people, brothers and sisters, husbands and wives, lovers and friends, those who stayed and those who left, those who killed themselves, those who reinvented themselves, and those who live on.

I arrived in Eastern Europe as the communist archives were opening. Archival work—reading pages from the lives of others—is a profoundly invasive act: it is staring at many things that were never meant to be seen. Often I have thought of Margaret Atwood's dystopian novel *The Handmaid's Tale*, recounting a woman's life as a reproductive slave in a terror-filled world, where the Eyes were always watching. In the novel's final chapter, set long after the gruesome events, historians sit calmly in a conference room, earnestly trying to understand a totalitarian hell that has by then long passed. They are aware that their sources are partial and leave many questions unanswered. They are aware that "the past is a great darkness, and filled with echoes." They are aware, too, that people may have conflicting motives: the self-interested and the sentimental are often entangled. "We must be cautious about passing moral judgment," says the historian presenting a paper about the recently discovered manuscript by "The Handmaid." "Surely we have learned by now that such judgments are of necessity culture-specific." The historians who appear at the end of Margaret Atwood's novel are doing nothing wrong, yet the reader feels something chilling in their scholarly detachment.

Being a historian in postcommunist Eastern Europe has very often felt disconcertingly like finding oneself in the last chapter of Margaret Atwood's novel. Empathy does soften detachment—yet this is an empathy itself born in voyeurism. Understanding the past is inextricably bound up with guilt: writing history demands an imaginative leap into a time and a place where one was not, an exercise insisting upon a simultaneous violation of and identification with the other. This book, in a sense, lays bare the ambivalent process of writing history. It also, I hope, reveals something about what it means to understand.

The Taste of Ashes

In April of 1995 I sat in a Prague café with Amanda, two days before the memorial mass she had arranged for Oskar. It was late. The spring was cold that year. We sat upstairs where it was dark and smoky, eating ice cream. Amanda insisted on paying for the ice cream because, as she said, she was "now an heiress." I was telling her about my young student, a smart girl with the rugged prettiness of a tomboy whose brown hair fell just below her chin. In an essay composed in her grasping English she wrote about the boy who had once held her hand and called her "sweetheart." One summer day he went off to his cottage in the countryside. When he returned he told her he had made love to an older girl. My student's tears and cigarettes, all of it too harsh for a fourteen-year-old girl. Her final sentence: *You know, I think that life can be very cruel sometimes*. And I had wanted to write on her paper: *Oh, but you don't know, it gets so much worse!*

But Amanda, the artist from New England whose Czech husband had just killed himself, told me, "No, that's it. That's as bad as it gets."

And I believed then that it was true.

Two days later I went with Amanda to the Catholic mass dedicated to Oskar, Oskar who had waited twenty-five years to return to Prague, only to find that he no longer had any home there. In the church tucked, as if concealed, behind Old Town Square, I took communion for the first time, although I was not a Catholic, although I was not even a Christian, although I did not believe in God.

Several hours later we were sitting in the apartment of Oskar's sister. She was matronly, prematurely aged, nothing like her brother, the stylish, cosmopolitan physicist. Oskar had been handsome, sexy well into middle age. His sister and brother-in-law lived on an upper floor of one of the many faceless high-rises built of gray concrete. In their time these socialist housing projects had created thousands of identical units for modern, single-family living. Now inside these run-down apartments there lingered the aura of communist-era bourgeois. On Oskar's sister's old wooden table there was food and wine, red wine in Bohemian crystal set against Amanda's beautiful silver hair. There were layers of aesthetic paradox: Amanda, the bohemian from Massachusetts, in the bourgeois communist apartment.

Oskar's brother-in-law poured the wine. Amanda and Oskar's friends, a woman named Korina and her husband, had come from Paris for the memorial service. They were scientists, young and attractive, eager to communicate. I translated, awkwardly, for Oskar's sister and brother-in-law.

Hours passed. In a few minutes it would be midnight. Amanda was consumed by the thought now: it was the first of May, the Czech holiday of love. *It was late in the evening, the first of May / May evening, the time of love / Voice of a dove calling to love / Where fragrance drifted from the pines.* With these lines Karel Hynek Mácha, Czech romanticism's greatest poet, had made it impossible for the communists to make the workers' holiday of May Day fully their own.

It was the first of May and Amanda wanted to give Oskar a gift.

We moved into the kitchen.

"Ask her for a pair of scissors," Amanda said to me, turning her head toward Oskar's unhappy sister.

I hesitated. I did not want to ask her, she would not want to give the American sister-in-law she barely knew a pair of scissors at a fragile moment. Amanda remained for her an alien, unfathomable creature from a decadent foreign world, with whom she shared no language, with whom she shared nothing but Oskar, who was now dead.

Amanda insisted.

"Why?" Oskar's sister asked.

I said nothing.

"Why?" she asked me again.

I shrugged, smiled weakly, Otto's sister brought the pair of scissors. I held Amanda's hand, and Korina, the scientist who had come from Paris to say goodbye to Oskar, took the pair of scissors in her hands. Amanda shut her eyes. Korina began to cut. A moment later she held between her fingers Amanda's long, silver ponytail. Beautiful, like sparkling ashes.

Now we left the kitchen and returned to the small living room where wineglasses still stood on the wooden table. I watched as Korina sat down on her knees on the wooden floor, reaching out to touch the porcelain. She put her finger into the urn and tasted Oskar's ashes.

In a moment Amanda was gone. She had fled the apartment, flown down the staircase. When I found her below on the dark Prague streets, her dress was already wet, the disembodied silver ponytail she held in her hand whisked about in the storm. Korina and her husband and I followed her, running drunkenly through Prague in the rain, Amanda clutching her ponytail, the rain-drenched silver turning to gray.

A Wrinkle in Time

One April morning in 1989 I saw the headline: Abbie Hoffman had killed himself. He had fought for civil rights and against the Vietnam War. He had thrown dollar bills from the roof of the New York Stock Exchange and held a séance outside the Pentagon to levitate its evil spirits. When, following the antiwar protests in Chicago during the 1968 Democratic Convention, Abbie Hoffman and seven of his friends were put on trial for conspiracy to riot, he appeared in the courtroom in judicial robes. His lawyer called upon Allen Ginsberg to read his poetry as testimony for the defense. The antiwar activists did not have a sympathetic judge: he issued more than two hundred citations, to the defendants and their lawyers alike, for contempt of court. "You are a *shande far di goyim*," Abbie Hoffman told the judge. You shame us in front of the goyim.

"Democracy is not something you believe in or a place to hang your hat, it's something you *do*," Abbie Hoffman continued to insist. The proper response to social injustice, he believed, was moral outrage. I was fifteen when I first discovered Abbie Hoffman's *Steal This Book* in a dusty college library. By then—1987—his onetime fellow revolutionary Tom Hayden had entered mainstream politics, and Jerry Rubin had abandoned his "Pig for President" campaign in favor of Wall Street finance. Abbie Hoffman, though, held tight to his earthy idealism. On the banks of the Delaware River he persisted, fighting to save the water from a nuclear power station's pumping project. Until, one day twenty years after the Chicago trial, when he was living in a converted turkey coop and making a one-dollar-per-year salary from a local environmental group, Abbie Hoffman gave up.

I felt crushed by the suicide of the man who had continued to fight for a better world even when the times were no longer his times. That summer, having just finished my junior year of high school, I traveled some two hours to a public memorial service for Abbie Hoffman in Washington Crossing Park, not far from the gentrifying countercultural enclave of New Hope, Pennsylvania, where I'd once bought a pair of peace-sign earrings. The park commission had not been receptive; its chairwoman believed this was an event honoring the wrong kind of person. The environmentalist organizers were undaunted, perhaps even pleased: they threatened a First Amendment lawsuit. The park commission relented. The gathering was named "Steal This Picnic." The program included some of the organizers' favorite Abbie Hoffman quotes: *"The Constitution does not begin, 'We the Philadelphia Electric Company.'" "The people must prevail if democracy is to survive."* At the picnic Allen Ginsberg read his poetry, Richie Havens played the guitar, and Bobby Seale of the Black Panthers sold his cookbook, *Barbeque'n with Bobby*, to raise bail money, he explained.

The mourners wore tie-dyed T-shirts and red, white, and blue buttons proclaiming, "Abbie lives!" Then came the scent of patchouli mixed with exhaust fumes as Vietnam veterans in black leather on Harley-Davidson motorcycles stormed the park, revving their motors and shouting, "Pinko commie fag!" and "We hate Abbie! Abbie is a commie!"

The motorcycle-riding veterans too, were soon to become an anachronism: these were the final days of the cold war. In the Soviet Union, Mikhail Gorbachev had already come to power. In Poland, the very same April when the American revolutionary Abbie Hoffman died, opponents of the communist regime sat down with communists at a roundtable and planned elections. That November the Berlin Wall fell. Within ten days, the Velvet

Revolution in Czechoslovakia began. The following month in Bucharest, at a mass rally for Romania's communist dictators, Nicolae
and Elena Ceaușescu, the cheers suddenly turned into boos. On
Christmas Day the Ceaușescus were executed by firing squad. Four
days later, on 29 December 1989, the dissident playwright Václav
Havel became president of Czechoslovakia.

Communism, as Americans had understood it, was over.

I knew very little about communism then.

▪ ▪ ▪

"WORKERS OF THE world unite!" Karl Marx and Friedrich Engels
concluded their *Communist Manifesto* in 1848. One day soon the
exploited working classes around the world would together rise up
and overthrow their oppressors, the bourgeoisie. Eventually private
property would be abolished and the state would wither away. Everyone would work according to his ability and receive according
to his need. Everyone would live in a just, peaceful, happy world.

The Communist Manifesto was not only a political program but
also a philosophy of history, a prophecy: history was moving inexorably in this direction. Feudalism had given way to capitalism,
and in turn capitalism would naturally yield to communism—as
soon as the working class came to understand its predestined
revolutionary role. And the working class *would* come to understand its role. "Being precedes consciousness," Marxism insisted.
This meant that a person's objective position in the socioeconomic
order—whether one was a factory worker or a factory owner, an
exploited employee or an exploiting employer—was determinate.
Consciousness—how a person thought—was derivative, following
naturally from concrete existence. Decades passed, the nineteenth
century neared its end, and in most parts of Europe the working
class remained rather small. Moreover, the workers seemed to be
taking some time to acquire class consciousness as Marx had understood it.

Then came the First World War. Suddenly the old Europe was
going up in flames. It was very dark and very cold in March 1917,

in the Russian Empire's capital of Petrograd. In a city drained by two and a half years of war, bread shortages inspired strikes, demonstrations, and mutiny among Tsar Nicholas II's troops. Unable to maintain order, Nicholas II abdicated his throne. The new provisional government convened a militia in the countryside; peasants revolted by seizing land and refusing to deliver grain. In the cities there were food shortages. A disenchanted population grew radical.

At this time the revolutionary Vladimir Il'ich Lenin was in Switzerland—perhaps the best place to be if one had to be in Europe during a European war. Lenin, though, wanted above all to get back to Russia. When in April 1917 he arrived in exhausted, hungry Petrograd, he and his fellow Bolsheviks—in Lenin's own words—"found power lying in the streets and picked it up." In the midst of anarchy, the Bolsheviks denounced compromise and insisted on acting at once. A child of backward Russia, Lenin had no desire to wait for feudalism to evolve into industrial capitalism, then for class consciousness to develop among the proletariat. This would take too long. Lenin was impatient.

When in November 1917 Lenin and the Bolsheviks stormed the Winter Palace in Petrograd, they were carrying out a workers' revolution in a country of peasants. The workers on whose behalf the Bolsheviks made the revolution were metaphysical ones, yet to come into being. In any case—Lenin believed when he made his separate peace with the Germans in March 1918—rushing History in slow-moving Russia would be anomalous only for a moment: any day now, the worldwide workers' revolution would come.

It didn't. Instead the First World War ended with the fall of four empires: the Ottoman, the Tsarist Russian, the Habsburg, and the German. At the negotiating table at Versailles, the victors—the French, the British, and the Americans—drew up a new map of Eastern Europe, creating nation-states and willing them to be democracies. Yet with the exception of Czechoslovakia, the new states remained democratic only for a moment. Liberalism soon fell out of fashion, victim to a spirit of polarization: the Right became ever more radical, the Left became ever more radical, and the center, in Marx's phrase, "melted into air."

In the meantime, in the former Russian Empire, a series of civil wars had ended with the Bolsheviks' victory. Yet just as the Bolsheviks founded the Soviet Union in December 1922, Lenin fell ill. His premature death in 1924 led to a power struggle between Joseph Stalin and Leon Trotsky. Stalin won. He collectivized agriculture and built industry—at an extraordinary human cost. While Stalin violently requisitioned grain to fund industrialization, millions of peasants starved to death. People were driven mad by hunger; there was cannibalism in the countryside. Stalin was unfazed: the Soviet Union had to catch up to the West, to History.

Socialism, Stalin declared in the 1930s, was now victorious—or nearly so. Yet he warned that it was precisely now, when the achievement of socialism seemed so assured, that the enemy became all the more malignant. At this final moment before socialism's ultimate triumph the class struggle intensified: the enemy, desperate, resorted to masking himself. He could be anywhere—including in the Communist Party's own ranks, including in one's own bed. Thus did the Soviet Union descend into terror. Arrests were made by night. False confessions were extracted by torture. Executions took place in prison chambers. Guilt spread like an epidemic. Everyone became infinitely powerful and infinitely vulnerable at once: anyone could inform on anyone else—and thus at any moment become his neighbor's executioner.

Throughout Europe, the 1930s were a dark decade. After coming to rule Germany in 1933, Adolf Hitler consolidated his power during the years of the Stalinist terror. When at the end of the decade the Third Reich began the Second World War, Eastern Europe was caught between Hitler and Stalin—the worst possible place to be. First Nazi Germany and the Soviet Union invaded Poland together. Then the Nazis betrayed their ally and invaded the Soviet Union. It was then, following their June 1941 attack on the Soviet Union, that the Germans murdered the Jews of Eastern Europe. Later German fortunes turned, and the Soviets returned to Eastern

Europe. For the most part, they stayed. The years between 1945 and 1948 were years of unstable coalitions and encroaching totalitarianism. In the end, Albania, Bulgaria, Czechoslovakia, Hungary, Poland, Romania, and Yugoslavia became communist states—as did the northeastern part of Germany that had found itself under Soviet occupation at the war's end. To many East Europeans, it was unclear whether they had won or lost the war. For after the war came Stalinism: in the Soviet Union's new satellite states East European communist parties imported the communist economic system and replayed the Stalinist terror of the 1930s—mass arrests, torture, show trials, executions.

Stalin's life was long. In Warsaw, in the 1990s, there lived still an elderly Trotskyite named Ludwik Haas, who had spent seventeen years in Stalin's gulag—for believing in the wrong kind of socialism. Unlike so many others, Ludwik Haas had endured—and survived. A deformed finger was a memento of his time there.

"I knew Stalin could not live forever," he said.

And this was true: even Stalin could not live forever. He died in March 1953. Three years passed after Stalin's death before Stalin's successor, Nikita Khrushchev, openly criticized his predecessor. In his "secret speech" of February 1956, Khrushchev conceded that under Stalin there had been "excesses."

With this very limited acknowledgment of Stalin's crimes, Stalinism came to an end. This meant the fall of some communists and the rise—or rehabilitation—of others. In Poland, the nationally minded communist Władysław Gomułka was quietly released from house arrest and appointed the new Communist Party leader. In Hungary de-Stalinization proceeded more vigorously. Hungarian premier Imre Nagy wanted socialism—only a more democratic version. But he went too far. After he proclaimed a multiparty system and an independent foreign policy, Soviet tanks put a stop to Hungary's revolution. Houses were burned and gutted; thousands of Hungarians were killed or imprisoned. In the years that followed the bloodshed, the new Soviet-approved government knew that it was unwanted. And so compromises were made: the Party would retain its monopoly on power, but terror would relent. The people would not challenge the authority of the state, which in return would allow them some private space. The Party would deem sufficiently loyal anyone not ostentatiously rebellious. A bit of prudent economic reform would raise standards of living. This was "goulash communism," and in time Hungary became known as "the most cheerful barrack in the Soviet camp."

Hungary, it seemed, had learned its lessons. Other Soviet satellite states had not. Twelve years later, in 1968, Czechoslovakia's Alexander Dubček led the region's next attempt to practice a more democratic socialism: a mixed economy, internal Communist Party democracy, freedom of speech. Dubček and his supporters had not forgotten Imre Nagy's fatal misstep: under Dubček's program the Communist Party would remain the single political party, and Czechoslovakia would remain a loyal member of the Warsaw Pact. Nonetheless history replayed itself. A century earlier Marx had written, *"Hegel remarks somewhere that all great, world-historical facts and personages occur, as it were twice. He forgot to add: the first time as tragedy, the second as farce."* Yet in this case the second time, too, was tragedy. Soviet—formally Warsaw Pact—tanks arrived in Prague as they had in Budapest a dozen years earlier. In this way hopes for "socialism with a human face" came to an end. Yet it was not a year without farce. In Poland, in the spring of 1968, the Polish United Workers' Party blamed student protests on "Zionist conspirators," using the demonstrations against censorship as a pretext to unleash an anti-Semitic campaign. Now communists propagated fantastical accusations of a Nazi-Zionist conspiracy against Poland. Thirteen thousand Polish Jews—many survivors of the Holocaust, believers in communism, Polish citizens deeply attached to Poland—gave up their Polish passports in exchange for exit visas.

The disillusionments of 1968 were the beginning of the end of European Marxism.

In 1975, inspired by a détente in the cold war, governments in the East and West met in Finland to sign the Helsinki Accords. Now the Soviet Union and its satellite states traded Western acceptance of the "inviolability of frontiers" for guarantees of human rights. Participating states promised to respect freedom of thought, conscience, and religion. Many believed that the communist governments' signatures on the Helsinki Accords were of merely symbolic value. This was true. Yet that did not prevent the Helsinki Accords from providing Western and Eastern Europeans with a new language of human rights—a language to replace Marxism. And in the years to come this would matter quite a lot.

▪ ▪ ▪

IN 1968, WHEN Polish students demonstrated against censorship, most workers, especially those older than the students, did not support them. Two years later, when Polish workers went on strike to protest price increases, the students paid them back—they did not join the workers' protests. It was only in 1976 that intellectuals reached out to the workers and formed the Workers' Defense Committee. Not long afterward, Krakow's Archbishop Karol Wojtyła became Pope John Paul II. In 1979, he made his first papal visit to Poland. A million people came to hear him.

"I must ask myself, as all of you must ask yourselves," Pope John Paul II said to his fellow Poles, "why it was that in the year 1978 . . . a son of the Polish nation, a son of Poland, should be called to the Chair of St. Peter. Christ required Peter, like the other apostles, to be his 'witnesses in Jerusalem, throughout Judea and Samaria, yes, even to the ends of the earth.' With these words of Christ in mind, are we not perhaps justified in thinking that *Poland in our time has become a land called to give an especially important witness?*"

A year later, in the summer of 1980, Polish workers—first those in the Baltic shipyards, then others throughout the country—went on strike. When members of the communist regime headed to the Baltic port city of Gdańsk, intellectuals from Warsaw traveled there as well and offered to help the workers negotiate with the government. Only in Poland, among all the communist bloc countries, did intellectuals and workers come together to form a mass movement.

This was how—in the wake of Pope John Paul II's visit and in the spirit of the Workers' Defense Committee—Solidarity was born. Solidarity was something special. It was not only a trade union but also a national experience of civil society. It was a name with real content: people of the right and left, Marxists and Catholics, intellectuals and workers—together some 10 million people—united against an oppressive regime. "History has taught us," Solidarity's program declared, "that there is no bread without freedom."

Solidarity's leaders considered theirs a "self-limiting" revolution: one that would not go too far. They would respect socialist ownership over the means of production; they would not challenge the Party's leading role in the state; they would not provoke a Soviet intervention. Yet like Imre Nagy in Hungary and Alexander Dubček in Czechoslovakia, now, too, Solidarity in Poland miscalculated: it overestimated how much independent initiative the communist government—and the Soviet Union—would tolerate. This time, though, Soviet tanks did not come. Rather, Soviet leader Leonid Brezhnev demanded that the Polish government itself resolve the problem. On 13 December 1981 the Polish communist prime minister, General Wojciech Jaruzelski, declared martial law. Solidarity was driven underground; its leading activists were arrested.

After 1968, opposition to the regimes existed in other, more modest forms throughout the communist bloc. In Czechoslovakia the human rights petition Charter 77 became its own movement, relying, like Solidarity, on *samizdat*—underground self-publishing. One Charter signatory, the Catholic dissident Václav Benda, described Charter 77 as a "parallel *polis*," a second society shadowing the official one, a nascent civil society forced underground.

Hungary, Poland, and Czechoslovakia, to varying degrees and in various ways, developed this parallel *polis* after 1968—Romania did not. There communist dictator Nicolae Ceaușescu broke away from Soviet domination only to lead Romania back to Stalinism, now in nationalist, dynastic form. Eager for more Romanians, Ceaușescu mandated gynecological testing and enacted draconian antiabortion laws. He demanded industrialization at any price, incurring foreign debt and then repaying it at the cost of his people. There were power shortages and food shortages; bread was rationed. In the winter people froze. Hospitals were unheated and infant mortality rates were high. Ceauşescu's secret police, the Securitate, were ubiquitous; living conditions more dire and repression more brutal than elsewhere in the communist bloc contributed to the absence of anything comparable to Solidarity or Charter 77. Ceauşescu's neo-Stalinism was no less a tragedy for being a farce: extravagant, crazed, and megalomaniacal, Ceauşescu had an insatiable appetite for praise. The Genius of the Carpathians, the Danube of Thought, the Shepherd and Savior of the Nation, and the Conscience of the World built a vast palace for himself and his wife, Elena, in Bucharest as the Romanian people starved.

"We are 22 million people living in the imagination of a madman," the Romanian novelist Alexandru Ivasiuc wrote.

On the day in December 1989 that the paratroopers captured the Ceauşescus, Nicolae was dressed in a dark three-piece suit that accentuated his lively white hair. Elena wore a long yellow coat and a satin scarf tied peasant-style under her chin. Loose strands of hair fell from a bun around her long nose. Sitting on small chairs designed for schoolchildren, Nicolae and Elena Ceauşescu held hands during their summary trial.

"You had palaces," the prosecutor said.

"No, we had no palaces, the palaces belong to the people," Nicolae Ceauşescu answered.

It was a very short trial. Afterward paratroopers tied the Ceauşescus' hands behind their backs and led them outside.

■ ■ ■

THE HUNGARIAN AND Polish communist regimes fell in 1989 after peaceful, if tense, negotiations. The new Hungarian government opened its border to Austria. Suddenly East Germans rushed through Hungary to Austria, and from Austria to West Germany. Disconcerted, East German authorities then made the decision to

open the border in Berlin. Since 1961 the Berlin Wall had symbolized a Europe divided by an "Iron Curtain." Over the years East
Germans had crawled through tunnels in the earth, desperate to
get to the other side. Above ground East German border guards had
shot to death those they caught trying to cross. Then one day—9
November 1989—the wall came down.

Two years later the Soviet Union itself ceased to exist.

The revolutions of 1989 spread from Poland to Romania via Hungary, East Germany, Czechoslovakia, and Bulgaria. They were like a
wrinkle in time: time, seemingly halted for so long, suddenly leapt
forward. To tens of millions of East Europeans the end of communism brought countless good things—above all a freedom the vast
majority of people never imagined they would live long enough to
see. Yet the end of communism also vindicated Freud's warning
that the repressed would return. For Freud the unconscious was
a dark psychic closet into which everything too disturbing for the
conscious mind was thrown. During the decades of communist
rule, the communist archives served a similar function. Freud, for
his part, had no illusions that coaxing the contents of that psychic
closet into consciousness would prove painless. And so it was with
the opening of the communist archives as well. *"A specter is haunting Europe—the specter of communism,"* wrote Marx and Engels in
1848. A century and a half later, communism, no longer a specter *to
come,* remained no less haunting as a specter from the past.

Truth

In February 1990, as the new president of postcommunist Czechoslovakia, Václav Havel came to Washington, D.C., to give his first speech there.

"Consciousness precedes Being," Havel told the American congressmen. "And not the other way around, as the Marxists claim."

No one knew what this meant, but it sounded very beautiful.

"If I could talk like that," said one journalist, "I would run for God."

In June 1993, I arrived in Prague to do research for my undergraduate thesis. In the city women carried small dogs in large handbags, and in the metro the escalators moved unsettlingly quickly. Next to the Hradčany metro station, over the speakers at the outdoor café, I heard Dolly Parton and Kenny Rogers singing "Islands in the Stream," then B. J. Thomas singing "Raindrops Keep Falling on My Head." Just a few feet away cobblestone stairs led up toward the castle.

Prague Castle sat on a hill overlooking the Vltava River. The buildings of the castle itself were broad rather than tall, painted in pale pinks and creams and beiges and opening onto spacious courtyards. Above all, though, that space was defined not by the bright neoclassicism of the New Royal Palace but by the dark neo-Gothic of St. Vitus Cathedral, with its stained-glass windows and towering spires. The castle complex formed its own charmed world, with twisting alleyways, one leading into the early Renaissance "Golden

Lane" lined with houses painted sky blue, sun-baked yellow, and deep rose, miniature dwellings as if built for elves. It was an enchanted place. Yet outside the castle's walls, on the streets, Czechoslovakia was not—or was not only—a fairy tale. Prague in the summer of 1993 was a city in which all the old rules were no longer binding. And no one yet knew what the new rules would be. The end of communism had brought robber-baron capitalism: "free market" taken literally as a free-for-all with no accountability and little restraint.

I met a social psychologist named Martina in her thirties. She had spent time at American universities and spoke English well; now the fall of communism had opened to her the possibility of a transatlantic academic life. About her own society she was both proud and critical: for years the public had been pacified with relative stability and low prices; they had lived a lie, knowing all the while they were doing so. Martina taught me the communist-era saying "We pretend to work, and they pretend to pay us." The transition to capitalism she described as a move from a zoo into a jungle: with the fall of the oppressive regime, crime had increased wildly. More and more women had gone into prostitution. Neofascist skinheads roamed the streets. Moreover, communist mafias were still powerful, and what the Czechs called "lustration" had thrown the country into a moral crisis.

Lustration, a word with Latin origins, meant "purification." It was both a political vetting and a purging from public life of former communist collaborators. This meant in particular collaborators with the secret police—a sizable portion of the population, as Czechoslovak citizens learned after the Velvet Revolution when a former dissident named Petr Cibulka took it upon himself to publish an initial list.

Would you like to know—Martina asked—whether your neighbor, perhaps your friend or your lover, was a secret police informer?

▪ ▪ ▪

A FEW DAYS later I left for Bratislava, the capital of newly independent Slovakia. While, after 1989, Germany had come together,

Czechoslovakia had come apart. By the time I had arrived in Prague that summer, Czechoslovakia no longer existed: as of 1 January 1993 the Czech Republic and Slovakia were two independent countries. This was the context in which I met Miloš, who a few years earlier had been studying physics at Bratislava's Comenius University. Never a terribly diligent student, he did not become a physicist. Instead, in July 1992 he ran for parliament on the ticket of Movement for a Democratic Slovakia, a nationalist-populist party led by a demagogue named Vladimír Mečiar. Somewhat unexpectedly to himself, Miloš won. Just months later, in January 1993, came the "Velvet Divorce": Czechoslovakia ceased to exist. There had been no referendum. Miloš explained to me that a referendum would have been impossible: a referendum among all Czechoslovak citizens would have been unfair because there were twice as many Czechs as Slovaks in Czechoslovakia, so the Slovaks could easily have been outvoted. And a referendum among only Slovaks would have been unfair because if the Slovaks had then voted to secede, under international law the Czech Republic would have inherited the rights of successorship to Czechoslovakia. There were many who doubted that either Czechs or Slovaks would have voted for a separation had they had the occasion to vote—which they did not. Instead Vladimír Mečiar and his Czech counterpart, Václav Klaus, took it upon themselves to negotiate the dismantling of Czechoslovakia. In the summer of 1993, newly independent Slovakia was voted into the Council of Europe, the Strasbourg-based organization working toward European integration and the promotion of democracy. Miloš, who had little political experience but was handsome and cheerful, became Slovakia's representative to the Council of Europe. Now he was looking for an English tutor.

In Strasbourg, at the Council of Europe, Miloš had to give speeches in English. It was a language he spoke a bit, more or less without grammar—a matter of little concern to him. He was charming and could always communicate. I tried to explain the verb tenses. He laughed—there were too many, he hardly had use for so many, he was sure they wouldn't be necessary. I tried to help him edit the texts of his speeches, but he would always interrupt: we should go to a bar, get another drink. There was no need to be so serious.

We were always close to a bar, even though Bratislava felt small and provincial. Slovakia's capital city had none of Prague's glamour, yet it had its own appeal. A round fountain in the main square was surrounded by mannerist and art nouveau buildings painted in spring colors. Along the winding cobblestone streets of the old town were dozens of sidewalk cafés and wine cellars.

At thirty, Miloš was energetic and flirtatious. Happy-go-lucky. He had a baby and a young wife, both named Maria. Miloš and the grown-up Maria had met at the physics faculty, where she had been the better student.

"My woman," he would always say when speaking of her.

"My wife," I would correct him.

He never remembered.

I tried to explain: "*Wife* indicates a relationship: my brother, my father, my daughter, my wife. *Woman* is a generic noun. And when you add the possessive to a generic noun, it sounds as if you're claiming ownership."

He contemplated that for a moment.

"Like property?" he asked.

"Yes, exactly, like property," I said.

"Yes, yes, exactly—like property!"

Miloš and the two Marias and I traveled together through Slovakia to the spa town of Dudince. People came "for the water," Miloš told me, although I didn't see any water and we were far from the sea, among white hotels surrounded by green farmland. We went swimming in the hotel pool and rode in a horse-drawn carriage through the countryside. We took walks and drank red wine mixed with Coca-Cola, and Miloš talked to me about the revolution.

A few years earlier, while a student, Miloš had organized a film club at the university. American films were generally banned, as were films from the Czech New Wave of the 1960s. But Miloš was amiable and gregarious; he befriended the head of the film archive

and in this way managed to show some censored films like the ad-
aptations of Milan Kundera's *The Joke* and James Simon Kunen's
The Strawberry Statement, a chronicle of the 1968 student protests
at Columbia University. Miloš was also a competitive distance run-
ner who had represented Czechoslovakia in cross-country races
abroad. He had seen the West, and he planned to emigrate.

Then one day—it was 18 November 1989—Czech friends from
Prague unexpectedly came to visit. The Communist Party still controlled the newspapers, the radio, and the television, so Miloš's
friends had come in person to deliver the news: there were demonstrations in the capital. Now computer-savvy students at the technical faculty bypassed censorship by communicating with Prague
via computer modem. Soon Miloš found himself, as if inadver-
tently, in the middle of the revolution. In Bratislava he organized
student meetings; he was among those who presented a proposal
to parliament demanding that the Communist Party relinquish
its leading role in the state. The parliament conceded. Miloš found
this quite funny: he and his friends had hardly expected this. It had
been unthinkable just a day or two before.

Many days during that summer of 1993 I spent with Miloš at the
Slovak parliament, where sessions began early. All were working faster
than they otherwise might have: Slovakia was a brand-new state,
and the parliament needed to enact a basic set of laws—before the
country realized these basic laws were missing. So legislation was
being passed quickly. Between votes the parliamentarians would
gather for beer at a small café on the ground floor. Drinking began
at breakfast time.

One day in July, in the corridor outside the chamber where the
sessions took place, Miloš introduced me to Jan Čarnogurský,
chairman of the Christian Democratic Movement and a leader
of the anti-Mečiar opposition. Just after the Velvet Revolution
Čarnogurský had founded the Christian Democratic Movement,
a party with close ties to the Slovak Catholic Church. The party
opposed abortion and pornography, supported private education,
and called for the restitution of Church property nationalized

by the communists. It supported, too, a free market economy and
Slovakia's integration into the European Union. Mečiar's nationalism, the Christian Democrats believed, was a threat to democracy. Yet despite their politically antagonistic positions, toward Jan
Čarnogurský, as toward everyone else, Miloš seemed to have only
authentically friendly feelings. For his part, Jan Čarnogurský was
very gracious. He told me about himself: he'd grown up after the
Second World War in a Slovak Catholic family. He'd grown up
under communism, a militantly atheistic ideology; from the point
of view of the communist regime, religious observance was sub-
versive. When one year the communist police discovered a prayer
retreat in a Slovak mountain cottage, they imprisoned both the
organizer and the priest. By this time Jan Čarnogurský had become a lawyer, and he defended them. He served, too, as a defense
attorney for other dissidents: signatories of the human rights petition Charter 77; readers, writers, and distributors of *samizdat*
literature.

In August 1989 Jan Čarnogurský, like so many of those he had
defended, went to prison. That November the Velvet Revolution
freed him; on 10 December he was nominated first deputy prime
minister and sworn in as a member of the Czechoslovak federal
government, which then still existed. He was placed in charge
of the secret police—who just weeks before had been his interrogators.

About his years as a dissident, Jan Čarnogurský was reflective:
there had been some successes. In the 1980s international phone
lines were installed in public phone booths. Dissidents would telephone friends in the West, who would pass the information on to
Voice of America or Radio Free Europe—radio stations that would
then broadcast the news back into Czechoslovakia. A circuitous
route, yet an effective one. There had been many failures as well—
yet even the failures had often been moral victories. As a defense
lawyer in a communist state, he had not managed to free his clients
from prison; there had been no chance of that. Yet those he had defended had understood this: by making the choices they had, they

had knowingly risked imprisonment. It was worth it to them to know that they were doing the right thing.

For Jan Čarnogurský Christianity and democracy were naturally of a whole, and Christian democracy was a path to Western-style liberalism. He said nothing—and I did not ask him—about the very different Christian politics practiced in Slovakia once upon a time, decades earlier. It had happened after September 1938, after British prime minister Neville Chamberlain had "appeased" Adolf Hitler at the Munich conference, and Nazi Germany had annexed a western region of Czechoslovakia called the Sudetenland. Six months later, in March 1939, Nazi Germany invaded what remained of Czechoslovakia. The Czech lands of Bohemia and Moravia became a Third Reich protectorate. Slovakia became a Catholic fascist state—nominally independent, albeit under Nazi tutelage.

In 1987, Jan Čarnogurský had been among a handful of Slovak intellectuals who signed an open letter of collective remorse for Nazi-allied Slovakia's deportation of its Jews, first to Slovakia's own labor and concentration camps, and later to Auschwitz, Sobibor, and Majdanek. I didn't ask Jan Čarnogurský about this singular precedent of Slovak independence, but later, sitting on the grass by the Danube River, I did ask Miloš. When I mentioned fascism, Miloš laughed.

Yet he was emphatic: "We made boots, the Germans bought boots. This was not collaboration. This was work."

Slovak independence was important to him, and the wartime years had been years of independence.

On the bookshelf in Miloš's apartment one day I noticed a copy of Allen Ginsberg's *Howl*, whose opening stanza had been so deeply ingrained in the American counterculture:

> *I saw the best minds of my generation destroyed by madness,*
> *starving hysterical naked,*
> > *dragging themselves through the negro streets at dawn look-*
> *ing for an angry fix,*
> > *angelheaded hipsters burning for the ancient heavenly*
> *connection to the starry dynamo in the machinery of night,*

> *who poverty and tatters and hollow-eyed and high sat up*
> *smoking in the supernatural darkness of cold-water flats float-*
> *ing across the tops of cities contemplating jazz*

Miloš had read the Beat poets; he'd watched *The Strawberry Statement.* A strange mixture of influences: Vladimír Mečiar and Allen Ginsberg, Slovak nationalism and psychedelic poetry. Miloš had campaigned with Mečiar in the countryside; he admired the way that Mečiar, unlike the intellectuals in Bratislava, knew how to talk to ordinary people, to people like Miloš's grandfather, who had been born in a house in a small village and who died an old man in that same house, never having spent a single night anywhere else. Miloš was not a fan of Václav Havel. He was not part of the romance of the dissidents, of the fairy tale of the persecuted playwright who went to live happily ever after in the castle. He laughed about Vladimír Mečiar—"My boss, he knows how to make propaganda!"—but Miloš had chosen precisely him: someone who was in some way heir to Slovakia's dark legacy of a clerico-fascist nationalism, someone whose language, unlike Havel's, contained no softness.

■ ■ ■

LIKE PRAGUE AND SO many European cities that came into existence in premodern times, Bratislava was built on a river. The Danube joined Bratislava, Vienna, Budapest, and Belgrade, and strong rowers could row their small boats between Bratislava and Vienna in a day. Only some fifty miles lay between the two capitals; there was no natural border, yet the two cities had long been separated by the Iron Curtain, and even four years later the distinction between the East and the West was a palpable one.

Prague lay 150 miles west of Vienna, but like Bratislava it was not the West. The trip between Bratislava and Prague lasted about six hours, and I began to make it often. It was a slow train ride across a new international border, and few were used to the border crossing. The currency had been divided with stickers: old Czechoslovak crowns with Czech stickers were now Czech currency; old Czechoslovak crowns with Slovak stickers were now Slovak currency. Exchanging currency meant paying a commission, so often travelers—Czechs and Slovaks, former Czechoslovak citizens—would gently pull the stickers off and paste on the others.

The economic transition—exploitative privatization, banking corruption, pyramid schemes—was not a romantic story. I wanted to learn about the novelists and the philosophers. I was interested in peace studies and human rights, and in particular in Charter 77—whose origins suggested that Václav Havel's essays were not so unsuited for the parking lot of a Grateful Dead concert.

As in Greenwich Village and Haight-Ashbury, in Prague and Bratislava, too, there had been a counterculture: *"angelheaded hipsters . . . contemplating jazz,"* poets and painters, saxophone players and psychedelic guitarists who played loud music, drank beer, and smoked marijuana, who believed in free love. In the 1970s, they would gather in the countryside for rock concerts held in barns. At that time in Czechoslovakia a band called the Plastic People of the Universe co-opted a young Canadian English teacher named Paul Wilson as its lead singer. It was a rebellious band, arrogant young men with long hair and a taste for saying "Fuck you" to those in power. They addressed a song to a communist apparatchik: *"What do you resemble in your greatness? / Are you the Truth? / Are you God? / What do you resemble in your greatness? / A piece of shit . . ."*

Paul Wilson and the other Plastic People were not great musicians. They had, though, a band manager who was a great personality. Ivan Jirous possessed the peculiar ability to persuade people to do things. In 1976, he met the playwright Václav Havel at an apartment in Prague. Havel, who was on his way to a party, never made it there: instead he spent the night at a pub, mesmerized by the long-haired Ivan Jirous and the rock music coming from his squeaking cassette player. The sound quality was poor, the musicians of mediocre talent. That mattered little: to Havel, here was authenticity, existential truth. For Havel that night with Ivan Jirous and his old cassette player was an epiphany.

"Suddenly I realized," Václav Havel later wrote, *"that, regardless of how many vulgar words these people used or how long their hair was, truth was on their side."*

Václav Havel's alliance with Ivan Jirous was a fateful one: nothing would be the same again. Serendipitously, the encounter had happened just in time: soon afterward the police came and arrested Ivan Jirous and his band. Paul Wilson was deported to Canada. The prosecutor instructed prison officials not to cut the hair or shave the beards of the accused: the regime wanted the musicians to appear on television as long-haired hooligans.

Now it was through Václav Havel that the older, "respectable" dissident intellectuals came to offer their support to the young rock musicians who called themselves the Plastic People. On 28 August 1976 the German newspaper *Frankfurter Allgemeine Zeitung* published an open letter on behalf of a handful of irreverent long-haired youth, signed by Czechoslovakia's intellectual elite, among them Václav Havel, Pavel Kohout, Karel Kosík, Jan Patočka, and Jaroslav Seifert. The signatories included playwrights and novelists, a future Nobel Prize winner, the greatest philosophers. The marriage was, from the outset, a seeming mésalliance, between the protégés of the philosopher Edmund Husserl and those of the guitarist Lou Reed.

Havel could not save his new friends. Ivan Jirous and three other band members were convicted; Jirous received the longest prison sentence. Yet something had happened, a certain magic conjured up by this unlikely alliance. It was 1976, the year when in communist Poland Adam Michnik and other intellectuals formed the Workers' Defense Committee. It was the year after the Helsinki Accords, when communist bloc leaders had traded their signatures to the Universal Declaration of Human Rights for Western acceptance of the inviolability of borders. The communist governments had never intended to honor that agreement. Nonetheless, the text was there. Now, perhaps unexpectedly, this détente-inspired document provided a new language, one that could possibly fill the void left after Marxism's death.

Ivan Jirous went to prison. Yet outside the courtroom where the Velvet Underground–inspired Plastic People were being tried, Havel felt a presentiment of something good. Havel was an able organizer, and by New Year's Day he had called into existence a collectively authored text that would become its own movement. Charter 77 lamented that human rights in Czechoslovakia existed on paper alone. The Charter's demand was morally—and legally— pure: it asked only that the Czechoslovak government respect the Helsinki Accords. Havel persuaded the revered philosopher Jan Patočka to be among the initial spokespersons. When the text was ready, the aging philosopher went to see the art historian Miloslava Holubová, his close friend of many years. Holubová was not a fan of the Plastic People.

"I didn't like them very much," she told me when I went to visit her at her apartment in Malá Strana, not far from Prague Castle. ". . . Maybe I'm old-fashioned . . . In the same song they talked about Jesus Christ and some sexual organs."

That was of little consequence: she signed Charter 77.

On New Year's Day of 1977, the Charter made itself public. And the signatories waited for the secret police.

"They came," Miloslava Holubová told me, "I think, for all of us in this first group during the night, the sixth or seventh of January."

By then she was in her midsixties, and she understood what arrest meant. A quarter century earlier, after helping her cousin cross the Czechoslovak border, she had sat in Stalinist prison for fourteen months. She didn't dare judge anyone who chose not to sign.

By 1977 the Stalinist years had passed. Torture was no longer common, although there remained, in the darkness of the interrogation rooms, "people who do this brutal work with physical consequences," the philosopher Radim Palouš told me.

Radim Palouš had felt the importance of being in prison. In prison, he said, he had felt "free in a deeper sense." We met at Charles University, where he was now rector. Radim Palouš, like his son, like Miloslava Holubová and Václav Havel and many others, endured and survived. But the philosopher Jan Patočka did not. He was sixty-nine and his health was poor. In March 1977, in the midst of draining interrogations, he died.

"It was shameful," Jan Patočka's friend Eva Stuchliková said. She was speaking of the funeral, where the secret police photographed the mourners, and the helicopters and motorcycles made it impossible to hear the priest.

At a café, I met Josef Hiršal and Bohumila Grögerová, an aging couple who in the past had together composed experimental verses and translated poetry from many different languages. They, too, spoke about Patočka's funeral, about the deafening noise and the regime's attempt to deny the service any dignity.

For all of the mourners at Patočka's funeral, the philosopher's death marked a rupture in consciousness. Everyone still saw so vividly those helicopters and motorcycles, heard their vulgar sounds.

Jan Patočka became the sacrificial martyr of Charter 77. Yet he was more than that. For Bohumír Janat, Patočka's death was the death of Socrates. The then twenty-seven-year-old Janat had intended to sign Charter 77 several months later, when he had finished his studies. Yet that day in March 1977, after he returned home from his professor's funeral, he knew what he had to do: he signed at once. He was cast out of the university. For the next dozen years, when he was not in prison, the young philosopher worked as a janitor and a stoker in a boiler room. This was the fate of intellectuals who chose to sign the Charter.

In Prague that summer of 1993 I was trying to understand Charter 77—what it was and what it was not. It was not anti-Marxist. It appealed for neither the restoration of capitalism nor the introduction of multiple political parties. It proposed no alternative political system. It called on the government only to take seriously its own laws. Everyone told me this; it was a kind of refrain. I was interested in democratic politics, but in Czechoslovakia the dissidents had been interested in "antipolitics." The Helsinki Accords had inspired a language that was not only post-Marxist but also postpolitical. Inside politics, the dissidents had believed, it was impossible to have clean hands. Political opposition would always imply something shared with the regime it opposed. The language of Helsinki was a language of human rights, transcendent of communist—or capitalist—ideology.

That power corrupts was inevitable, Bohumír Janat told me. The Velvet Revolution had returned him to the university after the many years of manual labor. His voice was emphatic, yet soft. He spoke about the funeral, about the helicopters and the motorcycles. He spoke about an opposition whose strength was rooted in individual moral choice—a moral choice to live in truth. There was a Manichaean distinction in his mind, but it was not between communism and anticommunism: it was between lies and truth. When I asked him about the communist regime, he began to talk about Fyodor Dostoevsky's *The Brothers Karamazov* and the tale of the Grand Inquisitor.

When I asked Bohumír Janat about the efficacy of nonviolence in opposing totalitarianism, he told me: "One who uses violence is a very big coward because he refuses to carry his own existential burden."

There was much that the signatories of Charter 77 agreed about: the inspiration of Jan Patočka's search for philosophical truth, the shamefulness of his funeral, the meaning of antipolitics, the opposition between truth and lies, the fact that they were a small ghetto of intellectuals. As a group they were both proud and self-critical; another of Jan Patočka's onetime students, the philosopher Ladislav Hejdanek, knew that in the last decades of communism, the years after 1968, most people had looked upon the dissidents as "stupid people who openly say what all know.

"I am afraid," he added, "it had no real political relevance."

In retrospect Charter 77 seemed to Ladislav Hejdanek a mere gesture. Bohumír Janat disagreed: he believed that Charter 77 had made a difference, that it had been "the silent and tranquil cause" of what happened in 1989.

This was the central point of the former dissidents' lack of consensus: in the end, had what they had done mattered?

On the other side of the Vltava River, in Malá Strana, tucked on a small street not far from the American embassy, I talked to Milan Otahal at the Institute for Contemporary History. A historian, he was certain that international politics—Gorbachev's renunciation of the Brezhnev Doctrine, in effect a promise of nonintervention; the domino effect of revolutions in Poland, Hungary, East Germany, Bulgaria—had played a large role. In 1989 the East Germans had poured into Prague, suitcases in their hands and children in their arms, headed to the West German embassy. This had an impact, psychologically.

No one, though, would ever know for certain how much Charter 77 or anything else had to do with communism's fall: it was impossible to do a control study on real life.

What was important was that the revolution had happened. In November 1989 there were demonstrations, first by students, then not only by students—dissidents gathered in the Magic Lantern Theater and called themselves the Civic Forum. Looking back, the art historian Miloslava Holubová saw the Velvet Revolution as theater, staged under Václav Havel's artistic direction. Outside on the streets the police arrived, as the demonstrators had known they would. There were beatings. Not long afterward someone spoke at a demonstration and told the crowd that there were two policemen present who had beaten demonstrators just days earlier. The demonstrators were furious. Then the speaker said that the policemen wished to ask for forgiveness. And the crowd began to chant: "We are forgiving! We are forgiving!" For Miloslava Holubová this was a miracle, a proof of Christian goodness and God's presence in the world.

After that things moved quickly.

In Bratislava, Miloš gave me a videotape of the November 1989 demonstrations, the crowds chanting on Wenceslas Square in Prague. There were literary references: "For whom the bell tolls," they shouted. "Liars!" "The truth will prevail!" Truth—*pravda* in

Czech—the dissidents used as the most concrete of nouns, as tangible as the keys in one's pocket.

▪ ▪ ▪

WHEN I ARRIVED at his Prague apartment one day in late August, the Charter 77 signatory Jan Urban opened the door for me. His small dogs came to the door as well, the adorable dachshunds who were then ubiquitous in Prague. His English was comfortable and refined, and he had a kind of jazz club hipness to him. Everything about him was engaging: he was articulate and self-reflective, his manner of being a fusion of self-possession and vulnerability.

"I didn't sign one bloody paper," Jan Urban said of the secret police's attempts to force him into collaboration. "Even a rat, when you push it into a corner, it jumps."

He was speaking of how the regime had threatened him and of how he had not broken. He had not, though, been immune to the fear: while he had learned to live with death threats, they stayed inside him. By summer of 1989 he was being detained more or less every fortnight, and the pressure was too much. He fled. Being in hiding was "a strange feeling," he told me. "This was my city and I was totally alone."

We talked about the communist regime, about fear, and about Václav Havel. The man who was now president had called the years after 1968, the years when belief and practice had parted ways, "post-totalitarian." These were the years of living "as if." No one any longer believed in communism—and no one, including those in power, any longer believed that anyone believed in communism. It was enough, though, that everyone pretended. In his 1978 *samizdat* essay "The Power of the Powerless," dedicated to the memory of Jan Patočka, Havel wrote of the seemingly innocent greengrocer, the ordinary man who every morning in his shop window, alongside the carrots and onions, hung the sign bearing the famous communist slogan "Workers of the World Unite!" The greengrocer did not believe this message, the words meant nothing to him; nonetheless he obliged the regime by displaying the sign.

Such a gesture was profoundly in the greengrocer's self-interest: it enabled him to live in peace. If one day he took down that sign, perhaps buried it at the bottom of a carton of rotten tomatoes, someone was likely to report him. The police would quickly arrive. Alone, the greengrocer was seemingly powerless. If he resisted displaying the sign, he would face harassment, persecution, eventually arrest, interrogation, and imprisonment. And yet . . . if one day all the greengrocers were to take down their signs, *that* would be the beginning of a revolution. Thus in fact the greengrocer was not so powerless after all. Because he was powerful, he was also responsible—and therefore guilty: for it was the greengrocers who allowed the game to go on in the first place.

Jan Urban had understood that the greengrocers were in the majority and that he and his friends were living in a ghetto. Most people in communist Czechoslovakia, he believed, had been happy—or at least content.

"It's very difficult to quarrel with or explain something to people who don't believe in anything," he said. Of course the regime was oppressive. Of course it was built on humiliation and the violation of human rights. Yet people—perhaps even most people—didn't mind. "Many people remember it as a very comfortable life," he told me, "nothing to really cry about."

Jan Urban was a warm person, but he did not speak warmly about "the people." He was not alone. Milan Otahal, too, was convinced that ordinary people cared much more for going abroad to the Yugoslav seaside on holidays than for free speech. The philosopher Ladislav Hejdanek, too, harbored no illusions about the masses. His fellow citizens, he believed, had been unwilling to risk anything. Eva Stuchliková described the majority as having reached a modus vivendi with the regime—in her mind like a dog chained to his house who doesn't want to upset his master. The experimental poet Josef Hiršal had friends who, under pressure, had signed the communist regime's declaration condemning Charter 77. They wanted his understanding: they had signed out of fear. Hiršal was unsympathetic: they were simply cowards.

The implications were disconcerting. In Czechoslovakia, I wanted very much to hear a story about the dissidents who spoke for the people, who led the people, who *were* the people. Yet now I began to see that even Havel, the hero of the revolution who became the people's president, he, too, had not had so much faith in the people. Alone in the studio apartment I rented, inside one of Prague's many faceless high-rises built of gray cement, I read Havel again and again. His tale of the greengrocer was both lyrical and merciless, the harshness of the accusation only thinly veiled by the aesthetics of the prose. The line between victim and oppressor, Havel wrote, *"runs de facto through each person, for everyone in his or her own way is both a victim and a supporter of the system."*

Ladislav Hejdanek agreed. "We have to be clear," he told me. "We are all responsible for the last forty years because we didn't react against it."

But of course, *he* did.

Miloš's attraction to Allen Ginsberg and *The Strawberry Statement* notwithstanding, the dissidents of Czechoslovakia had acted above all not on behalf of "the people" but rather on behalf of "truth." And "truth" in Czechoslovakia was generationally inflected. Once upon a time, there had been both terror and honesty. The Stalinists tortured and executed, but they were sincere: they truly believed they were ushering the people into paradise. Then came Stalin's death and his successor Nikita Khrushchev's revelations of Stalin's "excesses." Eventually Alexander Dubček came to preside over a "socialism with a human face"—which was never to be. Soviet leader Leonid Brezhnev decided that Dubček's liberalizing reforms had gone too far. In August 1968 Warsaw Pact tanks rolled into Prague and put an end to what might have been a different kind of socialism, a better kind.

In 1968 the arrival of the Red Army in Prague meant, paradoxically, the end of Marxism. In its wake, Marxist belief was decoupled from communist practice. The new hard-line government installed by Moscow brought "normalization": a return to dogmatism, to censorship and oppression, yet now without Stalinist terror.

Normalization-era socialism was no longer so bloody. Nonetheless, Ladislav Hejdanek believed, "morally it was much worse."

For "normalization" meant the reign of the opportunists.

At a Prague pub, Brad, a graduate student at Stanford, told me that during normalization, as the regime imprisoned dissidents, it took a chunk of its operating budget and transferred it from capital investment to consumer spending.

"The Czechs traded their freedom for new refrigerators," he told me. He said it not at all viciously, just as a matter of information.

The communist period, I began to appreciate more and more, had not been a homogenous bloc of time. The moral problems of Stalinism and normalization had been very different ones. I was thinking about this when I took the overnight train once more from Prague to Bratislava to meet the philosopher Miroslav Kusý. Slovakia was more provincial than the Czech Republic; even the capital felt like a town and not a city, and to have been a dissident in Bratislava was to have been even more isolated than to have been a dissident in Prague. Miroslav Kusý had been one of the isolated ones, and he, too, felt the sharp generational split. In the 1970s and 1980s, his secret police interrogators, he understood, were "pragmatic people": they belonged to a second, agnostic generation of communist apparatchiks, bereft of any ideals. One of his interrogators had graduated from the law faculty. Why, Miroslav Kusý had once asked him, had he joined the secret police? And the younger man had obligingly explained: it was a thousand-crown difference in salary.

Sincerity of ideology "definitely existed in the first generation . . . but nothing of it in the next," Jan Urban said. After our conversation, I thought again of Bohumír Janat and the Grand Inquisitor parable in Dostoevsky's *The Brothers Karamazov*: during the Inquisition, Jesus Christ returned to earth only to be imprisoned. While in prison, he received a visit from the Grand Inquisitor, who was not pleased to see him. Only slowly did their conversation reveal the Grand Inquisitor's one secret: he did not believe in God.

■ ■ ■

IN SOME WAY Jan Urban found the Velvet Revolution depressing: after all those years, the communists had simply run away.

"It's not that we won—it's that they collapsed. And we just had to step in, because there was no one else around."

For Jan Urban, "the power of the powerless"—of that small ghetto of dissidents—lay not in what they said but in that they said it. Those who signed Charter 77 stood apart only in saying aloud what everyone knew. They suffered, moreover, from a certain weakness: they were preoccupied with reacting to the regime's stupidity. They knew what they didn't want—that was obvious, everyone knew it. Jan Urban could not remember, though, any occasion from "the old days" when they had discussed the future, what would come after communism. There were no such expectations; the dissidents had no project, no future of their own. And this, he thought now, had been their great mistake.

They had been caught unprepared. Ladislav Hejdanek, too, was disappointed in 1989: he had believed that Charter 77 would form the basis for a postcommunist politics. That it had not—could not—had come as an unpleasant surprise. Others were not so surprised. The historian Milan Otahal was a pragmatist: the dissidents' entire strategy had been an "existential revolution"—a call to live in truth and in accord with one's own conscience. Antipolitics had been about the moral restoration of human beings; its objectives had never been political ones.

Miroslav Kusý belonged to those who believed in the Charter's efficacy. After all, in the very early days of communism's fall, it was the Charter signatories who had directed the critical first wave of changes. Kusý had been among them, serving as federal minister for censorship, given the happy task of destroying his own office. He was a philosopher, though, not a politician, and in the end he was skeptical about the possibility of a moral politics. To be engaged meant to forgo having clean hands. He opted out.

For the veterans of dark prison cells, the political engagement that followed November 1989 was a loss of virginity—and of virtue. The words I heard most often from them were *existential* and *truth*—both ill suited for politics. For the dissidents had found themselves in a philosophical trap: they had defined politics in opposition to truth. And then came the revolution. Perhaps they had made the revolution and perhaps they had not, but this no longer mattered. Milan Otahal told me that in 1989 Havel had insisted that his sphere of interest was the human being and that he did not want to become a politician. But he did—even as he gave speeches about authenticity and Being and the irreducibility of subjective human experience.

As I left the apartment with the angelic dachshunds, Jan Urban gave me a copy of an essay he had recently published. "The Powerlessness of the Powerful" was dated November 1992. The essay was a collective self-criticism, his friend Václav Havel was now the antihero.

> *The moment when the dissidents stepped out from their unreal world and through the few miraculous weeks of the Velvet Revolution entered the real world of the normality of political and public life, they were lost. Their old instincts did not work. Nearly all resistance movements in history ended this way. Their legitimacy is given by the existence of an enemy and is lost with his defeat. The dissidents in Czechoslovakia did not know a non-society they lived with. All they knew was their enemy and he—spiteful bastard—all of the sudden ran away. . . . The Old Velvet was a mess. We won it too fast and immediately forgot to think further.*

▪ ▪ ▪

SLOWLY, DURING THAT summer of 1993, I began to understand there was something more, still another layer of moral ambiguity: the neat opposition between the dissidents and the communists was in some way deceptive. For dissidence itself had often been born of communism. Many dissidents were former believers who once upon a time had been Marxist revisionists, supporters of Alexander Dubček's Prague Spring. They had believed that they could publicly acknowledge the evils of Stalinism and then make a fresh start; they had believed that Marxism could be democratized while still remaining Marxism. Even while, in the 1970s and 1980s, they were sent to communist prisons, some of these dissidents, the older ones above all, continued to hope for a "socialism with a human face."

Jan Urban's father had spent six years in the anti-Nazi resistance before he became a communist apparatchik. He was a believer. As a child, his son, too, had loved communist ideology.

"It was beautiful, we believed in it," Jan Urban told me. He still remembered with nostalgia the May Day parade of 1968, when no one organized anything but everyone flooded the streets. Then came the Soviet invasion; Jan Urban's father was in Finland as the Czechoslovak ambassador. A communist who supported Dubček's reforms, Urban's father was among the first diplomats whom Moscow demanded be recalled. In the years to come, the secret police began to detain him and tried to extract information about his son's oppositional activities. After a third brutal interrogation, Jan Urban's father died of a heart attack.

Among the dissidents, Jan Urban belonged to the younger generation. Many of his fellow signatories, older than he, had once been communists themselves, hoping for a gentler, more humane socialism. Josef Hiršal was the first one to tell me that many of the signatories were former Communist Party members. When the secret police had come for Hiršal, they had declared him to be in the ranks of the enemies of socialism.

"No," Josef Hiršal had answered them, "you put me in these ranks."

In the 1960s, the young philosopher Miroslav Kusý was writing as a critical Marxist. He was a Dubček communist: he believed both in communism and in reform, in the potential of a nondogmatic Marxism. Then came "normalization," and the professor of Marxist philosophy was expelled from the university. Living "as if" was a kind of game the people and the Communist Party played with each other, and Kusý did not want to take part in this game of pretend. He became first a librarian. After he signed Charter 77, he lost his job as a librarian and became a manual laborer. Time and time again he found himself arrested, interrogated, imprisoned. He had the chance to escape: the secret police told him that if he was not content in Czechoslovakia, he could go abroad. He told them that he would be content when they went abroad.

After the revisionist Marxists who made the Prague Spring were expelled, the Communist Party became a party of those who were left, those who cared little for the human face of socialism. This kind of socialism, Miroslav Kusý understood, could not be repaired. When I met him in Bratislava, we met at the university; the Velvet Revolution had restored him to his professorship. He was disappointed that in 1989 it had been too late for socialism with a human face.

"Hair Is Like Garbage"

That fall of 1993 I became immersed in the Czech novelist Milan Kundera, in his idea that the struggle of man against power was the struggle of memory against forgetting, and in his division of people into those for whom life was light and those for whom life was heavy. Through his books I came closer to the Stalinist years. Ludvík, the protagonist of Milan Kundera's first novel, *The Joke*, was a university student and committed Communist Party member. One day, resentful of the fact that a young woman had left him to go off to a Communist Party training camp, he sent her a sarcastic postcard: *"Optimism is the opium of the masses! A healthy atmosphere stinks of stupidity! Long live Trotsky!"*

After Lenin's death in 1924, Stalin had won the power struggle with Trotsky. Eventually Trotsky was forced into exile. Yet even very far from Moscow, he remained a threat to Stalin—until, in August 1940, one of Stalin's henchmen found Trotsky in Mexico and murdered him with an ice pick. For the remainder of Stalin's rule, Trotsky's name remained anathema.

Milan Kundera's protagonist Ludvík understood this. The postcard was a joke, but Ludvík was living in times without a sense of humor. He was expelled from both the Communist Party and the university and was sent to work in the mines. Everything else that happened in his life turned on that postcard, and in his mind he revisited obsessively the moment of his expulsion, when everyone in the room—some hundred people, including his professors and his closest friends—raised their hands to cast him out. Decades passed, but Ludvík never overcame that moment of alienation:

> *Since then, whenever I make new acquaintances, men or women with the potential of becoming friends or lovers, I project them back into that time, that hall, and ask myself whether they would have raised their hands; no one has ever passed the test: every one of them has raised his hand in the same way my former friends and colleagues (willingly or not, out of conviction or fear) raised theirs. You must admit: it's hard to live with people willing to send you to exile or death, it's hard to become intimate with them, it's hard to love them.*

■ ■ ■

THAT SPRING OF 1994 I invited to Stanford, where I was then a senior, a Slovak couple, Martin Bútora and Zora Bútorová, sociologists who had been dissidents. After the Velvet Revolution, Martin had become human rights adviser to Václav Havel. This was while Czechoslovakia was still a single country, before my parliamentarian friend Miloš's boss, Vladimír Mečiar, had engineered the "Velvet Divorce." At the San Francisco International Airport, Martin and Zora arrived with their eleven-year-old son, Ivan, who was charming and precocious. As we drove down the highway toward Stanford, they asked me about San Francisco. They wanted to know: where was City Lights Bookstore? Little seemed as peculiarly American as the Beat poets. What was it about Jack Kerouac, Allen Ginsberg, William Burroughs, and Lawrence Ferlinghetti that spoke to East Europeans? Yet something did. Miloš had a copy of *Howl* in his Bratislava apartment. Martin and Zora had read Jack Kerouac; they knew the story of City Lights Bookstore in North Beach, which Lawrence Ferlinghetti had founded in the 1950s.

Martin and Zora gave me a present: the English translation of their friend Martin Šimečka's novel *The Year of the Frog*. It was moving and sweet. Milan Šimečka, the author's father, had been imprisoned in the 1980s; when Havel became president, Milan Šimečka became his adviser on Czech-Slovak relations. Milan Šimečka, though, survived communism by less than a year: he died in September 1990, when he was but sixty. In *The Year of the Frog*, his son, Martin—who would have then been a university student had he not been the son of a dissident—wrote of his father's imprisonment. The arrest had come shortly after the birth of the Polish free trade union Solidarity, when the young Martin Šimečka was visiting Warsaw.

> *It all began approximately a year ago, if one can talk about the beginning, when they arrested my father. I happened to be in Warsaw then.... We had heard that there was freedom in Poland, and we wanted to see it.... When I returned home, instead of my father I found a male kitten with a pink nose and a silly face.*

Martin Šimečka wrote of his mother's grief and of the kitten she clung to in her husband's absence. He wrote of how he learned to be a pipe fitter but quickly forgot plumbing, and of how he found work as a hospital orderly and watched his patients die. He also wrote about his love for long-distance running, and for his girlfriend, who did not mind when her coffee got cold because she liked it that way.

During their visit Zora and Martin Bútora gave a talk at the Slavic studies house. They were wonderful speakers: smart and serious, warm and sincere. They were not at all like my friend Miloš: life—the past as well as the present—was heavy for them. They were engaged in a political world that they always understood in moral categories. It mattered to them very much that certain things be understood: that there *had* been fascism in Slovakia during the war, fascism and collaboration with the Nazis. That the Slovaks had participated in the Holocaust, that they had sent Slovakia's Jews to their deaths. And Martin and Zora feared very much that under Vladimír Mečiar, Slovakia would see fascism again.

Only now, belatedly, did I begin to understand that there were ethical implications to my friendship with Miloš. Martin and Zora's agonized grappling with Slovakia's uncertain transition to democracy contrasted so sharply with Miloš's good-humored pragmatism and lighthearted opportunism, with his laughter and good spirits. Miloš and I remained in touch: every so often he would call me from parliament, usually in the middle of the night or very early in the morning, California time. Once he called to tell me that in a day or two there would be a vote of no confidence and Vladimír Mečiar's government would fall. And so it happened. I read the story in the *New York Times* a few days later. Vladimír Mečiar, however, always came back. Once Miloš called very early in the morning, when I was still asleep, and began to ask me about President Clinton and education.

"This is a large topic," I told him. "Can you be more specific?"

"You know, the government—they give money to students," he said.

"University students?"

"Yes, yes, university students."

"Well, in 1992 there was a Higher Education Act."

"Good, good, Higher Education Act!" He was very pleased to hear of it.

"Miloš," I said, "why don't you tell me what you want this for, and I will try to help you."

"You know, the Slovak elections are coming in September, and I think it would be a good idea to say that the Slovak government will give money to Slovak students."

"What a nice thought. How can I help you?"

"I have an idea. Why don't you send me a copy of Clinton's law—and I will translate it into Slovak."

I thought then: I could be in the Slovak government too. But I liked Miloš very much, I promised I would try to find a copy of Clinton's law. A few days later I was having dinner with a friend. When I told him about my conversation with Miloš, he logged in to a government documents database and reappeared shortly thereafter with a copy of the 1992 Higher Education Act. I folded it into an envelope and sent it to Miloš.

▪ ▪ ▪

IN JUNE 1994 after graduation I flew from San Francisco to Burlington; I had signed up for an intensive Czech course at a small military college in rural Vermont. When I arrived at the airport one of the two instructors was waiting for me. Only because we had spoken on the phone did I know she was a woman, for Jarmila looked like a man. She was wearing khaki shorts and a man's tank top. She was very fit and entirely bald: her head was shaven.

Vermont was beautiful, and peaceful, the campus was small and green. We had class all morning and most of the afternoon, and in the evenings we went swimming in a nearby lake.

Jarmila was an excellent swimmer. In the weeks that followed I learned more about her: In the 1980s, growing up in a small village, she'd become involved in the underground church, in Catholic *samizdat*. While still a teenager she became the youngest person to sign Charter 77. Her parents were afraid, for themselves and for their other children. They tried unsuccessfully to dissuade her. Eventually they denounced her to the secret police, and so began a long series of arrests, detentions, interrogations, beatings. It seemed Jarmila held up well; she was obstinate and undeterred. Then came November 1989, when she joined Václav Havel and other Charter signatories in the Magic Lantern Theater and became one of the heroes of the revolution: a girl who looked like a boy. She met Shirley Temple Black, George Bush's ambassador to Czechoslovakia, and other American diplomats. After the communist regime fell in Czechoslovakia, Radio Free Europe sent her to the Balkans to report on the revolutions in Bulgaria and Romania. She was in Bucharest that December, when the cheers at the rally Nicolae Ceaușescu had organized in support of himself suddenly became boos and cackles, the opening act to the main drama: Nicolae and Elena Ceaușescu's execution on Christmas Day.

When Jarmila returned to Prague she studied theology at Charles University, taking classes in Latin and Hebrew. She did not, though, complete her degree. Instead she came to America—or rather was brought there, by a man named John Hasek—to join the U.S. Army. She attended a military academy in New Mexico, then transferred to the small military college in Vermont. She spoke about John Hasek often, although she did not explain what his role in the military was or how they had met or what their relationship had been. I understood it was a sensitive topic, for she was mourning his death: the previous year he'd been badly injured in Bosnia; he died a few months later in a Prague hospital.

I supposed Jarmila must have learned English well, insofar as she was serving in the American military, but with me and the other students she spoke only Czech. She enjoyed teaching; I sensed she enjoyed her time with us, her students who were more or less her own age. She would ask us to make up comic strips in Czech, with caricatured drawings and dialogue. She was full of warmth and goodwill. Yet I was disconcerted by her appearance—or rather by the indeterminacy of her gender, an indeterminacy that prevailed even over a Slavic grammar that allowed for very little gender ambiguity: in Czech men and women use different forms of adjectives and past-tense verbs.

Jarmila had her own mantra. "Marci," she would say, "you don't need hair. Hair is like garbage."

Then one day she was gone. From Marcela, our other Czech teacher, we learned that Jarmila was in the hospital. Marcela was at once an energetic and almost ethereal presence, entirely different from Jarmila. She was older, perhaps in her fifties, and beautiful; she wore her hair long, in soft blond waves. She had defected from communist Czechoslovakia long ago, coming to the States to marry an American filmmaker. In December 1989 she'd rushed to Prague to be part of the crowd on Wenceslas Square, the crowd she described as moving like an ocean, in currents and undertows. By the time I met Marcela she had a long career as a professor of engineering behind her. It had been only several years earlier that she'd decided on a radical change: she would leave engineering and become a Slavicist. She returned to the university and studied Russian and Czech literature. Languages came easily to her; she was warm and gentle and seemingly indefatigable. Something about her was otherworldly.

Between Jarmila and Marcela there was a subtle tension, though it was never articulated. It was Marcela, though, who drove us to the hospital to visit Jarmila. Only when we arrived did I realize she was in a psychiatric ward. She still seemed very much herself; she was happy to see us. Her head was no longer quite so clean shaven, and she asked whether, when I next visited, I would bring her a razor. No one in the psychiatric ward wanted to give her one.

"Everything I Know
about People I Learned in
the Camps"

I t was late summer in Prague, busy and bright. The city's usual
residents had long before left for their cottages in the countryside; by 1994, the Czech capital was transformed during the summer months into an English-speaking city, full of tourists. Prague's
fairy-tale glamour, though, was all in its old center. A few miles
away, in the unglamorous proletarian district of Žižkov, the wildly
successful financial speculator George Soros had conjured into
existence an English-language university that drew students from
all corners of Europe. It was a university designed to create a new
East European intelligentsia cosmopolitan in form, democratic in
content—benevolent social engineering by means of philanthropy.
There former dissidents came to teach those who were too young
to have faced difficult choices. Among those who lectured at the
new Central European University was the Slovak writer Martin Šimečka. He seemed less vulnerable than the narrator of *The
Year of the Frog*; still, like his autobiographical protagonist, he was
reflective—and saddened by the breakup of Czechoslovakia. He
spoke about the crisis of intellectuals in the post–Velvet Revolution
years. To be in prison, he explained, was its own kind of privileged
position: it meant that you had been recognized as a threat to the
powers that be. Now writers had lost that privileged position. They
were searching for a new place in this new world.

That August at Central European University I took a seminar

with Arnošt Lustig, a Czech Jew who alone among his family had survived Auschwitz. As a teenager, he had escaped from the camps and gone on to fight with the communists against the Nazis. I knew him from his novels, almost all of them set during the Holocaust. A certain motif ran through them: a beautiful woman—often a prostitute—in the midst of Nazi hell. Arnošt loved women; he wrote of sex as if it were redemptive. In his novel *The Unloved*, written from the perspective of a prostitute in the Theresienstadt ghetto, the heroine's eclectic earnings served as an almost musical refrain:

> August 28. *Three times. Two phonograph records. An eighth of a loaf of rye bread. Dostoevsky's* Crime and Punishment. *A travel manicure set. Twice during the night. A hot-water bottle. Four ounces of powdered sugar.*

> August 29. *Twice. A sheaf of pink stationery. A nail file.*

> August 30. *Five times. A collection of postcards from the most beautiful European cities and spas. An eighth of a loaf of rye bread. Two potatoes. Fifty marks in ten-mark notes. A leather frame for photographs. Once. A hand-knit woolen ski sweater.*

In the seminar we read Aristotle's *Poetics*. Arnošt liked to talk about Aristotle. He was full of good humor and countless anecdotes. His eyes twinkled. There was a kind of joie de vivre in him.

One day Arnošt told us the story of his affection for prostitutes, which was also a story of his father. In the Theresienstadt ghetto, awaiting their turn on the transport, his father had understood they would be going to their deaths. And he had a preoccupation: he did not want his son to die a virgin. Every night he would ask Arnošt if he had been with a woman. And every night Arnošt would say no—until one day the teenage boy lost his virginity to a prostitute in Theresienstadt. It was precisely on that night that Arnošt's father ceased to ask—and so Arnošt never told him. Soon afterward they were deported, and his father was gassed in Auschwitz.

Arnošt was not a dark person. He knew that people could be cruel—but also that people could be beautiful.

"Everything I know about people," he said, "I learned in the camps."

In Arnošt's seminar there was a Czech woman named Dorota, a student at the drama faculty. One day she told Arnošt that he used the word *beautiful* too much when he spoke English. Arnošt, who had been in Auschwitz.

Dorota was young and pretty and talented. She had won an English-language writing contest for Czech authors with a short story whose narrator was a young Czech man. The story opened: *"I like meat, sex, riding trams, and like most Czechs, I don't believe in God."* Some two years earlier, when she'd been working at one of the postrevolution McDonald's, she'd met an American tourist. Bret was in his midthirties, older than she by fourteen years. He was a geologist, or rather had been a geologist. He was also married, or rather had been married. He had left behind in California not only a good job but also a wife and two children. He was tired of geology and wanted to be a writer. Rainer Maria Rilke was his favorite poet; Rilke's stories had brought Bret to Prague.

It was Dorota who kept him there. She sold him french fries, and Bret became her first lover. He stayed in Prague, and they moved into a tiny flat in the same building where Dorota had lived with her parents. He wrote poetry and drank beer and made love to her. She studied at the drama faculty, and cooked and cleaned and ironed. She learned English extremely well, and she did everything for him: after two years of living in Prague, Bret still understood nothing in Czech. He seemed not to mind. Dorota took care of him. She loved him very much.

On Sunday nights Dorota and Bret would go out for beer and Czech crepes called *palačinky* at a below-street-level café called Barbar, not far from Na Kampě park and the John Lennon Wall, and it was there I met their American friends, nearly all men. One of them was a talented black American jazz singer who was sometimes harassed by the Czech police for no reason at all. Another was a thirty-year-old French major–turned–English teacher, "a tragic figure," Dorota called him. He was kind and loyal but also bitter and resentful toward a world that had not appreciated him—and above all toward women who had not loved him. A third friend, Scout, was older, perhaps in his midfifties, a hippie-turned–computer engineer from Berkeley who wore his long hair tied back in a ponytail and smoked too many cigarettes. He was fairly short and a bit heavy and always spoke emphatically, with his hands, with no concern for decorum, but also with no ill will.

Scout was a child of the cold war—and of the antiwar movement. After 1989 he'd come to Prague because he wanted to see who—or what—it was Americans were supposed to have been afraid of all those years. And immediately upon his arrival he'd concluded: what a joke. He stayed on in Prague, working as a computer programmer for a firm that supplied information to the Ministry of Transportation. He liked his co-workers. It seemed to him, though, that no one knew how to use a computer very well and so was unlikely to have contributed to a nuclear attack.

Dorota and Bret's friends who met at Barbar for beer and crepes were only a small part of a parallel, American Prague that numbered some twenty thousand people. They were expatriates, not tourists, because they were there indefinitely. They were not émigrés—for they might return to Boston or San Francisco, Madison or Columbus, at any moment. Few seemed to have any idea of what might come next. In the early 1990s, Prague was not expensive—one could live there for a long time on little money.

The expatriates were largely a twenty-something crowd; few were married, and most had come soon after college graduation. Flavoring the community was a certain hedonism: sex and beer and marijuana. Sellers gathered on a boat docked on the banks of the Vltava not far from Old Town Square. On tables set up on Charles Bridge and in Wenceslas Square, craftsmen and peddlers sold pipes alongside beaded necklaces and crystal earrings and cast-iron candelabras. The expatriates had degrees in English and French, history and sociology and comparative literature. They taught English and they wrote for the two competing English weeklies, *Prognosis* and the *Prague Post*. They founded literary magazines and organized poetry clubs. They sold used books and cappuccino at the Globe, and they waitressed and bartended at Radost'.

The Globe, located on an inconspicuous street in the unremarkable district of Holešovice, was an English-language used bookstore attached to a café that served lattes and absinthe. Radost' was something else. It was a vegetarian restaurant, a bar, a lounge, and a club—all brought together in a place named "joy." It was set in fashionable Vinohrady, and it served some of the very best food in Prague: spinach burgers and blueberry muffins and New York cheesecake. Many who worked there spoke no Czech, and the Czech clientele who did patronize Radost' were expected to speak English. The restaurant, the bar, and the lounge were upstairs; downstairs was a club for poetry readings and dancing. Everyone was young and attractive and writing the great expatriate novel. Radost' exuded pretentiousness. The model was self-consciously Paris of the 1930s, the Left Bank of Henry Miller and Anaïs Nin, of Pablo Picasso and Gertrude Stein.

The expatriates were partisans of postcommunist Eastern Europe, and they loved Prague. They felt both more and less sophisticated than the Czechs, and they related to the city's native inhabitants with a simultaneous condescension and insecurity. This—Douglas Coupland's Generation X, my own—was a wandering generation, searching for itself, unable to settle down, wary of commitment, longing for authenticity—an authenticity the expatriates hoped to reach by contiguity with the survivors of communism.

■ ■ ■

A YEAR EARLIER, in California in the fall of 1993, I had begun to study Czech. My teacher, Vlasta, had come to Stanford on a Fulbright. Her husband, Honza, had stayed behind, and she'd come to California with her thirteen-year-old daughter, Diana. Vlasta was not a teacher of Czech by profession. She was, rather, an Americanist, who taught Sylvia Plath and Edith Wharton to university students in Prague. She was also a translator of American literature. That December, her translation of Erica Jong's 1970s feminist classic *Fear of Flying* appeared. This Vlasta considered her Christmas present to Czech women.

It was in Vlasta's Czech class, on the very first day, that I'd met Amanda. She stood out because she was beautiful, and also because she was so much older than the rest of us in that small class. She was here, Amanda told us, because she wanted to know what her Czech husband was saying when he talked to his friends and family. She disliked being excluded.

"How long have you been married?" I asked her.

"Twenty-five years," she answered.

At the semester's end there was a Christmas party, and this was where I met her husband, Oskar. Like Amanda, he was strikingly attractive. There was a kind of glamour about them; years earlier, they had lived in Paris. They seemed very much in love.

Now, in Prague in August 1994, I saw Vlasta and Diana again, together with Vlasta's husband, Honza, who spoke no English but was relaxed and friendly with a playfully mocking sense of humor. He wore his hair long and played the guitar. He seemed to have none of Vlasta's awkwardness, none of her anxieties. He reminded me a bit of Miloš: happy-go-lucky, someone for whom life was light. Vlasta had a surprise for me: Amanda and Oskar were there as well. Perhaps in some way it was a surprise for them, too, an impulsive decision to leave their light-filled house with the garden in Menlo Park, their life in California, behind. Oskar had resigned his position at Stanford. He wanted to retire in Prague. He seemed very happy, and Amanda seemed both nervous and excited. She and Oskar talked about having a Halloween party, about introducing Oskar's Czech friends to America's favorite pagan holiday.

The balcony of Vlasta's Prague apartment, far from the city's center, looked out onto a lush green park beckoning from some half mile away. That afternoon the six of us spent walking the wooded paths, which felt so removed from the surrounding city. There was a mix of disparate emotions: for Vlasta, the return to Prague from California was a difficult one; for Honza, this very difficulty was a source of his exclusion. For Oskar, coming to Prague recalled a heavy past, one he did not share with Amanda. And for Amanda, coming to Prague ushered in an unpredictable future, one in which she would now be the foreigner.

"It Was Only a Small Revolution"

I answered an advertisement for an English teacher in a west Bohemian town, some three hours away by train. In late August of 1994 I left Prague for Domažlice.

This small town of perhaps ten thousand people was not unattractive. A gate hinged upon a clock-bearing stone watchtower led into an elongated town square, which every Wednesday was the site of an open market. Around the square, covered sidewalks were framed on one side by column-supported arches; the arcade buildings were painted a potpourri of greens and peaches and pinks. This was not true of the school, though, which in the small, not so dreary town of Domažlice was housed in a large, dreary building of four floors, a characterless construction of brick and stucco. There at the school the first people I met were two other English teachers. Jitka was a kind person, perhaps in her midforties, who had taught at the school for many years—first Russian, now English. Like nearly all of the Czech women I'd met, who were so pretty in their twenties, Jitka was prematurely aged. She was beaten down by everyday life, by waiting on her teenage son and her arrogant husband—a local bureaucrat with an apartment in town for his mistress. Every day Jitka would loyally return to their home in the small village several miles away, giving her husband his space in Domažlice, living in fear that he would divorce her.

Galina was different. Unlike Jitka, she had not had a previous career as a Russian teacher. She was, however, Russian—or rather, Russian was her native language. She had come from a Russian-speaking family in Soviet Ukraine and had studied English at the university in Kharkiv. A few years earlier she'd run away from an unhappy marriage, taking her daughter, Mara. For forty years Czechoslovakia had lived under the Soviet Union's domination. Now that had ended, but Soviet foreigners remained unwelcome among the Czechs. Galina, though, had arrived just after the Velvet Revolution, when English teachers were very much in demand. In Prague there was a surfeit of Americans and other native speakers, but it was not so in the provinces. And so Galina was given a job. By the time I met her, her Czech was fluent. The Czechs, though, could hear her accent, they knew she was from the East, and they avoided her. Her fellow teacher Jitka was the exception. She and Galina were friendly, if not close, and despite their differences felt something like affection for each other.

A few days later I walked into the classroom for the first time. The students rose at once, and above their heads I saw a large portrait of Václav Havel. They addressed me, as they did all their female teachers, as *Paní profesorka* (Mrs. Professor). Before the revolution, the students had said *Paní soudružka* (Mrs. Comrade).

I gave one class the short story Dorota had written in English, the one that began: *"I like meat, sex, riding trams, and like most Czechs I don't believe in God."* Dorota's story was, among other things, a play on the lack of gender inflection in the English language: only in the middle of the story did the reader learn that the narrator was a man. I wanted them to see how gender identity could be concealed in English in a way it could not in Czech. I wanted them to understand, too, the different ways that these languages structured thoughts: English verb tenses emphasized time sequence, in contrast to Czech verb tenses, which emphasized consummation: an action was either complete or incomplete, fulfilled or unfulfilled. Nouns functioned differently as well. The role of a noun in an English sentence was determined not by its suffix but by its position in the sentence. In contrast, in Czech a noun like *post office* had seven different endings, endings whose use depended upon whether one was talking about the post office, or going toward, inside, or around the post office, or sending a package by means of the post office.

I was learning Czech as I was teaching English, and my understanding of English changed as I absorbed the very different Slavic syntax. "Fine" or "okay" or "all is well" was *v pořádku*—literally "in order," which felt vaguely authoritarian. Friends greeted one another on the street with *Počkej! Kam jdeš?* (Wait! Where are you going?). Variations on the passive voice were the default mode of expression: human agency seemed to be obscured. Often the subject was depreciated to the position of indirect object. *I* was never warm or cold or well or sad—rather a nebulous "it" was warm or cold or well or sad *to me*. It felt as if the speaker had become the passive recipient of the world's caprices. Life was something that happened *to us*, fell *upon us*—and we dealt with it.

A year or so earlier, *pravda*—truth—had been the first word I learned in Czech. *To není možné* had been the first phrase: it was among the many ways to say that something was not possible. The realm of the not possible was vast. Very little was possible. Now I told my students not to translate *to není možné* into English.

"*Impossible*," I told them, "is a very strong word in English. Something has to be *literally*—physically, biologically—not possible."

For my students, though, especially the older ones, it was too late—they had already internalized the realm of the not possible. They had poignantly few ambitions—in any case, *ambition* was a word whose connotation was pejorative. My class of senior-year students composed essays on the topic "What I Would Like to Do When I Finish High School." The students wrote that they would like to go on to a university, they would like to study languages, or history, they would like to become lawyers or veterinarians. Yet they would cut themselves off: "*But I don't think that it will be possible.*"

My students were bright—they had been accepted to the only university preparatory school in their region—but they were also passive, in some sense deadened at sixteen or seventeen. They preferred memorization and rarely expressed any opinion. Communist content had been purged from that school, but a certain totalitarian form—or rather an acute sense of the world's restrictedness—lingered.

I worried about my students. I worried, too, about Galina's daughter, Mara, who was thirteen and a student at the school. From my first days in Domažlice, Galina was my only friend. Everyone else I met—the other teachers, the women wanting English lessons—seemed so reserved, in some paradoxical way so petit bourgeois in their intense concern for manners and prices and social status. Galina was open and revealing and so much less pragmatic, and our conversations were intimate almost at once. At the kitchen table in her small apartment hidden underneath the school's dormitory, we would sit for hours, drinking tea and talking about her fear of the headmaster. The headmaster was a man tiny in stature and authoritarian in bearing, who spoke not only to me but also to Galina and Jitka and each one of his colleagues as if to a member of a lower caste. He had a plain, heavy-set wife who towered over him and a lover who was the matron of the school's dormitory where I lived. She, too, was feared, and she reveled in being the mistress of a powerful man. The headmaster was suspicious of me—a foreigner, an American, a young woman—but he was openly hostile to Galina. A little man in a little town, the headmaster demanded unconditional obedience from her. After all, he would remind her, she was a homeless Soviet foreigner whom he had magnanimously agreed to employ.

Galina and I talked, too, about Czechs and Russians and Americans, about lost loves and sex and marriage, about languages and the ways they were so different, about how Galina had become a Christian, and about Mara.

Unlike her mother, Mara had quickly acculturated herself not only to the language but also to the accent and the mores, to the intricate local customs and social protocols. She knew who greeted whom first in public, and with what greeting, she knew when to bring cake and when to bring flowers, above all she knew how to be invisible. She was quiet and shy and possessed a kind of precocious wisdom. She wanted very much to be accepted. Yet although she did everything just as the Czechs did, she remained someone other.

▪ ▪ ▪

IN THE SENIOR class there was a seventeen-year-old girl with long blond hair named Lenka who was serious about dancing, had a natural talent for languages, and wanted to study at Charles University in Prague. Her classmates whispered that she was "ambitious." When Lenka returned from a bus trip to London she wrote in an essay:

> When I visited England, the people I lived with asked me whether the people in our country had been hungry or had suffered during the communist period. They thought that there had been great changes in our lives after the revolution. But it isn't true, at least in our family. In 1989 I was about twelve years-old and so I remember the communist era, the "tender revolution" and the events after it quite well. It is said now that the communist period was very cruel, that it was very difficult to live here, etc. I am not able to speak in general, but as for the people I knew very few of them suffered, we lived quite a normal life. Considering with our present life, it was nearly the same. There was no revolution in our town. Everything happened in Prague.

What Lenka wrote startled me. Everyone I'd met in Prague and in Bratislava had experienced communism's fall as a great drama. Its aftermath, too, continually ushered in new dramas: lustration, by exposing the names of informers, had destroyed not only careers but also friendships, families, and marriages. Václav Havel's general amnesty had emptied the prisons not only of political dissidents but also of ordinary criminals. The rise of nationalist politics had split Czechoslovakia in two.

Yet what was felt intensely in Prague was felt only mildly in Domažlice. Even the radical change of government was less radical in the provinces, where the lower and middle levels of bureaucracy remained embedded and where the teachers whose ideology the communist government had once deemed suitable for their profession continued to teach the same classes.

"I must say," one of my students wrote, *"that half of our neighbours were or are still communist. In offices and institutions are plenty of people, who were in StB (it's same as KGB in Russia). . . . And people are so, so impassive."*

"The system was destroyed," another student wrote, *"but people are still the same."*

"It was only a small revolution," wrote another, *"but it changed a lot of things."*

And it was true that even if people were still the same, this provincial town did experience other, different changes: above all the enormous inflation. The border to what had been West Germany was just a few miles from Domažlice, but until 1989 the border had been closed. Now everyone was free to go abroad, but soft currency and exchange rates made what was possible in theory very difficult in practice. Instead, it was the Germans who crossed the border to buy less expensive Czech products.

The students, like Lenka, understood this well—this was their lives—and while they spoke positively about the revolution they were not enamored of it. Before 1989, they had been too young to feel oppressed by censorship and too young to hate communism. Most real to them were the tangible changes in their own lives: Russian classes had ended and English and German classes had begun. There were new stores and new restaurants, new cafés and new bars. In the shops there were many things to buy but at high prices. The old buildings on the town square had been painted, and Domažlice looked much prettier now. Before the revolution, one girl wrote, *"everything was darker."*

A seventeen-year-old boy wrote of the May Day parades and of how he and his classmates would walk through town wearing red scarves, sending greetings to the Soviet Union and shouting, "Long live the Communist Party of Czechoslovakia!"

"Today it's amusing," he wrote, *"but in this time we were happy to have a day off from school."*

He lived not in Domažlice but in a nearby village, and he drew up a chart comparing his life before and after the revolution.

	Before	*After*
Town	*Staňkov (prefab house)*	*Staňkov (prefab house)*
Garden	*yes*	*yes*
Dog	*no*	*yes*
Money	*enough*	*a little shortage*
Equipment	*only essential things*	*more comfortable*
Freedom	*I can't say no freedom, but it was very little*	*almost completely*
Goods prices	*suited to my needs why? because almost everything was supported by state*	*for average wage too high*

I was happy he had a dog now.

The students were conscious of the fact that something called "freedom" had been achieved, yet they were conscious, too, of the fact that the world was still not open to them.

"The life in Domažlice before the revolution was not very differ-ent as now," one student wrote. *"We were going to the school, after school we were sitting on a bench and talking about our friends and school. But something changed after the revolution—we are free."*

In some ways Domažlice was a place where the revolution had barely happened—but then again it had.

▪ ▪ ▪

IN THE 1980S, when my Czech teacher Jarmila's parents had denounced her to the secret police, she'd taken refuge with her grandmother, a widow who lived alone in the small town of Ústí nad Orlicí, two hours or so east of Prague. And when Jarmila had left for the United States, it was her grandmother to whom she entrusted her papers: Charter 77 and Civic Forum documents, memoranda from the Velvet Revolution. Before I'd left Vermont, Jarmila had given me a letter introducing me to her grandmother: *"Receive her as you would me."*

In Prague I posted the letter. Jarmila's grandmother, Paní Bendová, wrote to me at once: it had been already several weeks since she'd had news from her granddaughter, and she'd been terribly worried. She hoped I would visit her soon and wrote of the beautiful countryside, of the castles and monasteries around Ústí nad Orlicí. I could come anytime, as soon as I liked, she was always at home. She would wait for me at the train station, under the clock, holding a photograph of Jarmila in her U. S. Army uniform. Paní Bendová was afraid for her granddaughter, so far away in America; she wanted very much for her to come home.

"I love her," Paní Bendová wrote of Jarmila, *"she's my sunshine."*

In Domažlice I wrote to Jarmila, who answered quickly: she was very glad to know that I would visit Ústí nad Orlicí. *"You'll have the chance to see places where I grew up, and moreover you'll be able to rest for a while from all problems and cares. You'll soon see that the Czech Republic is unlike America in many ways, that people live inside the attitudes of the last century, and that 'perhaps tomorrow' or 'it is not possible' is completely possible and normal."*

By now Jarmila had been in the hospital for eleven weeks. The doctors had diagnosed her with depression and post-traumatic stress disorder. They knew what was wrong but not how to help her.

"But don't tell my grandmother this," she wrote, *"she would worry unnecessarily. Insofar as I'm to end up on the streets in New York or somewhere else, I'll return to Prague."*

She hoped very much it would not come to that.

Days later I walked into my classroom to find a middle-aged man waiting for me. He was excited, or rather agitated, talking very quickly and in a colloquial language I couldn't make out at all. After some time I understood that he wanted me to come with him to his village, that he and his wife wanted to talk to me. Some minutes passed before I realized, suddenly, who he was: this man was Jarmila's father.

Some days later he returned. This time I got into the run-down car, and we set off for his village some ten or fifteen miles away. He was calmer now, and I understood more of what he said. When we arrived he took me first to a crumbling wooden building, a single room with a cross, a small altar, some flowers. It was their village church, and he wanted me to know that he and his wife did their best to look after it, to water the flowers. At their home, Jarmila's mother was waiting for me. She was nervous, excited. It had been four years since they'd last seen their daughter—the daughter they had once betrayed, who had now gone off to a far-away world.

It was midafternoon. Jarmila's mother poured Becherovka, a vaguely sweet Czech liquor that tasted of cinnamon but was deceptively strong, and we sat down in the kitchen, around a wooden table. She disappeared for a moment and then returned with a box of papers: Jarmila's childhood report cards. She had always had the highest grades in Russian. In the sixth grade she'd thrown chalk and an eraser at a picture of Czechoslovakia's communist leader, Gustav Husák. She'd also drawn three hairs on a picture of Lenin. Her parents had saved, too, press clippings from November 1989, the days of Civic Forum, when their daughter became a heroine of the revolution. And press clippings from a later time, when their daughter was already living across the ocean: Jarmila in her U.S. Army uniform, a Radio Free Europe journalist writing that Jarmila always appeared in every place where something was happening. She was fearless. When in November 1989 demonstrators were met with police violence, Jarmila—one article said—bore her injuries like a man. People called her "that pretty boy."

Jarmila's parents wanted me to know how proud they were of their daughter. And they wanted me to know how much they hated the communists, how much they had always hated the communists. When they had denounced their daughter to the secret police, it was only that they had two other children, that they were afraid. I understood what they meant: Jarmila's activities had put the entire family in danger.

They had a good Czech dictionary—an old two-volume dictionary of phraseology and idioms. They wanted me to have it. They wanted to do something for me—to help me, to feed me, to buy me things with money they surely did not have. I understood that their desperate generosity was a plea for forgiveness. But it was not for me to forgive them.

Some time afterward a letter arrived from Paní Bendová. She was happy I had met her son and daughter-in-law. *"They're good people,"* she wrote.

▪ ▪ ▪

IN DOMAŽLICE I took long walks and read Dostoevsky. *The Brothers Karamazov* absorbed me: Alyosha, who guessed that the Grand Inquisitor's secret was that he did not believe in God; Ivan, who insisted that if God was dead, then everything was permitted; Dmitri, who stared at Katya *"with a terrifying hatred, with the kind of hatred that is only a hair's breadth from the maddest, most desperate love."*

One night I walked to the town square and into a small café. It was empty but for one table of some half dozen young, attractive people—women in tight jeans and low-cut blouses and creamy makeup, their nails brightly colored, their hair dyed the same brilliant auburn, their boyfriends' arms hanging possessively around their shoulders. One of the men with tousled dirty blond hair called out, gesturing for me to join them. He introduced himself: his name was Libor.

Now some evenings I would go to the newly opened Italian-style café where Libor and his friends spent most of their time. One of them, Markéta, served as both bartender and waitress. She wore thick mascara and bright lipstick, tight black dresses cut low enough to hint at lacy lingerie. On the nights when she was not working she would come to the café as a customer, in jeans with a leotard top. Her girlfriends, the women I had met with Libor, would come to show her their new purchases, laying shopping bags on the bar counter and pulling out black stockings, auburn hair dye, violet nail polish, a red scarf. Markéta's boyfriend, adoring, would come, too. I admired Markéta: the way she enjoyed inhabiting her body, pouring drinks, being beautiful. And I was jealous of her—of her presentism and contentment.

Libor lived with his parents, not in Domažlice, but in a village a few miles away. As an adolescent, he had been sent to a vocational school and trained to work with machinery. He was eighteen when the revolution came and freed him from an officially assigned job. Instead he parlayed his charm into a relatively well-paying position at the local insurance company. Before the revolution he'd been unconcerned with politics: there was first love, there was soccer and ice hockey. Now, after the revolution, he was only slightly less unconcerned with politics. The time after work he spent at bars and cafés, he drank beer and chain-smoked, he played cards and read soft-porn magazines. He was very proud of his job at the insurance agency. It was a good job—he had his own business card—and money had become very important in these past few years. It had changed people. Once no one had had very much, but everyone had had some. Now some people had a lot, and some people had almost nothing. His parents struggled with this, but for Libor it was not a problem at all. On the contrary, he preferred it this way.

■ ■ ■

A LETTER ARRIVED from Miloš in Slovakia, who had lost his seat in parliament in the September 1994 elections. His tone was neither defensive nor sad: now he had more time for himself—and for his family.

"I think," he wrote in Slovak-inflected Czech, "that your Czech is similar to my daughter's Slovak, and that you two would understand each other. (That was a joke.) And now seriously. If you're feeling lonely, come to our place at least for a weekend. . . . You're warmly invited and my woman (wife), Maria, is now learning English (she's terribly ashamed), I'm not supposed to tell you."

In early October I decided to go to Slovakia to visit them. Miloš, together with Maria and little Maria, was now living in a small town called Topol'čany, two hours from Bratislava. Now again we drank red wine mixed with Coca-Cola and drove through the countryside to visit a castle. At the bookstore in Topol'čany Miloš picked out a dozen books and asked the bookseller to wrap them: they were a present for me. The books—some in Czech, some in Slovak—were mostly works of *samizdat* literature, originally printed in underground editions on thin paper and in small type. For years they'd been banned, now they were on display—in fact on sale at a large discount: no longer was there much interest in dissident literature. Communism was over.

The trip from Domažlice to Topol'čany was long, and on the way I had stopped in Prague, where Amanda met me at the train station. By now she had been in Prague for nearly three months. She was trying very hard to orient herself in this new life, to find a place for herself in this foreign city—while Oskar was trying to find a place for himself among the friends of his youth. Two disconnected projects. We wandered the city, stopping in pubs and cafés, drinking red wine and smoking cigarettes. I only pretended to smoke. I didn't inhale, I only liked to tap the ashes into the ashtray.

Later, after I returned to Domažlice, Vlasta wrote to me: there would be no Halloween party at Amanda and Oskar's apartment after all, as it seemed that for Amanda and Oskar life in Prague *"was not party-like . . . for various reasons."*

■ ■ ■

IN HER LETTER Vlasta added, *"I hope you are already feeling better, coping with Domažlice somehow, not letting the small world overwhelm you."*

Had my Czech been better, I could have learned much from my Ukrainian friend Galina's daughter Mara about this small world, about the students, the school, the teachers, the town. I was preoccupied with the language's grammatical intricacy, but I was slow to absorb the social codes that were so much more important. My colleagues, like the other adults in the town, kept their distance. It was the students who accepted me the most, especially the younger ones.

At the school classes were often interrupted by construction work, for the headmaster had a rather grandiose expansion plan: he wanted to enlarge the cafeteria, open it at lunchtime to local businessmen, and in this way make a profit for the school. Because the construction workers worked only during the day, and only on weekdays, the drilling and hammering often made it difficult to hear anything else. Several classrooms could not be used at all, so the headmaster had arranged for one class of fourteen-year-olds to be transferred to a decrepit building on the other side of the town, a fifteen-minute walk from the school.

Winter arrived in Bohemia early that year. One day in November I walked through the snow to reach the fourteen-year-olds' temporary classroom. When I came into the building something felt different. Inside the students were wearing their coats and scarves: the stove had broken and there was no heat. It was already the middle of the day, and the students were frozen. After a moment I asked them all to stand: we would do something that involved movement, they would warm up.

They all stood. And that was when I noticed they were wearing no shoes. By then I knew it was Czech custom to remove one's shoes indoors—at home or when visiting someone else's home. Stranger, though, was the shoe-changing rule at school: inside both school buildings, students—although not teachers—were required to remove their shoes and change into something resembling slippers. This remained true despite the construction that left sand and dust around the school, and this remained true in that small, dirty building on the other side of town where the stove had broken. Their shoes—much warmer winter boots—were piled outside the classroom door, and I told the students to put them back on.

No one moved. Then a girl in the front row, Tereza, asked if they could *really* put their shoes back on. Tereza was unlike the other students: her parents were from Prague, and even though she and her brother had been born and had lived all their lives in Domažlice, she was still in some way an outsider. She had been formed by Prague, where both of her grandmothers lived and where she visited often. She was a pacifist with the long, straight hair of a hippie. She dressed like a flower child, refused to eat meat, and loved the Beatles. Tereza's father was a lawyer who'd read *samizdat;* Tereza's mother as a child had lived for a year in India and spoke English. They were an intelligentsia family, exiled to the provinces by the capital's housing shortage.

A girl sitting beside Tereza added that in the morning, when they'd learned the heat was broken, their math teacher had warned them that she would report anyone wearing shoes to the feared headmaster. I hardly understood what to make of this. I only said it was cold, and they should put on their shoes. I promised to take full responsibility: no one would be reported to the headmaster. Still they hesitated, unsure, I saw, of whether to trust me—then Tereza got up, and the others followed.

I thought it was scandalous: students kept all day in a freezing building, no one responsible for fixing the heat. Public opinion, though, reached a different consensus: I was the one who was scandalous. What right did I have to suspend the shoe-changing rule? The headmaster was very angry. I was ostracized by the other teachers—for my audacity, for not respecting hierarchy, for believing I was above the rules.

I didn't apologize, I was too mystified—and in some way indignant: I felt protective of my students. I knew Tereza's mother a bit, and when I next saw her I began to tell her the story of the broken stove and the shoes and the headmaster's wrath. But she already knew; Tereza had told her. She'd even gone to the school board and put in a formal request: given that the heat was not working, perhaps the headmaster could formally suspend the shoe-changing rule until the stove was repaired. And the school board had responded: it was impossible to do this right away. The proposal would be considered at the next meeting, which would take place in a few weeks.

"But that's absurd," I said.

"Of course," Tereza's mother said, "but here we're used to that."

In the communist years, Tereza's father later told me, Czecho-slovakia was called Absurdistan. Around 1970 time had stopped; afterward there was no movement, only stagnation. He had never believed he would live to see a way out. People suffered in different ways, he explained, but the worst thing was the feeling of pow-erlessness: the obligation to take part in elections with only one candidate, to perform the empty rituals. He and his family did not go to May Day parades; every year he and his wife asked that their children be excused because the family would be away in the coun-tryside. One year the teacher appointed one of his son's classmates to spy on them: she suspected they had not really left town.

Someone who didn't live here, who didn't have these experi-ences, would never understand, Tereza's father told me. And it was true. I didn't really understand.

My older colleague Jitka, who had been teaching at the school for so many years, was both sympathetic toward me and terri-bly distressed by the headmaster's anger; she wanted me to un-derstand the context for the shoe-changing rule, and she tried to explain: "Everything is impossible here. It is impossible to make copies, because only the secretary is allowed to make them, and sometimes she's in a bad mood. It is impossible to argue with the headmaster. It is impossible to fix the lights, to allow a student to take a history class this year if a year ago she thought she wanted to study languages."

The realm of the not possible was expansive: it included the new, the uncommon, the difficult, as well as the vaguely inconvenient, the previously unconsidered, that which someone was not in the mood to do at the moment. And nothing could be done without the proper rubber stamp. To acquire the proper stamp it was usually necessary to acquire a series of them, each a prerequisite for the next. A given stamp was generally in the hands of a single person, a local bureaucrat who had been made inordinately powerful by such a possession and who might prove to be capricious, or greedy, or resentful—or simply absentminded, or ill, or lazy, or indefinitely on vacation.

My colleagues' wariness of me—a foreigner, a single woman— had become active distaste. Now, though, the students in that class trusted me, they talked to me. Among them I became a kind of heroine. It was not deserved: for I was a heroine only by virtue of a lack of acculturation.

∎ ∎ ∎

AFTER SOME TIME my impudent suspension of the shoe-changing rule gave way to more exciting news: a team of American scientists had discovered new evidence disproving Darwin's theory of evolution—and they had written to the headmaster announcing their willingness to include Domažlice on their European lecture tour. The headmaster was extremely proud—and vindicated in his sense of superiority: certainly it was not by chance that prominent American scientists had chosen his school.

The headmaster had not himself been able to read the letter, which was written in English. Jitka and Galina, though, had read the letter; and I asked to see it. I'd already guessed who the "scientists" were: American Christian missionaries were ubiquitous in postcommunist Eastern Europe.

I read the letter. And I insisted to Jitka and Galina that these were not scientists and that this had to be explained to the headmaster. They were being exploited, made fools of: these alleged American scientists understood perfectly well they would never be given a platform at a school in their own country. But I had no authority to correct the headmaster's impressions. He had already canceled classes for the day of the scientists' visit and announced the lecture to the entire town. All of the students would be required to attend; the public would be invited as well.

The day came. Five or six American born-again Christians appeared at the school with dozens of colored slides and an enthusiastic interpreter of moderate competence from a nearby town. There were hundreds of people in the room. The presentation began: the

slides of chimpanzees and orangutans, the slides of human beings, the slides outlining the differences between apes and human
beings. Students and teachers and local adults listened with rapt
intensity—and at a certain moment I realized that even the smart-
est among them, listening in Czech to the interpreter, could not
hear what I could hear painfully clearly in English: that these were
not educated people. Even had the claims not been so ridiculous,
the pretext for visiting Domažlice so improbable, among English
speakers their language would have given them away.

Then the slide show was over and it was time for questions. I
raised my hand, and began to speak—first in Czech, through the
interpreter, then—flushed, enraged—in English, directly to the visitors: how dare they? They had no right to come here to manipulate
my students—my students who, after years of communist propaganda, were just learning to think for themselves, and now these
fanatics had come here to trick them. Why didn't they just tell their
audience who they really were? Why didn't they just say they were
Christian missionaries who had come to talk about God? How dare
they pretend to be scientists? This was a lie.

The visitors were disturbed. They hadn't expected to encounter
another American. They defended themselves: after all, if these
were my students and I really cared about them, did I want them
to go through their lives believing they'd been descended from barbaric apes?

By now we were shouting at one another. The atmosphere of rev-
erence was broken. I had ruined what should have been one of the
headmaster's proudest moments. He—and my colleagues—would
now resent me as much as I resented the missionaries.

I regretted that I had done this to Jitka, who was so long-
suffering, and so good, and who could not entirely believe that the
American visitors were impostors. I pleaded with her, with Galina,
with my students to trust me.

By then it was already December, and the town square was covered with snow—and full of fish sellers: baking fresh carp was a
Czech Christmas tradition. The peddlers slaughtered the carp on

the spot, at the moment of purchase, and the white snow on the town square was saturated with the fresh blood of fish.

I knew I had to leave. And in January 1995 I did, having failed to understand the provinces and failed to find any place for myself there. I knew that I would see Galina and her daughter, Mara, again. Perhaps someday we would talk about the missionaries. The students whom I had allowed to wear their shoes bought me presents: chocolate and a stone charm of a silvery blue. Tereza's friend, the fourteen-year-old girl who had described her heartbreak over her boyfriend's betrayal in an essay, gave me a goodbye card: *"It's sad, that you must leave Domažlice. If I could I would say to you—'Marci, please don't go,' but I know, that it is not possible, that you must go.... —Life is cruel.... Bye and remember sometimes to your students from Domažlice."*

Pornography in Prague

I left Domažlice for Prague, where I moved into a room in an elderly couple's apartment. Pan Prokop and Paní Prokopová had been retired for some time; the inflation that followed communism's collapse had made their pensions now worth almost nothing. They could not pay their rent without taking in a boarder, and they could not imagine leaving their home of so many years: a small two-bedroom apartment with a tiny kitchen, some thirty minutes from the city's center in a district called Vokovice filled with identical housing blocks, the uniform gray concrete standing for a socialist aesthetic of equality. Just fifty feet from their building was Evropská ulice, the main thoroughfare leading from the end of the metro line to the airport. Just ten minutes by foot in the other direction, behind the complex of apartment blocks, the city ended and the woods began.

Pan Prokop and Paní Prokopová looked like so many other gray-haired couples in a country where youth passed quickly. Theirs was an ageless agedness: they might have been anywhere between sixty and eighty. As a couple, they were neither happy nor unhappy. Their relationship seemed harmonious if not affectionate, and they suffered most from boredom. They no longer worked, nor did they have the money to go to restaurants or concerts. During the days they watched television. American sitcoms from the 1980s now were aired with Czech dubbing, and they also followed *Dallas* intently: did I know who shot J.R.? If I'd once known, I no longer remembered. They spoke to me with great patience and attentiveness. Nearly every day we talked about Prague. The city had changed, and not in a way that Paní Prokopová liked. The new Prague frightened her. Under communism the streets had been completely safe. The Czechs remained unused to crime; once—not so long ago—there had been almost none. Time and time again Paní Prokopová warned me to be careful: the city had become threatening, there were thieves, gangsters, violent men who would steal my purse and perhaps assault me as well.

Paní Prokopová was preoccupied with prices: how much each item—each pot and pan, each plate, each box of kasha, each carton of milk—cost now, and how much it had cost "then"—before the end of communism. She was not devoted to communist ideology, and nothing that she or her husband ever said suggested that either of them had read Marx or Lenin. Yet they knew one thing: communism had been better for them than what existed now. What for Tereza's parents in Domažlice had been an unbearable torpor was for Paní Prokopová a comfortable stability. In the "normalization" years after 1968, there were men and women—if only a handful—who had willingly risked their lives to speak the truth. Paní Prokopová and her husband, though, had felt no need for uncensored literature, underground rock concerts, Radio Free Europe, or even open borders. The Velvet Revolution had brought freedoms they had no use for, and in any case had not the money to enjoy. Their whole adult lives they had worked under the communist regime, and that regime had promised they would be cared for in their old age. Now the social contract had been broken. For their generation the revolution had come too late. For Pan Prokop and Paní Prokopová, it would have been better had it not come at all.

▪ ▪ ▪

PRAGUE IN 1995 was a city in motion, transforming itself from one day to the next. Two decades of stagnation had ended, and now there was little stability and little security. Young Gypsy children playing accordions asked for money on trams and sometimes pick-pocketed. Everywhere there was new wealth and new poverty. Since 1991, refugees fleeing the bloody Yugoslav wars of ethnic cleansing had been arriving in Prague; desperate women roamed the streets, begging for money and holding their babies.

It was a time, too, when prurience was unabashed. Matchboxes, telephone cards, and plastic bags at supermarkets came decorated with pornographic pictures. In January a new billboard advertisement for Sony stereos pictured a young woman with bare shoulders, her chin resting on a pillow, a Sony stereo system beside her, and the slogan *"Muži chtějí ženy, které poslouchají . . . "* (Men want women who listen . . .). It was a play on words: in Czech the verb "to listen to" is the same as the verb "to obey."

And there were the men who ceaselessly called out to women on the streets. Sexual harassment—for which there was no word in Czech—was endemic, and not considered to be in especially bad taste. That spring a literary weekly published a long interview with my former Czech teacher Vlasta. She spoke about her American students, young women who resented the way Czech men shouted at them, mocked them, propositioned them. And I knew she was speaking of me.

In the interview Vlasta spoke, too, about *Fear of Flying*: yes, there was a lot of sex, but—she insisted—the book was not only about sex, it was also about the way sex became a prism, a way of perceiving the world. The heroine Isadora's escape into fantasies of the "zipless fuck" came from the feeling that she was unable to take not only her sexual life but also the whole of her life into her own hands. For Isadora, to "fly" was to act purely from her own will.

Since the book's publication, Vlasta had been receiving letters from readers: there were Czech women who appreciated what she had done for them. Yet this was not the only reaction. To translate *Fear of Flying*, Vlasta had needed to invent in Czech a new sexual vocabulary for women, and there were many Czechs who were not happy to see Erica Jong's feminist sexual explicitness imported into their culture. Among the many critical reviews it seemed to Vlasta only one had grasped the novel's essence—and that was the one published in *Playboy.*

Sexual explicitness from a man was taken for granted. My former teacher Arnošt Lustig had published a new novel, and now on the metro I began to read about "Tanga, the girl from Hamburg." The novel took place in 1943 at the prison in the Theresienstadt ghetto. There the narrator, then a sixteen-year-old boy, met the twenty-year-old Tanga, a circus artist and prostitute. Among her first words to him were: *"There isn't a woman in the world who wouldn't like to be a whore for at least an hour a day."*

Tanga herself emerged as a philosopher-prostitute figure—she was beautiful and noble, saucy and defiant. She was what was redemptive in the midst of horror. She had the power of redemption, not in spite of who she was, but because of who she was. I translated for an American literary journal a passage from the very end of the book: the narrator watched Tanga dress after they had spent their first night together. It was also their last, as Tanga had been summoned to the next transport to the East—that is, to Auschwitz.

She grew old even before she pulled the dress over her head. She fastened the buttons starting from the bottom. She was no longer looking toward the mountains. Perhaps in her mind she saw the devil. He was in her shadow, in my shadow. In the darkness that was receding. In the way she showed her teeth when she smiled; in the way I answered her with the same, short smile. In the way it grew light, even though it was still impossible to see the shadows; in the railway tracks to the east; in the hills, which—by the time morning came—she would no longer see, because she would be far away. She fastened the last button around her neck. She slipped on tall riding boots. I didn't tell her while she was dressing how often I would think of her. She was no longer sitting up. Perhaps she felt sick. Everything that made her a prostitute had melted away. She no longer needed it. She was thinking about what the elderly think about before they die, about how long it would last. Or she was thinking about nothing. She was beautiful and indifferent and dignified.

The story was so much an expression of Arnošt: of his lasciviousness, of his ability to find the beautiful in the awful.

▪ ▪ ▪

ONE DAY MY former student Tereza, whose grandmothers lived in Prague, came to visit from Domažlice. I decided I would take her to meet the long-haired Scout from Berkeley. When on a Saturday afternoon we appeared, unexpectedly, at his small, disheveled apartment in Malá Strana, he offered us avocados. They were terribly expensive in Prague, and they were Scout's single Western luxury. He did not make salad or anything else with them—he ate them just as they were. They reminded him of California. I introduced him to Tereza. She wanted to know about the 1960s, I told him. She wanted to know what it was like to be in California then.

We walked to Barbar and ordered french fries. Scout began to tell stories. I looked at them: Scout in faded jeans, his long graying hair tied back in a ponytail, the aging hippie computer genius. A character from People's Park in Berkeley, ebullient and irreverent. Tereza, a fourteen-year-old girl from a small Czech town with the long black hair and the flowing dress of a flower child, enraptured by his narration, by the authenticity of the encounter.

"The difference between us and you," Scout said, "is that here you don't protest anything. We protested everything."

Yet the American counterculture, the antiwar movement of the 1960s and 1970s, was a curiously resonant motif in Prague. There was a John Lennon memorial wall not far from Scout's apartment. During the November 1989 demonstrations protesters had carried flowers. I had a picture of my Czech teacher Marcela amid the crowd on Wenceslas Square, holding a rose. In 1965 Allen Ginsberg had visited Prague, where he'd met Václav Havel, who was then a student. After the Velvet Revolution they'd renewed their acquaintance, and Allen Ginsberg was impressed by how much the new president of Czechoslovakia had been influenced by Ginsberg's own counterculture: jazz music and the Beatles, Bob Dylan and Jack Kerouac.

■ ■ ■

IN THE EVENINGS that winter I spent much time with Pan Prokop and Paní Prokopová. In their apartment there was a certain comfortable rhythm to the days. They looked forward, I began to sense, to my coming home. Paní Prokopová in particular was full of concern about me—because I was a vegetarian, and because I was a woman alone. Many evenings she spent explaining to me why it was important to eat meat and why it was important to find a husband. Then, when it grew warm, Paní Prokopová and her husband began to spend more and more time at their cottage in the countryside. In the summer Paní Prokopová tended their garden and pickled vegetables and canned fruits to eat throughout the year. In Prague they took on a second boarder. I met Klaudie on the day she moved into the apartment with the help of her brother-in-law, a man in his thirties who worked for a computer company. There was something distasteful about him, a certain kind of crass arrogance. And he was very ugly. Paní Prokopová and Pan Prokop were at their cottage that day, and Klaudie, her brother-in-law, and I sat down around the table. Klaudie's brother-in-law tried to speak to me in English, which he spoke badly, barely at all. But this was not the reason I responded only in Czech. His demeanor was not subtle: he wanted to speak English with me because Klaudie could not, he wanted to show her that he was superior.

Klaudie I liked at once just as intensely as I disliked her brother-in-law. She was a medical student who had come from her hometown in Slovakia to attend Charles University in Prague a few years earlier, when Czechoslovakia still existed and Prague was the capital of her country. Then came the "Velvet Divorce"—the breakup of Czechoslovakia into the Czech Republic and Slovakia—and in the middle of her studies she lost her rights of citizenship and became a foreigner.

There was a kind of immediate intimacy between us. Klaudie was unusually expressive, and from the first day we met I understood her well.

From Klaudie I learned much about the medical profession—and the postcommunist economy. That year doctors and nurses were contemplating a strike: in the Czech Republic, as in the other post-communist countries, educated professionals received poverty-level salaries. To control inflation, the state had frozen state-sector wages. Czech teachers, too, were threatening a strike. Galina told me that in Domažlice the headmaster had called a meeting of the faculty, making it understood that he would not tolerate their taking part in any such thing.

"And they really were afraid of *him,"* Galina wrote of her fellow teachers.

For Klaudie, the financial crisis in the medical profession was only the most recent chapter in a life that was not—and had not been—easy. A single woman in her late twenties with no money and an exhausting course of study, she had for years sustained a long-distance relationship with a man twenty years older, a Slovak émigré who was a professor in Basel. He telephoned every day but came to visit only rarely.

Despite all difficulties, Klaudie had enormous energy and a peculiarly vivacious spirit. She was full of joie de vivre. Her eyes sparkled and she dyed her hair a glimmering red. When she returned late at night after assisting in some difficult surgery, her face would be glowing. She was extraordinarily resilient. And principled.

■ ■ ■

IT WAS VLASTA, who at Stanford had taught Czech to both me and Amanda, who called me one afternoon to tell me that Oskar had committed suicide.

"He wanted to come home," Vlasta said, "but for him there was no home here."

The morning mass Amanda had arranged in the church tucked behind Old Town Square was followed by lunch at the pub that was the favorite meeting place of Oskar's friends. In Massachusetts Amanda and Oskar's son, an anti–domestic violence activist and a counselor for men who beat their wives, had written a eulogy for his father. Vlasta had translated it into Czech so that today Amanda could read it to Oskar's friends.

"I'm told," Oskar's son wrote, *"to focus on the positive, but I can't help but be bitter."*

> *It didn't have to happen this way.*
> *It had everything to do with being raised male. . . .*
> *Who was there to listen to his disappointment when he returned to a country poisoned by the cheap mediocrity and plastic that seems to inevitably come with capitalism?*
> *This could have been a time of great promise, of great change in him. I was happy that he was finally confiding how he felt. But it didn't happen, it was cut short by this curse called "masculinity."*
> *And this kind of thing has gone on for generations but it can go on no longer. I pledge that it will stop with me. . . . I pledge to fight against these inhumane male roles, because they hurt gentle, dear men like my father and because they have killed him, and I wasn't done loving him yet.*

Vlasta was the perfect translator, but this was not the perfect audience—these middle-aged Czech men who did not understand why a twenty-eight-year-old man would criticize masculinity. Amanda wanted desperately to talk to them about what had happened to Oskar. But Oskar's friends did not understand why Oskar—who had long ago abandoned them for a freer and more luxurious life in the West, who had not suffered through those last two decades of communism as they had—should be pitied. They did not understand what this American woman who had aged so well, who was so much more beautiful than their own wives, wanted from them at all. As Amanda appealed to them and Vlasta interpreted, one by one Oskar's friends walked out of the pub.

▪ ▪ ▪

IT WAS ALREADY close to dawn when I left Amanda and returned to Paní Prokopová's apartment. A few hours later I had to be at the train station. I was going to Ústí nad Orlicí, to visit Jarmila's grandmother.

Paní Bendová had written to me often throughout the year, always worried about her granddaughter. She suspected Jarmila was hiding something and implored me to tell her if I knew anything more. I always answered her letters, but I told her nothing of her granddaughter's stay in the hospital. I was loyal to Jarmila, who wrote me warm letters, telling me not to fear people's whispers and not to fear making mistakes. *"And when you feel alone,"* she said, *"you can* always *write to me. Anything."*

That entire year I'd been in the Czech Republic Jarmila had spent in and out of the hospital in Vermont. The military college expelled her and revoked her scholarship. She had no insurance to pay for the psychotropic medications the doctors said were essential to her survival. They'd diagnosed her with post-traumatic stress disorder, whose origins lay in her secret police interrogations before the revolution and in the bullying she faced in the American military afterward. She never told me exactly what had happened to her in the army—or exactly what had happened to her during the interrogations. In her letters there were only dark allusions.

Jarmila wanted to study again, to return, now as an American, to the life of a young intellectual she had begun in Prague. She had, though, no money and no scholarship. Without a scholarship she could not enroll at another university, and without student status she could not renew her visa. Above all she feared deportation. She loved the United States with the passion of a revolutionary and was deeply convinced that she deserved to be there. Moreover, she did not believe she would be able to cope in the Czech Republic: she would go back only as a last, desperate resort.

On the day after Oskar's memorial service, I arrived in Ústí nad

Orlicí. Beneath the large clock at the train station stood a petite, elderly woman with fair hair, holding a large photograph: Jarmila's U.S. Army portrait. I looked at her and smiled. When Paní Bendová saw me, she began to cry.

We walked through the town square, which, like the square in Domažlice, was framed by arcade-style buildings painted pastel colors. Here the buildings were just a bit stockier and more robust, with curlicues and ribbons and other pieces of neoclassical ornamentation decorating the windows.

When we reached her apartment Paní Bendová began to feed me at once. She herself was thin, but she had an obsession with food, or rather with hunger. It was impossible to eat enough to please her. She fed me with a kind of fervent compulsion, as if she feared I might otherwise perish that very day, in her small apartment.

"But Marcelka," she said when I tried to explain that I couldn't eat any more, "I don't want you to be hungry!"

I wondered if this were an affliction of those who had lived through the war: they would never lose their fear of hunger. My landlady, Paní Prokopová, had a similar preoccupation.

Jarmila's grandmother brought me a box of papers. There was a picture of Jarmila as a teenage girl, looking much softer than I had known her, speaking to a handsome priest with the gentlest of gazes. There was something special about the priest—a look of such love in his eyes. As Paní Bendová talked I understood that it was he who had led this young woman—then only a girl—into the Catholic opposition, into the underground.

In the box there were other documents as well: a Charter 77 memorial for the philosopher Jan Patočka, bulletins from the revolutionary days of November 1989, an open letter from Czechoslovak students to Communist Party leaders:

> *Esteemed Comrades! Please understand that we will live in a wholly different world than the world in which your generation lived. . . . If the welfare of this country, this society, these*

nations actually weighs so much on your hearts, if the fate of your own party, the fate of socialism, of rebuilding, the fate of the young generation, that is, our fate, actually weighs so much on your hearts—please go away.

Most of the documents were Civic Forum declarations composed in November and December 1989 at the Magic Lantern Theater, where Václav Havel was then directing his greatest production. There were plans for a general strike and demands that all members of the Communist Party's Central Committee who had collaborated with the 1968 invasion resign at once. There were calls, too, for a free press and free artistic expression, for respect for the rule of law, for adherence to international human rights accords, and for the release of all prisoners of conscience.

"We strive," Civic Forum wrote, *"to help our country once again occupy a dignified place in Europe and in the world. We are part of Central Europe."*

I saw a photograph of Jarmila, sitting around a table at the Magic Lantern Theater with other members of Civic Forum, once dissidents, now improvisers of the revolution. There was a Christmas note from Václav Havel dated December 1989. By this time communism had already fallen and Havel was just days away from his inauguration as Czechoslovakia's first postcommunist president.

That evening Paní Bendová was reluctant to let me go. I was like a messenger from another world, her proof that Jarmila had not disappeared into an abyss, that it was possible to get from there to here, that she might yet see her granddaughter again. Yet while Paní Bendová wished desperately for Jarmila to come home, it was precisely this—coming home—that Jarmila feared most. She was determined to remain in the United States, and she despaired that she would be deported.

"I don't know," Jarmila wrote, *"what more to do. Perhaps only to go to church and pray..."*

God was important to her.

■　■　■

MY AMERICAN FRIEND Brad, who was writing a dissertation about the 1948 communist takeover of Czechoslovakia, wanted to go on a field trip: to the ghost village of Lidice. In May 1942, during the German occupation, soldiers of the Czechoslovak government in exile succeeded in assassinating Reinhard Heydrich, *Reichsprotektor* of Bohemia and Moravia. The Germans took vengeance. Lidice was the scapegoat: they razed the village and massacred the villagers, sending the children to be gassed at Chełmno. Lidice was just twenty miles from Prague, yet difficult to find because it no longer existed. Still, in the end we found this absence of a place.

This was the year the Czechs celebrated the fiftieth anniversary of their liberation from the Nazis. Victory Day had always been a communist holiday. Now, though, the emphasis had shifted: everyone wanted to forget the Red Army soldiers who had liberated Prague and remember instead the American troops who had liberated Plzeň, an hour and a half to the west.

In 1936 the Czech novelist Karel Čapek had published the apocalyptic *War with the Newts*, a tale of the world's takeover by hideous salamanders. At the novel's end, the overpowered world leaders gathered for a conference.

> *In a somewhat depressed atmosphere another proposal was put on the agenda: that Central China be yielded to the salamanders for inundation. In return the Newts would undertake to guarantee in perpetuity the coasts of the European states and their colonies. . . . The Chinese delegate was given the floor, but unfortunately nobody understood what he was saying.*

Karel Čapek's science fiction was eerily prescient: two years after *The War with the Newts'* publication, French prime minister Édouard Daladier, Italian fascist leader Benito Mussolini, and British prime minister Neville Chamberlain traveled to a hotel in Munich to meet with Adolf Hitler. At issue was the Sudetenland, a western region of

Czechoslovakia home to many ethnic Germans. Hitler wanted it—and Neville Chamberlain acquiesced. He was certain Hitler would be satisfied now—and certain he himself had done the right thing.

"How horrible, fantastic, incredible it is," the British prime minister said, "that we should be digging trenches and trying on gas masks here because of a quarrel in a faraway country between people of whom we know nothing!"

It mattered little that no one understood Czech, for Czechoslovakia had not been invited to the Munich conference at all.

And so Hitler's Third Reich annexed the Sudetenland, and Neville Chamberlain returned to London and told the British people, "I bring you peace in our time."

Just a few months later, in March 1939, Hitler invaded Bohemia and Moravia, while Slovakia became a Catholic fascist state, nominally independent, allied with Nazi Germany. Then on the first of September Nazi Germany attacked Poland. The Second World War began. Neville Chamberlain had been mistaken.

In English Chamberlain's decision was "the appeasement at Munich." In Czech Chamberlain's decision had always been *"zrada w Mnichově"* (the betrayal at Munich). Bourgeois democracy had failed to protect Czechoslovakia from fascism. The West had sold out Czechoslovakia to Hitler.

On the night of the fiftieth anniversary of the liberation I returned to the apartment to find Pan Prokop there alone. When I arrived he poured us drinks, and he began to talk about what had happened in his country a half century earlier. He had been a young man then, sent off to forced labor in Germany. We toasted the end of the Second World War.

It was the first time he had spoken to me of the war. It was also the last. The next morning Pan Prokop left again to join his wife in the countryside. Some days later I returned home to find Paní Prokopová there unexpectedly. She said to me at once, "He died, Marcelka, he died."

"The Human Being
Is Rather Perverse"

In Prague I continued to teach some English classes, now at a language school for adults. More of my time that spring of 1995, though, I spent working as an intern for an ethnic conflict project at an American-funded research institute, one of the many Western NGOs that had come to Eastern Europe since the fall of the Iron Curtain. Graduate students, mostly political scientists, passed through, but the institute was not run by researchers. The people who mattered there had come from other worlds, from politics and finance. I was assigned to do research on postcommunist Romania.

One day the institute's Prague director asked me to write a briefing on how best to promote bipartisan cooperation in the Romanian parliament. He was leaving the following day for Bucharest, with the intention of negotiating an agreement to provide research support to the Romanian legislature. Yet there was a flaw in the plan: there was no such thing as bipartisan cooperation in Romania. The Romanian parliament included over two dozen political parties breaking up and re-forming on a daily basis, like cliques in a junior high school. Soon afterward, the director called a breakfast meeting to determine how to create democratic culture in Eastern Europe.

This was not, though, the kind of problem that could be resolved over pastries and orange juice. Communism—it had turned out—was not a wicked witch, after whose death all could live happily ever after. Rather, the fall of communism had opened a Pandora's box, and ethnic conflict was just one among many demons to escape. It was true not only in what had once been Yugoslavia, where rapes of tens of thousands of women—mostly Bosnian Muslims—accompanied massacres in wars of ethnic cleansing.

At the institute, I researched issues of language rights, cultural autonomy, and political representation concerning Romanian's Hungarian minority—just over 7 percent of the country's population, some 1.6 million people, most of them in Transylvania. In the twentieth century this colorful region in the Carpathian basin was passed back and forth according to the vagaries of international politics. At the century's beginning, Transylvania had belonged to the Kingdom of Hungary, which had in turn belonged to the Habsburg monarchy. When the First World War brought an end to empires, Hungary lost Transylvania, and the beautiful wooded landscape that was home to Romanians, Hungarians, Germans, and Jews passed to Romania for the next twenty years. In 1940, during the Second World War, Nazi Germany awarded northern Transylvania to Hungary. In 1945, the Allies gave the region once more to Romania. By the 1990s, when revolutions seemed as if they might reopen territorial questions, this land of peasants had long found itself at the center of power struggles.

I read about Romanian history and Hungarian history, about battles over statues, about Transylvanian villagers and about the communist dictator Nicolae Ceauşescu's personality cult, about his hedonistic indulgences and sadistic practices. Through daily news reports I followed Romanian politics: personalities and parties, their shifting policies toward minorities, their ephemeral alliances, their capricious conversions.

Romanian politics was not simply a politics of opportunism inspired by the money and power available for the taking during the transition. More than that, it was a politics of ideological excess. Corneliu Vadim-Tudor, once Nicolae Ceauşescu's court poet, had reincarnated himself as the leader of the Greater Romania Party, conjuring up images of Western-Jewish-Hungarian conspirators who coveted Transylvania and plotted its conquest. Nicolae Ceaușescu was dead, and communism was over, but Corneliu Vadim-Tudor retained his flair for bombastic stylization, for pushing language toward the exorbitant. He was fond of speaking of "we" and "you," and he relished addressing enemies real and imagined.

> *No trespassing, dear Hungarian irredentists and highly cherished Romanian traitors, we do not believe in your variant of the Common European Home. That's how we are, more boorish, more primitive, we do not like being other people's servants and grooms, we want to be our own masters in our souls' home, you can make no headway, think better of it and rather colonize that steppe of yours or rent some lands in Siberia and Asia, but get used to the idea that Transylvania will be forever Romanian.*

Communism had exalted the worker. In his postcommunist incarnation, Corneliu Vadim-Tudor exalted the peasant—the Romanian peasant who was not to be trifled with, who was ever ready to use his spear to batter the heads of his enemies. *"And if UN intervention troops do come,"* Tudor announced, *"as some Hungarian extremists keep threatening us, the Romanian peasant will beat them down, at whatever risk, at any cost, because such a life in disgrace is not worth living."*

Corneliu Vadim-Tudor represented a certain continuity with Nicolae Ceaușescu's national Stalinism—which had been a dynastic communism, a rule by personality cult, a chauvinist megalomania with predilections for the macabre and the grotesque, including draconian pronatalist policies that left children starving in filthy orphanages. Corneliu Vadim-Tudor embodied just one variety of excess in postcommunist Romania.

Very soon after Ceaușescu's fall a student leader had founded the Movement for Romania. The "Movement" was based on oxymoronic "solid metaphysical grounds" as well as on the "exemplary model" of Romania's preeminent nineteenth-century poet Mihai

Eminescu, "the Last Romantic," who was sent to an asylum following a nervous breakdown. When Eminescu departed from this world before his fortieth birthday, his mistress professed she could never live without him and died a few weeks later. The Last Romantic was an exuberant nationalist, an eloquent anti-Semite, and a passionate worshipper of racial purity. For him, liberalism was a Western invention that had brought death to the spirit and had *"transformed Romania into a quagmire into which the social sewage of the West and the East is discharged."*

The Movement for Romania's leader called on the young—his own generation—to purify society, to return to the values of the peasantry. Recently his monthly newspaper had included an open letter saying, *"We are streams in one and the same river."* The letter was addressed to former members of the Iron Guard.

In Romania neofascism meant this: a return to the Iron Guard. In the 1920s, an archangel visited the prison cell of a young nationalist named Corneliu Zelea Codreanu. This angel, Codreanu later explained, had inspired him to create Romanian fascism. Codreanu's Iron Guard was not a political party. It was a cult and a crusade. Anti-Semitism was not a policy but a holy cause, and the nation not a political body but a mystical entity. Codreanu, "the Captain," mounted a white horse and set off through the countryside, where peasants received him as a savior. He was handsome and fearless and infatuated with death.

In 1936 one of the Iron Guard's leading figures broke with Codreanu. Soon afterward the defector fell ill with appendicitis and underwent surgery—and there in his hospital bed his former blood brothers found him. Again and again they fired shots into his body, with an ax they chopped up his corpse, they danced around the pieces of flesh, they prayed, they kissed, they cried with joy.

The Iron Guard glorified the peasantry and the primitive. Its ideology was anticommunist and anticapitalist, anti-Semitic and anti-Western, antidecadent and antimodern. Yet Codreanu—"the Captain"—found support among the most cosmopolitan and sophisticated intellectuals in Bucharest. French-speaking philosophers became ideologues of the Iron Guard. These were the brightest minds of interwar Romania, cultivated by a peculiarly seductive professor. The young philosophers, anguished by modernity, called for a spiritual regeneration transcendent of politics. Theirs was a self-conscious embracing of the excessive, an ecstatic antirationalism. *"I can only love a delirious Romania,"* Emil Cioran wrote.

Of the writers seduced by fascism, Cioran was my favorite. There was something perversely dazzling about his passionate self-hatred, his sadomasochistic exaltation of violence, his madness and despair.

Throughout the long years of communism, Emil Cioran and his friends, like the Iron Guard itself, had been taboo. Now the fascist philosophers had returned to fashion.

■　■　■

DESPITE HIS CONVICTION that the West was *"a sweet-smelling rottenness, a perfumed corpse,"* the once-fascist-sympathizing Romanian philosopher Emil Cioran lived most of his life in Paris. When he was an old man he explained to an interviewer how Romania was different from France: *"One simply goes too far. And what, basically, is the West, what is the great French civilization, the idea of courtesy, other than a boundary that one accepts on account of reason; just do not go over the boundary; it doesn't pay; it is bad taste, etc. As for the Balkans, one cannot speak of civilization; there is no criterion for it; there, one is simply excessive."*

Emil Cioran, who had always been drawn to cemeteries, had himself been buried in late June 1995, just days before I left for Romania.

When I arrived it was summer in Bucharest and very hot. The Romanian capital was a city with sharp edges—both terrifying and enthralling in a way that Prague, less urban and less intimidating, was not. The first person I spoke to there was Csortan Ferenc, the director of minority culture at the Cultural Ministry, who met me for coffee in the lobby of my hotel. An ethnic Hungarian engaged in minority rights issues, Csortan was a mild-mannered man approaching middle age. His comments were reasoned and thoughtful.

Nicolae Ceauşescu's reign had been more than brutal, in the winter there had been no heat, and Romanians had watched their children die from the cold. They had been educated to accept this, and this kind of education had a lasting effect on the psyche: Romania might now have a democratic system, but it did not have democratic people. Csortan was not an idealist. There would be no stepping into paradise.

"To bet on an optimistic scenario for the future would be a foolish mistake," he said. "We are in the middle of history. If the past was full of terrible things, the future will be full of terrible things."

Nonetheless, Csortan was working for change—for a more democratic Romania, a Romania more accepting of difference. He was working for change with the understanding that this meant working with real people in the real world.

There was something else. "We have a right to live the life you have," he told me as he stood up to leave. "By the simple fact that we were born here, to be condemned to a second- or third-rate life is not morally sustainable."

▪ ▪ ▪

THE NEXT MORNING I went to the Romanian parliament building in Bucharest. When I stepped inside the entrance hall, the first thing I saw was a large table with pictures for sale: glossy photographs of members of parliament, head shots in the style of opera singers or rock stars.

"There are crazy people everywhere," said a leader of the Democratic Union of Hungarians in Romania, the party representing Romania's Hungarian minority, "but here they're in the government."

It was true.

It was certainly the case of the current Romanian president Ion Iliescu's coalition partners, a pastiche of Far Right and Far Left, parties whose leaders included former members of Ceauşescu's regime like Corneliu Vadim-Tudor and extreme nationalists like the mayor of the Transylvanian capital of Cluj, Gheorghe Funar.

It was perhaps less true of the president himself. Ion Iliescu was of the Party of Social Democracy in Romania, and his was a national socialism less violent and extreme than that of his predecessor, Nicolae Ceauşescu. While not averse to allying himself with racists, he was not a racist himself. When political opponents accused Iliescu's wife of being Hungarian, then of being Russian, then of being Jewish, Iliescu did pause to remark that even if she were Jewish, this would not be a crime—before assuring everyone that she was, in fact, a pure-blooded Romanian.

I had asked Csortan Ferenc if President Iliescu were an opportunist.

"Don't say opportunist," Csortan answered, "say realist."

In Bucharest I met no one from Gheorghe Funar's or from Corneliu Vadim-Tudor's respective nationalist parties. It was the more moderate opposition who wanted to talk to foreigners.

A parliamentarian from the Democratic Party told me he longed for the banal: he only wanted Romania to be normal, ordinary.

Two parliamentarians from the Christian-Democratic National Peasants' Party explained that in Romania, unlike Poland and Czechoslovakia, there had been no real transition, nothing had actually changed, the same people remained in power. It was true that in other postcommunist countries the communists had now returned, but here was the essential difference: in Romania they had never left.

The Christian Democrats denied that there was ethnic conflict between Romanians and Hungarians in Transylvania. In their minds the "so-called conflictual" situation was the result of political manipulation, a power play among competing Romanian factions. Gheorghe Funar had exploited certain statements by Hungarians to win the mayoral election in Cluj. Had it not been for such self-interested exploitation, a democratic mayor would have been elected and the ethnic problems in Transylvania would not exist.

"But Gheorghe Funar," I said, "came to power in a democratic election."

"In any democracy, accidents can happen. Hitler came to power in a democratic process."

It was perhaps understandable, then, that these Christian Democrats felt warmly toward the prospect of the monarchy's return.

▪ ▪ ▪

ON A TREMBLING plane I left Bucharest the next morning for Cluj. It was sunny in Transylvania. A beautiful June day. Cluj was a bright city, a cheery city—in contrast to everything I had imagined about Transylvania: vampires and bats, cobwebs and castles.

Hungarian historians claimed that a Hungarian community existed in Transylvania by 896, long before ancestors of modern Romanians first appeared in 1222. Romanian historians claimed that, on the contrary, Romanians were descended from ancient Dacian tribes who'd arrived in the Transylvanian Carpathian Mountains two thousand years ago and had later become part of the Roman Empire. The year 896 marked a Hungarian invasion of an already-existing Daco-Roman community. Hungarian historians countered that there were no sources documenting the presence of Daco-Romans in Transylvania during the early Middle Ages. Romanian historians answered that the absence of sources was attributable to the fact that the Dacians were hiding in the Carpathian Mountains to protect themselves from the Hungarian invaders.

After the fall of communism, statues of Romulus and Remus appeared in ethnically mixed Transylvanian cities. These were the two sons of the Roman priestess Ilia by the god Mars, who founded Rome in 753 B.C.E. In the Transylvanian statues Romulus and Remus were depicted as two small human figures, standing with open mouths beneath the teats of a she-wolf: the wolf symbolized the Roman Empire, and the open mouths beneath the teats provided a touch of the erotic grotesque.

When in February 1992 Gheorghe Funar was elected mayor of

Cluj, the battle of the monuments was only beginning. In the city's Union Square had long stood a statue of the fifteenth-century Hungarian king Matthias on horseback, surrounded by six flags, each representing a land he had conquered. When Hungary lost Transylvania to Romania after the First World War, a Romanian historian announced that one of the flags—the Moldavian flag—was historically inaccurate, for Matthias had failed to conquer the Romanian province of Moldavia. In 1920 a new inscription was added to the Matthias statue: *"Conqueror of peoples, defeated only . . . when he tried to invade unconquered Moldavia."* When in 1940 Hitler returned Cluj to Hungary, this inscription was removed. When in 1992 Gheorghe Funar became mayor, he announced that the Romanian historian's inscription would be restored. That November Transylvanian Hungarians protested attempts to restore the Romanian inscription by creating a human chain around the King Matthias statue. Romanian soldiers arrived from Bucharest.

Then in May 1994 came the announcement that the statue of King Matthias might be removed entirely: Mayor Gheorghe Funar had plans for archaeological excavations aimed at uncovering the remains of a Roman forum beneath Union Square. The following month the Democratic Union of Hungarians in Romania, the largest Hungarian political party, decided on a twenty-four-hour-a-day guard presence to prevent the statue's removal. Young Hungarians declared themselves willing to "lie down around the monument and defend it day and night with their bare chests."

Cluj's mayor called the Hungarians "descendants of barbaric peoples, living in Europe for only one thousand years, this being not long enough for them to acquire the rules of civilized, European-like behavior."

Ariana, my Romanian interpreter in Cluj, was a very young woman, perhaps twenty years old, who spoke an eerily perfect, very American English she'd learned without ever having left Transylvania. She was wearing the kind of short, pretty dress that young women wore in the summer to stroll along the town square, laughing with their friends and flirting with boys. She was cheerful and animated.

We spoke with a Hungarian student who attended the university in Cluj. He was active in the Hungarian Student Union, although I could not imagine him lying down by the King Matthias statue, defending it with his bare chest. He was not a radical, nor did he seem very angry. Rather, he was contemplative. Perhaps he would be happier if Transylvania were a part of Hungary, but he believed it would be a mistake to make that happen: following Yugoslavia's example—changing borders by means of violent ethnic cleansing— was no way to solve problems.

Ariana liked him, I could tell. They were the same age, and there was a hint of flirtatiousness between them.

The Hungarian student was neither a fatalist nor an idealist. He understood that choices were circumscribed, that he lived in a part of the world where people were bound to the place of their birth. Somehow the Transylvanian Hungarians had to make things work here, in postcommunist Romania—where totalitarianism had come to an end but people were still afraid.

Fear now came from within. In Cluj I visited, too, Doina Cornea, a petite, energetic woman in her seventies, a professor of French with short gray hair who in the 1980s had been among Romania's most courageous dissidents. She spoke quickly and emphatically. She was preoccupied with the Securitate, the executed dictator's ominous secret police, among whose victims she had been. It was unknown what exactly had happened to them, these henchmen guilty of the crimes of the Ceauşescu era; she believed that they were still lurking, now enshrouded. There were signs of their presence: one day she received a newspaper photograph anonymously. The caption claimed it was she who was pictured there, and that the scarf she wore was pure silk from Bordeaux, the dress from Paris, the shoes Nina Ricci. On another occasion a newspaper published an article claiming that Doina Cornea's daughter had declared her mother insane. The daughter, living in Paris, sued the newspaper and won her case. The court awarded a certain amount of money, but both mother and daughter insisted that as compensation they wanted only a correction in the paper. After a year, their lawyer finally learned that the newspaper no longer existed and the author of the story had disappeared. The author, Doina Cornea believed, belonged to the Securitate, perhaps one of her former tormentors.

"You cannot have a democracy," she told me before I left her small house in Cluj, "with people who have a communist mentality, and that is a tragedy."

Everyone in the present opposition seemed to believe this. *Mentalité* was a preoccupation.

The Hungarian student from Kolozsvár wanted me to know that, despite informal segregation, at the university he had Romanian acquaintances and even Romanian friends. The Romanians who were part of his student world were not nearly as bad as Corneliu Vadim-Tudor and Gheorghe Funar—who, he hoped, would soon be gone.

"Because it's not fair," he said, "to have a city like Cluj, and a mayor like him."

I wanted to meet Gheorghe Funar.

My contacts at the Soros Foundation in Romania refused to arrange a meeting with Cluj's mayor. Their mandate was to build a democratic society. They would not talk to fascists. My interpreter Ariana, though, was quite happy to make the telephone call. She herself seemed unconcerned about politics. She was young and pretty and in possession of an especially marketable skill. She wanted to enjoy life. And it would be fun to go to city hall.

It was late afternoon, almost evening, when we arrived. Gheorghe Funar was not there, but one of his fellow party members from the city council had come in his place.

As we walked up the wide stairway, I said to Ariana, "I'd like to be very, very nice to this man. I'd like you to say whatever you need to say, so that we sound *extremely polite*."

"Of course," she said. "I always do that anyway."

I was hopeful: we were two young women in summer dresses, wholly unthreatening. I smiled at the city council member when he received us in his large office. I told him it was a pleasure to make his acquaintance, that I was very thankful for his time, that I understood there had been so many media distortions about Gheorghe Funar's city government, and that I would be grateful to learn directly from him what was true and what was not.

"With pleasure," the city councilman said.

Two of his teeth were black, and his smile was mildly terrifying. I looked at Ariana, sitting beside me with her legs crossed. She was adorable. He would not be in a hurry to part from us.

There was the issue of dignity. From now on, he emphasized, Romanians wanted to be treated as partners and as equal partners—in business, in politics, in everything. Romanians were not begging for anything. Perhaps they were not yet ready to integrate into Europe—but they would be. In another few years. Certainly by the turn of the century.

On the subject of ethnic discrimination in Transylvania he was adamant: Romanians were not the perpetrators but the victims. There were places in Transylvania, he said, where the poor Romanians who spoke no Hungarian could not get anything in stores.

Gheorghe Funar, he explained, had merely drawn attention to what Hungarians really wanted, for until very recently their desire for Transylvania had been masked. They wanted the borders modified but could not say this aloud. Instead they made up stories. They told lies. They falsified history. Recently they claimed that Romanians had inhabited Transylvania only since the sixteenth century. The real reason, he told me, that Hungarians were protesting the archaeological excavations in Union Square was their fear that evidence would be discovered proving that Romanians had been living in Transylvania for more than two thousand years.

Gheorghe Funar's was not an intolerant nationalism, his colleague insisted. On the contrary, his colleague had had the good fortune of having traveled through almost all of Europe, and among all European countries it was Romania who granted its minorities the greatest rights. Romanians had never been extremist in any way—neither against the Jews nor against other races. This had always been a very welcoming culture, open and friendly to foreign guests. Even during the Second World War, Romania—the city councilman explained to us—was the only country that had protected Jews and Gypsies. Romanians never took any Jews or Gypsies to German camps.

"The Romanian people," he said, "are one of the most tolerant peoples in Europe."

I smiled and thanked him. Ariana did as well. He radiated pleasure.

We left city hall and headed into town to a café. Ariana asked me if I were a vegetarian. All the Americans she'd met were vegetarians.

Yes, she said, now that we were talking just to each other, there were problems with the Hungarians, serious problems. Not in Cluj, not where she was. The people at the Soros Foundation were ethnic Hungarians. They were her employers and she liked them; they'd always treated her well. Her former boyfriend, too, was a Hungarian. She still liked him a lot. The problem was the other Hungarians, those she did not know, those who were somewhere else.

■ ■ ■

THE NEXT DAY I was in Bucharest again, where I went to see Nicolae Gheorghe, an activist for the rights of the Roma—who were more commonly called Gypsies. Nicolae Gheorghe, nearing fifty, was a striking man, bald with a long mustache and dark, slanted eyebrows. Born into a Gypsy family, as a child he had assimilated into Romanian culture. It was as an adult that he had returned to the community of his birth—now as a sociologist, a member of the Romanian intelligentsia, someone who was integrated not only into Romanian academia but also into a milieu of European human rights activists. He spoke quickly and emphatically, gesturing with his hands.

"We don't have a democracy," he said. Romania remained a peasant society accepting of authoritarian rule. Romanians understood not parties but personalities; they were eager to look to charismatic leaders.

I looked at him—so charismatic himself.

Western philosophy, he told me, offered no solution for people who preferred fascism.

Nicolae Gheorghe belonged to Romania's small human rights community. There were a handful of others, also in some way exceptional, coming together at the Helsinki Committee, a human rights NGO. At the Helsinki Committee I met Vera, the daughter of a dissident political scientist who was a veteran of Romanian prison. In the state census she had fought to be counted as an ethnic Jew, then refused to let the census taker list Judaism as her religion—after all, she did not believe in God.

Vera believed in marriage but not in wedding rings. She wore hers only when confronting critics who were likely to cackle that she would hardly be carrying on about this or that injustice if she could get a man. That week she had organized a meeting with members of the underground gay and lesbian community—underground because Romania was the only European country where homosexuality was illegal.

"I cannot agree," one Romanian senator said, "with the misuse of bodily organs that have well-established functions."

Another parliamentarian feared that the decriminalization of homosexuality would ruin the reputation of Romanian men as lovers.

At the Helsinki Committee I also met Gabriel. He had been a dissident under the old regime and, like Doina Cornea in Cluj, believed that former members of the Securitate still lurked behind the scenes, invisible and ubiquitous—forced by the greatness of their guilt to remain in positions of power. He knew that the old Ceauşescu people controlled the mass media, and he knew that they were watching him. The Helsinki Committee received mail that had been opened; their telephones and fax lines were tapped.

Like the Czech dissidents, Gabriel had little faith in "the people." They were, he believed, lacking in civic education and looking for scapegoats. Most had learned to hate communism but not how to create a democratic society.

"It's so simple to manipulate people in this country," he said.

He was thin and soft-spoken. Also gentle. And somehow frail, like a café intellectual who saw too little sun and lived too much on coffee and cigarettes.

Gabriel offered to walk me back to my hotel. It was a long walk, and we wound through one Bucharest neighborhood after another, avoiding the stray dogs who roamed menacingly in packs. The city had a wildness about it, something untamed like the feral dogs. Yet Bucharest radiated a kind of Latin hipness as well—even the ragged clothing looked fashionable, sexier than what people wore in Prague.

Gabriel spoke about Romanians' nostalgia for the old days, for the sadistic rule of Nicolae Ceaușescu.

"You know," he told me before we parted, "the human being is rather perverse."

■ ■ ■

IT WAS VERA from the Helsinki Committee who told me about the current efforts to rehabilitate Ion Antonescu. Marshal Ion Antonescu had been among the leading characters in Romania's unsavory interwar politics. At this time Romania was still a monarchy. In the years after the First World War, Ferdinand was Romania's king. Ferdinand's son, Carol, was married to Princess Helen. Prince Carol's true love, however, was Elena Lupescu from Iasi, a divorceé, and still worse, the daughter of a Roman Catholic mother and a Jewish father. Their affair caused a scandal; in 1925 Carol was forced to renounce his throne. Five years later, impenitent, he returned from exile to claim his kingdom, promising that "Madame Lupescu" would remain far away from his palace—a promise he did not keep.

Even while he brought his half-Jewish mistress to his palace, King Carol flirted with the fascists. In the end, though, the Iron Guard frightened the Romanian king, and Carol arranged for Corneliu Zelea Codreanu's execution.

Hitler frightened the Romanian king as well. In 1940 King Carol submitted to the German dictator and the Axis powers: he signed the Vienna Diktat, giving northern Transylvania to Hungary. Broken, he abdicated in favor of Marshal Ion Antonescu, an authoritarian of the Old Right. Very soon afterward, in September 1940 under Nazi auspices, Ion Antonescu and the Iron Guard led by Codreanu's successors joined forces to form the National-Legionary State. Like a marriage of convenience between the aristocracy and the *nouveau riche*, this was an alliance of convenience between the Old Right and the New Right. And it was an alliance that proved a macabre experiment. In January 1941, the Iron Guard led an orgiastic pogrom in Bucharest, murdering Jews in a slaughterhouse and hanging their bodies from meat hooks. Now Ion Antonescu had had enough. Orderly violence he approved of, but wild sadism he found distasteful. He used his army to crush the Iron Guard.

This was not where the violence ended. That June Marshal Antonescu's regime staged its own pogrom in Madame Lupescu's hometown of Iasi, murdering some four thousand Jews and deporting thousands of others. It was June 1941, and the streets of Iasi were strewn with corpses whose eyes had been gouged out. That same month Romanian troops joined the Wehrmacht in invading the Soviet Union; as a reward, Romania acquired a piece of conquered Ukrainian land between the Dniester and Bug Rivers, a territory Antonescu's government named Transnistria. There in the east, in Bessarabia, northern Bukovina, and Transnistria, Romanians and Germans massacred thousands of Jews, including some twenty thousand in the Black Sea port city of Odessa. Many were shot, and many others died of disease and starvation.

What the city councilman in Cluj had said was true: Antonescu did not deport Romania's Jews to the German camps. Instead he deported them to his own camps in Transnistria.

More than 700,000 Jews had lived in interwar Romania. Some 270,000 were killed during the Holocaust. By the 1990s only 10,000 or 20,000 remained. Vera was among them.

During the postwar Soviet occupation of Romania, Marshal Ion

Antonescu was put on trial as a war criminal and shot by firing squad. Today, the Gypsy human rights activist Nicolae Gheorghe told me, the marshal was once again "highly appreciated." Corneliu Vadim-Tudor's Greater Romania Party called for a statue of Antonescu to be erected in Bucharest. In 1991, the Romanian parliament held a moment of silence in honor of the marshal. Just months earlier an exiled Romanian millionaire, once a supporter of the Iron Guard, had sponsored the founding of a Marshal Ion Antonescu League. Its members now sought to rehabilitate Antonescu through a new trial that would posthumously overturn his death sentence.

Vera and Gabriel, devoted human rights activists, like Csortan Ferenc and Doina Cornea and Nicolae Gheorghe, harbored no utopianism. They understood only too well the difficulty of changing the way people think, of engineering the human soul.

■ ■ ■

ON MY LAST night in Bucharest Vera invited me to a jazz club with her friends. The club was in the open air, on the roof of a tall building in the city's center. And the music was not jazz but folk rock, the band's lead singer a man in his fifties with long, pale gray hair. A Romanian Bob Dylan. An actor, Vera told me. Her friend added that his lyrics were so mesmerizingly poetic, she barely noticed the melody. He had the most beautiful voice I'd ever heard.

Reason and Conscience

In the autumn of 1995 I was living in Toronto and reading about Slovakia: Prime Minister Vladimír Mečiar, in power once again, was waging battle against his nemesis, President Michal Kováč. That August President Kováč's son was kidnapped in Bratislava. His kidnappers brutalized him before he was found on the other side of the Slovak border, by the Austrian police, in the trunk of a car. The Slovak opposition suspected Mečiar's involvement, and the Christian Democrat Jan Čarnogurský demanded that the prime minister account for his whereabouts at the time of the kidnapping.

Vladimír Mečiar answered Jan Čarnogurský publicly: "Why don't you ask your wife where I was?"

In Prague, Paní Prokopová's life was less dramatic. In her letters that year after I'd left Prague she wrote of the early snow and the long frost. She wrote of price increases: the rent, the water, the telephone, everything was ever more expensive, and now that Pan Prokop had died, she had only one pension. She moved back and forth between her apartment in Prague and her cottage in the country, where she planted cabbage and flowers, yet everywhere she felt her husband's absence and nowhere did she feel at peace. *"I was used to him,"* she wrote. Perhaps it was simply that.

An American editor I'd worked with in Prague wrote long letters, often in a melancholic tone. In September he described one of Arnošt Lustig's public readings:

The saddest moment was the second appearance by Arnošt Lustig. I am pained to say this, not only because I know how you respect him but also because I was moved by his first appearance during the workshop, at the Globe.... This time, however, Arnošt took only one question, digressed from the answer into his employment by Playboy magazine, and began to maunder on the general themes of money and sex. One could not help suspecting that he had taken a glass or two before stepping on stage.... In view of the horror that Arnošt has survived and the beauty that he has created, no one has the right to judge him. This was only one unimportant evening in a long, important life. But with some shame I found myself that evening seeing him as one of his own characters: "Friday. Once. A lot of money from Playboy."

The connection with *Playboy* was not a literary fiction: Arnošt, with his receding white hair and forehead of kindly smiling wrinkles, had become editor in chief of the Czech edition. I saw him in Toronto, when in fall 1995 he arrived for a literary festival. Paul Wilson, the onetime lead singer of the Plastic People of the Universe, hosted a discussion with Arnošt. So it was true—Paul, full of good humor, asked Arnošt before an audience of Czech émigrés— that the famous Czech novelist of the Holocaust had accepted the editorship of *Playboy*?

And what could be wrong—Arnošt answered, wholly unoffended, smiling as he so often did—with being able to publish very good stories by his friends, the best Czech writers? Besides, Arnošt loved women. He considered their humiliation a great evil and would not allow it. On the contrary: his *Playboy* would celebrate the beauty of women.

Afterward Arnošt and I sat at a café and talked about the Stalinist years. About communism, as about sex, Arnošt was open: yes, he, too, had been a young Stalinist. After the war, when he returned to Prague from the camps, he had joined the Communist Party. He was not defensive, he only explained: during the war, in the camps—in Auschwitz—the communists were the best people. They were absolutely beautiful, wonderful people. Until they got into power. Then they were horrible.

■ ■ ■

THAT YEAR, IN the peaceful cosmopolitan city of Toronto, I began to study Polish. Pani Hanka, my Polish professor, was planning to retire soon, and I was among her last students. She was a traditionalist in her teaching methods and a puritan about form. The language was precious to her.

Pani Hanka was a large, tough woman in her sixties who lived alone and appeared to have no family. She was generous with her time. When I began to write a seminar paper about a long poem called "A Poem for Adults" by the avant-garde-turned-Stalinist poet Adam Ważyk, Pani Hanka spent hours translating it with me, line by line. Gradually I realized that, like the poet Adam Ważyk, she was a Polish Jew—although about this she said almost nothing. Many things we read together, alone in her office, had emotional weight to her. Yet she was always measured in her responses. I saw her cry only once: through an international child welfare agency, she'd sponsored a young boy in Africa. They had never met, but she became very attached to him. Every month she sent him money and in return she received letters. Until one day she received a letter not from the boy, but from the agency: the child had died, bitten by a poisonous snake.

I liked Pani Hanka. She was a serious philologist, articulate about etymology and syntax and comparative Slavic grammar. Most of the students in the class, though, felt somewhat differently: they were children of Polish émigrés who already spoke some Polish, if improperly, and there was an uneasiness between them and their professor. Only gradually did I see that, even beyond the classroom, there was a tension between Pani Hanka and the Polish émigré community, a tension whose origins did not lie only in her uncompromising stance toward Polish grammar. It was a tension that had to do with Jewishness—and with communism.

The vast majority of some 3 million Jews who had lived in pre-war Poland did not survive the Holocaust. Among the small number who did survive, though, and the even smaller number who survived and chose to remain in postwar Poland, there were disproportionately many communists. This came to an end in March 1968, when Poland's communist leaders claimed that student protests against censorship were incited by Zionist conspirators. The Party responded with violent repression against the students. There followed a collusion of the worldview of the anti-Semitic Right with the communist regime and the popularization of a theory of a Nazi-Zionist conspiracy. Newspaper cartoons depicted U.S. president Lyndon Johnson joining the anti-Polish campaign led by American Zionists; Nazis saluting Israeli tanks; and Israeli occupiers of the Gaza Strip reading the works of Adolf Eichmann and thinking, *"One should profit from experience."* The Party purged the universities and its own ranks; at the University of Warsaw, the philosophy department was forced to close, and Party general secretary Władysław Gomułka announced that Poland would open its borders so that those who "regard Israel as their homeland" could leave.

Some thirteen thousand Polish Jews—assimilated Jews, deeply attached to Poland—were sent into exile. Pani Hanka never spoke of this. Yet she, too, had left Poland in the wake of March 1968.

The history professor Stefan M. was more forthcoming. In some ways he was an unlikely source: a bearded man of perhaps forty, he had a demeanor dignified, austere, and somewhat distant. I asked him about Adam Ważyk, the author of the poem mourning the state of postwar Poland and invoking the refrain, *"Give me a piece of old stone / let me find myself again in Warsaw."* Adam Ważyk was a communist, in fact a Stalinist—but by 1955, when he wrote "A Poem for Adults," he already regretted who he had been and what had happened to Poland. One day when I came to see him, Professor M. closed the door of his office and told me that in Warsaw he'd known Adam Ważyk, who by now had been dead for over a decade. It had happened when he was a young man hiking with a friend in the mountains. It was beautiful there, peaceful and deserted. Then he and his friend saw two more hikers, young women, coming toward them. He fell in love with one of them. This young woman, he came to learn, was Ważyk's daughter. By then Adam Ważyk was an old man, broken and bitter, who believed in nothing.

■ ■ ■

THE EXPERIENCE OF communism could break people. My former Czech teacher Jarmila was a passionate devotee of *pravda* in the weighty Czech sense: truth as existential imperative. Yet she generously concealed much from her grandmother. Her failing grades at the military college in Vermont, just before her breakdown, had ruined her academic record. Now no school wanted to take her. Her visa had expired, and she could be deported at any moment. She was desperate.

"Why didn't the communists prefer to kill me during the interrogations in prison?" she wrote in a letter. *"It's very humiliating to die as a beggar on the street or in the woods of Vermont."*

She added: *"But whatever happens, at least you know part of the TRUTH and this is important."*

And it was the case that I knew only a part of the truth. In late January 1996 Jarmila sent me a long letter. She wrote in the philosophical idiom of the dissidents, and yet in her voice there was also a certain edge uniquely her own. By now her name was no longer Jarmila.

> *You have known me as one of those who disregarded their own safety and comfort, who decided to fight for TRUTH, who were very much oppressed by the lies of the totalitarian communist system. My fight was not only political, but also religious and legal, in the sense of the preservation of fundamental human rights and the dignity of man.*

Yet this was not her only struggle. The very first began long before, in early childhood, when—she wrote—*"I was fighting for my own SELF, my own I, for what I am and what I felt myself to be from the moment when my mind was able to distinguish the most basic things around me."* Her parents believed they had borne a daughter. This was not the truth. *"You see,"* Jarmila wrote to me, *"I have always been a man."*

Jarmila's parents had hoped she would grow out of this—but that never happened. Instead she fought to preserve her own self. She discovered Catholicism and determined to become a priest, as *"a way out of a desperate situation."*

"I believed," she wrote, *"that God is TRUTH, which must prevail."*

The battle against an oppressive regime was a battle by proxy for her own identity.

The narrative continued with Jarmila's decision to come to the United States. It was all part of a continuous whole, a story about *"the fight for TRUTH, which was the most unyielding weapon against the lies of communist rule."* In 1991 she had received a scholarship from a military school in New Mexico. She decided then to leave Czechoslovakia—not only, she explained, because she wanted an education free of Marxism-Leninism, but also and more importantly because she had become disillusioned with the postcommunist fate of the anticommunist underground: relations among former dissidents had begun to fall apart. No longer did it seem to Jarmila that they were standing purely for the truth they had once sacrificed themselves for; instead she saw her friends competing for positions, for power, for money.

So Jarmila had decided to leave. She found herself, then, in New Mexico, still as a woman. But the army was not kind to her. It was not tolerant and embracing, the way she had imagined American democracy would be. Instead she found the military to be an institution *"prepared to liquidate whatever or whomever was other, who differed in some way."*

Now Jarmila's new name was Todd James. Later, on the phone, she used an analogy: even if everyone around me were to tell me every day that I was a rabbit, I would know that it was not true. All the insistence in the world could not make me a rabbit, knowing—as I did—that I was a human being.

There was much in the story I did not understand: why Jarmila—now Todd James—believed he needed to come to the United States for an education free of Marxism-Leninism precisely at the moment when Marxism-Leninism was being so energetically purged from Czechoslovakia's universities; how he had come here; who her—his—patron, Major John Hasek, really was; why Todd James felt so betrayed by the United States yet so desperate to remain there.

A few weeks later I received from Todd James another long letter, again preoccupied with the themes of truth, struggle, betrayal. For Todd James the United States had always been the personification of the freedom for which he had unhesitatingly risked his life. Now he could not bear the way he had been treated in the army, the way that "America" had betrayed him when he had given her everything. The American military had pushed him to the brink of suicide in a way that the totalitarian state of Czechoslovakia had not—precisely because, I sensed, he had believed in America so fervently.

Todd James went on to tell me why, despite the betrayal of an unrequited love, he had chosen an American name: he had named himself after his American doctor. Strength had always been essential to Todd James. It was strength that had carried him through his parents' betrayal and his imprisonment, a strength that had come from the vision of revolution. Now, when he had lost himself in a new world that had also betrayed him, the support of his doctor had brought him strength again.

It was also important to Todd James to choose an English name; it was a symbolic gesture of separation from his previous life in Czechoslovakia.

I cannot forget about the suffering, the struggle and the pain I experienced in Czechoslovakia since childhood, but neither can I forget about the time of victory, when I organized demonstrations, led the procession on November 17th, 1989, founded with Havel and others Civic Forum, spoke on BBC, the Voice of America and Radio Free Europe, met Major John Hasek, who marked my life irreversibly, sent information to the US Congress, to the US Ambassador in Prague, to the CIA and US Special Operations, sat down to dinner with John Major, with Shirley T. Black, with people from the British parliament and the British information services. . . . At 12 I firmly believed in God and His strength, at 16 I was on my own, and at 18 I became part of the change that definitively changed the face not only of Europe, but of the whole world. For that victory I sacrificed everything I had and I was.

Todd James—at that time Jarmila—had believed so passionately in freedom and in democracy. That representatives of these things could suffer from envy, from vanity, from weakness, had led him to despair. He believed in absolutes: in Truth, in the Self, in the battle of Good versus Evil—in God, who had destined for him *"the life of a soldier, who marches from one battle to the next."* There was an eschatology in his thinking, a narrative uniting past and present and pointing toward the future. The end of communism had not meant happily-ever-after, and the fight was not yet over. There remained the imperative to speak truth to power, to create *"a better world, a happier world, where there will not be so much pain and suffering."*

"The revolution has not ended," Todd James concluded his letter, *"it's only begun!"*

▪ ▪ ▪

THE CANADIAN HISTORIAN Gordon Skilling had nearly single-handedly written the history of twentieth-century Czechoslovakia. Now he was in his eighties, long retired from the university.

"I remember my first research trip to Prague," he said the first time we met. "That was back in 1937."

His fiancée had traveled from New York by ship to join him; they were married in Prague's Old Town Hall. Of course, Gordon added, they had to leave a few months after the Nazis came.

Gordon and his wife departed Prague for England in the summer of 1939, when the city was already under German occupation. They returned in July 1948. By then Czechoslovakia was under Stalinist rule, and its president, Edvard Beneš, had seen the country he led taken from him twice: once in 1938 by the Nazis, a second time in 1948 by the communists. On both occasions he chose not to fight. In September 1948 Edvard Beneš died prematurely, just months after abdicating the presidency. Gordon was there for the memorial service held in Prague's National Museum.

During that 1948 stay in Czechoslovakia—nearly fifty years before my American friend Brad and I took a field trip to that village—Gordon and his wife visited Lidice, or what had once been Lidice. They found a brigade of young people laboring there, excavating the site where the Nazis had killed the villagers. Gordon and his wife could see the foundations of buildings that had once been. In one of the basements Gordon found a rough chunk of fused glass. He decided to keep it. A souvenir from a massacre.

Several weeks after our meeting at the university, Gordon telephoned. It had been a long time since he'd worked with graduate students, and now suddenly four had contacted him: myself, a musicologist, and two political scientists. A week or so later, in the living room of Gordon's Toronto apartment, the five of us inaugurated the Czech Living Room Seminar.

On one occasion Václav Havel's translator Paul Wilson joined us. A Canadian, he'd arrived in the Czechoslovak city of Brno in 1967 and had taught English for a while before learning Czech and drifting into a freelance career as a translator, initially of children's books. As it turned out, it was rather unintentionally that Paul had become the lead singer for the Plastic People of the Universe. He wasn't a singer at all, per se, but he was moving in circles with young musicians who believed English to be the proper language of rock and roll. And it was the 1970s, when Paul was one of very few native speakers of English in Czechoslovakia.

The Plastic People's manager Ivan Jirous, an art critic by profession, would schedule a lecture at a club in Prague. That was legal.

He would show slides of Andy Warhol's paintings, and the Plastic People of the Universe would play a set of Velvet Underground covers. Then the band would continue playing, moving on to their own music. For both the musicians and the audience, it was risky, but Ivan Jirous, Paul explained, "was a very persuasive guy."

"I was wondering," the musicologist asked, "if it weren't for Jirous, what would have happened?"

"It" never would have happened without Ivan Jirous.

Paul had been close to the girlfriend of the Plastic People's bassist, Milan Hlavsa.

"She stuck with Milan Hlavsa for years and years," Paul told us, "and then she finally hooked up with a young poet who eventually killed himself. She spent the next six months typing up all his poems and then killed herself. I remember talking to her one late night and remember saying, 'What do you think would have happened to Milan if he hadn't met Jirous?' and she said, 'He probably would have just been a normal musician.'"

Paul didn't want to demonize Ivan Jirous, his friend of many years. He only wanted us to understand the spirit of the time.

"Jirous," Paul continued, "—I mean I'm not blaming him at all—through the force of his personality, he just drew people into this kind of vortex of resistance. They were drawn voluntarily, I mean nobody regretted what they'd done, but it was just him that gave them a drive and a focus . . . I always saw him, as the French call it, as an *animateur,* someone who could animate others to do things."

Ivan Jirous the *animateur* paid a heavy price for his charisma: he was in and out of prison nearly until communism's very end. And after the revolution he never found a place for himself.

The years in the Czechoslovak underground—and the years in prison—marked everyone who took part in them. Some only proved more resilient than others. The poet and philosopher Egon Bondy had been one of the underground's gurus; the Plastic People had used his poems as song lyrics. After 1989, Bondy's name appeared on the lustration lists as a secret police informer.

Gordon Skilling, who had gathered us all there in his apartment, interjected: his name on a list didn't make it true.

But Paul, Egon Bondy's friend, believed that it was true: there were actual transcripts of what he had written. And the secret police had ways of making people betray their friends. They had put so much pressure on Bondy, Paul remembered Bondy's having been near collapse. He could believe Egon Bondy had been broken. This didn't make him evil, though.

Lustration had revealed that several people Paul had known well in the 1970s were informers. Often the friends who were their victims forgave them.

"Of all the people I knew," Paul said, "it was the people who were the most harmed by informers who were also the most forgiving of those informers."

■ ■ ■

IN TORONTO I thought more and more about the Stalinist years. In 1946, the communists had won a plurality in Czechoslovakia: 38 percent of the vote in genuinely free elections. The communist coup of two years later had not been carried out by a tiny minority: the communists had authentic popular support then. Understandably, no one wanted to remember that now.

In 1948, just a few months after the so-called "February Revolution" had brought the communists to power, Gordon and his wife arrived in Prague to find the windows of what once had been the American information office filled with displays of American capitalist horror: workers' strikes, lines of the desperate unemployed, beatings of blacks.

Yet in many ways what Gordon saw in Czechoslovakia in 1948 was still mild. When he returned to Czechoslovakia two years later, in 1950, it was already a time of terror. The show trial of Milada Horáková was under way. Milada Horáková was a Protestant, a Christian, a believer. She was also an activist and a democrat who in the interwar years had played an important role in the women's movement. When the Second World War came, she devoted herself to the anti-Nazi resistance. Imprisoned and tortured by the Gestapo, she behaved heroically. Hers was a strength seemingly not of this world.

One June night at ten o'clock Gordon listened as the verdict was delivered in the show trial: death by hanging for Milada Horáková and three of her co-defendants, including the surrealist literary critic Záviš Kalandra.

In the 1920s Záviš Kalandra had been a young radical, a student communist, part of avant-garde literary circles lending their support to the Bolshevik Revolution. Then news of the Stalinist terror of the 1930s reached Czechoslovakia. The show trials, with their self-flagellating confessions of Old Bolsheviks begging to be given the death penalty, seemed suspicious to him. Záviš Kalandra began to have doubts. For these doubts he was expelled from the Communist Party of Czechoslovakia. When interwar Czechoslovakia came to an end, his fate began to merge with that of Milada Horáková. Soon after the Germans occupied the Czech lands of Bohemia and Moravia, the Gestapo came for him. The long years of the war he spent as a prisoner, in Sachsenhausen and Ravensbrück.

Milada Horáková and Záviš Kalandra were among thousands arrested after the 1948 February Revolution that saw Czechoslovak president Edvard Beneš's defeat and the Communist Party's victory. The charges against them were fantastical: Trotskyite conspiracy on behalf of American imperialism; plots to destroy Czechoslovak people's democracy, restore capitalist exploitation, and initiate a third world war. The trial was theater: the play had been written in advance, the defendants tortured in preparation for rehearsals. Then the live performance was broadcast over the radio and the transcripts were published daily in the newspapers. Milada Horáková was all the more a monster for being a woman, a wife, a mother. In factories throughout the country signatures were collected in support of resolutions condemning the accused; thousands of telegrams poured into the Ministry of Justice, calling for execution. Women wrote letters demanding that all of the defendants be given the supreme punishment.

People wanted assurance that the glorious socialist future would not be spoiled.

The chief prosecutor was a young colonel in uniform, and after the trial Gordon listened as he addressed an open-air meeting in Prague's Stromovka Park. The young colonel spoke of the vileness of the West, the despicable nature of the defendants, the need for vigilance. His audience was wildly enthusiastic. Shortly afterward Milada Horáková and Záviš Kalandra went to the gallows.

In *The Book of Laughter and Forgetting* the Czech novelist Milan Kundera wrote of the day following those executions:

> *And knowing full well that the day before in their fair city one woman and one surrealist had been hanged by the neck, the young Czechs went on dancing and dancing, and they danced all the more frantically because the dance was the manifestation of their innocence, the purity that shone forth against the black villainy of two public enemies who betrayed the people and its hopes.*

After one woman and one surrealist were hanged, the show trials continued. Now the Communist Party turned against itself. Rudolf Slánský had been a devoted communist since before his twenty-first birthday. In September 1944 he was parachuted into Slovakia during the Slovak Uprising against the Nazis. Six years later, the Czechoslovak Communist Party held a fiftieth birthday celebration for him, the wartime hero who was now the Communist Party's general secretary. It was a wonderful birthday party. And Rudolf Slánský's very last. Soon afterward he was arrested—and before long was joined by other comrades, high-ranking communists like Rudolf Margolius and André Simone.

In the end there were fourteen defendants. Eleven were Jews. All were tried as *"Trotskyite-Titoist-Zionist bourgeois nationalist traitors and enemies of the Czechoslovak people, of the people's democratic order and socialism, who, in the service of American imperialists and steered by hostile Western intelligence services,*

*created a treasonous conspiratorial nucleus, undermined the peo-
ple's democratic order, obstructed the building of socialism, harmed
the national economy, conducted espionage operations, and weak-
ened the unity of the Czechoslovak people and the defense capability
of the republic, in order to alienate the republic from its unyielding alliance and friendship with the Soviet Union, to liquidate the
people's democratic rule in Czechoslovakia, to restore capitalism, to
bootstrap our republic once again to the imperialist camp, and to
destroy its independence and freedom."*

In prison the defendants' interrogators tortured them. Those
on trial all gave elaborate, self-condemning confessions. Their language was fantastical.

> PROSECUTOR: *Toward what goal did this hostile operation
> inside the Communist Party and its apparatus serve?*
>
> RUDOLF SLÁNSKÝ: *This operation served the goal of building
> the treasonous center's power inside the Party and exploiting
> these positions for our conspiratorial designs. By pulveriz-
> ing the Party with bourgeois and petit bourgeois elements we
> attempted to change the character of the Communist Party,
> so as to transform the revolutionary party of the working class
> into a party controlled by bourgeois and petit bourgeois ele-
> ments.*

The prosecutors were never satiated; they continually asked for
deeper self-incrimination.

> PROSECUTOR: *This is one part of your operation inside the
> Communist Party. Of course your hostile operation does not
> end with this . . .*

There was always more. Rudolf Slánský was obliging.

> RUDOLF SLÁNSKÝ: *I aimed the operation of the treasonous
> conspiratorial nucleus inside the Party directly toward the liq-
> uidation of the people's democratic order.*

The "treasonous nucleus" conspired with Zionists and Freemasons. It had support as well among the Communist Party's secret police, among supposedly trusted communist comrades. Slánský and his coconspirators were able to exploit this support, using it to conceal their hostile operations.

> RUDOLF SLÁNSKÝ: *I knew that intellectuals harboring cosmopolitan attitudes, bourgeois cosmopolitan politicians, who were pursuing the same goals as the conspiratorial treasonous nucleus at the head of which I stood, were organized in Masonic lodges. Their operation, too, was directed toward the restoration of capitalism in the Czechoslovak Socialist Republic and the liquidation of the people's democratic order. Their cosmopolitanism, their nationlessness served the imperialists, who could use these people as agents in their operation against the people's democratic order of the Czechoslovak Socialist Republic.*

The treasonous nucleus was infectious; the class enemy masked himself and could be anywhere.

The trial was broadcast live. The newspapers printed the transcripts every day. In Toronto, I began spending mornings at the microfilm room at the library, reading the Czechoslovak newspapers of 1952. Splattered across the front pages of the Party daily *Rudé Právo* were headlines: *"Death to the imperialists! Death to the fascists! Death to the traitors!"* Again and again, every day, women, children, wives, mothers, fathers, sons, workers—everyone demanded death. An orgy of bloodlust. A son disowned his father and supported his execution. Artur London's French wife disavowed her husband and demanded his punishment: she would never betray the Communist Party.

It had been a motif of the Moscow trials of the 1930s that the accused demanded for themselves the harshest sentence. It was a motif of this trial as well.

"There can be no thought of mitigating circumstances. . . . I ask the national court of justice for the most severe punishment," the journalist André Simone said in his closing statement before the

court. It was a statement too fantastical to have been believed in Moscow in the 1930s. In Prague in 1952—fifteen years after the Moscow trials—André Simone spit it back out. And the audience believed it. And they hanged him.

▪ ▪ ▪

IN *THE BOOK of Laughter and Forgetting* Milan Kundera wrote of his generation: *"And so it happened that in February 1948 the Communists took power not in bloodshed and violence, but to the cheers of about half the population. And please note: the half that cheered was the more dynamic, the more intelligent, the better half."*

The Stalinist years, Kundera described in that novel, were years of *"innocence dancing with a bloody smile."* Kundera, I slowly began to realize, had belonged to this "better half": he had been among those dancing. As had so many others I admired: Arnošt Lustig, Karel Kosík, Pavel Kohout, Stanislav Neumann, Jaroslav Seifert, Ludvík Vaculík. The best and the brightest young minds, caught up in an orgy of bloodlust.

It was this moment—the moment of the show trials, of the Stalinist terror in Czechoslovakia—when Milan Kundera wrote lyrical poetry affirming his love for his communist comrades, vowing never to distance himself from them. And he was far from alone: Pavel Kohout wrote court poetry to Stalin, *"who always knows, at every moment, what each of us hopes for, what each of us lives by."* Stanislav Neumann wrote a love poem to his Communist Party membership card, the place *"where my heart beats."* The young philosopher Karel Kosík published diatribes against *"cosmopolitan bandits and evildoers the likes of Slánský."*

Theirs was a generation whose founding moment of consciousness had been the betrayal at Munich. Bourgeois Western democracy had sold out Czechoslovakia to Nazi Germany; seven years later, the Red Army had liberated her. Liberalism had failed to protect against fascism. Stalin had defeated Hitler. The war had sliced time in two; in the new world to come, the betrayal at Munich, the German occupation, the gas chambers of Auschwitz would never be repeated. This generation of young communists came to communism during the war, through the war, when communism was already Stalinism—and Stalinism was coming to power in Eastern Europe. Some came directly from Auschwitz: in the camps, Arnošt Lustig said, the communists were the best people.

After Rudolf Slánský and André Simone and nine others were hanged that day in December 1952, their bodies were cremated. Someone, perhaps thoughtlessly, decided to store the urn holding the ashes inside a Communist Party automobile. One winter day when the roads were slippery, the Party chauffeur remembered the urn and scattered the ashes on the snow.

Stalin died in March 1953, just months after Rudolf Slánský and ten of his communist comrades had gone to the gallows. Three years later, Stalin's successor, Nikita Khrushchev, gave his "secret speech" at the Twentieth Party Congress of the Communist Party of the Soviet Union. During Stalin's reign, Khrushchev said, Soviet communism had suffered from a "personality cult." This had resulted in certain excesses: while the battle against class enemies was a necessary one, not *all* of the executions of the Stalinist era had been, strictly speaking, necessary.

In April 1956, the Czechoslovak Writers' Union met to discuss this "personality cult" and these "excesses." The writers were not ready to apologize. In any case, Stalinism was their language: they had no other language with which to critique it.

The poet Stanislav Neumann stood up to speak: his generation had grown up with Stalin's name. And with Stalin's name, as seventeen-year-old boys, they had come to the Communist Party. His best friends had gone to their deaths in Theresienstadt with this name. No, he would not apologize. He was not ashamed.

With time, though, there would be shame. In 1963 the victims of the Stalinist show trials in Czechoslovakia were rehabilitated. Posthumously. Quietly.

At the Writers' Congress held that year a young poet turned to his older colleagues: *"What kind of people were you, actually, and what kind of people are you?"*

Pavel Kohout was defensive: the poet, who was twenty-five years old in 1963, was too young to remember the First Czechoslovak Republic, too young to remember the social injustices, the poverty, the fatal weakness that had left the small country vulnerable to Hitler. Pavel Kohout had been most happy to be a poet of the Stalinist era. It had been an era of great faith.

"I am not ashamed of that faith," Kohout told the younger poet, *"if I called it Stalin or otherwise."*

At the 1963 Writers' Congress, Arnošt Lustig was less defensive and more melancholy.

"How was it possible," Arnošt asked, *"that the most beautiful idea of equality, justice, and dignity of man—which communism was—so perverted itself?"*

For Arnošt's generation, this would become the single most haunting question. None of them would ever fully escape it.

Yet with time the writers did construct a way out of Stalinist language. Gradually, they began to juxtapose words of the Stalinist era with other words: individual *persons* next to *the people; conscience* next to *class consciousness; truth* and *responsibility* next to *faith* and *belief.* They borrowed heavily from French existentialism, in particular from Jean-Paul Sartre. In a world in which there was no God, Sartre insisted, we ourselves were the creators of values. We had radical freedom—and radical freedom meant radical responsibility. The Marxist philosopher Karel Kosík began to rethink dialectics: perhaps Marxist teleology—in its reduction of people to mere objects of History—was in essence dehumanizing. For the inexorable progress of History rendered morality an *"alien encroachment, or, at most, an external addendum."* They had all believed that the terror of the Stalinist years had been dictated by the "iron laws of History." Yet what if History were only history, what if it had no iron laws? If this were true, then they were left—even if indirectly—with blood on their hands.

These, the 1960s, were the years of the Czech New Wave in film, and Arnošt Lustig was among the most active participants. It was a time of creativity, a time of weaving brilliant political allegories from yarns of the horrific and the absurd. In 1963 a Czech writer published a novel about the witch trials in seventeenth-century Bohemia. Afterward, a Czech director set about making a film. *Kladivo na čarodejnice* (*Malleus Maleficarum*, "A Hammer to the Witches") was more than graphic—it was vile. At the film's conclusion the women accused of witchcraft, after undergoing hideous tortures, approached the stakes where they would be burned. Yet they had forgotten something. Those overseeing their execution told them: *"You must say thank you."* And they did. Just as had the defendants at the Rudolf Slánský trial.

In 1967 Milan Kundera completed *The Joke*, the tragic story of Ludvík the young communist, cast out of both the Communist Party and the university by his own friends and comrades for having sent his would-be girlfriend a thoughtless postcard. At the Writers' Congress a few months later, Karel Kosík told the tale of a famous Czech intellectual, imprisoned for his refusal to abandon his convictions. The famous Czech intellectual, unnamed by Kosík, was the religious reformer Jan Hus, sentenced by the Ecclesiastical Council and burned at the stake in 1415. For more than five hundred years Jan Hus had been a Czech national hero remembered for his conviction that "truth will prevail." Now Karel Kosík told his colleagues of how a theologian had come to visit this intellectual in prison and had advised him that should the Ecclesiastical Council tell him he had one eye, even though he knew that he had two, he must acknowledge that the council was right. The imprisoned man replied that it would be of no consequence if all the world were to declare that he had only one eye. For he knew by his own reason that he had two, and a denial of reason was a betrayal of conscience.

I thought of Jarmila—now Todd James—and the rabbit analogy: even if I were to be told every day that I was a rabbit, I would still know that it was not true.

Toward the intellectuals who underwent such a radical ideological transformation, Gordon Skilling was sympathetic. Or rather empathetic. They were, he believed, neither opportunists nor fools.

"I can appreciate this myself," Gordon wrote to me, *"since I went*

through a similar process of evolution of thinking, of movement from faith to reason and conscience."

I liked that Gordon was forthright about his past as a fellow traveler.

Gordon's ideological sympathies, like those of his Czechoslovak contemporaries, had undergone a dramatic evolution as he'd grown older. In his later years, he'd lent his support to the dissidents, many of whom had become his friends. In February 1987, the year he turned seventy-five, Charter 77 issued a document sending him birthday wishes.

For a brief moment it had seemed that the Stalinists who had experienced a crisis of conscience might triumph: in January 1968 the Communist Party of Czechoslovakia changed course and embraced reform. Alexander Dubček, the new Party leader, promised "socialism with a human face." For the first time, the communist government publicly acknowledged the falsity of the show trials. The Prague Spring of 1968 was a time of great hope; and the once-young Stalinists-turned-revisionist Marxists were effusive in their support. Then in August, Soviet tanks rolled into Prague, and the Prague Spring was over forever. That winter the Czech student Jan Palach went to Wenceslas Square and set himself on fire. His death by self-immolation was a protest—not against the invasion itself but against his country's resignation. Stanislav Neumann could not bring himself either to support the crushing of the ideals that had brought him to communism or to oppose the Communist Party. In 1970 the poet who had seen his best friends go to their deaths in the Nazi camps with Stalin's name on their lips took his own life. He was forty-three years old.

It was impossible to know what "socialism with a human face" would have been.

▪ ▪ ▪

THE YEAR 1968 marked a break in time: afterward few true believers in communism remained. Now many of the young Stalinists-turned-revisionist Marxists became dissidents.

One day in Toronto a professor of European history overheard my conversation with a Czech student. The professor interjected—in perfect Czech, although he was not Czech himself. Later he told me he'd been born in Macedonia. During the Second World War, as a young child, he'd become separated from his parents. Still, he survived, and after the war found himself in a Czechoslovak orphanage, where he was raised by communist child care workers. He had been a ward of the communist state: his was a pure Stalinist upbringing. He cried when the social worker came to tell the children that Stalin had died.

"And the girls," he said, "the girls were sobbing."

Twenty years later he returned to Czechoslovakia, where he visited one of the social workers who had raised him. When they were alone she asked him: Could he ever forgive her?

"I already have," he answered.

And I saw that it was true: he was forgiving. His forgiveness was not only magnanimity but also equanimity—he was accepting: it had simply been the spirit of the times.

A Galician Summer

It was summer of 1996 when I left Toronto and arrived in Kra-kow. The dormitory cafeteria was crowded with foreign summer school students, boys wearing black denim and girls in flowered, sleeveless dresses. Above them light dust swirled in the cigarette smoke.

Behind the counter large women cloaked in white aprons, their hair tied in hairnets, poured ladles of borscht, mashed potatoes, and *żurek* from steaming cauldrons. Perspiration gathered along the webs of their hairnets. Boiled eggs floated in bowls of *żurek*.

I was sitting alone. A man stopped at my table and asked with excessive formality if he might not join me. Perhaps not formality, perhaps rather a bit of inappropriate grandeur. His Polish was stilted and formal, he spoke with an accent. Unlike myself, though, he pronounced the Polish nasal vowels correctly, as real nasal sounds spoken from his nose, grazing his throat and slipping from his mouth. Perhaps he was French.

"Of course," I answered him. He was much older and more well-dressed than most of the students in the cafeteria. He asked me if I were Polish in a hopeful tone.

"No, I'm not," I said.

"A pleasure to meet you."

He smiled with a kind of public warmness, as if he were a businessman, and perhaps he was.

Inside the cafeteria sundry languages wove a mask of incomprehensible sounds, soft consonants and deep vowels in varying rhythms. It was possible to hear everything and nothing at once.

"I have a great interest in the war," he said.

He was drinking weak lemon tea with his pierogies. They were coated with a sauce of lard, heated to the translucence of olive oil.

"My wife is Polish. I have a great affection for the Polish people. So noble, and so unlucky. Always the victims of foreigners—the Russians, the Germans, the Jews . . ."

I said nothing. I imagined that this man's wife was younger than he, and very beautiful. I wondered if she spoke to him in French.

"It is a paradox in some way that it was the Germans—historical enemies!—who resolved the problem. Forty years of communism did not do as much damage to the Poles as the centuries of economic exploitation by the Jews. Today they have a chance. Communism is over, and Hitler has taken care of the Jewish problem for the Poles."

His wife would not be saying this to me, I thought. Not here in Krakow. Not at the university.

I looked at him and said nothing.

"I do not say that I agree with everything, with his methods, of course. They were, I would say, extreme."

The Frenchman continued to talk. I stared into my glass of tea. Pieces of lemon swirled and drifted.

He stood up and extended his hand. "It was a pleasure."

■ ■ ■

IN KRAKOW BOYS pedaling rickshaws wobbled against the uneven spaces between cobblestones that reflected the shadows of turrets. Majestic Wawel Castle had once represented a Poland never to rise again: Nazi governor-general of Poland Hans Frank had made the castle his home when the Germans came to Krakow.

Yet in time the castle was cleansed of its Nazi taint, and Poland did rise again. It was not, though, the same Poland that had been before Hans Frank's arrival there. By the time the Second World War ended, Poland's eastern lands, with their Ukrainian and Belarusian minorities, had become part of the Soviet republics of Ukraine and Belarus. As compensation Poland had expanded its boundaries to the west, expelling the Germans who lived there across the border. And of the nearly 3 million Jews who had lived in Poland before the war, almost all were gone.

The exhibition *And I Still See Their Faces* opened in a Krakowian gallery that summer. Photographs of Polish Jewry from before the war: Ordinary people. Sisters. Grandfathers. Mothers and children. Babies. The religious and the secular. Men and women walking with goats on village roads and past shops on city streets. The wealthy wearing elegant hats. The impoverished in tattered clothing. Men holding puppies. Distinguished gentlemen and marriageable girls. Wedding banquets and family portraits. Boys studying and men playing chess. A family posing around a gravestone. The elderly in a rest home. Workers in a tailor shop. A school, a graveyard, a synagogue. Men carrying buckets of water. Rabbis and painters. Soldiers in the First World War. Young women playing the piano. Families on the beach by the Baltic Sea. Pretty girls sitting in gardens—some looking happy, some sad.

They were unspeakably beautiful photographs, all in black-and-white and sepia. They conjured up not only a lost Jewish world but also a lost Poland.

That summer in Krakow I also met Seth, who, as the Frenchman had, shared a table at the cafeteria with me one day. Like myself, Seth was there studying Polish. He was not especially friendly—but my roommate, a cheerful college student from the Midwest who loved beer and men and parties, chatted in his direction obliviously. We learned that he was nearly thirty and that he had once been American but was now Israeli. That he was a Zionist, but on the left, and that he wanted nothing in common with the barbarians on the right. When his army unit searched Palestinians at the border check, he always spoke to them in English: Hebrew was the language of the occupier, English was benevolently neutral. Now he was a graduate student in Jerusalem. He had come to Krakow to learn Polish, having already learned Hebrew and Russian and Yiddish. He wanted to write about the vibrant Jewish life that had once been.

This was how we met. Later we took many walks. It was summer in Krakow, and the cafés lining the square had all opened their doors to the Galician sun, which came and went abruptly. The days were fickle; powder white and dark gray clouds moved back and forth across the sky, brightness and darkness falling over them. At the outdoor cafés tables were clustered closely together and straw chairs wobbled on the cobblestones. The poetic title song of Grzegorz Turnau's new album *To tu to tam* was playing everywhere. A blend of lyrical pop and soft jazz, it was delicate and breezy. Young Krakowians wore brightly colored summer clothing—oranges and yellows and greens that were almost neon. Clothing that announced that it was summer and communism had ended.

Not all was new. In the background hooves tapped on cobblestone pavement as horse-drawn carriages emerged from alleyways onto the main square. Sounds of a Poland that had once been. Krakow still looked like a city of knights and princesses, a fairy tale preserved even during the war.

Krakow was beautiful, but Seth felt wrath toward the medieval city and toward the Poles who lived there. He refused to go dancing. For him Poland was a graveyard trampled upon by anti-Semites—who had gazed with veiled smiles as their Jewish neighbors filed into the trains that would take them to the gas chambers.

It was warm and sunny on the day that Seth and I made the hour-and-a-half-long bus trip to Auschwitz. The camp was now a museum. There were guides, a bookstore, a cafeteria. The camp itself was tight, condensed. Everything was close together: sidewalks and redbrick buildings. A once-electrified fence. Very little was growing there. In the center everything was gray and red, the color of dirt and bricks. There were cobblestones and well-defined paths. It was a miniature town, its own civilization. Inside the pavilions were exhibits: an entire room filled with eyeglasses, suitcases, shoes.

Birkenau was a ten-minute bus ride away. It was unlike Auschwitz. There were no redbrick barracks, no *ARBEIT MACHT FREI* cast in iron above the gate. Once upon a time Birkenau had been a forest. Now there was only dry earth and vastness, and one could easily become lost there. It was a long walk along a dirt path encroached upon by weeds to the crematoria. Amid the ruins it was dark and cool and quiet.

"Think About Whether or Not I Was Right"

At the Institute for Contemporary History in Prague's pictur-esque district of Malá Strana, Czech historians were revisit-ing the Stalinist show trials, that theater of horrors where some of the most talented had played the role of avant-garde directors.

That summer of 1996, after I left Krakow, I went to Prague, where at the film archives the archivist brought me the footage of Milada Horáková's show trial. I found the transcripts of the trial easily: after all, they had been published in multiple newspapers at the time. But I wanted to see something more. The interrogators, at the very least, knew how the script had been written, how the confes-sions had been extracted. Could the prosecutors have truly believed the defendants? What did it mean to truly believe? I wanted to see the staging, the clothing, the gestures, the expressions on their faces. I wanted to hear the rhythm of their speech and the tone of their voices. I wanted to imagine how it felt to be inside that room.

The film reels were in black-and-white. Watching them, it was dif-ficult to imagine there had ever been color in that courtroom. Mi-lada Horáková wore a tailored jacket, a straight skirt, wire glasses, and her hair pulled back tightly in a bun. She confessed to leading an espionage ring, to conspiring together with the West to begin a third world war that would overthrow socialism in Czechoslovakia and return nationalized factories to exploitative bourgeois owners. Like the Nazis, the Stalinists had tortured her. They had broken her . . . yet not to the end. Unlike Rudolf Slánský and André Simone and other victims of the Stalinist show trials, Milada Horáková had never been a communist. And she was not so obliging. There were moments when she hesitated, wandered from her script, subtly, as if shyly. *"I have a different position." "I cannot answer that."* Silence.

The prosecutor addressed Milada Horáková as *Paní obžalovaná*— "Madame, the Accused." It was a singsong phrase, especially in high-pitched Prague Czech, the first syllable stressed, the last elongated. *Paní obžalovaná!* Over and over again.

> PROSECUTOR: Paní obžalovaná, *you are confessing, then, that you worked in a criminal way against the state . . . against the people's democracy of the Czechoslovak Republic?*
>
> MILADA HORÁKOVÁ: *Yes—of that I feel guilty.*
>
> PROSECUTOR: Paní obžalovaná, *I am asking you again . . . did your program mean the return of nationalized businesses to the mill owners?*
>
> MILADA HORÁKOVÁ: *The return of the ownership of these factories.*
>
> PROSECUTOR: *Thus a program for millionaires—not for the people.*
>
> MILADA HORÁKOVÁ: *It was a program for the bourgeois strata.*
>
> PROSECUTOR: *Hence via that path there was to have been a renewal of capitalism here. What do you think, how might the workers of a nationalized factory accept their former master— being aware that he would exploit their work further?*
>
> MILADA HORÁKOVÁ: *I have a different position toward that matter.*

Every day the newspapers published the transcripts of the trial. Every day the papers published letters from readers. From angry readers. From readers demanding justice.

> *Here, before the faces of the working people, on the bench of the accused, concludes the shameful path of the bourgeoisie, of criminals united against the people of this republic in order to thrust a dagger in their backs!*

*With outrage we, miners, are following the trial against the
band of grand traitors and spies, who shrank from nothing, not
even the spilling of the blood of their own people and their own
nation, in order that their golden capitalist times be returned
to them.*

*Our workers, our peasants, our intelligentsia, our women and
our youth, who in the struggle with the great powers of yesterday are working for the establishment of a beautiful future,
express their deep disgust for them.*

This middle-aged woman, the prosecutor insisted, had been
plotting another world war, a war of the West against the East, a
war to restore capitalism.

> MILADA HORÁKOVÁ: *Wars of the Western powers against
> the East, that means against the people's democratic countries
> and the Soviet Union.*
> PROSECUTOR: *And, in such a case, on whose side would the
> former SS men of West Germany stand, and on whose side
> would you and your coconspirators stand?*
> MILADA HORÁKOVÁ:—*I cannot answer that.*
> PROSECUTOR: *You cannot? Thank you.*
> PROSECUTOR: Paní obžalovaná, *when the entire republic
> is working constructively and when against that a handful of
> people assist in preparing a war against their own republic, is
> that not a foreign and hostile element?*
> MILADA HORÁKOVÁ: *(silent)*
> PROSECUTOR: *Thank you, that is also an answer.*
> PROSECUTOR: *The only real conception was war,* Paní
> obžalovaná, *war against the republic, as the single condition
> for the realization of your plans.*
> MILADA HORÁKOVÁ: *We in the committee also thought
> about—with which I myself of course did not then agree, be-
> cause from an international perspective I did not regard it
> as somehow practical—about the possibility of a diplomatic*

road, about international elections, under international control, etc.

Then the prosecutor reminded the audience of the betrayal at Munich, that moment in September 1938 when Western bourgeois democracy had sold out Czechoslovakia, when British prime minister Neville Chamberlain had handed the first part of the small republic to Hitler.

> PROSECUTOR: *Do you recall a certain act of international control, which we paid for in 1938?*
> MILADA HORÁKOVÁ: *I do recall. And just for that reason in these conceptions, as I have stated here, we envisaged a war.*
> PROSECUTOR: *You envisaged a war and to war belongs the atomic bomb. At least so they threaten us.*
> MILADA HORÁKOVÁ: *I am, Prosecutor Sir, really about matters of war...*
> PROSECUTOR: *You were counting on the fact that in the case of war perhaps Prague as well would be struck?*
> MILADA HORÁKOVÁ: *If there were to be a war, we would have to count on striking all targets.*
> PROSECUTOR: *Among them even Prague? Is your sixteen-year-old daughter in Prague?*
> MILADA HORÁKOVÁ: *Yes.*
> PROSECUTOR: *Thank you. That is enough.*

During the trial, women and children, the adolescent and teenaged activists known as pioneers, factory workers and miners, wrote letters. They expressed their outrage at the evildoers. They expected justice from the communist state. They knew what they wanted: *"We, women from Vimperk, from a border town, we, who are devoted co-builders of socialism in our country, demand for all of the accused the highest punishment!"*

The legacy of totalitarianism was *"the spirit of the trial,"* Milan Kundera wrote.

Sitting in the small room alone in the film archives, I watched the trial conclude. Milada Horáková delivered her final words. They were words of advice: *"Do not do what I did, what I have done."*

That summer in a Prague bookstore I found Milada Horáková's last letters, written in the final hours of her life to her friends, to her sister and her mother-in-law, to her husband and her daughter, to her elderly father.

"'Though I walk in the valley of the shadow of death,'" Milada Horáková wrote to her mother-in-law, *"'I will fear no evil, for Thou art with me.'"*

She believed in God. She believed, too, in the world to come. *"If I depart before you do,"* she wrote to her husband, *"it is only to wait for you patiently..."*

She would wait there for her father as well.

> *Father, Papa, forgive me, understand me, don't harden your heart toward me! As I grew there grew in me so many of your qualities, even though otherwise directed. I know that this should not afflict your eighty-one years. I know that I should stand by you and kiss your dear hand, before the time of your departure to Mother arrives. It happened otherwise. Nevertheless I will stand by you just the same and with Mother I will wait for you... but as you see, we do not part for long.*

For her daughter, Jana, Milada Horáková wished independence. She wanted Jana to be courageous. She wanted her to study hard at school, to get regular exercise, to take care of her complexion. In Nazi prison she'd read the Habsburg empress Maria Theresa's letters to her daughter Marie Antoinette, queen of France, and had been impressed by the care the empress took to dispense practical advice, womanly advice. Now in her final hours, Milada Horáková, too, counseled her daughter about clothing, cosmetics, hairstyles.

> *You must, my little girl, find your own path. Search for it independently, do not let anything deter you, not even the memory*

of your mother and father. If you really do love them, you will not hurt them by seeing them critically—only you must not find yourself on a path that is dishonest, untruthful, false and unsuited to life. I have reconsidered many things, changed my mind about many values—yet what has remained unchanging for me, that without which I cannot imagine my life, is the freedom of my conscience. You, my young daughter, think about whether or not I was right.

That was not all.

There were inexplicable paradoxes. For the letter ended with a reading list: Czechoslovak Communist Party leader Klement Gottwald's *With the Soviet Union for Time Eternal;* Stalin's *The History of the Communist Party of the Soviet Union: Short Course;* literature by Stalinist court poets. She wanted Jana to read these books—when Jana did she would surely think of her mother.

The last letter was dated 27 June 1950, at 2:30 A.M. At 5:00 A.M. that morning Milada Horáková went to the gallows. The surrealist Záviš Kalandra had preceded her by some minutes. There were four executions that morning; hers was the last.

"I am departing without hatred," Milada Horáková told her executioners. *"I wish you, I wish you . . ."* She died before she finished the sentence.

Milada Horáková's letters were never delivered. But neither were they destroyed—neither discarded nor shredded nor burned. It would have been so easy: a few letters, one match from the package used to light the cigarettes the prison guard undoubtedly carried. Instead the letters went to the archives, where the paper yellowed and the door was locked.

Eighteen years later, when the Prague Spring came, Milada Horáková's family asked for her letters. The Communist Party said no.

Twenty more years passed. Then came the Velvet Revolution, when statues came down and streets were renamed. One was renamed in honor of the feminist democrat who had departed without hatred. Milada Horáková Street was one of the largest and busiest streets in Prague, quite close to Prague Castle.

Just months after the revolution, the forty-year-old letters found their way out of the dusty archives, and a new generation, a generation too young to have known their author, published them. Copies were on sale in ordinary bookstores. I bought one.

I was a voyeur, reading those letters.

The Other Side of Stalinism

In September 1996 I returned to Stanford. That fall Amanda, whom I had not seen since the night more than a year earlier when we had run through Prague in the rain, Amanda holding her disembodied ponytail, wrote to me from Massachusetts. It was wet and cold there, and she described her life as working her way through a fog. In that fog something distinct had emerged: a good-bye letter Oskar had left on his computer. The letter was in Czech. Amanda had pored over it with a dictionary, she could make out some phrases but not others. It was tormenting her. She enclosed a copy of Oskar's letter.

"If you find it a bearable task," Amanda wrote, *"could you take a look at it? If reading it is not too difficult, would you be willing to translate? You can just throw it out without reading it, I certainly would understand."*

I looked at the piece of paper. It written on 22 December 1994, at Prague's airport, by a man wrenched with despair.

She had sent the letter to Vlasta in Prague as well. Vlasta, though, had not been able to bring herself to translate it. I called Amanda. I would do it, I told her, but only if she was sure she wanted this. Was she?

Yes, she told me, she was.

I hung up the phone and began to type.

▪ ▪ ▪

SETH SENT LONG letters from Jerusalem. Even as he pleaded with me to come to Israel, he was apprehensive. Above all he feared that my ambivalence toward Zionism would inevitably become my ambivalence toward him, that I would fly away "disappointed and disgusted."

But Seth was wrong. There was much that drew me to Israel.

From my first visit, seven years earlier, I remembered vividly the greenness of the peaches and the saltiness of the Mediterranean. Mangos and falafel and coconut ice cream. Sundresses and beaded earrings and dancing on sand. The expanse of the Negev. The bright blue of the sea. The labyrinth of the Old City. The sun that set so quickly, vanishing just a moment after it began to slide downward in the sky. The wrenching beauty of Jerusalem. So many richly sensuous impressions, all uninnocent for being set against the backdrop of violence.

When classes ended in December I left on a flight from San Francisco. I was, after all, very happy to be in Israel again.

In Jerusalem, though, I was still thinking about Stalinist terror. On 8 June 1950 Milada Horáková and Záviš Kalandra were sentenced to death. Three days later the poet Stanislav Neumann's article appeared in the Communist Party's daily newspaper, *Rudé Právo*:

> *Here quite spontaneously in the middle of applause erupted the slogan: We want peace! Here are young people speaking about the future of our children, our pioneers—and over there are the condemned who speculated on war, who desired war, who helped to foment war.*
>
> *And this, too, is the whole difference. We love mankind, we believe in mankind, we know that the most precious thing in the world is human life. We are fighting so that the dreams of our parents not only become reality but also become small for us—we are fighting so that all of human life blossoms like an*

exquisite flower, so that our children do not recognize and our grandchildren forget the meaning of the words poverty, war, fascism.

They love nothing except themselves. They are willing to murder thousands of people so that the factories will be returned to them. They hate mankind, they despise mankind, they want to return to the past.

I thought about Stanislav Neumann's best friends going to their deaths in Theresienstadt with Stalin's name on their lips. I thought about Karel Kosík and Milan Kundera and Pavel Kohout, writing odes to the Communist Party while others were hanged. I thought of Arnošt Lustig, who said that in the camps the communists were the very best people. Arnošt had joined those people in the resistance. That generation had come to Stalinism during the Second World War, through the war—it was Auschwitz that was the other side of the Stalinist experience. If I really wanted to understand Stalinism, I would have to understand the war.

And so some days after I arrived in Israel I went to Yad Vashem, the Holocaust museum in Jerusalem. I went there to see Professor Yisrael Gutman—who had survived the Warsaw Ghetto Uprising, Majdanek, Auschwitz, and a death march to Mauthausen before going on to a new life in the new Jewish state as a historian of the old Jewish world. By now Yisrael Gutman was a man in his mid-seventies who had long been a central figure at Israel's Holocaust memorial.

Yisrael Gutman talked about the anti-Nazi resistance in the Warsaw Ghetto. These young men and women were not traditional, religious Jews but rather young revolutionaries of various kinds: Zionists, communists, and Bundists who rejected both Zionism and communism and instead embraced both a Marxism and a nationalism of a different kind. The uprising these young revolutionaries led in the Warsaw Ghetto had happened in the spring of 1943. This was some nine months after the *"Aktion"* of summer 1942 when most of the ghetto's residents had been gassed at Treblinka. Yet some remained. And when the Germans came to take the remaining ones, this small group of revolutionaries rose up against them.

It was a hopeless battle. In the end the Germans set fire to the ghetto, and the Jewish quarter of Warsaw burned to the ground.

Yisrael Gutman also talked about the Poles: the Jewish resistance had not intended to impress the Poles with their uprising—yet it happened that way. The Polish underground *was* impressed, despite their willful lack of interest, for they feared that an uprising in the ghetto would bring about a general uprising in Warsaw before the moment was right. They feared, too, that the Jews were communists.

If I really wanted to understand the war, I began to realize, I should be in Warsaw. For Czechoslovakia, the trauma of the betrayal at Munich was very real. Yet what had happened in Poland was a trauma much deeper.

Yisrael Gutman spoke to me about the Jewish resistance, the radical youth who rose up not only against the Nazi murderers but also against the existing Jewish authorities. In the ghetto—he was clear about this—the Jewish policemen had been a tool of German power, and the Jewish resistance had had no choice but to liquidate them. The *Judenrat* was similar—in the beginning the Jewish council's intentions had been good: the council members, like the Jewish policemen, had wanted to do what they could for their people. But power corrupted them, they came to believe in their superiority, and in the end this absence of solidarity demoralized the entire community. It was a community that, in any case, was decomposing with each passing moment: in the ghetto people grew more and more absorbed in their personal misery, and the social structures that held human relationships in place disintegrated. The underground emerged as a symbolic demonstration, a miniature society invoking past values.

Yet to most Jews in the ghetto, the demonstration by this handful of young radicals was incomprehensible. There was a complete disconnection, Professor Gutman insisted, between the Jewish underground and the surrounding Jewish society.

I saw how, all these years later, his heart remained with the Jewish resistance, the radical youth who were not understood.

And the uprising? I asked him.

The uprising was "something like a revolution"—but not a revolution to bring about a better future. Everyone understood this was the end.

And Israel?

Israel was the ghetto's foil, the Jewish future contrasted with the absence of any future. Zionist ideology had long ensured that our sympathy was more for the young radicals who rose up against the Nazis than for the majority who boarded the trains to Treblinka. Today, Yisrael Gutman believed, even Israelis were beginning to face the truth: that the entirety of the Jewish resistance represented only the smallest fragment of the Jewish population. The vast majority chose not to fight. Israelis had long preferred not to think about those in that majority, not to identify with them.

∎ ∎ ∎

AFTER I RETURNED to California in January 1997, an unexpected postcard came from a ski resort in Vermont. Jarmila—now Todd James—was there, hoping, he wrote to me, to qualify for the U.S. Ski Team. No longer was he a Catholic: after Jarmila had become Todd James, Todd James had become an Orthodox Jew. He did not explain why.

Galina, my fellow teacher in Domažlice, wrote too. Some months earlier the headmistress of a gymnasium in Plzeň—a small city closer to Prague—had offered her a job, and she and Mara had set off from Domažlice to begin life anew. Mara had been reluctant to move yet again, but Galina had insisted. In Plzeň Galina had embraced her new life but soon felt disillusioned.

Every time I meet new people I'm ready to open my heart to everybody, trust everyone, ready to love anyone. In the end: I usually cry, I'm upset, disappointed, misunderstood, punished by isolation, coldness if not worse.... Trustworthy, reliable recipe is to escape (here it is, finally, my favourite word!).

It was true: *escape* was her favorite English word.

With my widowed landlady, Paní Prokopová, I corresponded about the war. She had been fourteen years old in March of 1939, when the weather was gray, the spring would not come, and German soldiers occupied her small town. Everyone was afraid. The whole town was dimmed, quite literally: in the evenings the windows were darkened. There were rationing coupons and food shortages; in order not to go hungry people had to buy flour and butter on the black market. Trade happened by night. Paní Prokopová no longer remembered if anything had played at the cinema, but she doubted that anything had: life had simply come to a halt. Radio reports came from London and Moscow, but people were afraid to listen to them. The Germans were the rulers, although some Czechs cooperated with them, not many—but still, there they were, the others called them collaborators. They informed on their neighbors, denounced other Czechs to the Germans. Many of those other Czechs went to prison: the Czech patriotic *Sokolové* and the communists and the organizers of domestic resistance. It was enough for the Germans to catch one of them—they could extract by force the names of the others.

"It was worst for the Jews," Paní Prokopová continued.

In our town there was one doctor, a fabric merchant, and several who dealt in clothing and leather gloves. They had to wear a star until in the end all of them were deported and ended their lives in the gas chambers. We were sorry for them, we'd lived with them, but no one helped them. I don't recall that any of them returned.

▪ ▪ ▪

SOON AFTER I received Paní Prokopová's letter, Jan Gross came to give a lecture at Stanford. Jan was a Polish historian who, like my

Polish teacher Pani Hanka, had emigrated after the "anti-Zionist" campaign of 1968. His first book was set in German-occupied Poland during World War II. There he told the heroic story of the Polish wartime underground that created not only a partisan army but also a parallel society, which preserved values in a time of terror. His second book was set in Soviet-occupied Poland during World War II. There he told the story of the hell wrought upon eastern Poland: of hundreds of thousands deported to Soviet labor camps; of Poles shot and buried alive in pits; of noses, ears, and genitals cut off and eyes gouged out.

Now Jan wanted to talk about Polish Jews. He spoke about the rapid collapse of civility under the impact of war, about the plague of denunciations. He spoke, too, about how the Holocaust was not confined to gas chambers: in the east, executions of Jews took place in public, in the presence of their Polish neighbors—who by and large said nothing.

■　■　■

IN TORONTO THAT February of 1997 I went to see my former professor Stefan M. I was soon to leave for Warsaw, and he had offered to give me letters of introduction.

I sat down in his office. We talked about Poles—and about Poles and Jews.

"I feel like I'm sending this delicate young person into a nest of snakes," he said.

That struck me as improbably dramatic, if only given the demographics of present-day Poland. "But there can't be very many Jews left in Poland today—how bad could relations between Poles and Jews really be?"

"Imagine," he answered me, "that you have a little brother, and imagine that this little brother dies in some kind of horrible . . . 'accident.' For which you feel—*partially responsible*. Now, can you imagine how at subsequent family gatherings such an event could spoil the family atmosphere?"

The Locomotive
of History

In March of 1997 Warsaw was cold and gray. It felt like what it
was: a city that had been burnt to ashes and rebuilt in Stalinist
architecture. I had come to stay for nearly a year: I wanted to understand the war, that abyss out of which Stalinism arose in Eastern
Europe. I loved the bleakness.

On the streets sat men and women, mostly older, some with horrific deformations, boils, missing legs and arms; a man in a suit
jacket with only a head, arms, and a torso, wheeling himself on a
scooter down Krakowskie Przedmieście, Warsaw's most elegant
shopping street; a man outside the Palace of Culture with half of his
face grotesquely deformed, a form of an eye hanging where a nose
should have been. Gypsy mothers and their children and refugees
from the Balkan wars begged for money. The children chased after
me. In the early evening when the stores closed, the streets quickly
emptied of all but gangsters and drunks, staggering and falling. The
gangsters wore gold chains under their Adidas track suits.

On certain days packs of young men wearing peacock-like head-
dresses prowled the streets. They were gangs of fans—often violent, each attached to its own soccer team. A taxi driver advised me
not to leave my apartment on the days of soccer matches: barroom
fights easily spread onto the streets.

"Poland for the Poles," someone had written in spray paint on
a building near my apartment. A Star of David was hanging on

spray-painted gallows. On other gallows hung the names of soccer teams. Polish graffiti: a discourse of gallows.

At the Miodowa bus stop on Krakowskie Przedmieście I read the black writing on the red wall. *"Adolf Hitler was right about the Jews. He murdered them. No mercy for the enemies of Polishness."* Nearby there was more graffiti: *"Jews to the gas chambers."*

But there were no more Jews here. Only the elderly could have remembered the time when there was a Jewish quarter of Warsaw, and graffiti was the expressive medium of youth.

All during the day I heard the tapping of horses' hooves on the cobblestones beneath my window. The scent of urine and horses and vodka. On Good Friday I looked out the window onto the narrow cobblestone street and watched hundreds of people singing in Latin, carrying enormous wooden crosses, holding fire on sticks. Walking, chanting, kneeling, rising.

In the Old Town, on Piwna Street, I rented a one-room apartment from a middle-aged couple, who before Solidarity's 1989 victory had used the studio as an underground art gallery. Now capitalism had arrived, and the former site of democratic opposition had become a real estate investment: they rented the studio to foreigners. With the additional income they had bought a car—and for the first time in his life my landlord had begun to drive. In the beginning he had been fearful, but the thrill quickly overshadowed the fear. He became passionate about driving and infatuated with speed.

My landlord was a painter who liked to talk about philosophy. Once he sat by the window in the studio and told me of a conversation he'd had with his students at the art academy—a conversation about numbers, and about numbering, about the many ways in which we were all numbered: our apartment number, our passport number, our bank account number. Then someone brought up the numbers tattooed onto the arms of inmates at Auschwitz.

"And suddenly," my landlord said, "the joking came to an end. Some of those victims were undoubtedly, by chance, bad people, thieves or criminals. It doesn't matter, we forgive them everything, we forgive them because it was such an inhuman situation."

He paused, then said, "It's easy for me to talk—how can I know how I would have behaved in such circumstances?"

I, too, had no confidence that I would have behaved well. On the contrary—I suspected I would have been a coward.

▪ ▪ ▪

IN POSTCOMMUNIST POLAND, as in the Czech Republic, a criminal underworld had come into being. There was a new trend: teenage hooligans and Mafia-style gangsters, not infrequently wearing Adidas track suits, murdered one another with newly imported baseball bats. Around the city billboards began to appear with pictures of baseball bats and a rhyming slogan: *"Służy do grania, nie do zabijania"* (This is for playing, not for killing). As if the misuse of the baseball bats were, perhaps, only a misunderstanding.

To the Polish graduate student Mikołaj, Warsaw's violence seemed almost natural. He had moved to the capital from a smaller town in 1988 to begin studying at university, and he remembered the Warsaw of those last days of communism as *"dangerous, impoverished . . . but with some charm."*

"That time was really exciting," Mikołaj wrote to me from Budapest, *"demonstrations, happenings and cheap bistros with vodka served with a heavily oiled herring."*

I wrote to him about the graffiti and the billboards.

"Envy, insanity, racism and hooliganism," he answered me, *". . . the pillars of the Polish reality."*

In March 1989 he had been knifed in Warsaw, Mikołaj told me. Who had knifed him?

"It's hard to identify the f——rs who knifed me 8 years ago," he answered.

"I guess they thought of themselves as cool skinheads though after some years I think they were simply some asswipes trying to get my precious GDR-made reporter's tape recorder. I had my short moment of triumph before the 2nd of them knifed me (which I discovered a few minutes after, bleeding like a slaughtered pig). I smashed the prodigious balls of the 1st assailant. Hey, old good Rumanian military boots.

Now Mikołaj was spending weekends in Zagreb, where his girl-friend lived.

"Croatia," he wrote, *"reminds me of Poland in the late '20s and early '30s. Freshly achieved independence, strong man's rule and the overwhelming battle spirit. Let's hope they won't pay the same price as we did. Memento mori and death to our friends!"*

■ ■ ■

IN APRIL I took the train from Warsaw to Bratislava, where I visited Zora Bútorová, the sociologist who had once come to Stanford. Three years earlier, she and Martin had returned to Slovakia after a year in the United States. Their homecoming had not been a happy one. She and Martin had arrived full of impressions and new ideas from their yearlong stay at Princeton—but no one wanted to hear any of that. Their friends and colleagues were resentful that Martin and Zora had abandoned them for the West. Leaving was a betrayal—even if one returned—and they learned to say nothing about the United States, and nothing about their time there.

About Slovak politics, Zora despaired. Vladimír Mečiar, in and out of power, often ruled as a quasi-dictator. People were easily manipulated, accepting of absurdities: a recent survey had revealed that a majority of Slovaks looked favorably upon the clerico-fascist wartime state—and that a majority of Slovaks looked favorably, too, upon the Slovak National Uprising of August 1944—which was against that very same collaborationist state. It was a wholly uncritical affirmation of Slovak identity: any show of Slovak power was good. Zora feared that the next generation would be raised with a similar understanding. Under Mečiar schoolchildren were memorizing nationalist slogans.

Now, in the spring of 1997, Zora told me that Slovakia's new history textbooks described the transports carrying Slovak Jews to the gas chambers as if they were trains to a summer camp. She didn't want her son Ivan learning from those textbooks.

I thought of my friend Miloš, so amiable and warm, so undeniably a part of all this.

▪ ▪ ▪

WHEN I RETURNED from Bratislava to Warsaw, I walked out of the train station to face the monumental Palace of Culture, Stalin's postwar gift to the Poles, built with the labor of prisoners. Stalinism rising from Warsaw's ashes. *"The whole nation builds its capital,"* announced the communist slogan carved into the stone building at a prominent downtown intersection. Today prostitutes with brightly dyed hair and tall spiked heels walked the corridors of the Hotel Warszawa. The dark dining room in the hotel where I felt as if I were still among the balding apparatchiks now served as an ersatz brothel. Blikle, an old literary salon before the war, was now overdone and artificial, and Isaac Bashevis Singer's Krochmalna Street in the heart of Jewish Warsaw, a street so full of color in his novels, remained so only in my imagination.

In her 1934 guidebook for English-speaking tourists, Grace Humphrey wrote of the maze of streets connected by short, crooked alleyways that was the Jewish quarter. *"Shabby and smelly and sordid this section of Warsaw is,"* she wrote, *"yet full of character and interest."*

Sidewalks and doorways are crowded with people crying their wares, trading and bargaining, doing their business in the streets—this for five days a week. But go on a Friday evening or on Saturday, and what a difference! Dignified men and women in their Saturday best, moving along slowly, carrying striped prayer shawls and well-worn books, talking quietly. . . .

A circle and you swing into Marszalkowska, past the railroad station, then west and north via Karmelicka, Dzielna, Gęsia, Franciszkańska. The crowds on the sidewalks and the signs in Yiddish will tell you that you're in the heart of the Ghetto—the Jewish district of Warsaw. The men in long black coats, high boots, very small black caps with tiny vizors, with corkscrew curls hanging in front of their ears; the women in brown wigs; everybody talking at once, bargaining, gesticulating, doing all their business on the street; the numerous little shops, plastered over with advertisements, price marks, and pictures of their wares—that is the Ghetto.

This was when "the ghetto" was simply a Jewish district of the city, when no one could have imagined that it would one day soon be indelibly associated with trains to Treblinka. Now, in 1997, no longer were there men in long black coats and high boots with corkscrew curls. And no longer were there signs in Yiddish. Instead the site that was once a ghetto was marked by the communist-sympathizing sculptor Natan Rapaport's enormous granite monument, his homage to the ghetto fighters—and by a wall of names at Umschlagplatz, the place from where trains had departed for Treblinka fifty-five years earlier.

The war was complicated in Poland: Jews were not the only victims, and Germans were not the only enemies. In August 1939 Hitler's Germany and Stalin's Soviet Union signed a nonaggression pact. On 1 September 1939 Germany invaded Poland from the west. Sixteen days later, the Soviet Union invaded from the east. Both occupations were merciless. In the beginning, Polish citizens in each occupation zone tried to escape to the other, convinced that the other could not possibly be as brutal as the first.

Now, a few blocks away from Umschlagplatz on Muranowska Street stood a bronze cast monument: enormous railway tracks, a wooden cart overflowing with staggering crosses, a small Jewish tombstone among them. Names of towns were carved into the tracks. These were places where Poles deported to the Soviet Union, to Stalin's labor camps, had met their deaths. A monument to those *"murdered in the East."*

■ ■ ■

IN THE EVENINGS I took walks through what had once been the ghetto, through a neighborhood called Muranów, which was now full of communist-era apartment blocks, wholly unexceptional. On the way home to my apartment on Piwna Street, I vomited into the bushes. I felt numbness and nausea, and I did not even want to escape it. On the contrary: I was looking for a way to enter the war.

I was not the only one. Hundreds of Jewish teenagers, from the United States, from Israel, from dozens of other countries, were coming to Poland. They came to Poland wearing Stars of David. They came on tours of the death camps, to mourn the dead in the country they regarded as a cemetery. The tours were called Marches of the Living, and they concluded in Israel: the new world, the new hope, the land of the New Jew. The Jewish teenagers did not want to talk to Polish journalists—they did not want to talk to Poles at all.

They didn't come to Poland for dialogue, one boy told a Polish reporter. They came to say kaddish for their dead.

A Polish girl who lived today in the town the Germans called Auschwitz and the Poles called Oświęcim said to the visitors who were her own age, "My grandmother remembered that when the wind blew, they could smell the stench of burning Jews."

The visitors were angry. They wanted to know: "Why didn't you say—the stench of burning *people*?"

Yet they themselves had come as Jews.

When Poles tried to talk to them, these young Jews wanted to know how they could live there—in a land that was a cemetery. They wanted to know why the Poles had not saved the Jews. They believed it was not by chance that the Germans had chosen Poland as the site of the death camps. They didn't know about the heroic Polish underground. They didn't know that Poles had also died in Auschwitz. They didn't want to know.

The young Jews who came to Poland and wanted to see nothing more than the remains of crematoria did not offend only the Poles. They also offended the few remaining Polish Jews.

A Jewish university student in Warsaw joined a March of the Living and traveled to Israel with the group for the journey's conclusion. The final evening the students spent on an Israeli army base. They were all young, they held hands and danced.

In Poland we were reviving a memory, here we were to feel like Jews. In Poland we'd suffered, here we rejoiced, tasting the flavor of Israel. And suddenly everything revealed itself to be an illusion. When representatives of forty-three countries, participants in the March, were called to the stage so that they could each say a few words in front of the microphone, Polish Jews were passed over. It was the greatest humiliation of my life.

The student was part of a nascent Jewish community, supported by the New York–based Lauder Foundation. The foundation sponsored, too, a new Polish-Jewish magazine called *Midrasz*.

"Do you have Jewish roots?" I read there.

Is it a problem for you? Or a secret? Or perhaps a passion, a pride, a hope? Perhaps you feel shame because of your Jewish origin? Perhaps you're afraid? Does it happen that you conceal it? Perhaps you don't know what to say to your wife or husband? Or to your friends from school, your boyfriend or your girlfriend? And what should you tell your children? . . . Perhaps something about this is painful for you, perhaps you feel alienated? Perhaps you think that anti-Semites have something of a point?

You did not have to face these problems alone, the advertisement promised. For those struggling with their Jewish identity, a confidential hotline was now accepting phone calls.

"We promise discretion," the advertisement concluded.

∎ ∎ ∎

IN POLAND THERE had been too little working through of the Jewish question; in Czechoslovakia there had been too little working through of the Stalinist question. In 1952, three of the fourteen defendants in the Rudolf Slánský trial were sentenced to life imprisonment. Eleven of the fourteen were sentenced to death. All went to the gallows with the same last words: *"Long live the Com-*

munist Party of Czechoslovakia!" Rudolf Margolius was the exception: he went to his death in silence.

Now, in 1997, I took the overnight train from Warsaw to Prague. I was going there, on behalf of the journal my former Czech teacher Vlasta edited, to interview Heda Margolius—the widow of Rudolf Margolius.

Heda had left Prague after the 1968 Soviet invasion. The next quarter century she had spent in the United States, working at Harvard. Now, in her old age, she had returned to Prague, and I visited her in a light-filled apartment not far from Wenceslas Square. Rudolf Margolius's widow was animated and articulate. Just before he went to his death, in the prison during their last meeting, Rudolf Margolius had told his ill and despairing wife that she looked beautiful. Nearly half a century later Heda Margolius still radiated traces of her younger beauty.

I'd just arrived from Warsaw, and as I asked her questions I mixed up the Slavic languages, the Czech words and the Polish words becoming entangled in one another. I began to apologize, but Heda stopped me: it wasn't a problem at all, mixing up Czech and Polish. When she was in Auschwitz—she said reassuringly—she used to talk to the Polish girls in Czech, and they spoke to her in Polish, and everyone always understood one another.

She spoke of these girls warmly, almost with nostalgia, as if she were speaking of her girlfriends from childhood: *the Polish girls she met in Auschwitz.*

Heda survived Auschwitz. Late in the war, she escaped from a death march and made her way back to Prague—where her old friends would not take her in. It was not that they didn't care whether she lived or died. It was only that they were afraid: during the German occupation, sheltering a Jew could bring the death penalty.

I wanted to know: How could she not hate them?

But it was true: she did not hate them. She bore no resentment. Rather she was full of a philosophical equanimity: she had a right to try to save her own life, she explained, but not to ask others to risk their lives to save hers.

▪ ▪ ▪

LATER, STILL IN Prague, I talked to Vlasta about my interview with Heda Margolius, and Vlasta wanted to know: Had I asked her about the earlier show trial of Milada Horáková? After all, Rudolf Margolius had been a high-ranking member of the communist government then, and his wife, too, had been a Communist Party member. Had they believed in Milada Horáková's guilt?

"I wanted to ask her—but I couldn't . . ." I told Vlasta. After all, this was a woman who—as she was once described in a Czech novel—had been to hell twice. What right had I to judge her?

"I understand," Vlasta said.

Digging around in the Institute for Contemporary History, I found a newspaper clipping of an interview with Heda Margolius during the expansive days of the Prague Spring, the days when the rehabilitations of Rudolf Margolius and those who went with him to the gallows had been belatedly made public. In the interview Heda spoke of how she and her husband had survived the Holocaust and come to join the Communist Party. It had been in the Nazi camps that she had come to so admire the communists:

> They were in fact the best people in those camps, they were the only ones who didn't think only of themselves and of the horrors confronting them personally, but actually about what kind of world there would be when the war was over. And that gave them such strength and they were such wonderful people, they simply enraptured everyone around them. All of us . . . above all my husband . . . in '45, it was the first thing that we did, when we came back from the camp, we applied for membership to the Party. . . .

▪ ▪ ▪

ONE DAY AFTER I'd returned to Warsaw a policeman came to see me in the studio on Piwna Street. He was looking for my landlord's wife.

I told the policeman where they lived; it was not far away.

"What happened?" I asked him.

There had been a car accident: my landlord had been driving, undoubtedly too quickly, and he might have been drinking as well. He was in the hospital now, in critical condition; it was uncertain whether he would survive.

▪ ▪ ▪

IN WARSAW DURING the day I sat in the archives. It was July of 1951, and the Polish communists whom the war had brought to power had put on trial the German officers who had "liquidated" the Warsaw Ghetto. The final liquidation of the ghetto had come in the spring of 1943. By that time most of the ghetto's 350,000 original inhabitants had already been gassed at Treblinka. Only some 60,000 remained.

Now eight years had passed, and SS officers Jürgen Stroop and Franz Konrad pleaded not guilty.

Slowly I read the transcripts of the trial of Jürgen Stroop and Franz Konrad, the "liquidators of the Warsaw Ghetto." Next to me the women working at the war crimes archive who had brought me the files drank tea and played ABBA tapes on an old cassette player.

The trial was victor's justice—and communist theater.

"One must think dialectically," one witness for the prosecution said.

Marek Edelman, the Bundist commander of the Warsaw Ghetto Uprising, also testified. Edelman, a hero, was not a romantic; his account was devoid of pathos or grandiloquence. He talked about the burning of the ghetto.

"I won't describe here," Marek Edelman told the judge, *"the scenes that took place, because it's obvious that if a house is burning, then people are burning alive."*

The whole ghetto was in flames. Corpses were lying on the streets. Nothing was mystical to Marek Edelman—neither having led the ghetto uprising nor having watched Warsaw Jewry consumed by flames. Everything was crudely human—even when it seemed not human at all. He described how the Germans succeeded in finding the last Jews hiding in the remains of the ghetto: *"With the aid of a horsewhip it's possible to find out everything from a five-year-old child. By beating the child with the horsewhip, the Germans brought him to such a state, that, dripping with blood from head to toe, the child crawled to the stairs and showed them that they needed to remove the beam and here were the Jews.*

"The only way out was the sewers." That was how Marek Edelman himself survived. But this was a different story.

On 18 July 1951, the prosecutor questioned the accused Franz Konrad about his membership in the Nazi Party.

> PROSECUTOR: *For how long had you been a member of the party?*
> FRANZ KONRAD: *Since 1932.*
> PROSECUTOR: *Then you, the accused, were familiar with the theory of the party, with the party's ideology?*
> FRANZ KONRAD: *I was uninterested in that.*

"Dancing Queen" was playing in the background as I read the trial transcripts: Jürgen Stroop was aloof, proud of his good breeding and refined manners. He insisted he'd always conducted himself as a gentleman.

"In my life I've always tried to behave chivalrously," he said. *"This is the most important asset my wife and children possess. I have tried during my life to extend to other women the chivalry with which I relate to my wife."*

During the uprising Marek Edelman came upon what had been the hospital on Gęsia Street.

> *In one bed lay a newborn suffocated with a pillow, in another lay a woman with her stomach ripped open, in a third lay a woman who had probably given birth and been killed together with her child. That's how the gynecological ward looked. And how did the surgical ward look. There were wounded people*

lying there, they had their legs in plaster, all of the wounded were burned alive on the beds that were set on fire.... What I'm going to say I saw by the entrance to the ghetto on the corner of Gęsia and Zamenhof: A woman was sitting with a child in her arm, likely she'd no longer been alive for twenty-four hours, but apparently someone with a keen sense of humor had halfway undressed the woman and pushed her breast into the child's mouth. That's how it looked.

"Jürgen Stroop," testified one communist historian, "is responsible for the organized murder of the last part of Warsaw's Jewish population."

"It wasn't so important, what I did," Jürgen Stroop told the court. Another witness took the stand. His Polish was awkward, ungrammatical.

As the flames gradually spread through the house, the fire began to go out to the balcony, and a young woman was talking to General Stroop. I still remember some fragments: that he should be ashamed, that this is a nation that has such great ancestors as Goethe, and what is it that you're perpetrating, I'm not asking here for any mercy, because I know that none will come to me from your hand, but remember, for what is happening to us, it's you who will pay, not me. That's all I remember, after all I was vulnerable, the police and the SS were there, and it wasn't good for me to be listening to that. By then the fire had gone out to the balcony and begun to roast them and those people didn't have any choice but to jump: first an old woman, an old man jumped behind her, and a mother took her child by the hand and jumped from the balcony with the cry "Long live Poland"; behind her jumped a man. It was Stroop, he was sitting down, then he stood up and advised the SS men to go finish off those who'd jumped from the balcony.

The witness added that he had seen Franz Konrad taking pictures. In his closing statement SS General Jürgen Stroop elaborated:

racial matters had always been incidental to him. He had been raised as a soldier, and as a soldier he had carried out his duties, duties he had believed necessary for his fatherland. He had merely obeyed orders; it was the responsibility of his superiors to examine their content. That he had found himself in Warsaw—he added— was purely by chance.

General Stroop's defense attorneys pointed to mitigating circumstances: The first asked the judges to consider that *"Jürgen Stroop's intellectual capacity is in fact less than paltry."* The second asked the judges to consider that *"Jürgen Stroop was a wretched servant of dark capitalist powers."*

The attorneys' pleas for clemency were halfhearted, pro forma.

Through the windows of the archive I could see the clouds moving. The sky was growing darker. In a few minutes it would rain again.

The verdict was delivered on 23 July 1951. It was summer, and Jürgen Stroop and Franz Konrad were sentenced to death.

■ ■ ■

IN LATE SPRING of 1997 I flew back to Israel. It was already summer there, and I wanted to stay by the water forever, feeling the heat and the sun. On the bus the religious Jews with their ringlet *peyes*, their tall black hats, and their cellular telephones, did not— would not—look at me.

In the Old City of Jerusalem, watching the sunset, I wanted to read the notes that those who came to pray tucked inside the cracks in the Wailing Wall. A voyeuristic impulse.

There in the Old City a pretty young woman told a man with a very long beard that her parents did not approve of him. He was gaunt, thin, unattractive. To my left another man lit a cigarette for a woman and told her that here, in this spot, there was no one else between himself and God. "In all other places there is someone else," he said to her. I didn't feel God this way, and I found him pretentious.

When in the summer of 1989, as a seventeen-year-old, I'd gone to Israel, I'd studied history there with a teacher named David. Like

Seth, David was an American who had become Israeli. Now, eight years later, David came to meet me at a café in Jerusalem.

We talked about history. For David there was a single historical narrative: the narrative of anti-Semitism, proceeding inexorably and inevitably toward the Holocaust—and necessarily resolving itself in Zionism.

"You understand nothing!" I told him. "You obscure from your students what the war really was: the cataclysmic event of modernity, the failure of the Enlightenment, that which forces us to question the meaning of modernity—has it meant civilization or has it meant terror?"

David only smiled. Perhaps I was right, but would his students understand anything if he were to tell them that?

"And besides—" he laughed "—what is going to make them good Zionists?"

Yet it seemed to me that the Zionists, in appropriating the Holocaust this way, had paradoxically marginalized it.

▪ ▪ ▪

WARSAW AND JERUSALEM: the dialectic of the Old World and the New World was draining. Now in Warsaw all around me I saw broken pieces of gravestones, fragments, dislocated pieces of the past.

Professor Tomaszewski, a kind, liberal-minded historian who had been born nearly a decade before the Second World War, described the postwar years as a Time of Missing People.

"For instance," he said to me, "there were no tailors."

Modernity, a Time of Missing People. Missing People and Former People, the *byvshii liudi* of the Stalinist years: people who not only were no longer but were considered never to have been. The presence of absence, this was Warsaw.

A letter arrived quickly from David, continuing our conversation at the Jerusalem café. The Zionist movement and the waves of East European Jews emigrating from Europe to Palestine were the product of anti-Semitism, David wrote.

In other words, when they realized that the Enlightenment was a farce as far as they were concerned, and that they would never be accepted in the Christian world, they began the modern Zionist movement. Therefore, it should be no wonder that the Enlightenment reached the pinnacle of its failure with the Holocaust.

At Warsaw University I watched Andrzej Wajda's film *Korczak*, the story of the Polish-Jewish pedagogue Janusz Korczak, who became the beloved director of a Jewish orphanage in the Warsaw Ghetto—and chose to go to the gas chambers with the orphans. The film was not a romantic one. By the time he led the children to Umschlagplatz, the Janusz Korczak in Wajda's film was a broken man.

In Wajda's film Korczak lowered himself to collect money for his orphanage from the ghetto elite: a handful of wealthy Jews, some collaborators, others smugglers and businessmen who had managed to profit from the misery around them. A friend was appalled: did Korczak have no dignity?

"I don't have dignity," Korczak answered, *"I have two hundred children."*

When it was their turn for the transport, the orphanage's directress told the children: *"Fifteen minutes. We're going on an outing. . . . Put on your best clothes, take the most essential things . . ."*

She knew where they were going—and that even the most essential things were not essential there.

I left the university through the main gates and thought of David, and the Zionists' ideology of redemption. One missed the point: there was no redemption, the war was an abyss.

I wrote to David, *"Zionism is an ideology of modernity and can never be an antidote to it."*

■ ■ ■

IT WAS THE first day of August 1997, and time was suspended as the city remembered that just over half a century before, after five long years of unbearable waiting, the Polish Home Army's general had said *yes, now*, and so began the Warsaw Uprising—the Polish uprising. An ecstatic, desperate sacrifice. A sacred martyrdom. Sixty-three days later what had been Warsaw would be ruins.

The Polish Home Army, the anti-Nazi resistance subordinate to the Polish government in exile in London, had waited as long as it could—Stalin's Red Army was camped just on the other side of the Vistula River, and waiting any longer would mean losing the chance to liberate their own capital. When I came to Warsaw and saw the Vistula River for the first time, its narrowness startled me: the Red Army had been *right there*.

In London, Polish prime minister Stanisław Mikołajczyk and Polish ambassador Edward Raczyński pleaded with the British for support. I had read the correspondence in the archives. Winston Churchill was firm. *"An accommodation should be reached between the Polish Government in London and the Soviet Government,"* he told Mikołajczyk and Raczyński during a meeting on Downing Street. That was on 31 May 1944.

But the Polish prime minister and the Polish ambassador knew better: the Soviet Union had already invaded and occupied Poland once during this war at its very beginning. Moreover, during that spring and summer of 1944 Polish leaders in London had been receiving reports from Polish Home Army divisions in the east. They knew that when Polish partisan soldiers encountered the Red Army they were treated as enemies, not allies. They knew that, east of Warsaw, Soviet soldiers heading westward had disarmed Polish soldiers, arrested them, at times murdered them.

The Polish prime minister appealed to Churchill and Roosevelt to intervene with the Soviets. By the end of July, Stanisław Mikołajczyk could wait no longer.

On 28 July 1944, Polish ambassador Raczyński heard from the British permanent undersecretary for foreign affairs: *"I am afraid that, quite apart from the difficulties of co-ordinating such action with the Soviet Government, whose forces are operating against the Germans in Polish territory, operational considerations alone preclude us from meeting the three requests you made for assisting the rising in Warsaw."*

On 1 August Warsaw rose up.

"We were all talking," the Polish poet Miron Białoszewski wrote in his memoirs, *"suddenly we heard shouting. Then, it seems, heavier weapons. We could hear cannons. And all sorts of guns. Finally a shout, 'Hurrahh...'*

"'The uprising,' we told each other at once, like everyone else in Warsaw. Astounding. Because no one had ever used that word before in his life. Only in history, in books."

In the days that followed, the Red Army sat in Praga, on the other side of the Vistula River, and watched. On 4 August, the Polish Home Army command appealed to London: *"Request categorically immediately assistance."*

The English-language report from Warsaw read:

> *The Germans are setting the City on fire constantly. Numerous fires are raging, all attempts by the civilian population to extinguish them are opposed by the enemy. There are more cases of murdering civilian population. German bombers are very active and operate with no interference from the Soviet Air Force.... Incessant appeals addressed to the Allies since the first day of the Battle for dropping ammunication has given no result as yet.*

In London, Polish prime minister Mikołajczyk begged Roosevelt and Churchill for help. In response Roosevelt and Churchill insisted that Stalin would come to Poland's aid, that the Poles should cooperate with the Soviets. It was the Soviets who were so close to Warsaw—just across that narrow river—surely they would come to help. After all, they were all allies in this war against Hitler.

But the Red Army did not cross the river, and the Soviets did not come to help. Days later, Prime Minister Mikołajczyk's emissary, in awkward English, made another appeal to the Western Allies:

I am proud to state that nobody, not even in the least, has collaborated with the Germans. We were first to fight the Germans and fight them on end, though we are lonely. The present tragic battle of Warsaw is the best evidence. I say it with great sorrow because I am aware of the fact how great hopes our country put on America and England and what sufferings it must cause to our people to know that the Allies have not recognized the Polish Underground Army as a combatant and that they did not protest against the German mass murders on the civilian population.

Polish literature had a great romantic tradition, and *uprising* in Polish was the most romantic of words. Yet the poet Miron Białoszewski—like the Warsaw Ghetto Uprising commander Marek Edelman—was not a romantic, not even about uprisings.

That a short period of time appeared long is no cause for wonder. Every day people would say, "It's already the twelfth day of the uprising. . . ." "It's the thirteenth day of the uprising already. . . ."

It seemed as if we already had entire years of this behind us, and what was there ahead of us? As if there never had been, nor would there ever be anything else—only the uprising. . . . People kept track of time incessantly.

People lost each other as suddenly as they found each other. They'd be close for quite some time. Then others became close. Suddenly these were lost and new people became important. That was common.

On 14 August, Polish ambassador Edward Raczyński received another letter from the British government:

In general, while His Majesty's Government are, of course, anxious to give every assistance in their power to Polish forces fighting against the common enemy, they cannot overcome the serious geographical and other operational difficulties which unfortunately hamper the provision of such assistance. They are, therefore, reinforced in the view which they have consistently held and frequently represented to the Polish Government, as also to the Soviet Government, that it is most desirable in the general interests of the allied war effort to promote practical means of cooperation between the Polish and Soviet forces.

"*After that, I just ran on,*" Miron Białoszewski wrote, "*a long time. Through streets. But they didn't. They were afraid. Because they weren't used to it. To shells and bullets. It really was a matter of becoming used to them.*"

During the uprising, in the working class-neighborhood of Wola, Germans had murdered tens of thousands of Polish civilians and burned their bodies in pyres. Now, in 1997, in a Wola amphitheater, the elderly came to remember this. A military band marched back and forth across the grass, and a veteran took the microphone, believing himself to be a hero. But the host cut him off: the former resistance fighter had been talking for too long.

"*For Poland, the most important thing about Warsaw was that it was burning,*" wrote Miron Białoszewski.

On 10 September 1944 Polish prime minister Stanisław Mikołajczyk wrote to Roosevelt and Churchill:

Mr. President, The Reports which the Polish Government receive from Warsaw show that the situation is desperate and that the fight against the overwhelming German power may cease at any moment, unless sustained from outside.... I therefore beseech you, Mr. President, and you, Mr. Prime Minister, to take a bold and immediate decision which could save Warsaw and its inhabitants from total destruction.

Franklin Roosevelt did not take a bold and immediate decision. Nor did Winston Churchill. On 2 October, the Polish Home Army commander signed the capitulation. Like the legendary Polish uprisings of centuries past, this Polish uprising, too, ended in failure. After the Polish Home Army surrendered, the Germans went from neighborhood to neighborhood, from block to block, burning down those buildings that still stood.

In January, after the survivors had been sent away to German prisoner-of-war camps, the Red Army walked from the other bank of the Vistula River and took the empty city. When the war finally ended, there were those who proposed to leave Warsaw as it was, a monument of ruins and ashes.

"Everyone is gray," Miron Białoszewski wrote, *"From the ruins. Covered with smoke."*

Then communists came and rebuilt the little streets in the Old Town to look as if they were old. In Warsaw's downtown, Stalin came and built great tall buildings on top of the ashes. Half a century later the city remained the color of ashes, and I loved the grayness. It was bleak and beautiful.

▪ ▪ ▪

A YOUNG WOMAN my own age escaped Poland for a new life in Israel, only to find herself at a Jerusalem market that just minutes later would explode. It was her first experience of the terrorist attacks that colored everyone's life in Jerusalem. The man who sold her bananas the day before was no longer alive, her husband, who came from Minsk and was now Israeli, told me. In his eyes there was the vaguest trace of sparkle, as if such were the arbitrary malice of fate, which must, in its own way, be respected. A youth spent in the Soviet Union had left its mark.

The young woman's husband led groups of Russian Jews on tours of Jewish sites in Poland. Those on this trip were young—teenagers, men and women in their early twenties. They cared nothing for Judaism and very little for Jewishness. Poland was the West to them—they wanted to go shopping in the capital.

Their guide was disgusted.

He took the group to Treblinka. Seth and I came with him.

When we arrived we were nowhere. We walked through the forest until we came to a clearing. Treblinka was unlike Auschwitz. It was only a cemetery in the woods, a symbolic graveyard and fields of green earth surrounded by dense trees. Vastness. Once upon a time Treblinka had been a forest.

It was impossible to see the gas chambers. They were gone. The Germans had dismantled them before the Soviets had arrived. The crematoria, too, were gone.

Afterward Seth and I took the train to Lublin, southeast of Warsaw, then a city bus to Majdanek. It was quite close to Lublin's center.

I looked up into the sky, into the colossal monument that now stood in place of a gate leading into Majdanek. Poised, precarious, dizzying. It was everything Natan Rapaport's monument to the ghetto fighters was not: by 1969, when the Majdanek monument was unveiled, socialist realism was over; this was all abstraction.

There was a plaque thanking God for salvation.

Obscene, I thought.

I walked underneath the monument, down the hill, into the abyss that was Majdanek. The death camp was now a kind of public park; children were riding their bicycles through Majdanek. There were few cars and wide open spaces. At the bottom of the hill two boys were playing with a graceful wooden airplane.

There was a mausoleum—a disc and inside, a mound of ashes. For Seth this was Poland: an enormous mound of ashes, ashes and anti-Semites. Like the young people on the Marches of the Living, Seth, too, saw coming to Poland as a pilgrimage—and like them, he resented the Poles for living as if their country were not what it was: a Jewish graveyard.

It was a long walk along a dirt path encroached upon by weeds to the crematorium. The barracks were wooden, but the crematorium had cement walls and a long chimney reaching toward the sky.

Outside the crematorium a young woman in a short, tight dress, her blond hair teased and set with hairspray, was flirting with the guard.

I walked on, into the crematorium. Inside there were signs:

corpses were baked at 700 degrees Celsius. I looked inside the ovens. A capacity of a thousand corpses daily. I reached through the metal grating to touch the shoes. I smelled my hands, inhaled the dust on my fingers.

I moved backward from the crematorium to the gas chamber, Hannah Arendt's *"factories to produce corpses."* The ceiling was very low, and I could see the rat-size opening for the gas. The walls of the gas chambers were made of cement. Inside it was dark and cool and quiet. Enclosed.

I looked through the small window built into the cement: this was how the guards had watched the gassing.

Vertigo. Outside blackbirds were descending. Hundreds of blackbirds.

■ ■ ■

IN KRAKOW I saw the historian Jan Gross again. We took a walk through the city and he made a suggestion: at the Jewish Historical Institute archives there was a little-known collection, papers of the postwar Central Committee of Jews in Poland. He had looked at some of the material; it was very interesting.

Later in Warsaw, at the Jewish Historical Institute, the archivist gave me the files. I started from the beginning: the Central Committee of Jews in Poland had come together shortly after the Warsaw Uprising, in November 1944, with the goal of presiding over the remnants of Polish Jewry. It was an ecumenical committee, including Jewish communists, Zionists across the political spectrum from the center to the radical Left, and Bundists who were Yiddishists and diaspora nationalists and who sought a Jewish socialism here in Poland, alongside their Polish neighbors. The committee members represented a handful of activists, many who had fought in the resistance, including devoted communists who had survived the war in the Soviet Union: Grzegorz Smolar, Michał Mirski, Szymon Zachariasz.

Among the committee's tasks was organizing commemorations of the Warsaw Ghetto Uprising. Even as they struggled to find resources to rebuild a devastated community in a city of ruins, the committee, under the labor Zionist Adolf Berman's leadership, undertook an international fund-raising campaign for the purpose of constructing a monument to the ghetto fighters.

There were only a dozen or so active members of the committee's presidium, and from the transcripts of the meetings their personalities emerged. The communist Szymon Zachariasz was harsh and dogmatic. The Marxist Zionist Adolf Berman was energetic, in fact inexhaustible, and idealistic. He cherished visions of solidarity, and believed that the worst was over and that the new world was about to be born. Striking about those meetings was something else: the warm relations between communists and Zionists. Communists were supporting the creation of a Jewish state. Left-wing Zionists were speaking of a Soviet Palestine. Having passed through hell, they, the avant-garde of the world, were all about to live happily ever after.

This was my first glimpse into how the Jewish question was hopelessly entangled in the communist question. The closeness between communists and the many Zionists who embraced socialism of some kind was only one part, I began to see, of a desperately complicated story about the involvement of Jews in communism. In April 1948, on the fifth anniversary of the Warsaw Ghetto Uprising, the sculptor Natan Rapaport's enormous granite monument was dedicated in a grandiose unveiling ceremony. Here was the posthumous glory of the ghetto fighters, portrayed as epic heroes. There was a touch of classicism, a likeness to Zeus. The men carved in granite exuded valor and virility. Natan Rapaport's monumental creation represented Jewish socialist realism rising from the ghetto's ashes, dedicated atop a field of ruins. The ruins had been too heavy to shovel away, so before the ceremony began workers had poured cement over them.

In the few years following the end of the war, communists came more and more to dominate the story of the ghetto uprising— and the Central Committee of Jews in Poland. The usurping of the narrative—the emphasizing of the role of the communists, the downplaying of the role of Bundists and Zionists—was subtle. After all, the Zionists and the communists shared an aesthetic, and a manner of speaking.

I wanted to know: Could relations between communists and Zionists really have been this close? I asked a Polish graduate student writing about the postwar Zionist movement in Poland.

Her name was Tamara, and the first time we met we sat in a café on Nowy Świat, near the gates to the university, and Tamara cried. She cried because her grandfather had not crossed the border into Czechoslovakia after the war, because he had not crossed the border to Czechoslovakia from where he could have gone on illegally to Palestine—as had so many others, whose children and grandchildren, unlike Tamara, were now Israelis.

Tamara was consumed with self-pity because her own family had not left for Israel after the war. And so she was born in Poland, where she did not feel like a Pole. She could not escape from this moment of her grandfather's refusal to cross the border, this moment of decision, the moment when her life might have been a different one. She could not forgive her grandfather for having misunderstood History, for having made the wrong choice—and so, having thrown Tamara from the current of History.

▪ ▪ ▪

THAT FALL *GAZETA WYBORCZA*—a very successful daily newspaper, many of whose editors and journalists had once been opposition activists—published an article about university students who earned extra money through unusual part-time jobs. One of these students belonged to the collective "Ten Religious Jews." The members rented themselves to other Jews who needed extra men to make up the ten-man minyan required by Jewish law for certain occasions—for instance, when a family wanted to have a proper Jewish funeral. The charge was several hundred złoty per hired religious Jew—about $200.

I told Seth that this was prostitution, that the Jewish community had made a mockery of itself. He was furious and would not—could not—speak to me. He hated the Poles for printing this, for laughing once again at the Jews. I told him that the editor of the paper was Adam Michnik—a Jew by birth himself.

Seth was disgusted with me.

"You think it's a joke?" he asked. "This is what happens when you decimate a community."

When Tamara arrived she told us that yes, it was true—but *Gazeta Wyborcza* never should have published it. The collective "Ten Religious Jews" represented a certain demoralization that was unavoidable in today's Poland.

At night Seth cried in his sleep that I did not love him, that I would never love him because he was a Jew and a Zionist and I was a rootless cosmopolitan—and a self-hating Jew.

■ ■ ■

THE POLES WERE fascinated by cemeteries. On 1 November, the Day of the Dead, all were drawn to the graveyards where the stones glowed in the candlelight. It was something extraordinarily beautiful: the city coming into its own, baring its soul.

Now it was late in November, and the conference commemorating the hundredth anniversary of the mass Jewish workers' party called the Bund began in the morning with a tour of the grave sites of Bundists. So Polish. And so Jewish.

At the conference the Warsaw Ghetto Uprising's hero Marek Edelman had the status of God, whom Edelman distrusted.

"I feel as if I want to touch him," a woman sitting beside me whispered.

Edelman spoke about the Bund, about the uprising, about the battle for human dignity. Irena Klepfisz, who was in her fifties, had come from New York, and Marek Edelman treated her as a child, as his child.

"He buried her father," the same woman whispered to me.

And now I remembered the story of Michał Klepfisz, who during the Warsaw Ghetto Uprising had used his body as a shield so that Marek Edelman and the others in his unit could pass through the wall of gunfire and continue fighting the Germans. There were rows of bullet holes in his corpse, which Marek Edelman and his comrades, singing "The Internationale," buried beneath the rubble of the ghetto.

"We do not even pause to consider how it happens that Michał Klepfisz jumps straight onto the German machine pistol firing from behind the chimney," Marek Edelman wrote just after the war. *"We only see the cleared path. After the Germans have been thrown out, several hours later, we find Michał's body perforated like a sieve from two machine-pistol series."*

Before the conference I had spent a day in the little apartment on Piwna Street reading a long interview with Marek Edelman from the 1970s. By then he was a prominent cardiologist who intertwined reflections on the Ghetto Uprising with those on his attempts to save the lives of his patients.

"God is trying to blow out the candle," Marek Edelman tried to explain, *"and I'm quickly trying to shield the flame, taking advantage of His brief inattention. To keep the flame flickering, even if only for a little while longer than He would wish. It is important: He is not terribly just. It can also be very satisfying, because whenever something does work out, it means you have, after all, fooled Him."*

A satisfying radicalism—subtle and ironic: And where was God? He was there, but on *their* side, Edelman teasingly suggested.

Very few survived—as the ghetto fighters had expected. *"It was only a choice as to a manner of dying"*—this was Marek Edelman's refrain. Afterward, when the Germans set fire to the ghetto, Edelman led the last surviving ghetto fighters in escaping through the sewers.

"Everybody got in, I was the last one, and one of the girls asked whether she could join us in escaping to the Aryan side. And I said no. I only ask you one thing," he said, *"don't make me explain today why I said no then."*

For two days they waited for their contacts, Polish communist partisans. Underground, inside the sewer, the water reeked of feces and methane. They were suffocating. There wasn't enough air for all of them, and Marek Edelman made the decision to send eight of his comrades to a wider sewer. Finally their contacts among the Polish communist partisans arrived and lifted the manhole cover on Prosta Street. Suddenly there was light and air, and Marek Edelman sent one of the men to get the others. But there was no time. Their rescuers insisted they had to drive off immediately, another few seconds and they could all be caught and killed. And so the eight—plus the one sent to call them back—were lost.

The conference to commemorate the Bund's anniversary was held in the Hotel Europejski, on Krakowskie Przedmieście. Warsaw's oldest hotel, broader than it was tall, encompassed a whole square block close to the university. The lobby conveyed an aging grandiosity: the entrance opened to swirled marble floors, marble walls, a marble staircase with faded carpet. A blend of nineteenth-century and communist-era luxury had now become a dated opulence. The hotel was home to an elegant café and a large conference hall where time now collapsed: the Bundists and the Zionists, the Yiddishists and the Hebraists all accused one another. The battles of the 1920s and '30s again consumed them—and us.

For the elderly Bundists had not forgotten that the new Jewish state had been ashamed of the old Jewish world. Had Yiddish not been persecuted in newly independent Israel? Had there not been laws banning Yiddish publications there? A bombing of a Tel Aviv kiosk selling Yiddish newspapers? A handful of the very last Bundists, old men in their eighties, shouted at the young Israeli professors who had come to give papers on the history of the Bund.

"You persecuted our language, you killed our culture!" an elderly man yelled.

One of the young Israeli professors stood up and answered him, "The Zionists didn't kill the Bund, the Holocaust killed the Bund!"

After all, it was not as if, had the Bund—or the Zionists—made the right decision, history would have been different. The war was an abyss, inescapable.

Another elderly man stood up with difficulty and pointed his finger in the air. "This is a Bund conference, I want to speak Yiddish!"

"Yes, yes, speak Yiddish, speak Yiddish!" A much younger Yiddishist from New York felt passionately about this. After all, the Bund had been a Yiddishist movement; its leaders had believed in the need to speak to the Jewish working masses in their own language.

Pandemonium. And bitterness. The kind of anger that could never be made okay. And this was only the Jewish-Jewish question. No one had yet even begun to talk about the Poles.

"They forget nothing," Tamara said, "and they forgive nothing."

Today I spoke to her in English. I could no longer bear the tension, the dialectics of Polish and Hebrew, Hebrew and Yiddish in this room.

▪ ▪ ▪

TAMARA INTRODUCED ME to her friend Bogna, the Last of the Diaspora Nationalists, who was teaching herself Yiddish and who hated Israel for seducing Tamara away from her. Later Bogna invited me to Shabbat dinner at her apartment on the other side of the Vistula River, where once the Red Army had waited, watching the Germans burn Warsaw to the ground. It was a small apartment with old furniture. On the table were potatoes and salad and candles. Around the table were the last of the twenty-something Polish Jews—with the exception of Tamara, who had just gone off to Oxford on a fellowship. Hostility, affection, passion. Bogna's friend Halinka was silent; she spoke to no one apart from Bogna and then only in whispers, and only in Yiddish—the language of the Polish Jews who were no more, a language Halinka had learned at Oxford.

Bogna's friend Dagmara wore a fiery red sweater and a Star of David dangling around her neck. Dagmara was feisty and saucy and full of anger. She hated the Israelis, who did not even want to talk to the few remaining Polish Jews they encountered on their pilgrimages to Poland. She hated as well the Israeli government, who was so dismissive toward her and her friends, who declined to acknowledge their voices.

"And what are we?" she cried. "Only the guardians of grave-stones?" She wanted apologies, trials, vindications.

Their friend Romek rejected this. He was in favor of education.

"And what then?" Dagmara shouted at him. "Maybe my great-great-great grandchildren will see the results . . ."

Romek wore a jacket and tie and a yarmulke and looked as if he were a child dressing up as an adult. He'd come with Lea, who wore a long black shawl draped over her shoulders and a hat covering her hair, although she was not married, although she might not even have been religious. She paced in and out of the kitchen, smoking cigarettes.

Dagmara continued to shout at Romek, who rejected her insistence on both collective and inherited guilt.

"Should Bartoszewski also apologize to the Jews?" Romek shouted back at her.

Władysław Bartoszewski was now a member of the Polish parliament. During the war, as a very young man—and a Catholic—he had risked his life to save Jews. And he had saved many. Romek did not believe that the Poles were, on the whole, so hostile. He, too, would stay in Poland—unlike Lea, who had spent a year at a women's yeshiva in Jerusalem and would perhaps make *aliya*.

"There is no such thing as inherited responsibility!"

Now it was Lea who was shouting at Dagmara. No one could apologize to Lea for her grandmother's death in the Holocaust: those to whom apologies were owed were dead, and therefore no apologies were possible. In any case, the Poles were guilty not of extermination but of apathy, which was a responsibility of a different kind. Lea demanded apologies from no one—it was just such collectivized thinking that had led to the Holocaust in the first place.

Dagmara protested: Lea's was a philosophical argument, and Dagmara was speaking of politics.

"And who am I?" Lea shouted, trembling now. "My father and my uncle built communism. Am I also responsible for that?"

"You're speaking personally!" Dagmara answered. She was thinking of symbolic apologies, political statements.

Yet of course here the political was always personal.

It was late when I left with Romek and Lea. We waited at the bus stop, talking quickly, Lea and Romek still agitated. Some young men arrived to wait for the bus, and Romek and Lea suddenly, nervously grew silent. On the ride across the river we did not talk at all.

▪ ▪ ▪

CELINA WAS BEAUTIFUL, as if she had appeared from an old photograph taken in the 1940s: a young woman in a cranberry hat, thick black glasses, a flared cream coat. She felt guilty because it was Shabbat and we were violating the Sabbath by taking the bus the few miles from the synagogue to her apartment. Inside twenty-six candles stood on the table, for today was Lea's twenty-fifth birthday. We drank tea, and Lea and Celina read their poetry. Lea wrote about Adam and Eve in the Garden of Eden. No, she was not beautiful, Lea wrote of Eve. It was Lilith, Lilith bearing a soul created by Satan, it was she who was the beautiful one.

When Celina was sixteen she had fallen in love with an anti-Semite. In the end he had left her to marry a Christian woman: he did not want his children to be Jewish. Now Celina was married to a Jew, but it was not her husband but rather this anti-Semite who had awakened her femininity, she confessed shyly.

"You are that man whom I don't want / You are that man, whom I desire," she read to us.

Celina, like the others, had not been raised as a Jew. She came to Judaism later, as a young woman. For a time, she was a Buddhist, sitting, breathing, meditating, watching her thoughts flow in and out of her mind. The Buddhist master had told her that she was going through life with her hand closed and that this was wrong, for her hand should be open, open so that things could pass in and out, could come and go.

Romek read a poem he had written a few years earlier to his then unborn son. It was the first time I learned that Romek had a child—or that he had once had a wife. He looked like a child himself.

Lea begged Romek to read more of his poems, and I saw now that she was in love with him. Lea who had spent a year in a women's yeshiva in Jerusalem, where the nineteen-year-old Orthodox girl who was her tutor did not want to teach her about women's impurity and the *mikvah* because she was embarrassed. But Lea had insisted. She was not an anti-Zionist like Bogna. After all, it was because of the Holocaust that there was a Jewish state—in Lea's mind, the Jews *did* win the war.

Bogna was enraged. How could Lea speak that way about the war? Yes, since the Holocaust there had been no ghetto benches at universities—because there were no Jews! Would she have been baptized had it not been for the Holocaust?

Bogna spoke of her Catholic baptism as of a rape, an unforgivable violation done to her. Lea had been baptized as well. They had all been. It was 1982, martial law, and their parents had given themselves to Solidarity, the great opposition movement, in atonement for the sins of their own godless parents. And Solidarity had given itself to the Catholic Church. It was a sign of moral freedom.

"I was a Catholic, I was religious, I believed!" Bogna cried, consumed with guilt and hatred. She would never forgive her mother.

Celina tried to comfort her.

"Was it Bogna's fault that her mother did not bring her to the synagogue when she was a child?" Celina asked all of us. There was no synagogue. None of them had been taught how to be a Jew.

Romek and Bogna shouted viciously at each other, and the women began to cry.

"Bogna has no right . . . ," Romek said.

"And who are you to judge Bogna's rights?" Lea shouted at him. Their anger was more than anger. In it was a kind of malice and pain and betrayal.

Bogna despised Israel for having stolen her few friends. When she had once visited there, she had met her cousin for the first time. Why was he there and she in Poland? If it had been Bogna's grandmother who had been the one to make a different choice . . .

She and her cousin said nothing to each other. They just stood and looked at each other, and then walked away, having said neither hello nor goodbye.

Soon Bogna's lover Halinka would leave for an Orthodox women's yeshiva in Jerusalem, Halinka who sat with us all silently, who rarely spoke, except to Bogna and then only in Yiddish. When Halinka was out of the room Bogna whispered to me that according to traditional Jewish law Halinka was not really Jewish, perhaps only on her father's side . . . She was going to Jerusalem to study for an Orthodox conversion. Bogna would stay in Warsaw; she did not think that Halinka wanted her to come with her to Jerusalem.

"We live in Warsaw," Bogna said. "The city of two uprisings during the war, and of many uprisings before that. You can never forget that here. Our grandparents were never happy—there was the war, the Holocaust. Our parents were never happy. There was communism, martial law, the memory of the Holocaust. We grew up, and we could never be happy. It was impossible, obscene, to be happy. Anything that gave pleasure was bad. Celina once wrote a poem . . ."

Romek interrupted her. He did not want to talk about the poetry they had written as teenagers.

Bogna cried out, "I let you talk! Why must you interrupt me if I feel I need to say two more sentences, to explain myself?"

"Read the poem," Lea encouraged her.

But Bogna could not now, she was too angry at Romek. We all waited until she grew calmer, until she began to read Celina's poem. It was a poem about swimming, about coming back to the water after having been away for a long time, about feeling her body in the water, *"the pleasure between my legs."*

"This poem helped me," Bogna said. "For years I remembered it and it helped me. When we were growing up, it was as if everyone were in mourning."

They spoke endlessly at an unsustainable pitch. All the angst of the past converged with that of the present until there was no distinction.

▪ ▪ ▪

I WAS SITTING in Hebrew school, in the basement of a synagogue in Pennsylvania. It was 1982, the era of Ronald Reagan, of the cold war and the Evil Empire, of demonstrations by American Jews in support of the *refuseniks*, Soviet Jews who were not permitted to leave the Soviet Union. The teacher was showing us a film about an Israeli kibbutz. The sunniness of communal life. Everyone equal, everything shared. A wonderful world.

And suddenly the question came into my ten-year-old mind; I raised my hand.

"Isn't that just like in Russia?' I asked.

I knew so little about Russia then—and so little about communism. I knew, though, that under communism there was no personal property, that everything was shared. And I remembered the teacher's anger, and my humiliation.

"They have nothing at all to do with each other!"

The teacher's voice was very sharp.

Now it was 1997. Tamara had given me a list of the postwar Zionist newspapers, and during the day I sat in the library of the Jewish Historical Institute, reading them. And now I saw that, on the contrary, they had everything in the world to do with each other.

More and more it began to seem obvious: socialism and Zionism had grown up side by side in the Russian Empire. The Zionist propaganda posters from the 1930s were nearly indistinguishable from the Stalinist collectivization posters. Theirs was the same aesthetic: socialist realism.

Tamara, I realized, must know this. She had read the same material I had. When I found her in the reading room at the Jewish Historical Institute, I asked her, "What were relations really like between communists and Zionists after the war?"

"Warm," she said, looking down at the table. She did not want to talk about it.

Something else became clear: the unveiling of Natan Rapaport's monument to the ghetto fighters was the beginning of the end. In

Poland, just as in Czechoslovakia, Romania, Hungary, and elsewhere, 1948 marked the consolidation of communist power—and a Stalinist campaign against both "right-wing deviationists" and "rootless cosmopolitans," by which Stalin meant Jews. "Right-wing deviation" meant "bourgeois nationalism"; its pairing with "rootless cosmopolitanism" was a nonsensical one. But if the communists Szymon Zachariasz, Grzegorz Smolar, and Michał Mirski noticed this, it changed not at all the fact that they were displeased with the course the dedication of the Rapaport monument had taken; they accused Adolf Berman of co-opting the unveiling ceremony into a Zionist demonstration.

Michał Mirski expressed the opinion that in Adolf Berman's left-wing Zionist party something was *"not in order."* Mirski added: *"This is—as Comrade J. Berman has called it—a conspiracy of silence."*

Comrade J. Berman. J. was for Jakub—Adolf's older brother who was not a Zionist at all. At the moment Mirski was speaking, Jakub Berman was one of a triumvirate of Stalinist leaders in postwar Poland, in charge of the notorious security apparatus during the bloodiest years. Today his name was anathema in Poland.

A few months later the communist members of the Central Committee of Jews in Poland gathered for a separate meeting.

"I have been criticized as if I had declared that Zionism were progressive," Szymon Zachariasz said there. *"I once claimed that Zionism was a reactionary theory. . . . The anti-imperialist Zionist wing is currently progressive, but tomorrow it could become unprogressive. Only we are consistently progressive. We were, we are, and we always will be progressive."*

Zionism was now a bourgeois nationalist-cosmopolitan ideology, and Adolf Berman was no longer a good Marxist.

In the Party archives I found Szymon Zachariasz's notes. Sometimes he wrote in Polish, sometimes in an illegible Yiddish. There were doodles as well: phallic mushroom rockets, a man with a long nose in a tall pointed cap, a faceless head in a similar cap. Rockets and lanterns in a drawing that could be turned a full 360 degrees,

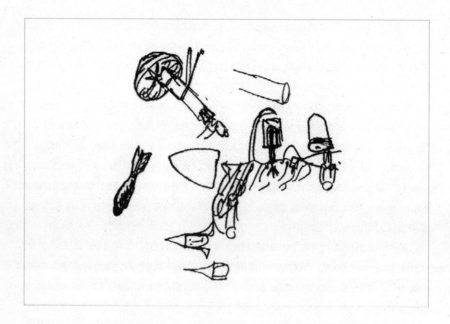

any angle was equally probable, it was unclear where was the bottom and where was the top.

At the Jewish Historical Institute I continued to read the files of the Central Committee of Jews in Poland. It was now 1949, and Michał Mirski was especially vicious toward Adolf Berman and his Zionist comrades—for their "lack of vigilance," for their failure to combat "right-wing deviation," for their nationalist inclinations.

That April Szymon Zachariasz told Adolf Berman that he had very much wanted to help him be a Marxist but that Adolf Berman was digressing from Marxism. The communist members of the Committee, Zachariasz explained, were now forced to depose him from the chairmanship of the Central Committee of Jews in Poland.

Adolf Berman stepped down without a word. The communist Grzegorz Smolar took his place.

An era drew to a close: the communists and the Zionists, a brief love affair brought to an end with Stalin's "anticosmopolitan" campaign. Now Adolf Berman decided to leave Poland. In January 1950, on the eve of his departure to the new state of Israel, he wrote a farewell letter to his communist comrades: *"A common battle for peace, progress and Socialism, for the freedom and independence of nations, against imperialism, reaction, and reformism, united us and will continue to unite us unto eternity."*

Once Adolf Berman was deposed, the legacy of the Warsaw Ghetto Uprising belonged exclusively to the communists. Now they told the story of the uprising in their own way: it was communist partisans who had brought the idea of battle to the Jews. The Jewish resistance movement became a movement for Poland's liberation. When the Central Committee of Jews in Poland's new chairman, Grzegorz Smolar, spoke on the anniversary of the uprising, he alluded to the possibility that purges of Jewish nationalists would follow: *"And when we find among ourselves people who, like annoying flies, make noise about some higher and more essential allegedly Jewish national goals, we will eliminate those people from our society, just as the fighters in the ghetto cast away from themselves those who were fainthearted and cowardly."*

The allusion was an ominous one: the first people the resistance fighters in the ghetto had killed were not Germans but Jews—Jewish collaborators.

A Jewish communist historian who had spent the war in the Soviet Union, who had not been in the Warsaw Ghetto at all, returned from Moscow after the war to become the director of the Jewish Historical Institute. When he wrote the official history of the Warsaw Ghetto Uprising, it no longer had anything to do with Zionists or Bundists, it no longer had anything to do with Jews at all. Instead it had everything to do with Polish communism.

This was the time when Adolf Berman's older brother Jakub was the member of the Politburo responsible for cultural policy.

■ ■ ■

SZYMON ZACHARIASZ DIED in 1970. In 1997 his daughter was still living in Warsaw. Pani Ryszarda had been born shortly after the war; recently she'd been among the founders of the confidential hotline for Poles struggling with their Jewish identity. She greeted me with tea and raspberry cheesecake; we sat at her table and she talked to me about her father. While he had never spoken to her about his life before the war, there were some things she knew from her mother: that her father had come from a poor Orthodox family with some dozen children; that at least one brother had remained a religious Jew, while another had become an anarchist. In 1917, when her father was still a teenager, he joined the same Marxist Zionist party as Adolf Berman did. The following year, though, Szymon Zachariasz changed his mind: in 1918 he became a communist. He remained deeply attached to Jewishness, but he came to believe that the Jews' fate would be improved only when all men could live as brothers.

Pani Ryszarda's mother was educated. Her father was not—or rather, he never finished school. When he was a child his parents sent him to a traditional religious school—until one day the teacher caught him reading a Yiddish translation of *Robinson Crusoe* under his desk and expelled him from the *kheyder*, leaving the thirteen-year-old to be sent to work in a factory. Szymon Zachariasz's real education came only later—during his time in prison. The period between the two world wars lasted two decades; half of that time Szymon Zachariasz spent in a Polish prison, together with other communists, studying Marx and Engels and Lenin.

When he was thinking about something he would pace diagonally between the window and the door. He said he had learned that in prison. This was typical, Pani Ryszarda told me; many of his friends had the same habit.

"Rigid," Pani Ryszarda described him. Firm in his beliefs, and in his behavior.

The only guests in their home were Jewish communists. Her parents taught her to address everyone as "comrade." The first grown-up word she learned was *revolution*.

"How was he as a father?" I asked her.

"As a father he was . . . he wasn't. He didn't engage with me. He was there, I knew that he was there, that he loved me, that he gave me a certain stability. Of course I knew that he loved me, but it was as if nothing followed from that, because all the time he sat and read. He went into the bathroom with a book, he went on a walk with a book. When I would go on a walk with him, he would read the paper. I would hold his hand, looking around."

Szymon Zachariasz was a man who cared only about politics.

"He didn't have anything to talk to me about," she added.

Pani Ryszarda was still living out the clash between the world presented to her in childhood and the world as she later came to understand it.

"In the Stalinist period—that is, until 1956, until the time when I was ten years old, the world was very homogeneous in my eyes. The whole world that I knew, it was these comrades, and they were almost all Jews. I knew that somewhere out there, there was a different world, but that different world was not good, or at least it was foolish for not subscribing to communism. And so it was natural, everything was homogeneous—communism, Jewishness, Polishness."

Pani Ryszarda encouraged me to eat more cheesecake.

She was thinking of the Stalinist years, the years of her childhood. These were the years of the brightest colors—and the brightest conviction: that they were right. They were ushering in a new and happier and more just world for all. About the trials of the Polish Home Army soldiers who'd heroically fought the Nazis, the torture in prisons, the executions, she'd known nothing—during her childhood there was no terror, it didn't exist, it didn't penetrate.

"At that time," she said, "we were the avant-garde of the world. Such a Jewish feeling . . ."

Perhaps, she added, it was simply that everyone remembered her childhood as colorful and harmonious. But I knew this was not the case: I didn't remember my childhood that way.

It was only later in her life, when she was no longer a child and had made Polish friends, that she heard about the 1940 Soviet massacre of more than twenty thousand Polish citizens near the forest of Katyń. And even then she did not believe it, she thought it must be anticommunist propaganda.

Her parents had felt themselves to be Jews. But they had also felt themselves to be Poles. Even her father—a native Yiddish speaker who never learned Polish well, who until the end of his life spoke with a heavy accent and made grammatical mistakes—was very attached to Poland.

"The only thing was," Pani Ryszarda added, "he didn't know Poland at all."

The year 1968 was the caesura. But even then, during the "anti-Zionist" campaign, her parents did not leave the Party. Her father was enormously pained—but unable to accept that he had given his entire life for nothing. That he had wasted it. Or worse.

This was what Pani Ryszarda believed her father had felt and thought—by nature, though, he was a closed person. He didn't speak to her about what had happened in 1968, when the Party embraced anti-Semitism and purged itself of Jewish communists, purged the army of Jewish officers and the universities of Jewish professors, when some thirteen thousand "Poles of Jewish origin"—including my Polish teacher Pani Hanka and the historian Jan Gross—left Poland.

After the "anti-Zionist" campaign of March 1968, Ryszarda's father did, though, go to Israel for the first time. Szymon Zachariasz, who had attacked Zionism so harshly in the Stalinist years, found himself warmly received in the Jewish state: so many of his old comrades were there. He marched with them in the May Day parade. Yet in the end he returned to Poland, where he lived for only another two years.

I had the impression, I told her, that many of the Jews who remained in Poland today were—or had been—communists.

"Of course, the majority," Ryszarda said. "Of course, because anyone who wasn't a communist would have left."

"The reality was such," she added, "that there were very many Jews in the Communist Party both before and after the war."

In the Stalinist years, it was a pleasant thing to be the daughter of someone so respected. Since then it had not been so easy. Time and time again she was asked the same question: "Are you the daughter of *that* Zachariasz?"

"And I have to answer: Yes, I am."

Ryszarda lived alone, in what had once been her parents' apartment in Warsaw. She was here, in this room where we now sat, when Stalin died. She was in kindergarten and she heard it over the radio, she saw her father grab his head with his hands.

"Thousands of years of Jewish history," she told me, looking at the place where the radio had once rested, "led to this . . ."

▪ ▪ ▪

LEA TOLD ME that she woke up every morning in Warsaw and asked herself: "Should I be in Poland—in the diaspora—or should I be in Israel?"

"And when you were in Jerusalem?" I asked her.

"And when I was in Jerusalem I woke up every morning and asked myself the same question."

Her real home, she felt, was on the flight between Warsaw and Tel Aviv, when she was suspended in the air between Poland and Israel.

Lea's father was a communist who had survived the war in Soviet Russia. Later—like Milan Kundera and Arnošt Lustig and Karel Kosík—he became a revisionist Marxist. Like her father, Lea too believed in socialism—if it were to be an authentic socialism.

Lea's father, who was buried in the Jewish cemetery of Warsaw, had not wanted his daughter to be Jewish. When he'd died in 1979, Lea had been seven years old. We were sitting in the loft in the café by the synagogue. Today we spoke in English and pretended not to understand the drunken conversations among the Mafia men and prostitutes taking place in Polish alongside us.

When she was a child Lea would hear her father singing quietly to himself in Hebrew, but when she asked him to sing these songs aloud, when she told him she wanted to learn them too, he would sing only "The Internationale," and only in Russian. Everything had been a mystery to her then, including the small Torah, which her father had told her was "stories for adults." She converted to Judaism only after his death, when she was a teenager. She felt that she must be Jewish, that she was already Jewish, that her father's burial in the Jewish cemetery had marked her for life.

■ ■ ■

I WENT TO see a young professor of literature. I asked him about the Jewish Historical Institute.

"Between us," he began. All important conversations were "between us" in Warsaw. The institute's history was bleak; its leading figures had compromised themselves under Stalinism. Now, of course, there were new people—still, they were bound to the past, laboring under its burden. I would find no openness there, he warned me.

In Toronto Stefan M. had given me a letter of introduction to his colleague at the Jewish Historical Institute, a historian named Paweł. When I went to see him it was not yet evening, but inside his apartment it was dark; we sat at a wooden table in a kitchen with no lights. On one of the shelves in the kitchen sat a small menorah—although he celebrated nothing, he told me.

Paweł stood up and began to pace around the kitchen. About everything he was passionately negative. A world with no meaning.

I asked him about the communists and the Zionists, and about the uprising in the Warsaw Ghetto.

He told me that it was only the communists who bestowed the word *uprising* upon the Jews who fought in the ghetto. In Polish *uprising* was a sacred word, a word the Poles would never have shared with Jews. Even under communism, the head of state never attended the commemoration.

At the Jewish Historical Institute I bought a copy of Paweł's most recent book: an annotated collection of articles from Poland's wartime underground press. The material was striking: in the spring of 1943 it was clear that it was the Left—the communists, but also the socialists—which was unequivocal in its support for the Jewish resistance fighters. At its center, the Polish underground was restrained. The Polish government in exile in London was supportive, yet cautioning: the revolt against the Germans could not be allowed to spread beyond the ghetto walls, the time was not yet right for the Poles—the Home Army was still lacking in weapons, the Germans were still too strong. The nationalist Far Right was still more ambivalent, its compliments prefaced with anti-Semitic qualifications:

> We are not, and never have been, philo-Semites. The Jewish question in Poland was a sore point in our domestic politics. There existed a good number of reasons for the distaste of the broad Polish masses toward the psychically and culturally alien Jewish element. This question had to be resolved and undoubtedly would have been settled in the new independent Poland in consideration of the interests of the Polish nation. Yet today, at the moment when the remaining Jews are fighting for their lives, we declare that the whole of Polish opinion, regardless of personal sympathy or antipathy, feels deeply the tragedy of this battle.

Very few of those who fought in the ghetto survived. One of the survivors was the Bundist Marek Edelman. Two others were his friends, a young couple, left-wing Zionists named Yitzhak Zuckerman and Tzivia Lubetkin. After the war they went to Palestine and founded a kibbutz dedicated to the ghetto uprising. Yitzhak Zuckerman, an extraordinary hero in Warsaw, did very little else for the rest of his life. Eventually he agreed to speak his memoirs into a tape recorder—under the condition that they be transcribed only after his death.

Now Yitzhak Zuckerman was no longer alive and his memoirs had been published. I found them at the National Library and read of the Polish Home Army's cold response in April 1943, its failure to provide more weapons, to offer more support:

> Even if I don't attribute that to clear antisemitic intentions, even if I don't accuse them of this Nazi sin, of wanting to annihilate us—it's clear that as a battling bloc, we were like thorns

in their flesh, they didn't need us. They wanted peace in Poland, in Warsaw, to amass forces, until they found the right moment. History paid them back.

But Yitzhak Zuckerman felt no schadenfreude. On the contrary: he went on to fight in the Warsaw Uprising of 1944 himself. As did his wife. As did Marek Edelman.

The Warsaw Ghetto Uprising broke out on 19 April 1943—as the Germans began the final liquidation of the ghetto. By then Yitzhak Zuckerman was no longer in the ghetto: his comrades had sent him to the "Aryan Side," where he was in contact with Polish communist partisans, coordinating possible military support.

The young poet Miron Białoszewski was also in Warsaw then. Later he recalled that *"famous, beautiful, late Easter eve of 1943. The Aryans—we were still called that—were in the churches, dressed up for the holiday, but over there, in that hell, we knew, there was no hope. There were those who helped. There were well-wishers. There were even some who were indifferent. The height of the conflagration was on Easter eve itself. There was fire in the sky."*

Inside the ghetto the young Zionist Mordechai Anielewicz led his small, poorly armed unit in battle against the Germans. On 23 April he wrote a final letter to Yitzhak Zuckerman:

> *I can't describe to you the conditions in which the Jews are living. Only a few individuals will hold out. All the rest will be killed sooner or later. The die is cast. In all the bunkers where our comrades are hiding, you can't light a candle at night for lack of oxygen. . . . Be well, my friend. Perhaps we shall meet again. The main thing is the dream of my life has come true. I've lived to see a Jewish defense in the ghetto in all its greatness and glory.*

Adolf Berman translated the letter into Polish.

In September 1942 Adolf Berman and his wife, Basia, had escaped from the ghetto to the city's "Aryan Side." Inside the ghetto, Adolf already had contacts with Polish communist partisans. Now outside, he assumed the name Adam Borowski and became a founding member of a group named Żegota, the Council for Aid to the Jews. It was a small, conspiratorial group, supported by the Polish government in exile. Among the founders was a twenty-year-old Catholic named Władysław Bartoszewski who had recently returned to Warsaw after having been imprisoned in Auschwitz. Adolf Berman knew him by the pseudonym Ludwik. The two men became friends; it was with Żegota's aid that Adolf and Basia Berman survived in hiding.

On 16 May 1943 Jürgen Stroop reported that *"the former Jewish quarter in Warsaw no longer exists."*

After the war, the Zionist Adolf Berman's brother Jakub was the member of the Polish communist Politburo in charge of overseeing the security apparatus. These were the years of a lingering civil war between communists and former Home Army partisans loyal to the London government. The communist-sympathizing writer Jerzy Andrzejewski wrote his greatest novel about this moment: the novel's protagonist, a young, handsome Home Army soldier, has been ordered to execute a communist. In 1958 the director Andrzej Wajda made *Ashes and Diamonds* into one of his greatest films. It was set during an era when thousands of Home Army officers were imprisoned. Among those who sat in prison during Jakub Berman's reign was Władysław Bartoszewski.

Just before Jakub Berman's death, a Solidarity journalist asked Jakub Berman why his brother, who had survived the war with Władysław Bartoszewski's help, did not speak up when his friend was imprisoned. There was time: Bartoszewski spent nearly seven years in prison.

Adolf had spoken to him about it only many years later, Jakub Berman answered.

This year, in 1997, Władysław Bartoszewski was elected to the Polish parliament.

■ ■ ■

TAMARA HAD GONE to Jerusalem because she no longer wanted to be different, and because one could no longer be a Jew in Poland.

In Jerusalem, Tamara thought, she had found herself. Really she had lost herself, though, lost herself in her dissertation, lost herself in her own narrative of determinism. She hated her grandfather for not crossing the border into Czechoslovakia, for not emigrating to Palestine. She was obsessed: here was the fatal error, the moment before her own birth when she was thrown off the train of History and became lost, exiled, an aberration.

Now she was determined to leave Poland. Her life was a *szpagat*, she lived in a split. In Israel her friends could not understand why, each time she was in Jerusalem, she used her return ticket to Warsaw.

At a café with Tamara and Seth, I asked Tamara again about relations between the communists and the Zionists after the war. I knew that in my question there was something almost cruel: she did not want to talk about it. And I did not want to let it go. She looked down into her cup of coffee. Now she turned to Seth and they spoke in Hebrew, as if I were not there, and I supposed that for them I was not.

I went to see Kostek Gebert, the editor of *Midrasz*, the new Polish-Jewish magazine that publicized the confidential hotline for those struggling with their Jewish identity. It was not a joke: the magazine, Kostek explained, was aimed at Jews who were still in the closet.

I'd subscribed to *Midrasz*. Each issue arrived in my mailbox in an undistinctive brown envelope with no return address.

"Tamara feels as if she's been thrown off the train of History and must, at all costs, get back on," I said to Kostek.

"I'm not on a first-name basis with History myself." He said this with a smile.

We spoke about fascism, communism, Zionism.

"And Israel exists," I said to him.

"Yes, it exists."

"Every time I go there I'm surprised that the country exists at all."

"Me, too. Only I am also surprised that Poland exists at all."

We spoke about the war. Kostek told me that for the Polish Right the war was a war between nations. For the Left it was a war between ideologies. If I were a Jew in Poland in September 1939, wouldn't I, too, greet the arrival of the Red Army with cheers? The Poles could never forgive them.

Or did he say, "The Poles could never forgive us"?

Kostek told me about his friend Staszek Krajewski, also a Jew and a former Solidarity activist, and the son of Stalinists. Staszek believed that the Jews should make a collective apology for communism.

I was fascinated. But Kostek, who was also the son of Stalinists, did not agree.

"Fascinating? No, it's stupid. I feel responsible for communism as a person on the Left, but not as a Jew."

I asked him about Adolf Berman, who had watched Władysław Bartoszewski imprisoned under his brother's rule and apparently said nothing to his brother.

"Perhaps he was silent as a gesture of goodwill," Kostek said with irony. "After all, he might have spoken out against Bartoszewski. . . . There were Jewish communists who did speak out against Poles who had saved their lives but who had now become the political enemy. They must have thought of it as a gesture of selflessness, self-sacrifice, political faith—to turn against those to whom you were closest and most indebted in the interest of the greater political good."

I would never understand, Kostek insisted, how betrayal was not really considered betrayal at a moment when lives were expendable. To not betray, to be silent—as Adolf Berman presumably had been—indicated some special decency, but to betray was simply a mandate of History.

Kostek remembered Jakub Berman: he had put Kostek's communist father in prison when Kostek was a child. Afterward Jakub Berman would visit their apartment, bringing Christmas cards and candy for the children.

"My father did sit in prison for a while, but then he was released . . ."

Overall, Kostek's childhood—like Pani Ryszarda's and like those of other children of prominent communists—had been a privileged one.

Kostek suggested I call Marek Edelman, who through all these years had remained in Poland. After the war he'd become a cardiologist in Łódź. The choice bore a certain logic: After all he had been through, how could any stakes lower than life and death have any meaning? For years Marek Edelman was quiet and inconspicuous. Then in the 1980s he reemerged, engaged again in the political world, this time on the side of Solidarity.

"He loved the comradely brotherhood. At that time, Solidarity wasn't a trade union, it was a new utopia," Kostek said. "Edelman drinks a lot. He still loves chasing skirts. He might be willing to talk with a young woman, if you catch him in the right mood."

■ ■ ■

I TOOK THE train to Łódź to visit Marek Edelman. He spoke like my Yiddish-speaking grandfathers had: sarcastic, crude, devoid of sentimentality. Yet underneath there was a kindness and a warmth.

"And you suggested that God was there, but on their side?"

"It was a joke. Anyway, God is an invented thing."

For Marek Edelman, the legacy of the Holocaust was nihilism. Before the war, "to destroy human life—that was something." By the time the war was over, to destroy human life—this was very little. But Edelman himself, a cynic, was not a nihilist: on the contrary, for Marek Edelman the moral imperative in the wake of the Holocaust was to resist nihilism by valuing human life—and human love.

The loss of the Jews was sad for Poland, he told me, because a single-nation state was never a good thing. This applied to both Poland and Israel alike: Zionism remained for him now, as ever, rather stupid. The history of Jews in Poland was over. There were no more Jews. It was sad for Poland. There was nothing to discuss.

I thought about Kostek, the son of communists who now wore a yarmulke and observed the Sabbath, the Solidarity journalist who now edited *Midrasz*. What about the Jewish revival, the new Jewish community in Warsaw?

"But how many? Twenty people. That's a performance, a kind of folklore, entertainment."

I asked him about the Central Committee for Jews in Poland, about the relations among Zionists, Bundists, and Jewish communists, about their convictions that they were the avant-garde of the world.

"I can say that, too. I'm the avant-garde, too, everyone can say that. Hitler said it, too. . . . It's nothing so great. It's insolence. Or arrogance. It's not a nice thing if someone considers himself the avant-garde of the world."

I wanted to talk about Adolf Berman. Marek Edelman must have known him.

"Adolf Berman, he was an idiot."

"Did you know him?"

"I knew an idiot."

"And what did Adolf Berman do that was stupid?"

"Everything he did was stupid. First of all he was dishonest."

Żegota, the Council for Aid to the Jews, was the initiative of the Polish government in exile in London. Adolf Berman was simultaneously an active participant in the Soviet-dominated, Polish communist protogovernment formed while Poland was still under German occupation. By this time the Nazis were nearly defeated, and the Polish Home Army loyal to the London government and the Polish communist partisans were on the verge of a civil war.

I didn't believe Adolf Berman was dishonest, only perhaps quixotic.

Marek Edelman put it another way: "You can't dance at two weddings with one *tukhes*."

The hero of the most hopeless of all the hopeless Polish uprisings, Marek Edelman had nothing of a romantic in him.

"A person is a very poor creation," he told me, "he only has three hundred billion of those brain cells."

■ ■ ■

THE YEAR 1897, which saw the founding of the Bund in Vilnius—
then Vilna—in the Russian Empire, also saw the first World Zionist
Congress in Basel, Switzerland. At a 1997 conference in Warsaw
marking the hundredth anniversary of Zionism, a Polish historian
named Dariusz told the story of Ignacy Schwarzbart, the last Zionist of the interwar Polish Republic, loyal to the Polish government in exile until the end. A hero who lost all battles. Only two
Jews had sat in the Polish government in exile in London: the Zionist Ignacy Schwarzbart and the Bundist Szmuel Zygielbojm.
They hated each other and did not speak. Theirs was the animosity
still—absurdly—felt at the conference marking the hundredth anniversary of the Bund.

At the conference Władysław Bartoszewski spoke with great
animation, while Tamara, who so wished her own grandfather had
been a Zionist, paced nervously outside the conference room, cir-
cling the table of coffee and greasy Polish doughnuts.

"After the war," she said, when it was her turn to present her paper,
"the Jews left because they had no one, because they felt alone."

Afterward I asked Władysław Bartoszewski if he would be willing to talk about Adolf Berman. He said yes with no hesitation.

When I arrived at his office a few weeks later, Władysław Bartoszewski, now a member of the Polish parliament, greeted me with
a yellowed folder of Adolf Berman's letters. Bartoszewski, despite
his age, was intensely energetic. He spoke quickly and emphatically; about both the war and the Stalinist years, he spoke with
no defensiveness. He was, I realized, one of the very few people
who feared nothing, who had nothing to hide. The moral clarity he must have had as a young man—as a teenage boy who had
joined the Polish Home Army, who had survived Auschwitz only
to jump again into the resistance—was still there, like a calming
presence in the room.

He showed me postcards from Israel and Switzerland, from

Australia and Argentina. Adolf Berman had signed them "Adam Borowski," or sometimes only "A."

"If someone travels around the world and for years continues to think about that other person and send him postcards," Bartoszewski said to me, "that means that there's no opportunism or obligation; it means that he feels in some way connected to this person."

During the war "Ludwik" suspected that "Adam Borowski" was working with the communists as well as with Żegota, the Council for Aid to the Jews. It bothered him, but he said nothing. He had tried to justify it to himself: the Jews were in such a desperate situation, they were looking for contacts absolutely everywhere possible.

Only after the war did "Ludwik" and "Adam Borowski" learn each other's real names. "Adam Borowski's"—that is, Adolf Berman's—wife, Basia, was pregnant then, and Władysław Bartoszewski was very happy—it was a sign that life went on. Adolf offered him a job in the Central Committee of Jews in Poland, any position he liked, but Bartoszewski politely declined. He did not want to tell Adolf Berman that he was still connected to the former Home Army, taking orders from London.

In 1945 Bartoszewski was arrested. He was not detained for very long, yet the following year he was arrested again—and this time released only some eighteen months later. On both occasions a friend alluded to Adolf Berman's intervention on his behalf. Bartoszewski never spoke to Adolf Berman about it. Then in 1949 he was arrested for the third time. This time he sat in prison for five years. A Polish Catholic, he was accused of, among other things, collaboration with the Zionists. These were the years when Jakub Berman was overseeing the security apparatus.

By the time Władysław Bartoszewski was freed, in 1954, Stalin was dead, and Stalinism was coming to an end. The young resistance fighter became a historian and set to work collecting accounts of Poles who had saved Jews during the war. He resumed his

friendship with Adolf Berman. Bartoszewski traveled to Israel to
do research; Adolf Berman helped him there.

Władysław Bartoszewski was at once manic and calm. His
voice was full of warmth, even nostalgia. Even after the war, all
the way until Adolf Berman's death, Bartoszewski told me, he and
Adolf Berman always called each other by their wartime pseu-
donyms. I wanted to know the answer to the same question I had
asked Heda Margolius, whose friends in Prague had declined to
shelter her after she'd escaped from the death march: Was he not
resentful?

Bartoszewski seemed not to understand: Why would Adolf have
had an obligation to free him from prison? He never would have expected any such thing. Neither would he ever have turned to Jakub
Berman for anything—he regarded Jakub as a man responsible for
the deaths of thousands of people: his friends and acquaintances,
as well as strangers, decent people.

"I didn't know Jakub Berman and I never met him," he told me.
"But he knew about me, their whole family knew about me. Well,
and I continued to sit in prison, although I must say—and I don't
know whether there's a causal connection—I wasn't among those
treated the worst. I was subjected to all kinds of severities, I experienced all kinds of unpleasantness, I was beaten—but I wasn't
tortured. And it's one thing to punch someone in the face or to
kick him, and another thing to break his arms or rip off his nails.
There's a difference. So I wasn't tortured. And further: all the investigating officers who interrogated me were Poles, not Jews. They
never let a Jewish officer around me."

Yet in fact Władysław Bartoszewski did meet Jakub Berman.
Once. Much later. In the 1960s and 1970s Adolf Berman would
make trips back to Poland. He always got in touch with Bartoszew-
ski, and they always saw each other. During one of these visits,
Bartoszewski saw Adolf with his brother Jakub at the theater, and
Bartoszewski meant to walk by silently; after all, they were family
and he had no place there. But no, Adolf called him over: "*Panie
Ludwiku!* Allow me to introduce you to my brother."

And Władysław Bartoszewski was in some way moved. He told me the story so that I would understand how close they were, how genuine the friendship was, that he would be included on a rare family evening.

▪ ▪ ▪

IN DECEMBER I went to the edge of the city to see Stefan M.'s colleague, a historian of the Polish underground who spoke dismissively about the uprising in the ghetto. *Uprising* remained for him a sacred word. What had happened in the ghetto, he told me, was no uprising, it was self-defense. He was resentful: during all those decades after the war, all those decades of communism, the true Warsaw Uprising, the Polish uprising, was falsified and neglected. It was only in 1964, twenty years after Warsaw had been burned to the ground, that the communist government issued the first commemorative postage stamp of the real Warsaw Uprising—and this was after three had already appeared to commemorate the much lesser event in the Warsaw Ghetto. No one spoke of the Polish underground; his schoolteacher reacted with indignation to the suggestion that there might have been anyone in Poland resisting the Germans apart from the communists. The harshest trials in the Stalinist years were those against the leaders of the Warsaw Uprising—the uprising whose existence was de facto denied, when it was not explicitly condemned.

"A famous communist principle," he said, "as long as something is not spoken of, it does not exist."

Before I left, his wife came into the library, and the historian's tone softened. I asked him a question then: The current director of the Jewish Historical Institute, who under communism had been the director of the Party archives, did he know anything about Jewish history? Or was he simply a bureaucrat? An apparatchik?

"Married to Jakub Berman's daughter," he told me, "between us."

"Did she change her name?" I asked.

"Of course."

"And what is she like?"

"A very nice person."

"She didn't choose her father," his wife said sympathetically.

■ ■ ■

AT THE JEWISH Historical Institute, I finished reading the files of the Central Committee of Jews in Poland. I was about to leave the archive, when I had another thought: the inventory listed a collection of one of the Committee's leading communist members, Michał Mirski. I asked to see Michał Mirski's correspondence.

The archivist returned with the file. I sat down by the window and began to read. The first letter was dated 10 July 1956, from Tel Aviv.

> *Dear Comrade Mirski!*
>
> *Twenty years ago, in 1936, we met for the first time. As you remember, this was during the time when together we created the Progressive Cultural Front. In my consciousness it's as if it happened in a former life, before the bloody deluge. Yet it happened and it had its own meaning. Do you remember our visits together to Wanda Wasilewska, to Wiktor Alter. . . . I send you warm greetings on the occasion of the twentieth anniversary of the Cultural Front.*

It was signed by Adolf Berman.

Now for the first time I cried for the Zionists. For the Zionists and for the Marxists, for the believers. Tamara hated me, had grown to hate me, for my unbelief, but she did not understand that I hated myself as well—for the same reason.

■ ■ ■

READING ADOLF BERMAN's letters to Michał Mirski, I realized something else: that these postwar relationships I was trying to understand were not really postwar relationships. That it had all begun long before the war.

Adolf and Jakub Berman were not the only children in the Berman family. In the beginning there were five siblings. A brother and a sister were murdered in Treblinka. Adolf Berman died in Tel Aviv in 1978. Jakub Berman died in Warsaw six years later. Only the youngest sister was still living.

Pani Irena was elderly and frail. She was also a lifelong communist who remained distinctly bourgeois. Certain things she wanted to impress upon me: she, her brothers, and her sister were from a good family. They spoke pure Polish, the very best, without a Yiddish accent. They always took care of their parents. Every year on Passover, her brothers all came to the seder, even though they did not believe in God. And even Jakub, active in the Communist Party at the time, even he was married under a chuppah, because it was important to their mother. And they loved their mother very much. Their Yiddish-speaking Jewish mother who had done so much for her children: her sons went to the very best Polish schools in Warsaw.

Pani Irena had spent the war years in the Soviet Union, where she had nearly died of hunger. It was Jakub who'd helped her to survive the war. And it was only later, when the war was already coming to an end, that she met her brother Adolf in Lublin and learned what had happened in Poland: that the Nazis had murdered 3 million Polish Jews, among them most of her family.

After the war, when Warsaw was still in ruins, Irena gave birth to a son. The baby survived for only three and a half months. Later she had two daughters—both of whom had by now emigrated to the United States, leaving their mother, in her old age, alone in Warsaw.

It was sad for her that Adolf and Basia had left Poland for Israel. And very sad for them, for Basia did not live long in her new homeland. Soon after they arrived in Israel, she fell ill and died. They had been a couple very much in love.

Adolf had then been left alone with their young son, Emanuel, who'd begun to teach his father Hebrew.

"I often think," Pani Irena said, "that in Israel Adolf didn't achieve what he wanted to achieve. He wanted to achieve some kind of peaceful life, where no one would be killing anyone else."

She was sorry Adolf and Basia had gone so far away, but she also understood there were problems in Poland: that Poland was a very strange country, that there was much anti-Semitism here. Even now, it was returning.

Among communists, though, there hadn't been such problems.

"If someone was a communist, he wasn't an anti-Semite. He couldn't be. Among communists there were a lot of Jews. That's a different matter. There were a lot of mixed marriages. There was no problem. Even Gomułka had a Jewish wife—a hideous one, after all. She was very primitive; she came from a Hasidic family."

It was Władysław Gomułka, the Polish communist who had married into a Hasidic family, who had presided over the "anti-Zionist" campaign of March 1968.

■ ■ ■

THE BUNDIST REPRESENTATIVE to the Polish government in exile in London, Szmuel Zygielbojm, was familiar to me. A few years earlier, in the Hoover Archives at Stanford, I'd found a letter he had written during the uprising in the Warsaw Ghetto. The uprising had begun on 19 April 1943. The letter was dated 11 May, and it was brief: *"My dear friends, should you ever see Mania or one of my children please tell them that I never could forgive myself for having left them behind."*

He enclosed a signed telegram he had written in English. Would they cable it to New York?

> *The responsibility for the crime of murdering all Jewish population in Poland falls, in the first instance, on the perpetrators, but indirectly, also weighs on the whole of humanity, the people and Governments of the Allied States, which, so far, have made no effort towards a concrete action for the purpose of curtailing this crime. By the passive observation of this murder of defenceless millions and maltreatment of children, women and men, these countries have become accomplices of the criminals. . . . I cannot be silent and I cannot live while*

*the remnants of the Jewish people in Poland, of whom I am
the representative, are perishing. My comrades in the Warsaw ghetto perished with weapons in their hand in their last
heroic impulse. It was not my destiny to perish as they did,
together with them, but I belong to them and to their mass
graves. By my death I wish to express my strongest protest
against the insensitivity with which the world is looking on
and permitting the extermination of the Jewish people. I know
how little human life is worth, especially to-day. But as I was
unable to do anything during my life, perhaps by my death
I shall contribute to the breaking of the indifference of those,
who are able and should act in order to save now, maybe in
the last moment, this handful of Polish Jews, who are still
alive, from certain annihilation. My life belongs to the Jewish
people in Poland, and therefore, I give it to them. I wish that
this handful which remained from several millions of Polish
Jews could live to see, with the Polish masses, the liberation,
that it could breathe in Poland, and in a world of freedom
and in the justice of socialism. For all its tortures and inhuman sufferings. And I believe that such a Poland will arise
and that such a world will come.*

In December I went to what was once the ghetto to see the new
monument to Szmuel Zygielbojm. A shimmering black, the vaguest outlines of bodies, all modernist abstraction. *"I cannot be silent
and I cannot live while the remnants of the Jewish people in Poland are perishing."* Visitors had brought flowers; their reflections
glistened upon the black wall of the most contemporary of office
buildings in Warsaw.

▪ ▪ ▪

BOGNA'S MOTHER WAS a teacher. Every year on Teachers' Day her
students would bring her flowers. And every year she would give
the flowers to Bogna and tell her to take them to Umschlagplatz—in
memory of the Jews who had boarded trains there to Treblinka.

The evening of Christmas Day I spent with Bogna, at her small apartment on the other side of the Vistula River. We talked about her father, who had spent his childhood in a Siberian orphanage, where he was constantly hungry and where he was treated as "an enemy of the people." Like so many Polish communists, his communist parents had fallen out of Stalin's favor.

I asked Bogna about her grandparents, her father's parents.

"My grandparents? They built communism. They built it before the war. And they also built it after the war."

Her father was a Jew by birth, her mother was not. In the 1970s he became involved in the opposition. In 1979 and 1980 he was a political prisoner; in 1982, during martial law, he was again imprisoned for over a year. Afterward her father was periodically detained, and their apartment was wired to aid the secret police in eavesdropping.

Many of Bogna's friends, twenty-something young Jews, had parents who had belonged to the opposition, casting their lot with Solidarity—in rebellion against, and perhaps atonement for, the choices made by their own parents, who had been among the builders of Polish communism. Pope John Paul II was Solidarity's greatest patron; for the parents like Bogna's who baptized their children, this Catholic ritual was an act of freedom.

Bogna, though, remained bitterly resentful of having been baptized: had she lived in a free country, there would have been no baptism. She would have been a religious Jew, she would have had a bat mitzvah. Or so she believed. Now it was too late for a bat mitzvah, but not too late to learn Yiddish, the language she saw as preserving the essence of her identity.

Communism Bogna described as a "frozen time." The ideologies and emotions she had encountered as a student in the 1990s, she believed, were the same ones that had been frozen some half century earlier, "as if that time hadn't been, as if there hadn't been those fifty years." The anti-Semitism of the present day she understood as prewar anti-Semitism. Like so many other ideas and attitudes, after 1989 anti-Semitism had thawed, emerging in the same form in which it had been frozen.

Yet in some way Bogna, too, lived in the prewar years; she had re-created those years in her mind. Her way to Jewishness was through not only Yiddish but also Yiddishism: she was ideologically com-mitted to the Yiddish language; she defined herself as a diaspora nationalist and took impassioned part in debates against the as-similationists, the Hebraists, the Zionists. In fact the greatest of her wrath she reserved not for Polish anti-Semites but for Zionists.

Yet Bogna was close to Tamara—despite their ideological an-tagonism.

"When I talk with Tamara," I told her, "often I have the feel-ing that she feels as if her entire life here were a mistake. That she should be in Israel . . . that in a certain sense she was thrown off the current of History."

"I feel this entirely differently," Bogna said. "I consider myself as having been absolutely in the center of the current of History—and this I can only regret."

Regret was at the heart of both Bogna's and Tamara's very dif-ferent sentiments. Bogna did not lament that her grandparents had not crossed the border into Czechoslovakia and from there gone on to the land that became Israel. On the contrary: it would have been terrible if they had.

When the Jewish tours of the Nazi camps called Marches of the Living began, Bogna was a teenager, and by some conjuncture of events found herself invited along. She accepted—she thought the program was about the Holocaust; no one had told her it was a Zi-onist program. When, after visiting the death camps, she left with the group for Israel, she thought they were going to the Holocaust museum Yad Vashem. Instead she learned that the time for talk-ing about the Holocaust was over. The group's time in Israel was a time for celebration, and there were songs and marches—in which Bogna refused to participate. When it was time for her to return to Poland, the young Israelis told her she was betraying her country.

Bogna was offended. The truth was precisely the opposite: she was returning to her country.

Later she met more Israelis, and more American Jews, as they passed through Warsaw on the March of the Living. She was not fond of them: they were aggressive, they hated Poland, and they couldn't understand why Bogna and her friends remained here.

"But that's their problem," she added.

Bogna knew who she was—and this was the most important thing.

"Well, and now I'm twenty-five, and only now am I learning to be happy," she told me.

We were sitting on her worn sofa, drinking tea.

"Because when I was a child, it wasn't a time for childhood. It was actually a war. When I was ten years old and they announced martial law, that was a war in my life. And had it not been for martial law perhaps it would have been okay for me to laugh. Things were so bad that it wasn't okay to laugh. And all the more so for children whose parents were in prison. It's very hard to learn how to laugh. That is, we were always laughing, but it was a terrible laughter. I was raised in a tradition in which we had to identify with the situation of our country. That situation was horrible, our country was unhappy. And so it wasn't okay to be happy."

So she was only now learning to be happy—although if she had to choose she would have rather lived in another time.

"I'd like to have lived before the Holocaust," she told me.

■ ■ ■

AT THE UNIVERSITY I met Kostek's friend Staszek, whose father had remained a Stalinist even after, in Moscow during the Great Terror, his own mother and father—Staszek's grandmother and grandfather—were killed by Stalin.

When Staszek and his wife had first met in the 1970s, Staszek had been a hippie, interested in Eastern philosophy and involved with the opposition, watched by the secret police. Discovering Judaism became part of a larger project, a search for freedom. It all began in the seventies, spontaneously, at Kostek's apartment, at the apartments of Pani Ryszarda and a handful of others. When Staszek and his wife hosted their first Passover seder, the atmosphere was euphoric: they were doing it for the first time, perhaps making mistakes, but that was of little importance—they were doing it themselves. During the seder, when they said the prayer that included the phrase *"Today we are slaves, tomorrow we will be free,"* they added a prayer for a free Poland.

Today Staszek was a mathematician preoccupied with moral philosophy. He was also the leading activist in a society for Jewish-Christian understanding. For many years he had been struggling with one of the most painful issues between Poles and Jews: the relationship between Jews and communism. Even after the fall of communism, Polish anti-Semitism was fueled by the stereotype of "Judeo-Bolshevism": the impression that communism in general and Stalinism in particular had been a Jewish conspiracy against the Poles.

Staszek was the son and grandson of Stalinists; his great-grandfather had been among the founders of the Polish communist movement. For Staszek "Judeo-Bolshevism" was much more than an anti-Semitic stereotype. Jews were like a family, Staszek believed, and when someone in your family did something wrong, you felt bad as well. And so perhaps the Jews could collectively . . .

"I did not use the word *apologize,*" he insisted, "but perhaps *acknowledge, engage in dialogue . . .*"

The Jews who had survived the war had usually survived by themselves, without their families. After the war they had found themselves alone, in a void, surrounded by emptiness—the result was a desire for radical change. This was such a large phenomenon, it should not be taboo to speak about it.

Pani Ryszarda's mother had told her that when she returned to Poland after the war she felt as if she were in a cemetery.

Staszek spoke to me as well about Jewish tradition, a tradition he had acquired as an act of will—through much effort and study, for there had been no one to pass it on to him. It had happened when he was already an adult, during the Solidarity years, the years of the underground Jewish Flying University: seminars held in private apartments, where Staszek and his friends studied non-Marxist philosophy and traditional Jewish texts. He began to see the deep affinities between Judaism and Marxism: the role of the *tsadik*, the tradition of textual commentary, the messianic hope. Stalin had become the messiah—at a time when it seemed that one had to choose between Stalin and Hitler. For Staszek the tragedy was not that the Jews chose Stalin over Hitler but rather that they confused Stalin with the messiah. Only in 1968 did they learn that communism and fascism were alike.

Before he left the café at the university, Staszek put on a black yarmulke. Poles respected him more, he believed, now that he was openly Jewish.

"Otherwise it's much worse," he said. "They accuse you of 'concealing your origins.'"

As he began to walk away, Staszek turned to me one more time.

"The locomotive of History," he said in parting. One was about to collide with the locomotive of History.

Cemeteries

In June of 1998 I returned to the small apartment on Piwna Street. In the end my landlord, the painter, had survived his gruesome car accident in Łódź, but his face was disfigured, and he was now blind. And yet he was somehow unchanged. Unable to paint, he had begun to write. He had written a story about Adolf Hitler, his rejected application to the art academy in Vienna, and his unfulfilled artistic ambitions—instead of *Mein Kampf*, it could have been *Meine Kunst*. Gallery openings in London and New York. If only . . .

■ ■ ■

IN THE WARSAW archives I found Jakub Berman's notes for his memoirs, which had never come into being. By now I recognized his handwriting. The notes had been composed in telegraphic form, on scraps of papers of various shapes, staccato, abbreviated, tiny, torn.

In 1956, Jakub Berman was in Moscow for the Twentieth Party Congress of the Communist Party of the Soviet Union, where Nikita Khrushchev gave his "secret speech" about Stalin's "cult of personality." When Jakub Berman returned to Warsaw, he submitted his resignation to the Politburo. It was less that he accepted his guilt—and more that he accepted himself as a scapegoat for the "excesses" of the Stalinist era. He offered to sacrifice himself so that the Party could remain strong.

At the Politburo meeting devoted to his resignation, Jakub Berman denied having known of the methods employed by his security apparatus. Jakub Berman, I had come to believe, was a deeply principled man. Yet his claim of ignorance could not have been true. He had been a Party member since the 1920s. He had seen the purges of his comrades in the 1930s; he had spent the war years in the Soviet Union. He knew what Stalinism was.

Jakub Berman accepted being cast out of the government, but what was still to come was much worse: in 1957, the Central Committee revoked his Party card. This he could not bear. He had never needed to be in power, but he did need to belong to the Party. He understood that he should bear some costs of Stalinist crimes, but he could not accept the loss of his Party card. In the archives I found his response to the Central Committee: *"I cannot reconcile myself to the thought of being excluded from the Party to which I have been joined for thirty-four years."*

I found a second letter, dated three years later. This one was addressed to Władysław Gomułka, now—in the wake of de-Stalinization—the general secretary of the Party. Jakub Berman was pleading for his Party card back.

"In the course of these three years," he wrote to the man he had once imprisoned, *"I have felt, as in the years preceding, indissolubly joined to the Party, to the Party's daily efforts. . . . I beg to be accepted back into the Party, so that in the ranks of the Party I can serve the cause that is the essence of my entire life."*

Jakub Berman had considered the wording very carefully: there were several drafts.

Władysław Gomułka said no.

In the archives I did not find, though, what I had been looking for: a letter from Adolf Berman about Władysław Bartoszewski.

"Adolf told me about Żegota, but only after many years," Jakub Berman had said to his interviewer at the end of his life.

But of that missing conversation I found nothing.

I went to see Kostek at *Midrasz*'s editorial office on Twarda 6, the gathering site of what was still a nascent Jewish community in postcommunist Warsaw.

"Fascism, communism, Zionism—the three great utopian ideologies of the twentieth century," said Kostek. "You can't understand communism with the arcane apparatchiks of the Brezhnev era, you have to think of the forties—in the forties, communism was sexy."

Then Kostek suggested I visit Adam, the longtime editor of a small Yiddish-language periodical.

Adam's office was across the street—not even a street, but rather a path through the grass—just a few yards away at Warsaw's Yiddish Theater. The Yiddish Theater was the alter ego of *Midrasz*'s office on Twarda 6: it was the old Jewish community, the meeting place of the elderly, the Jews who had stayed in Poland after the war because they believed in building socialism.

The year before I had come for the first time to the Yiddish Theater, where I saw scenes from *Fiddler on the Roof* and listened to the whispered conversations among the American Jewish tourists seated around me.

"Treblinka, that's what I really came here to see," one middle-aged woman told her neighbor. "Last night—the Hotel Bristol. Today—bread and cheese in the car on the road to Treblinka. It's good for the soul."

However well intentioned, it had felt like the Theater of Grotesque Kitsch. A farce. The director had once been a communist and was now an old man.

"Was he a believer?" I now asked Adam, one of his friends.

"He believes in that which is to his advantage," Adam answered.

He smiled gently. He himself was neither an actor nor a director, but rather the editor of a publication already long an archaism, its tiny readership literally dying by the day.

As a child, Adam had spent the war years fleeing east with his family. The winter in Siberia was beautiful, he told me.

He felt some resentment toward Kostek and Staszek, whom he understood to be the new "court Jews," whose wives had converted to Judaism, who spoke American English but could not read the Yiddish pages of his magazine, who found it curious that he even bothered to publish in Yiddish anymore. Adam was soft-spoken and generous with his time—more than that, he seemed happy to talk. He was sensitive to the fact that Kostek and Staszek had become the spokespeople for the Jewish community. They monopolized this role—not by aggression but by English. Adam's own trilingualism in Polish, Yiddish, and Russian was no longer of very much importance in this new, postcommunist world.

Adam spoke to me about the postwar years. It had been a difficult time: Poland was in the midst of a civil war, Jewish survivors were killed by bandits. Yet Adam insisted on a distinction: while postwar Polish society was anti-Semitic, the communist government was not. Under the communists, there *was* a space for Jewish culture, it only had to be a secular Jewish culture. As for Michał Mirski, Grzegorz Smolar, and Szymon Zachariasz, the communist representatives in the postwar Central Committee of Jews in Poland—the contribution they had made to postwar Jewish culture was very real.

It would be a mistake, Adam believed, to describe the Stalinist years as a negative time for Jewish culture. After all, the Yiddish Theater had been much better then.

Adam's own father was a communist who before the war had spent seven years in Polish prison. Adam himself had never joined the Party, but he understood his father's choice—after all, at the time there was no choice.

"If the Jews accepted the communists," Adam said, "it was only because the communists were the only ones who accepted us."

"Staszek believes the Jews—himself, too—should in some sense apologize—for communism ... ," I began.

"Let him do so in his own name," Adam said.

Later, at a café in Mokotów, I met Dariusz, the historian who had described the animosity between the Zionist Ignacy Schwarzbart and the Bundist Szmuel Zygielbojm, the only two Jewish representatives to the National Council of the Polish government in exile during the war.

Dariusz and I talked more about Adolf and Jakub Berman, about Michał Mirski, Grzegorz Smolar, and Szymon Zachariasz. Dariusz was excited: he—a Polish Catholic—could never tell this story, this tragic story of the Polish-Jewish communists, for he would be branded a Polish anti-Semite. But I could.

Marxism, Dariusz now suggested, was for these figures a post-Jewish alienation.

That came to an end in 1968, of course. Dariusz was working on a book about the so-called anti-Zionist campaign. A revolution always devoured its children, and March 1968, Dariusz said, was the story of the last children to be eaten.

Dariusz told me about a letter he'd found in the archives. It was a letter written by Grzegorz Smolar, the communist who in 1949 had taken Adolf Berman's place as chairman of the Central Committee of Jews in Poland. Grzegorz Smolar was a professional revolutionary, a communist since the age of fifteen who before the Second World War had spent five years in Polish prison; his wife had spent nine. In 1949, the year when they deposed Adolf Berman from the chairmanship of the Central Committee of Jews in Poland, Grzegorz Smolar and Szymon Zachariasz were campaigning to stop immigration to Israel. A year or so later, the door was closed: Jews could no longer leave Poland. Dariusz believed that Grzegorz Smolar had wanted emigration cut off so as not to lose his constituency.

Then, in the wake of March 1968, Grzegorz Smolar—a devoted communist for some half century—was removed as the editor of the newspaper he himself had co-founded and was cast out of the Party. Now it was his children who were in Polish prison for their participation in student protests against censorship. It was then that Smolar wrote a pleading letter to the Party general secretary Władysław Gomułka. He bargained: he was willing to leave Poland and never return if only Gomułka would free his sons.

"I am writing at a moment," Grzegorz Smolar told Władysław

Gomułka, *"when the despair that has overtaken me has begun to turn into desperation."*

Grzegorz Smolar's whole life had been devoted to the cause of the Party: he had been in Polish prison in the 1930s; had taken part in armed battle in defense of the Bolshevik Revolution; had helped to create some seven partisan divisions during the Second World War; had organized the Bolshevik underground in Minsk during the German occupation. For twenty years he had been the editor of the best Yiddish-language communist newspaper; he was also the author of the only postwar book in Yiddish dedicated to the battle against Jewish nationalism. Now he stood accused of Zionism by the Party to which he had devoted his life. He had only his children left, two boys whom he had tried to raise as honest citizens and ideologically committed communists—and who now, together with his daughter-in-law, the mother of a three-year-old child, faced prison sentences. In despair, Grzegorz Smolar offered himself in exchange for his children: *"Perhaps, as has been suggested to me by various parties, the situation would undergo a fundamental change if I were to express a desire to leave the country. In light of the situation that has developed, I declare this: If soliciting permission to leave the country can save my imprisoned children, I am ready to carry this out."*

The following year his two sons were released from prison. The older son tried to persuade his father to leave Poland. In the end, Grzegorz Smolar did.

In the summer of 1998 I met the older son. After being released from Polish prison, Alik Smolar had gone to Bologne, then to Paris, where he found he had little in common with his contemporaries, veterans of 1968 in Western Europe. Now, after two decades in France, Alik Smolar commuted between Paris and Warsaw. In the years since his release from prison in 1969, he had become an eminent political scientist and the chairman of a foundation established by George Soros to support democratic civil society.

Alik spoke quickly and brusquely—but, I sensed, quite honestly as well. He told me that as a child, he, too, had been a good communist.

Alik's father had been devoted to the communist cause throughout his entire life. This was true even though he feared Stalin. During the Stalinist purges of the 1930s, Grzegorz Smolar, like so many other Polish communists, was summoned to Moscow. He remained in Poland only because he was then in Polish prison. Otherwise Alik believed his father would have followed the Party's orders and gone to Moscow—even knowing what awaited him there: almost certain execution. The 1930s were the years of the Terror, the years when Stalin had more than a hundred thousand people shot as Polish spies, including almost all of the leading Polish communists.

"I think," Alik said to me of his father, "that he knew about Stalin very early."

Looking back on his life in his old age, Alik's father had been happiest with his biography during the war years—heroic years when he'd organized the Jewish resistance in Minsk, when he'd worked with the anti-Nazi Belarusian resistance to save many lives. It was a gruesome war, yet nonetheless the most satisfying chapter of his life, when the divisions between good and evil were clear.

And as for Grzegorz Smolar's postwar work in the Central Committee of Jews in Poland—his taking the place of the ousted Adolf Berman—this was work done, Alik's father had believed, to save Jewish life in postwar Poland. The communists who worked "on the Jewish street" believed that Jewish life would continue in Poland, that a secular Jewish culture was compatible with communism.

In the end, Alik said, his father had left Poland because he was a professional Jew in a country where there were no longer Jews. By then his father understood that his generation had been corrupted by the times. Emigrating to Israel was a moral and intellectual defeat.

At the end of his father's life, Alik visited him in a hospital there. It was then that the father told his son that they were very similar: for although Alik had gone to prison for protesting the very system his father had devoted his life to building, they were both devoted to an important cause.

My questions were invasive: What had his relationship with his father been like?

Alik respected his father and his father's courage. Yet he—much like Pani Ryszarda—had also understood from a young age that he was the son of a professional revolutionary whose primary concern was not his family and who did not know how to deal with his children.

I told Alik about the letter Dariusz had found. Alik was dismissive: he knew his father. His father would never have written such a letter.

▪ ▪ ▪

IT WAS SUMMER in Warsaw. I was talking to a literary scholar named Jacek at an outdoor café on Krakowskie Przedmieście.

Jacek was working on a book about the Warsaw Ghetto. He told me of a famous Polish actress, who was now an elderly woman. In his research he had come across newspapers from the ghetto and realized that as a very young woman this actress had performed there, in the cabaret in the ghetto. He went to visit her then, and she agreed to speak to him, but only if he promised to keep her secret. Jacek wanted to know: Why should it be a secret? After all, she was a celebrated Polish actress at the end of a splendid career; nothing could happen to her now. And she explained: she had two grandsons, two boys who would continue to live in Poland. She did not want to burden them with a Jewish grandmother.

Jacek himself was not a Jew. He had grown up, though, in Muranów, in the space that was once the ghetto, on the street named to honor the fallen hero of the ghetto uprising Mordechai Anielewicz. From his window, Jacek could see the Jewish cemetery, less than a mile in the distance. He used to go for walks there; when he was young it was an act of daring to walk through the graveyard at night. It was a fantastic place, as if in a Gothic novel: a quiet wildness crowded with slanted tombstones, overgrown by weeds, nearly reclaimed by forest.

Once, some fifteen years ago, when Jacek was no longer a child, he was walking in the cemetery with the woman who would become his wife. Suddenly they encountered, walking toward them, an older man, Jacek's professor from the university. Jacek was wearing a hat, not a yarmulke but a hat, because it was a Jewish cemetery, and the other man, his university professor, was also wearing a hat, a multicolored beret. At once upon meeting each other they begin to explain, to reassure each other: of course they were not Jews, they were simply wearing hats . . .

"Why?" Jacek asked me over the wobbly plastic table.

"Only in Poland," he answered himself.

▪ ▪ ▪

WHEN I TOOK the train from Warsaw to Bratislava, I remembered that I used to love the trains. Now they filled me with anxiety. I had read too much about the trains, the trains that carried Prague's Jews to Auschwitz, the trains that carried Warsaw's Jews to Treblinka, the trains that carried some three hundred thousand Poles—including many Polish Jews—to Soviet labor camps in Kazakhstan and Siberia.

In Bratislava it was overcast. At a conference organized by Czechoslovak émigrés I spoke about Milada Horáková's show trial, and the letters she'd written before her execution. I continued to think about the person who had saved those letters, who had read them perhaps, and who had marked them "for the archives." This was Lenin's legacy: the perversity of preservation.

The audience had other preoccupations, though. In my talk I mentioned that during the trial several thousand petitions had been sent to the Ministry of Justice demanding the immediate execution of the accused.

"It makes you wonder what kind of nation you belong to," said one Czech man, pained.

A woman in the audience told me how, in the 1950s, schoolchildren were asked by their teachers to draw pictures of the gallows and to pencil in the figures.

Several other people wanted to know if I had found the people who had written those letters to the newspapers, demanding Milada Horáková's execution. They wanted to know if the letter writers were still alive. There was a subtle rage in the room, a demand for accounting.

▪ ▪ ▪

MY OLD FRIEND Miloš, no longer a Slovak parliamentarian, had become an entrepreneur—although exactly what he sold was unclear. He picked me up that evening at the conference hotel in an ostentatiously expensive car. I'd called him on his cell phone when I arrived in Bratislava. Postcommunist Eastern Europe was a land of leapfrog technology: a transition directly from phonelessness to cellular phones. We had drinks at an expensive restaurant. The waitress, when Miloš opened his wallet to pay her, gasped when she saw all the bills.

Miloš was among the winners of the transition—unlike my former landlady, Paní Prokopová in Prague. A few months earlier she had written to me of the current political scandals. The newspapers were full of very unpleasant things: millions of crowns in bank loans had not been repaid, and now the banks were on the verge of collapse. Prices of basic goods had become a horror. The doctors were on strike.

"Politics," she wrote, *"is a horrible thing."*

From Bratislava I went to Prague, again by train. Now a widow, Paní Prokopová's pastimes were few: She made jam, she visited her husband's grave at the cemetery. In the summer, she lived in her cottage in the country, tending her garden. Klaudie, though, was in Prague. She had passed her medical school exams and was searching for work. She remained poor and in debt, caring for her sister's children.

The brother-in-law I had found so arrogant was not only distasteful but also violent. He could frighten his wife into submission but not Klaudie. She spoke back to him, until one day he struck her too. Unlike her sister, though, Klaudie responded not with fear but with fury.

"This will cost you dearly," she told him.

And it was true: it was Klaudie who guided her sister through the divorce trial.

It was summer and Paní Prokopová was away at her cottage. Klaudie and I were sitting alone in Paní Prokopová's living room, far from any walls. Klaudie grew nervous when we sat too close to walls, for someone could be listening. Nearly a decade had passed since communism had ended, yet some anxieties could not be uneasily unlearned.

"Did you testify at the trial?" I asked her.

"Yes," she said.

"How was it?"

Klaudie's eyes lit up. It was a triumphant story: she had testified not only as the battered wife's sister but also as a physician. I saw then that it was her strength that had carried this divorce. There was something marvelous about her.

But the divorce lawyer could not perform miracles. Klaudie's sister was granted the divorce, but she could not force her now former husband to leave the apartment they shared, and she herself had nowhere else to go. And so they continued to cohabitate. The physical violence, however, did end. The lawyer warned Klaudie's former brother-in-law that the woman who had once been his wife now legally bore no relationship to him: now, if he hit her, it would be an ordinary assault. He would go to prison.

■ ■ ■

SOON AFTER I returned to Warsaw from Prague, I left again for Berlin, where the old Jewish graveyard was now a small park. Dogs were running about; the only gravestone was a reconstructed one for the eighteenth-century philosopher Moses Mendelssohn, the founder of the Jewish Enlightenment who had insisted on the compatibility between reason and God. I thought of what Marek Edelman had said of Adolf Berman: "You can't dance at two weddings with one *tukhes*."

In the tiny café by the synagogue the only picture on the walls was a dark painting of a Hasidic Jew. Nearby, in a café named Mendelssohn, a new generation paid homage to the dead with cappuccino.

The street where the synagogue had once been was now lined with the most fashionable cafés. After midnight prostitutes came to move among the crowds of café-goers. I thought of Arnošt Lustig's *Tanga: "There isn't a single woman in the world who wouldn't like to be a whore for at least an hour a day . . ."*

My friend Fabian had grown up in West Berlin, on the good side of the wall, on that Western island in the midst of the East. His mother was a Berlin politician, and Fabian could not escape the guilt of his aristocratic German heritage. He took me to a cemetery with gravestones of German soldiers fallen in the Second World War. He pointed to the gold paint on the inscriptions: the paint was new. Inside the graveyards Germans fallen in the two very different world wars mingled. Fabian felt disgusted. I wanted to say something to make him feel less ashamed, but I could think of nothing.

In a few days it would be the thirtieth anniversary of the Soviet invasion of Prague.

In the spacious, imperial Café Eisenstein in Berlin, Fabian's girlfriend told me of the city's plans for a new Holocaust memorial: a stone maze in which visitors could literally become lost. The newspapers were saying it would become merely a dropbox for wreaths.

"Can you imagine," Fabian said, "erecting an enormous monument in the center of your capital to commemorate the worst thing your country ever did?"

"Aestheticizing the Holocaust," his girlfriend said. She was against it.

Broken Families

Adolf Berman had spent the last decades of his life in Israel. It was from Tel Aviv that in 1956 he had written the nostalgic letter to Michał Mirski, reminding him of their visits together to the then-socialist activist Wanda Wasilewska and the Bundist leader Wiktor Alter. Now I wanted to find the other half of Adolf Berman's correspondence with Michał Mirski.

In Tel Aviv I met Adolf Berman's son, who was born in Poland and was now Israeli and who spoke to me in American English. And like more than one child of devoted Marxists, Adolf and Basia's son had grown up to become a psychoanalyst. Like his father, Emanuel Berman was an engagé intellectual with deep moral convictions. He was not a dreamer, though. While the communists strove to create a "New Man" and the Zionists a "New Jew," Emanuel Berman criticized the idea of the "purified New Person" as a "utopian fantasy," liable to backfire, to claim victims, not at all innocuous.

Dr. Berman was introspective. He spoke thoughtfully of his father. His parents, he told me, were marginalized when they came to Israel. That his father became a member of the Israeli Knesset was in essence an accident. It was 1951 and he barely spoke Hebrew. His son, a young child then, was the ghost author of his Hebrew-language articles.

"Perhaps it's just my family pride," Dr. Berman mused, "but I think that Jakub, if he were not Jewish, would have been number one in Poland, and Bierut . . . perhaps number three. Bierut was not as bright as Jakub."

Of this there was a broad consensus: after the war, Jakub Berman had been the best-educated member of the Party's Central Committee. Stalin would have gladly made Jakub Berman the central defendant in a show trial, the Polish Rudolf Slánský. But Poland's communist leader, Bolesław Bierut, protected Jakub Berman: after all, Bierut needed him.

Jakub Berman had lived until his eighties. Adolf's son, though, believed his uncle's life had been shortened by a car accident that preceded his death by some three years. Jakub had been driving through Warsaw to the Jewish cemetery to visit family graves. Had it really been an accident? Dr. Berman wondered if perhaps Jakub had been a scapegoat.

Emanuel Berman's cousin, Jakub's daughter Pani Lucyna—he told me—still remembered how the three brothers used to argue in the years before the war. I had written to Pani Lucyna several times. She had never answered. Emanuel Berman urged me speak to her, and I saw that he didn't understand that she did not want to speak to me. And at that moment, I also saw how in some sense the Zionist dream had come true: in Israel, in a way that could never have been true in Poland, Emanuel Berman had grown up free.

I told him that in Warsaw I had met his aunt, Pani Irena.

"Irka—Irena," he said, "was the least intellectual, intelligent but not intellectual, a communist, the adored little sister, kept on the sidelines."

I showed him the protocol of the 1949 Presidium meeting of the Central Committee of Jews in Poland when Adolf Berman was deposed and replaced by Grzegorz Smolar.

"The demotion must have insulted him very deeply," Emanuel Berman said to me of his father.

In 1952, Adolf Berman broke with his leftist Zionist party in Israel over the Rudolf Slánský trial: he refused to take an anti-Soviet line against the Communist Party of Czechoslovakia. Afterward he became a member of the Israeli Knesset representing the Communist Party of Israel.

Now, Emanuel Berman told me, he understood better his father's decision: "Even if they were not loyal to him, he would be loyal to the cause. He needed to prove that his labor Zionist party really was a leftist party; when it turned out otherwise, he left. By 1956 my father was a communist; he could write to Mirski and say, implicitly: I have a Party card, after all that has happened, I am loyal."

His father had made peace with all of them, he said, with the exception of Szymon Zachariasz: he had always despised Zachariasz.

After his father's death, Emanuel Berman donated his father's papers to the Diaspora Research Institute at Tel Aviv University. The university was closed—the Israeli labor movement had called for a general strike—but the Polish-speaking archivist, a Belarusian émigré to Israel, let me into the archive.

Inside that archive I learned that Adolf Berman had had many friends—Poles and Jews, poets and political activists, famous people and ordinary people.

Before the war, Adolf Berman had been a teacher of psychology and philosophy at a Warsaw high school. In October 1945 his former student Aleksander Masiewicki wrote to him from the town of Olsztyn. Five years earlier Aleksander Masiewicki and his wife had been among some three hundred thousand Polish citizens deported to labor camps in the Soviet interior. Now the war was over, and Masiewicki had been repatriated from the Soviet Union to Poland, where he had accepted a good position as director of a regional Office of Press Control. Yet his tone was anguished. He felt painfully aware that the current leading positions of Polish Jews like himself were the result of the weakness—or rather absence—of a "democratic Polish intelligentsia." People like himself and Jakub Berman would not be in these roles otherwise; that they were necessary was only the result of a sick organism. Poland—and Polish Jews—needed more drastic medication.

"Today, at once, we must approach our question with a surgical

knife, not with a philosophical prescription," he repeated twice in that long letter.

Aleksander Masiewicki was a communist. He would stay in Poland and build the new world there. He did not believe, as Adolf Berman and the Zionists did, that emigration offered any hope: *"I have taken pains to exert my imagination, but I cannot see a place for myself there. And besides—there is no place for us anywhere. We are all eternal wanderers.... To this I must add: I do not like Jews. Specifically I find Jewish mannerisms reprehensible, Jewish ways of behavior offend me tremendously. Often I'm ashamed of Jews. Yet I am one of them!"*

During that same year, 1945, letters also arrived from another old friend, this one across the ocean. In the years before the war, Chaim Finkelstein had been the editor of Warsaw's largest Yiddish newspaper. He and Adolf Berman had known each other for a long time. Chaim Finkelstein knew Jakub well, too; he knew the whole Berman family. Adolf and Jakub's mother had considered him one of her own children. And she had loved her children very much.

Now Chaim Finkelstein was in New York, desperately hoping for news of his family, pleading with Adolf Berman to find them. He was a man in despair, driven nearly to insanity by the hellish years of waiting, helplessly and far away, for news of the people he loved. Without them life had no meaning for him. Again and again he begged to know something of the fate of his wife and two daughters, of Jakub and his family, of Adolf and his wife Basia, of their brother and sisters.

"With a beating heart I await news from you," Chaim Finkelstein wrote *"About myself I can tell you only that I'm alive (in truth I don't know what I've done to deserve such a punishment)."* The letter was dated 20 April 1945, less than three weeks before the Germans surrendered.

That summer of 1945 Jakub Berman sent a telegram: neither Chaim Finkelstein's wife and older daughter nor Jakub's sister Anna and brother Mieczysław had been found.

"Is this the final verdict? How can I believe it and how can I recon-

cile myself to it? And how to live?" Chaim Finkelstein wrote to Adolf that August after the war ended.

Yet one of his two daughters had been found. Awiwa was now fourteen years old; she had survived the war in hiding on the "Aryan Side" of the ghetto walls. At some point she managed to contact Adolf and Jakub Berman, and they helped her. In the months after the war ended, Jakub, Adolf, and Basia Berman managed to arrange for Awiwa to join her father in New York. Europe was still in chaos, and it was a long and difficult process, but in the end they succeeded.

From the moment he learned she was alive, Chaim Finkelstein was desperate to have his daughter with him. Every further hour of separation tormented him. Yet when Awiwa did finally arrive in New York, it was not easy for the father and daughter. Both were in mourning, both were ensconced in guilt. Awiwa did not know why she had survived when her mother and her sister had perished, and she urged her father: they should kill themselves together.

In his letters Chaim Finkelstein said very little about politics. Once, though, he responded to the news of Jakub Berman's success in postwar Poland:

> It's understood that I'm happy about the news that Jakub has acquired a "higher rank." But I'm afraid that my pleasure doesn't originate from the same source as does yours. For me this was only a confirmation that Jakub is still managing to survive, because truthfully stated, what kind of a life is it and how much value do those offices have, if even a man of Jakub's merit and position does not have the right, or the courage, to write to his brother?

It was true: since 1949, when it became apparent that there would be no Soviet Palestine, that the new Jewish state would not join the Soviet bloc, relations between communist Poland and Israel had not been good. These were the years of the "anticosmopolitan" campaign. Contact with Zionists would not have been in Jakub

Berman's interest. So even when Adolf's wife, Basia, died so terribly prematurely in 1953, it was Jakub Berman's daughter, Lucyna, who wrote with condolences. His sister, Irena, too, wrote on Jakub's behalf. She wrote frequently, though her letters nearly always began with apologies for her long silence or with chastisements for Adolf's. They were warm letters but nearly devoid of deeper content. There were always reports on the family's health, on Jakub's heart condition, on who was going on holiday and where. In the letters she never seemed to grow older, never seemed to change.

In the archives, though, the years passed quickly. Chaim Finkelstein's letters continued uninterrupted for decades.

The "anti-Zionist" campaign of March 1968 had a dramatic effect on Adolf Berman's correspondence. Friends and comrades he had not spoken to for twenty years now found him again. One of these was his former student Aleksander Masiewicki, and he had a story to tell Adolf Berman.

It was March 1968. A beautiful, sunny morning. Aleksander Masiewicki stared at himself in the mirror—and saw before him a man perhaps about to take his own life, perhaps about to hurl a bomb. Instead he went to a Party meeting, where without saying a word he handed the secretary a piece of paper on which he had written:

"In connection with the campaign being conducted by the Party concerning student activities, a campaign unworthy of the great traditions of our Party and hence villainous, I ask that you remove my name from the list of members of the Polish United Workers' Party." I submitted my resignation and signature and still without a word left the room of farewells deep in silence. I felt then a tremendous relief; the nightmare that had throttled me for many years departed. Already long ago I had entertained the thought of finally tearing off of myself that "burning shirt of Deianeira"; I lived in unceasing conflict with my conscience, choking me with disgust. The decision was a difficult one, as it meant self-annihilation, the negation of my entire life. Yet now that this was behind me, I felt absolutely

indifferent as to the consequences. I could not have acted dif-
ferently. I called my wife. I said: "You can congratulate me!"
She did not ask what for, at once she understood. For a mo-
ment she was silent, then she spoke: "If you've made your deci-
sion, then good. Now it's my turn!"

Two years later, now in exile in Brooklyn, Aleksander Masiewicki was pained above all by the separation from his friends.

And how many families have been broken into pieces as a re-
sult of these events, how many children have found themselves
far from their parents, how many wives have separated from
their husbands, how many of the closest friends have been
scattered over various continents. In the bill of injuries, which
perhaps some day will be presented to that band of gangsters,
these torn-apart families and broken friendships will surely
not find themselves in last place.

Aleksander Masiewicki, a communist since his youth, now was
convinced that the image of an ideal, just society, happy and free,
was but a utopia born in the minds of nineteenth-century dream-
ers. To his former teacher Adolf Berman he wrote:

I no longer nourish illusions that at some time the "ultimate
goal"—which generations of fighters for the so-called "better fu-
ture" have dreamed of—will be achieved. For in reality that "fu-
ture" will bring (as it cannot be otherwise) new problems, just as
(and often still more) complicated as the old ones and bringing
upon the ordinary man only the calamities of unhappiness and
disillusionment. I have my doubts as to whether "history goes on."

The Polish-speaking archivist knocked on the door of the room
where I sat alone reading Aleksander Masiewicki's letters and told
me that Kenneth Starr's report on Bill Clinton's relations with
Monica Lewinsky had just been published on the internet.

And then that rare thing happened: I found the other half of Adolf Berman's correspondence with the communist Michał Mirski, who in the Stalinist years had attacked Adolf Berman so harshly for "bourgeois nationalism." I learned that in the 1960s Mirski's daughter had been very ill and that Mirski had sent her to Israel in Adolf Berman's care, in the hopes that an extended stay in the warmer climate would cure her.

Then came the "anti-Zionist" campaign.

"I am a political emigrant and my homeland is Poland," Michał Mirski wrote after he'd arrived in Denmark.

The Eternally
Wandering Jew

In autumn of 1998, at Stanford, I began to study Yiddish. My teacher, Harvey, was nearing fifty. He spoke several languages and had had at least nine lives: among them as a grape picker, a hat importer, a cabinetmaker, a restorer of old houses, a klezmer revivalist, a teacher of Yiddish. Harvey was a native Yiddish speaker; he'd grown up in New York, the child of Holocaust survivors. His mother was from Romania, his father from Poland, and Yiddish had been the family's common language.

Harvey had recently visited Warsaw. He described it as "a city that could turn on you at any moment."

About his parents Harvey said, "People don't come out of a history like Jewish history healthy."

The sounds of Yiddish helped me to imagine the years before the war, the years when Warsaw was unimaginable without those sounds. In the end, this was the most important thing I had learned from Adolf Berman's correspondence with Michał Mirski: that— despite the war, despite the Holocaust, despite everything—these postwar relationships were epilogues to prewar relationships. And if I wanted to understand the convergence of the war and Stalinism, I would have to go back in time, to the decades between the two world wars.

When my friend Mikołaj had come from Budapest to Warsaw the previous year, he'd brought me a present: a book called *Lucifer*

Unemployed, a collection of stories by the Polish poet Aleksander Wat. The tales, written in the 1920s, were parabolic, antiutopian, nihilist. In "The Eternally Wandering Jew," Nathan, an orphaned Talmudic student from an isolated shtetl named Zebrzydowo, traveled through all of Europe to America in search of his wealthy benefactor. The story, set during a moment when Europe was "cannibalistic, impoverished, mystical, sadistic, prostituted," invoked as its refrain, "There is always mud in Zebrzydowo." In New York, now as his wealthy benefactor's secretary, Nathan conceived of the ideal social world as one that reconciled communism and Catholicism. He insisted that all Jews convert to Catholicism, and the yeshiva student himself became pope. The story ended hundreds of years later, when the last anti-Semites came upon Nathan's shtetl of Zebrzydowo. There they converted to Judaism and restored the ancient Hebraic traditions.

Aleksander Wat was a friend of Adam Ważyk, the author of the "Poem for Adults" I had read with my Polish teacher Pani Hanka in Toronto. In the early 1920s, as young men, Aleksander Wat and Adam Ważyk had been futurists and Dadaists, enamored of the avant-garde poets Guillaume Apollinaire, Filippo Tomasso Marinetti, and Vladimir Mayakovsky. Later, at different moments, they became the most fanatical of communists. It was to Sepp, a professor of literature who had abandoned Bavaria for Northern California, that I came with the question: How did these poets make the leap from Dadaism to communism, from radical contingency and radical nihilism to radical utopianism and radical determinism?

Sepp was writing a book about the year 1926. It was the era of the avant-garde—painters, poets, graphic artists, organizers of "happenings"—when art began to understand itself as no longer reflecting the world but rather creating it. For the avant-garde, Sepp explained, the pleasure—the thrill—was in the moment of crossing the boundary, leaping across the border from representation to transformation.

"Once you've crossed," Sepp told me, "you have nowhere else to go."

There was only pure contingency—which was misery, unbearable. And so, in a world of pure contingency, the existential imperative was to make a choice, to take some decisive action.

This—the imperative to choose, to embrace one's freedom and one's responsibility—was the philosophy of Jean-Paul Sartre, the French existentialism that had so haunted the Czechoslovak writers in the 1960s.

∎ ∎ ∎

I CONTACTED YIVO in New York. YIVO, the Institute for Jewish Research, had once made its home in Vilnius. Now, since the Second World War, the institute resided in New York. I asked the archivist there about Chaim Finkelstein, who had once been the editor of interwar Poland's largest Yiddish newspaper.

Yes, the archivist told me, the scholars at YIVO had known Chaim Finkelstein well; he had worked with YIVO for years and had lived a long life, dying just several years earlier.

I wrote then to Emanuel Berman in Tel Aviv, asking if he knew how to contact Chaim Finkelstein's daughter, Awiwa, who by now would be in her sixties. Emanuel responded with Awiwa's address. A few days later he wrote again: he had spoken to his cousins, Jakub Berman's daughter and son-in-law in Warsaw, and they believed that Chaim Finkelstein was still alive.

This seemed unlikely: if Chaim Finkelstein had grown up with the Berman brothers and lived still, by now he would be very, very old. I was headed to New York for a conference, and I sent a letter to Awiwa, giving her the phone number of my brother on the Upper West Side.

The very first day I arrived my brother and sister-in-law got a voice-mail message. They were very excited: the message was from Chaim Finkelstein himself, back from the dead.

I telephoned right away. Chaim Finkelstein was indeed still alive, and living with his second wife in a modest apartment in Co-op City in the Bronx. He had been born in the nineteenth century and was now one hundred years old.

He was small, shorter and thinner than I'd imagined. And terribly sarcastic. His was the very same Yiddish sarcasm of Marek Edelman, an acerbic humor that resonated through the boundaries of any other language. I asked him about Adolf and Jakub Berman.

He had met their older brother Mieczysław first, Chaim Finkelstein told me. It must have been 1909 or 1910. They were friends from school, and Chaim Finkelstein began to come home with Mieczysław in the afternoons. Warsaw was still part of the Russian Empire then, and Chaim Finkelstein and the Berman boys spoke Russian together.

Chaim Finkelstein spoke slowly, repeating the phrases he thought important, ending his sentences with ellipses.

"They were not Orthodox, but they were not not-kosher either. They wouldn't eat not-kosher products at home." In any case, where the Berman family lived, in Warsaw's Jewish quarter, there was no place to buy nonkosher products.

"The house where he grew up—Jakub—was a Jewish house, a typical Jewish house. The parents spoke Yiddish, the children spoke Polish, and Russian . . ."

Jakub's mother was a nice-looking Jewish woman, Chaim Finkelstein told me, repeating "nice-looking" twice.

I wanted to know what had happened in the 1920s that had drawn all three brothers toward such different ideological choices. How did it happen that Mieczysław joined Poalei Zion–Right, while Adolf joined Poalei Zion–Left, and Jakub joined the Communist Party of Poland? How was it that Adolf became a Zionist and Jakub became a communist?

"You have no idea of what you're talking about, you know? You have no idea about the situation," Chaim Finkelstein answered me.

His wife, who was in her eighties, was in the kitchen preparing lunch. I had to warn her that I was a vegetarian.

"So you're a vegetarian," Chaim Finkelstein said to me.

I nodded.

"And you have brothers?"

"Yes."

"And your brothers, are they vegetarians?"

"One is," I told him, "but not the youngest one, the youngest one isn't."

"So there, you see?" Chaim Finkelstein said. "One brother—*is* a vegetarian. The other brother—*is not* a vegetarian. So—Jakub was a communist and Adolf was a Zionist!"

His wife, who had been listening, interrupted. "Chaim, you're being stingy with explanation! Chaim, the girl came all the way to the Bronx, tell her! You can explain why Jakub became a communist. This is not so difficult . . . so answer it!"

She was sharp, animated, in her way philosophical.

"What can I tell you? What can I tell you?"

"My husband is very stingy in explanation."

Chaim Finkelstein's wife believed that the underlying cause was anti-Semitism—and its economic implications.

Chaim Finkelstein interrupted, now in Yiddish, *"A shikse bay a rov ken oykh a shayle paskenen"* (The rabbi's shiksa servant knows the answers to the questions people come to ask the rabbi).

"The lack of possibility to live as normal persons," she continued, "the background was lack of economic possibilities to make a living." She began to explain: there was very much anti-Semitism, there were not enough Jewish places to work, and Jews had no possibilities to find work . . .

"You, lady, come here, don't listen to her," he said to me.

"I am sorry I interrupted, but he is so stingy with words!"

He turned to me. "You have the best intention. Perhaps the right question, too." He paused. "What should I tell you? What should I tell you?"

Yet there was something he wanted to tell me.

"Very seldom can you meet a person so straightforward as he was," Chaim Finkelstein said of Jakub Berman.

He wanted me to know something else: he wanted me to know that despite everything, Jakub Berman was a good Jew.

"To me he was Jakub. And I was a person who visited the house very often."

Chaim Finkelstein was absolutely lucid, absolutely sharp. I was sure he remembered—perhaps not everything, but at least very much. But there was little he was willing to tell me. I could feel that it seemed pointless to him, for how could he communicate this world—*his* world that by now had no longer existed for over half a century—to a young person from a wholly other world?

"You already know too much," he said, "too much and not enough, and nothing."

The Dead and the Living

That August of 1999 I visited Amanda in the house in the woods where she now lived. An hour's drive from Boston, it was a wonderful, impractical house with a large kitchen where we made pesto with basil Amanda had grown herself. There was a studio outside where she would paint . . . when she was ready to start painting again. In the time since I'd last seen her, Amanda's hair had grown longer; now it nearly reached her shoulders.

"He was the love of my life," Amanda said.

We were talking about Oskar. She'd made a resting place for his ashes next to a small pond with a large goldfish whom she'd named Rybička—"little fish" in Czech.

A few days later I flew back to Warsaw, where violence lingered on the streets. Through the window of a taxi I watched a gang of boys move toward an older man who was no longer sober and perhaps never had been. The taxi driver watched, too, as one of the boys struck the first blow. Sudden, rapid violence. We drove past them. The driver said nothing.

Yet even so, by 1999 Warsaw was no longer nearly so frightening as it had been just two years earlier. The city had changed much in two or three years: The power of the taxi mafias at the train station had been broken. Large, bright supermarkets had opened. Late at night near the train station, on Marszałkowska Street and Aleje Jeruzalimskie, middle-aged prostitutes still solicited customers. Yet they were no longer alone on the streets otherwise dominated by staggering drunks and gangs of men in Adidas track suits: along with new shops and department stores, new restaurants and cafés had appeared. They stayed open in the evenings, and the streets were no longer empty at night.

■   ■   ■

AT THE UNIVERSITY I went to see Professor Tomaszewski, the historian. We talked about the Berman brothers, and about Polish-Jewish history. Professor Tomaszewski told me a Polish-Jewish joke: "A Polish client goes to a Jewish tailor and orders a pair of pants. A week passes. Two weeks. The client hears nothing from the tailor, so he returns to the shop and says to the tailor, 'Your God created the world in one week. And in two weeks you can't manage to make a pair of trousers?' And the tailor answers him: 'Take a look at God's world. And then at my trousers.'"

We took a walk to the university bookshop, where Professor Tomaszewski showed me the literary theorist Michał Głowiński's new book, *Czarne sezony* (*The Black Seasons*). Had I read it yet?

"You must," he said.

At home in the small apartment I now rented just off Plac Trzech Krzyży on Mokotowska Street—a beautiful, prewar apartment with high ceilings—I opened *The Black Seasons*. It was a memoir by a Polish literary scholar who had once been a Jewish child in the Warsaw Ghetto.

> *In my memories the color of the ghetto is the color of the paper that covered the corpses lying on the street before they were taken away. The corpses belonged to the permanent landscape, as the street was a place of death: not only sudden and unexpected death, but also slow death—from hunger, from disease, from every other possible cause. The season of great dying lasted in the ghetto without interruption. These bodies covered with sheets of paper never failed to make an intense impression on me, and that paper itself became for me one of death's em-*

bodiments, one of its symbols. I'm unable to describe its distinc-
tive color; afterward, I never again saw such paper, yet I think
that the description "discolored" would be closest, most fitting.
Precisely that color without color—neither white nor ash nor even
gray—defines the colorscape of the ghetto and imparts its tone.

I was struck by the softness of the language, horror described gently.

In one scene Michał sat in the attic where he, his mother, and his aunt were hiding on the "Aryan Side." A Polish blackmailer found them, and Michał waited to see if they would find the money to buy their lives or if the man would turn them in to the Gestapo. When his aunt set out in search of ransom, Michał, a young boy, remained in the attic with the blackmailer—who suggested they play a game of chess while they waited. And so they did. The game was never completed: Michał's aunt returned. She had found, somehow, just barely enough money.

In another chapter a second aunt left young Michał alone in a pastry shop while she went in search of a telephone. The women in the pastry shop grew suspicious; their gazes fixated on the young boy, they suspected he was a Jew. They came closer, they began to examine him, to ask him questions. Among themselves they whispered, *"We have to let the police know."*

It was, despite itself, a coming-out-of-the-closet book: coming out of the closet as a Polish Jew.

Later I met the book's author at his office at the Academy of Sciences.

"In my book, I say nothing about relations between Poles and Jews," he said.

"But of course the whole book is about that," he added after a moment.

Later we spoke about the chapter set in the pastry shop. He was uneasy about such scenes being taken out of context—that is, used in English translation as evidence of Polish anti-Semitism. After all, he was a Pole, too. And in the end he, a Jewish child, was saved

by Poles: the magnificent Irena Sendlerowa, Władysław Bartoszewski's and Adolf Berman's coconspirator in Żegota, the Council for
Aid to the Jews, arranged for his trip to a place called Turkowice.
And in that distant, impoverished convent, a priest and many nuns
risked their own lives to save his.

Michał Głowiński spent a long time in Turkowice. Months
after the Red Army had liberated the area from German occupation, Michał's Jewish mother found him there. At a loss as to how
to thank the nuns for saving her son's life, she consented to his
baptism. Yet unlike Bogna and her friends, baptized in the 1980s
in very different circumstances, Michał Głowiński did not think
of his baptism as a violation—on the contrary: it was something
he had desired very much at the time. While he did not remain a
Catholic, he had no regrets—the religious feelings he developed in
Turkowice were real: in those years that church, that convent, was
his sanctuary. He was protected there from the Germans.

■ ■ ■

AT THE JEWISH community center on Twarda 6 I learned that
Bogna, the young Yiddishist and diaspora nationalist so filled with
hostility toward Zionists, had gone to Israel and not come back.

Others, though, had arrived. The Lauder Foundation, hoping to re-
invigorate Jewish life in Poland, sent to Warsaw a young American
couple in their twenties: Rachel and Yonah were *baalei teshuva*—
born-again Jews. Both had come from secular Jewish homes, and
both had become devoutly observant while in graduate school at
Oxford. They'd married in California and moved to Jerusalem. Now
they were in Warsaw with their enchanting six-month-old baby.

Rachel had gone to university in the Pacific coast town of Santa
Cruz, on a beautiful wooded campus on a hill. The university was
known for the presence of the revolutionary Angela Davis, Bobby
Seale's fellow Black Panther activist, and for the legacy of the counterculture and its colorful movements: animal rights and environ-
mentalism, feminism and gay liberation, civil rights and pacifism.
Rachel had embraced feminism.

Now she wore only long skirts, covered her hair with a wig, and devoted every Friday to preparing Shabbat meals for some two dozen guests.

I began to spend Saturdays at Rachel and Yonah's apartment, sitting through long, slow lunches and playing with the baby. A handful of Rachel and Yonah's Warsaw friends were almost always there as well, including a man in his late twenties, a young father who was smart and sarcastic. Often he came with his five-year-old son, who was obsessed by *Star Wars*, which had recently appeared in Polish.

"Niech Moc będzie z tobą!" the little boy declared, raising his fist into the air. May the Force be with you!

"Niech Moc będzie z tobą!" I answered.

"That's not so bad, but it's not *exactly it*." He was referring to my intonation.

One day Rachel asked me if I would go with her to church. It was a liberal church, in the northern district of Żoliborz, where a tolerant priest had agreed to Staszek Krajewski's project: a Jewish-Christian ecumenical celebration of Simchas Torah—the festival celebrating the conclusion of the past year's reading of the Torah and the beginning of the next year's reading. Rachel was reluctant to go alone.

After the service there was a reception. I stayed downstairs among the pews, waiting for Rachel. There the priest found me. He was young and gentle and asked me: Was I here as a Christian or a Jew?

"I'm not a believer," I told him, "only a friend of Rachel."

He introduced himself, and guided me upstairs to the reception. I told him that until fairly recently Rachel had been secular as well.

"I wasn't religious either," he told me.

"And so . . . was it that one day, suddenly . . . ?"

"No, not one day. But perhaps in the course of one month."

He was speaking softly now, in the corner of the room, where the other parishioners could not hear him. Even today, even now, it was still difficult for him to believe in God, he admitted.

I was grateful to him for saying this to me, an American, a stranger, a nonbeliever.

▪ ▪ ▪

POLAND HAD BEEN independent for just days when on 29 November 1918, at nine in the evening, Antoni Słonimski was among the handful of young poets who held their debut poetry reading at a Warsaw café. That night was a dazzling success.

"A pleiad of talent one encounters once in a hundred years," Aleksander Wat wrote many decades later.

This group of five poets, who named themselves Skamander, was unique in those years. It was, Adam Ważyk later wrote, *"the only formation in Europe of that time that . . . lit the lantern of the heart."*

Of the Skamander poets Antoni Słonimski was the most sardonic. Acerbic and irreverent, he held nothing sacred. He was not only a lyrical poet but also the Warsaw intelligentsia's favorite satirist. In his weekly feuilletons published in a literary newspaper he spared neither Right nor Left.

In 1936 Antoni Słonimski devoted a column to a right-wing, anti-Semitic publicist: *"Mr. Piasecki claims that Jews invented communism. If one considers the fact that Jews invented capitalism as well, it could seem that in relation to us their accounts are all squared. We could likewise add that Jews also invented Christianity, but let's not complicate Mr. Piasecki's ideological situation, which is already so complicated as it is."*

On April Fools' Day of 1937, Słonimski published a full-page fictitious report describing Stalin's coronation as *"emperor of the proletariat, king of the bourgeoisie, and the grand prince of technical experts and the intelligentsia."*

Vacillating between the lyricism of the Skamander poets and the radicalism of the futurist poets was a young man named Władysław Broniewski, whose room was adorned with ancestral daggers. I learned that during the gray Polish winter of 1922, this young poet was dreaming of a tempestuous romance with a demonic woman. Instead he fell in love with a pretty girl named Janina.

Broniewski lived then among the artistic elite of prewar Warsaw. Evenings he would spend with a small group of writers who gathered on the upper floor of a café called Ziemiańska. The young poets were, for the most part, Poles and cosmopolitans, like Antoni Słonimski, "non-Jewish Jews." Władysław Broniewski was an exception, an ethnic Pole, and among the poets most heir to the legacy of nineteenth-century romanticism. It was Broniewski who came out of Polish leader Marshal Józef Piłsudski's military Legions, who had fought against the Soviets in his youth—before he became a proletarian poet. For Janina he composed florid love letters in the language of epic novels. Janina loved him as well, as she would for her entire life. Her deepest love, though, would be for Adolf Berman and Michał Mirski's friend Wanda Wasilewska, who was a tall woman with a large voice in a man's world.

Władysław Broniewski, the romantic, fell in love first with independent Poland, then with revolutionary Russia. He was a poet and a soldier who could not live without passion, a man of extraordinary vanity who longed to sacrifice himself to a greater cause.

Władysław Broniewski's friend Antoni Słonimski responded to the existential imperatives of the interwar years very differently: Słonimski, a lyrical poet, never lost his acerbic wit. As Hitler rose to power to Warsaw's west, and Stalin to its east, Słonimski mocked them both. He harbored no illusions: unlike so many of his friends, he was not fooled by the Moscow show trials. In the 1930s, Słonimski's was among the very last sober minds in Eastern Europe—if not in Europe as a whole.

In September 1939, when the Nazis came, Władysław Broniewski went east, Antoni Słonimski west. The following years the poet with the acerbic wit spent in England. There the war—and the end of Polish Jewry—broke him. When after the war he returned to the city that was his one great love, he embraced the Stalinist ethos. And when in 1951 the poet Czesław Miłosz defected from communist Poland, Słonimski addressed to him a vicious open letter:

You are an enemy of workers, peasants, and the intelligentsia, who for the first time in the history of our country have stood in battle to cast off the harm and exploitation of the capitalist system. You are an enemy of our workers' and peasants' sons, who fill the schools of higher education, who crave learning and work, you are the enemy of the architects and bricklayers who are rebuilding the capital, of engineers who are working out plans for new factories, of Party workers who are fighting against ignorance. . . . Each Polish success, each stage victoriously overcome, each new factory, new collective, each good book by a Polish writer evokes your hatred. You feel joy at every adversity that the ravaged country encounters on the path to socialism.

Antoni Słonimski, the satirist who in 1937 had harbored no illusions about Stalin, had now mastered Stalinist discourse:

You are an enemy of our present, but what frightens you most is our future. You know that the fulfillment of the six-year plan will make a great and strong socialist country of Poland. You don't want every person in Poland to have work, bread, and education. You don't want hundreds of new factories and hospitals, dozens of new universities and laboratories to arise on this land, you don't want the works of the great writers of the world to reach the working masses in hundreds of thousands of copies, you don't want the liberation of your own nation from the capitalist yoke.

What do you want? What is your program? Let's be honest. You want only one thing. You want war. A war more terrible than all past wars. On the new corpses of millions of children, women, and men, on the new ruins of cities today rebuilt, do you rest your hopes.

I recognized the language: it was the language of the show trials of Milada Horáková and Rudolf Slánský.

▪ ▪ ▪

IN SEPTEMBER 1999 *Gazeta Wyborcza* published an open letter to Polish Jews written by an Israeli woman, a young philosophy professor named Shoshana Ronen who was living in Warsaw.

Shoshana was unimpressed by Poles—*"even those worldly and intelligent Poles"*—who reacted with embarrassment when she introduced herself as a Jew. She was still less impressed by the confidential hotline for closet Jews listed alongside the confidential hotlines for alcoholics and AIDS patients.

Above all, she was unimpressed by Warsaw's "Jewish revival." With condescension she pointed out the pathetic character of the "rediscovered Judaism" of people like Kostek and Staszek—who, in deciding to return to Jewishness, had chosen the most narrow-minded kind. Moreover, half of them were not even Jewish according to Jewish religious law, and that they would not be accepted by Orthodox Jews elsewhere rendered their constructed identities still more absurd—and hypocritical.

> *The choice of Orthodoxy by "New Jews" in Poland points not only to a lack of understanding of the essence of Judaism and of what it means to be a Jew. It seems to me that it also testifies to a feeling of inferiority, to a lack of self-confidence. . . . I claim that it's possible to be a Jew in many ways, and the way chosen by the "New Jews" in Poland is the worst of them all.*

Shoshana herself suffered from no inferiority complexes, and she advised Polish Jews to follow her lead: proposing secular Jewishness—liberal, tolerant, and pluralist—in the spirit of Spinoza, the Jewish Enlightenment philosophers who came after him, and modern luminaries like Freud, Einstein, and Kafka. It was the secular Jews who were the more secure, the more intelligent, the better Jews.

"A nonreligious Jew," wrote the young philosophy professor, *"has a sufficiently strong Jewish identity to acknowledge that in a short story by Kafka there can be more wisdom than in several chapters of Talmud."*

Kostek was angry. He responded in the same newspaper: today very few Jews remained in Poland. Those who were living in Poland were dispersed throughout the country, entirely assimilated, speaking neither Hebrew nor Yiddish, and unable to create their own distinctive culture. It was not anti-Semitism—although this remained present—but rather demography that was the main obstacle to rebuilding a Jewish community. In these circumstances only a religious identity gave this handful of Polish Jews an opportunity to engage immediately, in some sense fully, with the Jewish world. Only Judaism provided a framework for Jewish spiritual growth.

It was a reasoned defense. But in the end Kostek could not bear Shoshana's condescension and added:

In the name of intellectual curiosity, I'm prepared to countenance the possibility that one story by Kafka, as she writes, can contain more wisdom than several chapters of Talmud. It's difficult for me to believe, though, that in speaking of the Talmud, she knows what she's talking about. And even about Kafka I'm beginning to have my doubts.

Soon afterward, Rachel came with me to the Yiddish Theater, where a public debate had been announced between Kostek and Shoshana: "How to Be a Jew in Poland?"

Staszek was there, and the aging leading actress of the Yiddish Theater. Most of the room was filled with elderly Polish Jews, the oldest generation of Holocaust survivors—the last to remember the large Orthodox community that for centuries before the war had made its home in Warsaw. The ones who stayed in Poland because they were committed to building socialism here. Atheists and communists. Old enough to be Shoshana's grandparents, sharing no language with the young Israeli professor. People, in turn, about whom she could only have known very little.

Yet they had come to cheer for Shoshana—Shoshana, who wrote about Nietzsche and Wittgenstein and was too young even to remember 1968, who spoke in English through an interpreter, who had hardly been thinking of these long-forgotten aged people who'd been devoted to building socialism when she wrote her open letter to Poland's "New Jews." Shoshana had been writing as a young secular Israeli. The audience members were expressing their support as elderly Polish Jewish socialists.

A woman in her seventies introduced herself by saying that she had lived the first fourteen years of her life before the war.

"To live through all of it and be normal—this is too much," she said.

Nobody applauded for Kostek.

"These are my people," he said to me a few days later, "and they hate me."

Now he tried to comfort himself with the thought that God would also like to be making the world with better Jews than He had.

We were at a Jewish book festival that Rachel and Yonah had organized at Twarda 6. The historian Jan Gross had come from New York; he led me to a table at the café where Stephanie was waiting for him. She was my age, dressed all in black and without any pretentiousness radiating a Greenwich Village–art café hipness. She was glamorous without any makeup. And sensitive.

▪ ▪ ▪

STEPHANIE WAS SPENDING the year in Krakow. I saw her again in late October, when we met at a prewar-style inn named Klezmer Hois, on Szeroka Street in Kazimierz, once Krakow's Jewish quarter. At Klezmer Hois there was a small, perfect black cat. He jumped on Stephanie's lap, lying down on her black skirt, becoming invisible.

I'd come to Krakow that day to see the poet Czesław Miłosz, and when we'd sat down in the living room of his Krakow apartment, I was immediately struck by his laughter, unusually deep.

He was an encyclopedia, he told me. The only one left.

Miłosz dismissed Jean-Paul Sartre and existentialism. It had been after all, only "a short-lived fashion in Paris, for a while they started to wear black sweaters."

And the connection between the avant-garde and Marxism?

"It would be a wonder if such a connection didn't exist," he told me, pointing out that in the interwar years all of New York was Marxist, either Stalinist or Trotskyite. Such was the zeitgeist.

Of Adam Ważyk, the prewar avant-garde poet, Apollinaire's translator-turned-"terroretician" of postwar socialist realism, Miłosz said, "We were good friends . . . even in the time of Stalinism Ważyk sort of winked at me."

And Antoni Słonimski, who had written the diatribe against him?

Despite everything, Czesław Miłosz had remained good friends with Antoni Słonimski. In 1948, when Miłosz was serving as cultural attaché in Washington, D.C., Słonimski told him: "Listen to an old Jew, stay as long as possible abroad." Three years later Miłosz defected. Then came the vituperative attack. Miłosz explained it to himself by the fact that Słonimski was "clearly out of his wits from fear."

"Then he came to Paris and we became friends again," Miłosz said.

Again that deep laughter.

"Because I forgave him."

■ ■ ■

IT WAS ONLY, I thought, on November first, the Day of the Dead, that Warsaw came into its own. The city was never more consumed by its past, never more ensorcelled by death, never more itself. The cemeteries were beautiful: vast and aglow. Warsaw by candlelight.

Now the days became ever shorter; the sun had barely risen before it began to set again. In Warsaw I walked with Stephanie along Nowy Świat, pausing inside shops, looking at tall leather boots and black dresses. In one boutique Stephanie tried on a long silver coat. It was stunning, she was stunning. Suddenly here, with Stephanie's bright eyes and black hair, I saw interwar Warsaw, with its cabaret glamour.

Later we sat in my kitchen. Stephanie lived in Brooklyn. She knew Awiwa, the once-fourteen-year-old girl who had miraculously survived the war to join her father in New York. I showed her Chaim Finkelstein's letters. I told her that after the war his daughter could not believe her father would love her, the only one who survived, and begged him to commit suicide with her, and Stephanie cried.

∎ ∎ ∎

DARIUSZ HAD BEEN in his midtwenties and already married when the revolution of 1989 had come. Now, a decade later, from time to time the same nightmare returned: the Iron Curtain had not yet fallen. Dariusz had been in the West, he had crossed the border back into the East, but he had forgotten his wife on the other side, and there was no longer any way to get back to her.

Over coffee at a café in Mokotów, he told me, too, of his meeting several years earlier with an intelligence officer who wanted to recruit him. Dariusz was a good candidate: well educated with excellent English. But he refused.

"You won't tell anyone about this conversation," the agent told him in closing.

"On the contrary, I will tell everyone," Dariusz answered.

Now he told me, "If I had agreed to keep the secret, that would have been the first step."

∎ ∎ ∎

DARIUSZ WAS FINISHING his book about March 1968. More and more I thought about the letters written to Adolf Berman by those "last children to be eaten."

A Polish journalist asked me if he could publish some excerpts from the letters I'd found in Adolf Berman's Tel Aviv archive. I agreed. Among them was the letter from Aleksander Masiewicki telling the story of the day in March 1968 when he returned his Party card—the day that *"meant self-annihilation, the negation of my entire life."*

A week or so later I was asleep in my apartment when the phone rang. It was an elderly man who spoke in Polish but told me he was calling from New York. He was upset, and it took me some time to realize who he was: he was Aleksander Masiewicki. Adolf Berman had been dead for more than twenty years, and Aleksander Masiewicki had never suspected that his letters had survived. How was it that I, a stranger, had gotten them? And how could I have published them?

He was right: How could I have?

Later I sat drinking wine with Jan and Stephanie in the living room of the apartment with the high ceilings on Mokotowska Street. I showed Jan the letter Dariusz had given me, the letter Grzegorz Smolar had written to the Party general secretary Władysław Gomułka in 1968, pleading for the release of his sons. Should I send it to Alik Smolar? Neither decision could be innocent: Grzegorz Smolar had been dead for many years, and he had never meant for his children to know about the letter. I had no right to give the letter to his son—and yet no right to keep it from him either.

Jan read the letter. He had known Alik Smolar for many years.

"You should send it to Alik," he said.

"What does it say?" Stephanie asked.

"It's a letter written by a man in despair," Jan said.

The next day I photocopied the letter and posted it to the son who did not believe his father would have written such a letter.

■ ■ ■

FIVE YEARS AFTER Oskar's suicide, Amanda returned to Prague for her sixtieth birthday. I took the train from Warsaw to meet her, and together we went to a club to see the debut poetry reading from Vlasta's daughter Diana's punk feminist journal *Bloody Mary*. The journal had adopted an English slogan: *"Only a dead fish flows with the stream."* Diana and her friends called themselves the Riot Girls, and Diana wore a turquoise dress, her hair dyed in streaks. No longer a child, she was coming into her own as a feminist. After Diana's performance, Vlasta and I danced. She was glowing for her daughter.

Before I left Prague, I promised Diana I would write an article about postcommunist Poland's antiabortion laws for *Bloody Mary*. Not long before, in the Polish town of Lubliniec, the police had received an anonymous phone call accusing a doctor of having performed an abortion. Two policemen were sent to investigate. They burst into the doctor's office and encountered there a gynecologist, an anesthesiologist, and a patient. They searched the office and confiscated surgical equipment and the remains of an aborted fetus. They took the patient for forced gynecological testing: the only way to prove her crime.

It was a chilling story. A conservative senator explained to the press that the antiabortion law existed to protect women's "natural dignity."

■ ■ ■

PAN SŁAWEK, THE kind and generous curator of the Władysław Broniewski Museum in Warsaw, had once wanted to be an actor. Today he had no real regrets, although he missed the costumes very much.

"I felt splendid and apparently looked just right in a tail-coat, in the attire of the old Polish nobility—a kontusz, *or an uhlan uniform from the Napoleonic era."*

Instead Pan Sławek studied Polish philology and remained nostalgic for the bohemian atmosphere at the drama school.

It was there at the museum that I found a poet's letters to his friend Władysław Broniewski. The letters were written in the textile town of Łódź in the 1920s. The poet had returned to Poland from Ukraine during the Russian Civil War, bringing with him Vladimir Mayakovsky's poetry. Władysław Broniewski's friend from Łódź was a futurist and a proletarian poet, a manic-depressive and a graphomaniac, a self-absorbed individualist with a fatal attraction to revolution.

"Revolution is a painful tragedy, a glorious fire, in which you must burn yourself, descend into savagery, into barbarism—in order to discover in yourself the simple joy of life," he wrote.

He went on:

Joy gives me the conviction that I'm disposed with my entire being toward life, toward everything that matures, that fights for its right to existence, that is healthy, manly. . . . I know that

I'm a true futurist-constructivist. That means: All the force of my decision is directed toward the future—and the present is only a joyful ladder toward the approaching future.

This last letter was eight pages long, written in black ink, as if by a feather, in prewar calligraphy. Pan Sławek helped me to make out the words I could not read. He was taken by my enchantment. He had not spoken of the graphomaniac poet from Łódź in a long time, and he had much to say.

Pan Sławek was a Catholic. One day he told me that, notwithstanding his Catholicism, he, too, had his own communist past. He had joined the Party in 1966, when he was twenty-three years old. Later—in 1968, again in the 1970s—he thought of returning his Party card ... but he did not.

"Why?" he asked me, or perhaps himself. We were the only ones in the room. "An instinct for self-preservation? Cowardice?"

I wanted to reassure him, but I could think of nothing to say.

Pan Sławek invited me to give a lecture in the house in Mokotów where Władysław Broniewski had once lived, at the museum dedicated to the poet who had died an alcoholic thirty-eight years before I'd arrived there. Pan Sławek used a new graphics program on his computer to print invitations with a red star and Lenin's profile.

I began with the author of "The Eternally Wandering Jew," with Aleksander Wat's feeling of unbearable guilt, his insistence, in the conversations he had with Czesław Miłosz in the 1960s, that his engagement with communism had been a pure, free choice. That he had chosen it himself, that there could be no excuses. The Marxist literary monthly Wat had edited between 1929 and 1931 had appeared for only twenty issues, two of which were confiscated. Yet for the rest of his life Aleksander Wat was haunted by those twenty issues, *"the* corpus delicti *of my degradation, the history of my degradation in communism, by communism."*

"It was in a communist prison that I came fully to my senses," he told Czesław Miłosz, *"and from then on, in prison, in exile, and in communist Poland, I never allowed myself to forget my basic*

duty—to pay, to pay for those two or three years of moral insanity.
And I paid, and paid."

"I say to Aleksander Wat, yes, fine, I understand," I said at one
point during my lecture, "but tell me: Who managed to escape
from those years with clean hands?"

And yet, I told the audience, it was a rhetorical question, inspired
by empathy, perhaps pity—because in the end I did believe that history was made by making choices.

I spoke, too, about Władysław Broniewski's letters to Janina written during their courtship, about how—despite the romanticism of
those letters—he wrote crudely of the woman in Krakow who was
then pregnant with his child. Broniewski insisted she have an illegal abortion. He wanted nothing to do with her.

The audience was scandalized. How dare I?

When I finished speaking, an older woman in the audience said
to me, "You, a young person from another continent, you're unable
to understand Poland."

▪ ▪ ▪

ON ŚWIĘTOKRZYSKA STREET, I stopped by the table of an outdoor book vendor. The birthday of Rachel and Yonah's friend's *Star
Wars*–obsessed son was coming up, and I wanted to buy him a
present. I chose a book with brightly colored illustrations of Princess Leia and Luke Skywalker. As I handed the bookseller the
money, I saw that, alongside the children's books, he was selling
a variety of anti-Semitic literature, books about Jewish-Masonic
conspiracies. I knew that I should leave, that I should put the book
down, that I should refuse to patronize him. Yet I lacked the poise.
The bookseller had already taken my money. I took the illustrated
guide to the *Star Wars* characters and left quickly, but when I gave
it to the little boy I felt as if I had touched something I should not
have, as if I were giving him a tainted gift.

Among the other Shabbat guests at Rachel and Yonah's apartment one *Star Wars*–filled Saturday was an elderly woman who
had been born in Warsaw in 1915, during the First World War. Now

she lived in Belgium, and today she had returned to Warsaw for the first time in sixty-seven years. Every few sentences she would drift from Polish into French or Yiddish. The place where you were born, she believed, always drew you back. She told us how, in 1961, her husband had taken their savings and gone to Israel to see the trial of Adolf Eichmann, organizer of the Nazis' "Final Solution." Fifteen days later her husband returned, having been unable to bear watching Eichmann in the glass booth.

Mo, whose father survived in the Warsaw Ghetto, was also among Rachel and Yonah's guests that Saturday. He told us of how in April 1943, during the uprising when the ghetto was in flames, his father had encountered a man covered in burns, crying out from pain. The man handed Mo's father a knife and pleaded with him to kill him. It would be a mitzvah, the man whose skin was burning pleaded.

Mo's father stood there before the burning man and deliberated: Was it a mitzvah or was it not? The man claimed it was . . . yet if it were not, to kill a man would be an unforgivable sin. In the end Mo's father did not take the knife. He walked away. But the picture of that man, tortured by his burning skin, dying a slow and agonizing death, tormented Mo's father for the rest of his life.

■ ■ ■

DARIUSZ TOLD ME that I was a true product of modernity: I was homeless. It was spring in Warsaw and we were sitting outside at the Hotel Europejski café. Dariusz was the only one to have ever asked me why I felt so close to Władysław Broniewski, Aleksander Wat, Adam Ważyk, and these other angst-laden futurist poets, to their lives defined by idealism and disillusionment, by faith and betrayal. And so I told him.

"It's a beautiful story," he said.

We talked of the provinces, and I told him of my stay in Domažlice, of how the townspeople had treated me as if I were not quite a person. And Dariusz told me that I could not blame them, for only intellectuals could be held accountable for their prejudices, *we* could be held accountable. But simple people, people in villages—theirs was an innocent xenophobia. They were not responsible.

"At least," he said, "unlike you, they are not homeless."

Dariusz was a Catholic, a believer, a liberal wary at moments of his own liberalism, a historian who lived in enormous gratitude toward his ancestors, who had given him so much while asking for nothing in return. He believed in both God and the devil. When he began to speak of God I thought of the Hasidim doing somersaults, singing of their faith in the coming of the Messiah, dancing along the path to the gas chambers. This, too, was unbearable. It was not their passivity that humiliated them, it was their faith. At this Dariusz smiled.

"Now I finally see," he said, "that you are a believer. I can see it: you accuse God. An atheist would be indifferent."

■ ■ ■

STEPHANIE BECAME INVOLVED in a documentary film project about Gentiles who saved Jews during the Holocaust. One day I went with her to meet an older woman named Pani Jadwiga. I went as her translator, although Stephanie's Polish was getting better every day and soon she would no longer need me. She had a talent for languages. Her mother, herself a hidden child during the war, was a Belgian Jew, a cosmopolitan woman who knew many languages and had spoken French to her daughters.

Pani Jadwiga had two dogs. One of them, whom she had found on the street some fifteen years before, was shy, recovering from an operation. There were bits of yellow around her tail. I talked to Pani Jadwiga about her dogs; they looked as if they were sisters, although they were not.

Gently, always gently, Stephanie began to ask Pani Jadwiga how she had survived the war.

Pani Jadwiga was ashamed that she had to talk to Stephanie through me, she, who had come from an intelligentsia family, a multilingual family: her mother a translator of English literature, her father a famous teacher of Polish philology. Pani Jadwiga, though, had never attended a university. She knew no other languages, she spoke only Polish. After the war, people who had known her father found it shameful that the daughter of the famous teacher had remained uneducated. Pani Jadwiga had become a seamstress.

I wanted to disappear then, so that she would not be ashamed. Instead I looked away from her, toward the small dogs.

Pani Jadwiga showed us a photograph of her mother as a child, dressed up very augustly for such a young girl. In another photograph her father was a toddler, wearing a cape and a cone-shaped hat that made me think of Szymon Zachariasz's strange doodle.

Stephanie was so warm and so sympathetic, and Pani Jadwiga began to slip back, unwillingly yet more and more easily, into the time when she had been a child, into the war. Her family was living then in a village outside Krakow. One night the Germans came for her parents. She clung to her mother's legs, but her mother said, *"Już do cioci!"* She was sending her daughter away: *Right now—to Auntie's house!*

I knew before she told us that these were the last words she ever heard her mother say.

"And that was all," Pani Jadwiga said, but felt she had to explain: She had been taught that when her parents told her to do something, she was to listen. She hadn't wanted to leave them, she had never wanted to abandon them to save herself, it was only that it would have been unthinkable to disobey. Her mother told her, *"Już do cioci!"* And that was that. She ran right under the legs of the German who was holding on to the edge of a washbasin, she ran in her nightgown to the aunt who was not really her aunt but rather a close friend of her family, who lived not so far away, in any case no farther than a few kilometers. And so in the middle of the night little Jadwiga—who was not Jadwiga then—arrived in her nightgown.

Her aunt took her in. She changed the girl's name to the less-Jewish-sounding Jadwiga and fastened a large bow in her hair to distract attention from her Jewish face. But the bow proved inadequate: a local seamstress surmised the truth and blackmailed Jadwiga's aunt and her family. And so Jadwiga was led to a Catholic orphanage carrying a container of sugar and a figurine of the Virgin Mary as a signal to the nuns. Later the nuns told her that her parents would come for her. They never did.

After the war ended Jadwiga boarded a train back to Krakow. She slept on the floor of the train car, using candle wax to kill the mites beneath the wooden planks.

When fifty years later a support group for child survivors of the Holocaust formed in Warsaw, Pani Jadwiga joined it. She did not go to the meetings, though. She was afraid someone—a neighbor, perhaps—would notice her, that someone would spray-paint her door with anti-Semitic graffiti, that around her people would begin to whisper that she was a Jew.

■ ■ ■

HER NAME WAS Nitzana, and I liked how it sounded at once: it conjured up a graceful Jewish femininity. She was fortunate to have close friends. They were a threesome of young women—Nitzana, Malwina, and Izabela—and when they graduated from high school, Nitzana and Malwina went to Warsaw to study French at the university. In the capital, they shared a room. Yet after a month Nitzana left, returning to their small hometown in the eastern provinces. Perhaps she felt insecure about whether she would succeed at the university, where most of the students came from urban intelligentsia families. Or perhaps she disliked city life or was simply homesick. In any case, she returned home, married, and began to study agriculture.

It must have been that same year, or perhaps the next, when the war began. In September 1939 their town in eastern Poland was occupied by the Soviet Red Army. Then in June 1941 the Red Army retreated, and the Wehrmacht arrived. Nitzana, her husband, and their infant daughter were herded into the ghetto. Then the ghetto was sealed. Nitzana escaped with her baby; she ran to her friends, to Malwina and Izabela, who hid her. But Nitzana could not bear life in hiding—the isolation, the claustrophobia, the confinement in the apartment she could never leave, not even for a moment. She returned to the ghetto, to her young husband who was among the Jewish policemen there, and whose fate—her friends believed—she wanted to share to the very end. The baby girl, though, she left with her friends.

Nitzana's parents were among the first to be taken. Her mother died during the transport; her father survived the transport to die in the gas chambers of Treblinka. Then they came for Nitzana and her husband. When she reached the train, Nitzana poisoned herself—and Izabela thought this was as it should have been. I didn't learn if Nitzana had offered to share the poison with her husband, if he refused it, or if she needed it all for herself. He did not take his own life as Nitzana did, though: he boarded the transport to die in the gas chambers of Treblinka.

Their baby remained with Malwina and Izabela, who arranged to take little Esterka to an orphanage and then to come for her. They wanted to disguise her past, to erase all traces of the ghetto. And so they did. Malwina and Izabela took care of Esterka in turns; neighbors whispered that the little girl had been born out of wedlock. Perhaps before the war the two young women from the small town would have felt wounded by the gossip, but now it no longer seemed important.

It was spring in Warsaw and Stephanie and I sat in the living room with Pani Izabela and Pani Malwina, who cried, as did Stephanie, as finally did I. Nearly sixty years had passed; Izabela and Malwina were elderly women now. Pani Izabela was sharp, energetic, and dignified.

Pani Izabela's sister had a young son, who became Esterka's older brother, as Stefanek, Pani Malwina's nephew, became Esterka's younger brother. In photographs Esterka and Stefanek had their arms around each other; as young children they were in love. Esterka was a stubborn child who would relent before no one—except for Stefanek. She melted before Stefanek.

Today they no longer remembered each other at all.

Eventually the war ended. Malwina and Izabela found Nitzana's brother, who before the war had left Poland with a group of young Zionists bound for Palestine. Izabela wrote to him, and he answered: yes, he did want his sister's child. In Warsaw the rabbinate was gathering orphaned Jewish children to send to Palestine. The children set off from Warsaw but were detained in Paris: Israel did not yet exist as a state, and the British had blocked Jewish immigration to Palestine. Malwina, who had resumed her study of Romance languages, won a French government grant and went to Paris, where she managed to visit Esterka in the temporary children's home. Esterka seemed to her very unhappy there.

When Esterka finally arrived in Palestine, her uncle was waiting for her. She went to live with him, yet soon he and his wife had their own child, and Esterka was terribly jealous. Esterka's aunt and uncle began to fear that their niece would do harm to the new baby, and they abandoned Esterka to a communal upbringing on a kibbutz.

As the women told the story, I understood how much they regretted having offered Esterka to Nitzana's brother. More than half a century had passed, and they had not forgiven themselves. At the time, though, they had believed it was the right thing: he was the only family the little girl had left. And family was important.

When Malwina returned from her studies in Paris, she went to work at the French embassy in Warsaw. There the Stalinist security apparatus approached her. Would she cooperate? She refused. They threatened her. She lived in perpetual fear and in the end could not endure it. She fell ill with schizophrenia, and I watched the tears well in her eyes, the eyes of a woman now nearly eighty.

■ ■ ■

I WATCHED ANDRZEJ Wajda's film *Korczak*, now for the second time, with my friend Amelia from Harvey's Yiddish class who had come to visit on her way to Vilnius.

"Za pietnaście minut. Idziemy na wycieczkę..." In fifteen minutes. We're going on an outing....

At Umschlagplatz Janusz Korczak and the children from his orphanage boarded the train that would take them to Treblinka. In the film's last scene, the camera suddenly shifted into slow motion, the unrelenting realism was broken, and the cattle car carrying Korczak and the children floated away from the train. The doors opened, the children jumped down, and together with Dr. Korczak they bounded into a lush field, toward a sunlit clearing.

The ending was not in color—I had colored it in my mind, yet even so I agreed with the critics: I did not like the aura of redemption the fantasy ending implied. The walk to Umschlagplatz, the trains—the film should end there, with this abyss.

A few days later I joined Amelia in Vilnius. In 1897, when the Bund had been born there, Vilnius was a city in the Russian Empire. Later, when Czesław Miłosz was a university student there writing catastrophist poetry, it was a city in interwar Poland. Now it was a post-Soviet city, the capital of newly independent Lithuania. Like Bratislava, Vilnius was a small and unintimidating capital, for Eastern Europe a bright and cheerful city, its university painted in pale peaches and yellows. Amelia and I jogged through the city and into an expansive green park filled with trees and flowers. In the evening we went to the Soiuz Pisatelei, the Writers' Union club that by night turned into a small disco where people waltzed to ABBA songs and danced cheek-to-cheek a bit like cartoon characters. There was a soft wildness to the dances, conjuring up an Andy Warhol–like aesthetic. Smoky air and Lithuanian-accented Russian.

In the stores of Vilnius everyone spoke Lithuanian, yet when Amelia and I entered the large restaurant where a Passover seder was being held, I heard only Russian: the language of Lithuania's atheist Jews. Everyone began to eat at once, and soon I realized there would be no seder, per se—no one even read the Four Questions, although the text was distributed in Cyrillic transliteration of Hebrew. After the kiddush over the wine, a woman in gold lamé with spike heels took the microphone and began to sing. She was accompanied by flashing lights, fake smoke, and a disco klezmer band playing pop versions of Red Army war songs.

"Israeli kitsch meets Soviet kitsch," a professor of Yiddish remarked to us, although I saw little that was Israeli about it. There was something almost degrading, and yet at once strangely appealing, about these post-Soviet remains of a once-vibrant Jewish tradition. The band played "Rock Around the Clock" and Amelia and I joined in the dancing. It was a disco seder.

■ ■ ■

THE MOST SIGNIFICANT issue of Bogna's magazine, *Jidełe*, appeared in print only after her departure to Israel: it was the issue devoted to "the grandchildren of Judeo-Bolshevism." The twenty-something editors of *Jidełe*—Bogna and her friends—had organized a discussion among Polish Jews of their own generation on the topic of Jews and communism. Bogna coauthored the introduction:

> *Often it is repeated to us that a Jew who becomes a communist ceases to be a Jew. Not wanting to become entangled in a futile discussion about the Jewishness of Jewish communists, we must be aware of a fundamental fact: a considerable, if not the dominant, portion of ourselves, people regarding themselves as young Polish Jews, have grandfathers and grandmothers who were once engaged in creating a communist system.*

Bogna's coeditor began the discussion with a vexed question: *"If we're proud of Freud, how, then, should we treat Jakub Berman?"*

A decade had passed since the revolutions of 1989 had opened the Pandora's box of Poles, Jews, and communism. And yet the discussion was only beginning. The most painful part was still to come.

That spring Jan Gross was visiting again from New York; he and Stephanie were staying with me in Warsaw. One afternoon Jan came back to my apartment carrying a large box: the first copies of his new book, *Neighbors*.

The book was a microhistory. The story took place in Poland's eastern provinces, in a small town called Jedwabne, within just a few days in early July 1941. Hitler's Germany had just broken the Nazi-Soviet nonaggression treaty and attacked the Soviet Union. The Red Army had retreated and the Wehrmacht had just arrived, although the new occupation regime was not quite yet in place. The small town, caught between two totalitarian occupiers, experienced a window of semianarchy. And in that window the newly arrived Germans told the Polish townspeople: they had a few days, they could—or perhaps should—take care of the Jews. It began with stonings and lynchings, with murders by farm tools. Later the townspeople forced several dozen of the strongest Jewish men to take down the Lenin statue; to carry it to the cemetery; to dig a grave for its burial. Then the Poles threw the bodies of those Jewish men into the same grave. Germans were there, not participating, but rather observing, taking photographs—as Franz Konrad would when the Warsaw Ghetto burned.

Then, on the afternoon of 10 July, the local Poles forced Jedwabne's several hundred remaining Jews from their homes and into the town square. The townspeople herded their neighbors into a barn. Then they set the barn on fire.

Neighbors was a "postmodern" book. The graphic details—the burial of the burnt corpses; the brothers playing a clarinet and accordion to drown out the cries of Jewish women and children; the murderers' plucking out a Jew's eyes and cutting off his tongue; the children picked up by the legs and hurled into the fire—Jan himself did not describe. The truly vile images emerged not from his own words. Rather Jan let his sources—the Polish peasants of times past—speak for themselves. The book was a mosaic, a dialogue between the author and his sources, and the contrast between Jan's self-reflective, literary Polish and his sources' rough spoken dialect—full of grammatical mistakes and crude formulations—itself told a story about the historian's position vis-à-vis the ghosts of the past.

That night I joined Stephanie and Jan at the very fashionable Qchnia Artystyczna café attached to a modern art gallery. My former landlord, the painter who was now blind, had recently exhibited there a collection of miniature human figures named *Geonauci*, pensive and smooth and cast in bronze. He had sculpted them in the years since the car accident in Łódź, his hands shaping what his eyes could not longer see. Now at Qchnia Artystyczna Jan saw a colleague who joined us for a time. They spoke about *Neighbors*.

"They'll resent this coming from an outsider," the colleague said to Jan.

"I resent being thought of as an outsider," Jan said.

▪ ▪ ▪

IN JULY MY eccentric and delightful Yiddish teacher Harvey came to Poland. He wanted to see the shtetl where his father had lived before the war, and he had managed to learn that in that small town of still no more than a few thousand people there lived an unofficial town chronicler.

And so when Harvey arrived in Poland he rented a car and we set out to the former shtetl of Nowy Korczyn. There we visited the town chronicler, who was heavy-set with greased-back hair and a belly that hung over his belt. He and his sons kissed my hand when we arrived, in an old tradition of Polish chivalry. He showed us his fourteen homemade volumes—the Chronicles of Nowy Korczyn.

The town chronicler and one of his sons accompanied us to what had once been the synagogue, a simple rectangular construction of stone-covered brick built in the eighteenth century. Amid the ruins a front portico and a pediment recalling a classical Greek temple were still visible.

The chronicler's son was young and bright and sweet. Later, when we were alone, the son told me of how he had been studying to become a priest but had been expelled from the seminary in Krakow: rumors had reached the seminary that his father had been meeting with Jews—Jews making a pilgrimage to the shtetl where their parents and grandparents had once lived. The seminary gave him seven days to leave; he was then quickly drafted into the army. He did not seem bitter, though.

"When God closes a door, then you must look for a window," he told me.

"But Not in the Ovens"

When I returned to the United States in September 2000, I went to Brooklyn to see Aleksander Masiewicki. As we walked from the subway stop to his apartment Aleksander talked to me about his wife, Olga. They had been together for sixty-five years: in Poland, in Russia, in the Soviet labor camps during the war. It had been a very difficult life, but a very good marriage. In all sixty-five years they had been together, he told me, between the two of them there had not been a single bad day—not even in the camps.

I asked him, then, about the camps: in the months after the Red Army had occupied eastern Poland in September 1939, he and Olga had been among hundreds of thousands of Polish citizens deported to forced labor settlements in the Soviet interior, where nearly all froze and suffered from hunger, and many did not survive. They remained there until the general amnesty that followed Hitler's June 1941 attack on the Soviet Union, and the Wehrmacht's march to Moscow. Their Soviet experience had been brutal, yet after the war they returned to Poland as they had left it: as believing communists.

And here in Brooklyn Aleksander Masiewicki explained to me: yes, there were people dying in the Soviet camps, *"ale nie w piecach"* (but not in the ovens). At the time of Auschwitz and Treblinka, this was a nontrivial distinction.

■ ■ ■

IT WAS NOVEMBER in Northern California. A cool, sunny Saturday morning. I was at the farmers' market, buying apples and apricots, when Stephanie, now back in New York, called me on my cell phone to tell me that I should go home right away and see what *Gazeta Wyborcza* had just published.

By then some six months had passed since Jan Gross had brought the first copies of *Neighbors* to my apartment on Mokotowska Street. Since then, very little about the book had appeared in the press. Now I went home and found in the internet weekend edition of *Gazeta Wyborcza* a long interview with the Polish historian Tomasz Szarota.

About *Neighbors* the interviewer said, *"That book is an atomic bomb with a long fuse."*

Now it was happening, I thought.

And it was only now, anticipating the publication of the English version of *Neighbors*, that *Gazeta Wyborcza*'s editor in chief, the former dissident Adam Michnik, relented and decided to pursue the Jedwabne story.

The historian Tomasz Szarota expressed much skepticism about the allegedly minimal role of Germans in the Jedwabne massacre and questioned how some 1,500 strong, healthy people would allow themselves to be led to death by fewer than a hundred people armed only with sticks. He made disparaging comments about Jan's "emotional, essayistic style." Tomasz Szarota did not doubt that the massacre had happened—that the Jews of Jedwabne had died at the hands of their Polish neighbors—but he asked readers to consider the context: a terrorized small town, the local anti-Soviet partisan movement betrayed to the Soviets, the betrayed Polish partisans arrested and murdered by the NKVD, a desire to settle accounts: at the time townspeople had believed that the informer was a local Jew. And there was the ever-present image of "Judeo-Bolshevism," and the widespread belief that the NKVD—the notorious Stalinist security apparatus—was made up of Jews.

The next week, Jan responded in *Gazeta Wyborcza:*

> *Let's say, that in fact a German police battalion was in Jed-*
> *wabne that day and that Poles—under pressure (by local*
> *scum? the town administration? public opinion? German gen-*
> *darmes?), embittered with the conviction that during the So-*
> *viet occupation Jews cooperated with the NKVD . . . murdered*
> *their Jewish neighbors: women, children, old people—everyone*
> *whom they fell upon that day. The first question: Do there exist*
> *some parameters, pressures, and embitterments that would*
> *cause the Jedwabne murder committed by Poles of Jews to*
> *be—"understandable"? Can we imagine a sequence of events*
> *leading to the murder in Jedwabne that would allow us in con-*
> *clusion to say something in the way of "Aha, I understand," or*
> *"It was a monstrous crime, but after all . . . ," or "It's terrible,*
> *unforgivable, well, but yet . . ."?*

That weekend edition of *Gazeta Wyborcza* broke the silence. Soon more than a hundred texts were appearing each month about Jedwabne.

The Polish Catholic Church was divided. Some of the clergy were defensive—and furious.

"Clearly," Cardinal Józef Glemp said of *Neighbors,* "the book was written 'on commission' from someone."

Others felt very differently. Father Stanisław Musiał told Jan that the place of Jedwabne's priest should have been in the barn with the Jews.

In Warsaw, at the Władysław Broniewski Museum, Pan Sławek followed the debate over Jedwabne with pain. He did not doubt Jan's story, and he did not defend the Polish peasants who had killed their Jewish neighbors. He was angered, though, by a public discussion that cast Poles as unreformable anti-Semites.

During the war, when the Polish Home Army courier Jan Karski had risked his own life to bring news of the Holocaust to London and Washington, who—Pan Sławek asked me in a letter—failed to react? And when in London in spring 1943 Szmuel Zygielbojm committed suicide, was this a protest against the murdering of Jews by Poles, or a protest against the Allies' failure to react to the information Jan Karski had brought them?

Pan Sławek apologized for his tone. These were rhetorical questions. We both knew the answers.

"In the whole of this very painful and in fact monstrously muddled issue, one thing still astounds me," Pan Sławek wrote to me that year.

> *Why is it Poles who are regarded as the worst anti-Semites? Why Poles and not the Germans, who planned and carried out the Holocaust? Why not the Soviets, who during the war cynically played the Jewish card.... Why is there not talk about present-day Russian anti-Semitism...? Of course this in no way diminishes our national guilt and responsibility, for the fact that someone else also acts shamefully is no justification for evil deeds.*

We corresponded more about Poles, about Jews, and about anti-Semitism. In Poland I'd encountered American Jewish tourists who would ask me: How can you live in this horrible anti-Semitic country, this country where Poles go to the movies in the place that was once the Warsaw Ghetto, where they live on Jewish graveyards, going about their lives without regard for the dead?

In some way I, too, was offended by the questions. For I saw much more anti-Semitism in Poland than the tourists saw. I saw more because I understood Polish, I knew what the titles of the books being sold on the street meant, I could read the graffiti and the headlines of the right-wing tabloid press. But I also understood how Poles could live here. After all, I lived in Warsaw and I thought about the war every single day—and I also went to the movies.

"On the subject of treating Poland like a cemetery, I agree with you completely," Pan Sławek wrote to me. *"This is all well and good for people who drop in for a short while and very quickly are on their*

way. But regarding the claim that it's so cruel to live a normal life, to have fun, to go to work and such in a place where so many people died, I have one small question: I'm sorry, but what should we do with ourselves? Should all of us emigrate? And besides, it's our cemetery, too."

An older and much respected historian, once an active participant in Solidarity and Jan's longtime colleague, Tomasz Strzembosz, was much more enraged. There was an irony in this, for Jan had first begun to write about Jedwabne for Tomasz Strzembosz's *Festschrift.*

"Did the Polish inhabitants of Jedwabne and the surrounding villages enthusiastically welcome the Germans as saviors?" Tomasz Strzembosz asked Jan. *"Yes, they did! If someone pulls me out of a blazing house in which I could burn to a crisp in seconds, I will embrace and thank that person. Even if the next day I regard him as yet another mortal enemy."*

That was not the only thing Tomasz Strzembosz had to say. There was more: namely, it was understandable that in 1941 the Poles in Jedwabne resented the Jews. After all, twenty-one months earlier the Jews had not mourned the end of the Polish Republic. On the contrary, they had welcomed the Red Army, they had collaborated in deporting Poles to Soviet labor camps.

Jan was very angry. It was not true, he argued, that it was the Jews who had sent Poles to Siberia. After all, Polish Jews had been overrepresented among the victims of those deportations, they had suffered at least as much as non-Jewish Poles had under the Soviet occupation.

"The whole stereotype of Jews supporting the Bolsheviks and communists," Jan told Tomasz Strzembosz, *"is nonsense."*

But the colleague with whom Jan had once had warm relations did not accept this. That the Jews had suffered as well under the Soviet occupation regime hardly meant that Jews had not collaborated with that regime.

"Why?" Tomasz Strzembosz asked. *"Because that was a system that devoured its own children."*

Jan was misunderstood, portrayed by his critics as a Polish-Jewish émigré who relished the opportunity to expose Poles as anti-Semites. The truth was in some sense the opposite: Jan very much felt himself to be a Pole. Wandering upon that first account of the Jedwabne massacre in the archives had been devastating for him. He was haunted by the Jedwabne story—and by why his friends and his colleagues, why he himself, had left that material untouched for so long.

"I have one question," Jan at a certain moment asked Tomasz Strzembosz and other colleagues. *"How is it that for fifty years not a single historian dealing with the German occupation and Polish-Jewish relations has uttered so much as one word on the dramatic fate of the Jews of Jedwabne? This question is addressed to you in particular, Tomasz, because as a historian you cover not just that period but that very region. Why have you never written about it? Didn't you know anything about it?"*

Tomasz Strzembosz defended himself. He was not a historian of Polish-Jewish relations. He had been writing about other things, in particular about the Polish opposition to Soviet occupation between 1939 and 1941, before the Jedwabne massacre.

He added, *"If I had gone any further, I might have been found dead in the mud. That was made clear to me."*

Jan refused to accept this.

"In spinning these reflections," Jan said, *"I am in no way attempting to affix onto Strzembosz the label of an ignoramus. Because the conjecture of ignorance is a very kind explanation for the silence about the fate of the Jews in his work. An alternative hypothesis would be that he knew about the fate of the Jews and wrote nothing."*

Tomasz Szarota, the historian whose interview in *Gazeta Wyborcza* had opened the Jedwabne debate, responded to Jan's question as well.

"Gross cannot understand," Tomasz Szarota wrote, *"why no one had studied Jedwabne earlier. After all, he says, it was enough to go there, go into some corner bar, and start talking with people. My answer to that is that history is not written by going into bars."*

A meeting was held at Warsaw's Historical Institute. Jan was there. And Tomasz Strzembosz. And Tomasz Szarota. And Marek Edelman.

Afterward Tomasz Szarota wrote, *"I must candidly admit to the participants in the meeting at which Professor Gross took part at the Tadeusz Manteuffel Historical Institute, where I have worked for thirty-eight years, that it was one of the most unpleasant experiences of my life."*

▪ ▪ ▪

WHEN TOMASZ STRZEMBOSZ insisted to Jan that it was the Polish Jews who had collaborated with the Bolsheviks, Jan asked him in return, *"Do you think Wanda Wasilewska, one of the main collaborators, attended synagogue?"*

Like many others, this, too, was a rhetorical question.

Wanda Wasilewska was not Jewish at all. And she was indeed one of the main collaborators.

A fascinating figure who chain-smoked and drank endless cups of black coffee, Wanda Wasilewska captured my imagination with her inimitable amalgam of Stalinist dogmatism and feminine sentimentality, her philo-Semitism and her various lovers, her passionate ideological convictions and her peculiarly moving friendship with the poet Władyław Broniewski's wife, Janina Broniewska.

During the war Wanda Wasilewska was a fervent believer in the Soviet project—she was Stalin's confidante, and some said his lover as well. When in April 1940, in newly Soviet Lvov, the NKVD "accidentally" murdered Marian Bogatko, her more skeptical husband, she accepted their apology and never wavered in her loyalty to the Soviet Union.

When I'd visited him in Krakow, Czesław Miłosz had not wanted to speak of Wanda Wasilewska and Janina Broniewska at all.

"I don't want to hear of those two women," he told me.

Of Janina Broniewska he said only, "One of the most dangerous females." Of Wanda Wasilewska he added, "I feel a horror at the very mention of this name."

Janina Broniewska and Władysław Broniewski had one child, a daughter named Anka. She died tragically young, while in her twenties, yet not before she herself had given birth to a daughter named Ewa. After Anka's death, Janina Broniewska raised her granddaughter. The letters Wanda Wasilewska wrote to Janina Broniewska, Pan Sławek told me, had never been given to the Broniewski Museum. Likely they remained in Pani Ewa's possession.

Pan Sławek learned that Pani Ewa, by then around fifty, had recently married a man from Greece and had gone to live with him by the Aegean Sea. I wrote to her there, and she answered me. We began to correspond about her grandmother and about Wanda Wasilewska. Their letters, Pani Ewa told me, were not easy to decipher.

> *The correspondence is a dialogue between two intelligent, emancipated women, who wittily and in a specifically women's way describe their daily lives: writing, home, children, later grandchildren. They smuggle political information in a way so complicated and known only to themselves, that to this day no one apart from them has been able to decipher it.*

Her grandmother, Pani Ewa told me, had been married three times. All three husbands disappointed her.

"*She was a strong woman,*" Pani Ewa wrote.

> *She taught that to me. And I taught it to my daughter . . . even though my grandmother would caution: Remember—the weak, fragile ones come out ahead, as for the strong ones, men know that they'll always manage on their own. And here my grandmother would tell of how, at the beginning of the war, her two husbands, en route to the front, appeared in turn (and my grandmother had her ten-year-old daughter from her first marriage and was pregnant with her second husband's child) and both of them voiced more or less the same text: Oh, but you're so capable, you'll certainly manage on your own.*

Janina Broniewska looked down upon weakness. She was disdainful of hysteria and unhappy with Władysław Broniewski's behavior at their daughter Anka's funeral: his sobbing, his throwing of himself at the coffin. In the presence of other people, Janina did not cry. Nothing broke her. It was her philosophy that even when faced with the most horrific dramas one had to pick up the pieces and move on.

Pani Ewa's grandmother was wise and competent, responsible to a fault, the one person her granddaughter could trust completely. She insisted on honesty and transparency. On courage. Wanda Wasilewska was similar. Both women could not stand anything that contained the slightest trace of "bourgeois mentality": artificiality and pretentiousness.

From her childhood Pani Ewa remembered Wanda Wasilewska as a large woman with big feet, friendly and warm, surrounded by the aroma of perfumes.

The perfumes surprised me. But that was only one side. Janina and Wanda were honest and straightforward, they treated Ewa with warmth and friendship. Yet there were secrets, things they shared only with each other. As a girl, Janina's granddaughter was jealous of their conversations, from which she was so often excluded.

"After all," Pani Ewa wrote, *"those were the Stalinist years."*

They were years when adults did not speak of politics around children. About Wanda Wasilewska's much-adored second husband, murdered by the NKVD, Ewa was only ever told, *"Marian perished."*

About her grandmother's precise role during the Stalinist years Pani Ewa knew little. Until today she felt that period of her life to be a dark hole: the secrets kept by adults, the death of her mother, her loneliness. She disliked returning to those times.

"I slammed them behind me," she wrote in one letter, *"like a heavy door."*

Pani Ewa's own political coming of age came in Warsaw in March of 1968. It was her first year at the university, where she was studying sociology. She was nineteen years old then, already married to a fellow student and eight months pregnant with their child.

It was because she had a doctor's appointment that morning that she arrived late to the university, where the demonstration protesting the arrest of Adam Michnik and other students had already begun. She was looking for her husband. Instead she heard the clicking of boots, then saw the lines of armed militiamen coming toward her. With her enormous stomach, she began to run in the direction of the library. The militiamen with their shields and helmets and batons chased her, and she was saved only by a librarian who pulled her into the building and slammed the door. Through the windows of the library she saw, then, students being beaten, covering their heads, the screaming and the blood, then the glass from the shattering windows falling into the library.

When she and her husband returned home, Janina said to them: *"Kids, this is a provocation, these are jousting matches inside the Party. Don't let yourselves be so foolishly exploited."*

"Of course," Pani Ewa wrote, *"we didn't want to listen."*

On behalf of her unborn child, Ewa was more cautious after that. Her young husband, though, continued to take an active part in the student demonstrations. They continued to live with Ewa's grandmother, who did not interfere. Janina Broniewska believed they were adults and had a right to decide. She did more than that, though. She also took in her granddaughter's friend, a student of Polish literature with a three-month-old daughter. The young woman's husband was among the arrested university students, and she and her baby found themselves homeless. Ewa gave birth as well, and for some time they all lived together. Pani Ewa believed her grandmother—a former teacher and the author of children's books—enjoyed having the two infants at home. She had always liked children.

I wanted to know: How did Janina Broniewska—who had so many Jewish friends—come to terms with March 1968?

Pani Ewa had no answer. She knew only that those were no longer her grandmother's times, that her grandmother's times had *"ended together with Stalinism."*

Her grandfather, on the other hand, had he still been alive, would have certainly been in the university courtyard, demonstrating with the students. Władysław Broniewski was an incorrigible romantic. Pani Ewa had no doubts: *"Had he lived to see Solidarity, he would have been in the front row, bolting to the shipyard—and perhaps would have even ended up in prison yet again."*

Later, in the 1970s, when as a young woman Ewa joined the opposition, her grandmother looked on with concealed affection. She told her granddaughter that what Ewa was doing now reminded her of her own youth. Yet Janina Broniewska remained, until the very end, on the "other side of the barricade."

All her life Pani Ewa fled from the awareness of what Wanda Wasilewska and her grandmother had done. All of her life she tried to separate what was private—her grandmother's care and wisdom, her love and their bond—from the role her grandmother had played in Poland's history.

> *Wanda Wasilewska knew Stalin. She had to have known that this man was a monster. She knew about the crimes. It was true that she did pull people out of prisons and camps. She helped individuals, but she remained in a system where political crime was the daily bread. . . . This is the distant past, but for me it remains on the frontier of horror or socio-psychological science fiction. Why did Wanda and my grandmother, knowing about the monstrosities, not recoil? Perhaps, as in the Mafia, past a certain degree of involvement there was no turning back?*

Pani Ewa never spoke to her grandmother about Jakub Berman. She avoided conversations about the war and the Stalinist years that followed. She never read the books her grandmother wrote during her years as a war correspondent in the Soviet Union. She never read her grandfather's famous poem about Stalin. She avoided reading about Wanda Wasilewska. So many times people had attacked her for her grandparents' past—as if grandchildren could somehow go back in time and undo the sins of their grandparents. Of course she herself bore responsibility for nothing. Everything had happened either before her birth, or when she was too young to have taken part. She knew that. And yet it was difficult to escape the guilt.

■ ■ ■

PANI EWA SENT me the letters Wanda Wasilewska had written to her grandmother. I learned to decipher the handwriting; it became familiar. By then I could also distinguish Adolf Berman's handwriting from that of his brother. I knew that Wanda Wasilewska chain-smoked, that Aleksander Wat's wife, Ola, mixed chocolate into her coffee, that in the interwar years the editor of the best literary weekly brought his two small dogs with him to Café Ziemiańska.

I read Władysław Broniewski's letters and those of his friends and sometimes wondered: Did they need to be so harsh? Sometimes I became irritated at their pretensions, their condescension, their graphomania. At other times I was overwhelmed with sympathy for their angst, their suffering, their guilt—the whole enormity of their drama. For after all, how could one be dispassionate about revolution? The question I asked during my lecture at the Władysław Broniewski Museum I continued to ask to the futurist-turned-communist Aleksander Wat, when later in his life he descended into despair at his unbearable guilt: *But tell me, who managed to escape from those times with clean hands?*

Yet there were others, like Adolf Berman's younger friend, the Catholic resistance activist Władysław Bartoszewski. His moral clarity. He never agonized, never vacillated, what was right was illuminated for him.

Slowly I began to see the arc of how their story unfolded.

■ ■ ■

IN AUTUMN OF 1922 the young poet Władysław Broniewski made the acquaintance of the "extreme futurist" Aleksander Wat. In December 1922 Broniewski noted in his diary that at Café Ziemiańska he had been meeting with a small group of writers, Wat among them: *"All Yids. People of much intelligence and erudition.... I have benefited much from that—above all because I've become acquainted with the new Russian poetry.... Mayakovsky, the most important of them all, has revealed to me completely new worlds."*

At that time, in the new Polish capital there lived a small group of young futurist poets, Poles and cosmopolitans, often "non-Jewish Jews." They lived in a city of cafés and cabarets, of rickshaws and streets paved with cobblestones; they dabbled in nihilism and catastrophism. They were the avant-garde of Milan Kundera's imagination, possessed by the ambition to be in harmony with the future.

Soon the Krakowian Bruno Jasieński met the Warsaw futurists. Jasieński had returned home to Poland after having spent his teenage years in Russia; in Krakow he went to the university, where he soon became a futurist. He was the dandy, nineteenth-century elegance dressed in black with a top hat and a wide tie and a monocle on one eye. Girls fell for him.

Older writers accused the futurist poets of snobbism, of imitating foreign fashion. Yet this charge was not nearly the harshest. Later critics would accuse the avant-gardists of having been harbingers of Stalinist culture. For it was the avant-garde who had striven for transparency, who had sought to erase the boundary between art and life. Now art aspired no longer to represent life but rather to transform it—and it was the crossing of this boundary that was the fatal step.

One evening the futurist Aleksander Wat met the lovely young drama student Ola at a drama school ball. She was said to be among the most beautiful women in Warsaw: her dark features were exquisitely delicate, her eyebrows were tweezed into thin moons. Afterward he ran to a friend with the wonderful news: such a beautiful girl—and she wanted him! The girl who had aspired to become an actress gave up her dowry to marry the young futurist. Years after Aleksander Wat had swallowed many pills and left a note for Ola pleading with her not to save him, she wrote of how she would get goose bumps whenever she thought that she might not have been at that ball, she might never have met him, and her life would have been wasted.

I found photographs. It was true: Ola was very beautiful, dark hair and dark eyes against porcelain features.

They were all young when they met. It was a time of decadence, experimentation, carnival. None of them would escape with clean hands. All of them would die too young—beginning with their Russian futurist friend Vladimir Mayakovsky.

The futurists introduced Pani Ewa's grandfather Władysław Broniewski to Mayakovsky's poetry. Soon all of Café Ziemiańska, the waiters as well, were reciting Mayakovsky's "Left March"—*Left! Left! Left!* resounded throughout the café. The mesmerizing Russian futurist—the rhythm of his words—seduced them with revolution. Radical nihilism and radical contingency proved unbearable; in the end they could not endure it. They fled. From nihilism and contingency to utopianism and determinism. It was in the air: the existential imperative to make a choice.

The choice itself, my professor Sepp said to me, was not as important as the act of choosing.

Sepp was of Pani Ewa's generation: born in the years after the war, afflicted with a feeling of guilt by contiguity. When Sepp was a child it had been his grandfather whom he'd loved the most. And this grandfather, Sepp told me one day in his ebullient English that was always so fresh precisely because it was a little bit off, "was a big-ass Nazi," a member of Hitler's party since the 1920s. Sepp had been a talkative child, and it was from his grandfather that he'd learned to tell anti-Semitic jokes and repeat stories of Jewish conspiracies. He was only a boy of ten or so when his grandfather died, but later there was his *Doktorvater*, Hans-Robert Jauss, the famous literary theorist and—it eventually emerged—a former member of the SS.

"*I began to become obsessed,*" Sepp wrote, "*with the famous question how I would have acted myself before 1945—if somebody like Jauss, by whose mind I felt so attracted, had been a Nazi until the apocalyptic end.*"

Sepp, the very European intellectual from Bavaria, had decided to take American citizenship. It was his final act of atonement for a certain *"shameful moral contiguity between my birth on the one hand and the Third Reich and the Holocaust on the other."*

"They're all smoking, aren't they?" Sepp asked me after he'd read the first chapter of my dissertation.

In the microfilm room I read the *Literary Monthly*, the Marxist journal Aleksander Wat edited between 1929 and 1931. The paper appeared for only twenty issues—two of which were confiscated. Aleksander Wat never joined the Communist Party, yet for the rest of his life he was unable to escape the guilt of having been that legendary paper's editor.

On the pages of the *Literary Monthly* Wat recanted his decadent, anarchistic futurist youth: futurism was *"the crooked mirror in which Caliban gazed at himself with a grimace of abomination."*

The saddest issue was the one dedicated to the Russian poet Vladimir Mayakovsky.

It was neither Marx nor Lenin but rather the breathtakingly handsome Russian futurist who had brought the Polish avant-garde poets to the Revolution. In the spring of 1927, Mayakovsky had paid a visit to Warsaw. He was their most passionate love affair—a love affair that was, the Polish poets believed, the beginning of the future, of the new world.

Mayakovsky was an enormity, and at once tender, those large hands, but most moving of all was his voice. Rooms trembled when he read his poetry. *"A superhuman of cosmic melancholy,"* Aleksander Wat described him. In that colossal voice was the threshold of the new world.

"I assume," Wat said of an evening that spring with Mayakovsky, *"that chills went up the spines of quite a few of the people there, for that truly was an imperious power. That wasn't a man, that wasn't a poet; that was an empire, the coming world empire."*

Bruno Jasieński was not there. He was no longer in Warsaw; he met Mayakovsky in Paris, where he lived in the lower Montmartre, by the Impasse de la Poissonnière. There he wrote *I Burn Paris*, the wild apocalyptic tale of a deathly plague transmitted via contaminated water that destroyed the debauched, bourgeois European capital; only those in prison—the communists—were spared. For this the French deported him, and Jasieński forsook returning to Poland in favor of arriving as a hero in Leningrad.

When in Moscow in April 1930 Vladimir Mayakovsky took his own life, the first detail that reached the Polish poets who so loved him was the phrase from his suicide note *"liubovnaia lodka / razbilas' v byt'"* (The love boat / crashed against the everyday).

My Russian friend Ksenia wrote to me from Moscow, enclosing a newspaper clipping: the last photograph of Mayakovsky's lover and muse. In the photograph the incomparable Lilia Brik was already a very old woman with a gaunt face and thick eyebrows, her long hair pulled into a low ponytail, heavy necklaces resting beneath her throat. She wore dark clothing, and she sat with her arms on the armrests of a large chair, gazing not into the camera but elsewhere.

I fell in love with Mayakovsky from his 1910 photograph, in his black cape and cone-shaped hat. I imagined his deep, sonorous voice, the voice to move civilizations.

"Why are you American girls all in love with Mayakovsky?" the middle-aged Russian woman working at Mayakovsky's archive in Moscow asked me.

I only smiled, embarrassed, and handed her my file requests. But I thought: How could one *not* fall in love with Mayakovsky?

In September 1931 the police interrupted a *Literary Monthly* editorial meeting and arrested the editorial staff. Now came their much-anticipated ritual baptism in prison. Ola Watowa sent care packages with notes for her husband tucked inside the head of a herring. Władysław Broniewski sat in the cell, translating Gogol and reciting his own poetry. He was that kind of poet, Aleksander Wat remembered, the best kind—poetry in any circumstance.

When they were released several months later, they began receiving invitations again to receptions at the Soviet embassy, where the Soviet diplomats fed them caviar.

When a Polish writer visited Moscow, the dandy Bruno Jasieński hosted an extravagant dinner party in his filthy apartment. A table set with silver and crystal and glasses bearing the insignia of the last emperor; the table strained from their weight. Beluga caviar and crystal. Spiderwebs covering the iron doors of the stove. There was no need to freeze the vodka; there was frost in the room.

Sepp wanted to know: What kind of caviar did Bruno Jasieński serve that night? Was it red or black?

How could I know? I didn't.

There were not many dinner parties remaining for Bruno Jasieński. Nineteen thirty-seven arrived, the year of the Great Terror. Bruno Jasieński was arrested. In prison they tortured him. In September he confessed to Polish nationalist sympathies and espionage on behalf of Polish counterintelligence. Several days later he recanted his testimony: in confessing to crimes he had not committed, he had hoped to buy himself a speedier death. In January 1938, in a prison cell awaiting execution, he wrote of his favorite poet Vladimir Mayakovsky, who had brought him to the October Revolution.

In the archives I found a crushed fly inside Bruno Jasieński's NKVD file.

Interwar Warsaw came to an end. Occupied on one side by the Germans, on the other by the Soviets, Poland disappeared from the European map. Most of the once-futurist poets and their friends fled east, to the city of Polish Lwów, which quickly became Soviet Lvov. In the opulent Hotel George, in the center of the once-cosmopolitan Habsburg city of Lemberg, the Ukrainian playwright and apparatchik Oleksandr Korneichuk, charged with organizing cultural affairs, held court.

In now-Soviet Lvov a friend who was a stage designer invited the Polish poets to a dinner party at a fashionable restaurant. Aleksander Wat was curious: Perhaps it was his birthday? The scenographer refused to reveal the occasion: it was to be a surprise. That evening he was especially generous, ordering delicacies and vodka for everyone. Then someone provoked a brawl. Aleksander Wat was hit in the jaw. Blood poured from his face; he collapsed. Adam Ważyk, now the editor of a Stalinist newspaper, helped Ola to revive him. The scenographer fled the restaurant. Aleksander Wat and Władysław Broniewski were among those arrested, driven in a black limousine to prison. Having been communists in interwar Polish prison, now they were Polish nationalists, Jewish nationalists, Zionists, Trotskyites, spies, and provocateurs in Soviet prison.

The chain-smoking Wanda Wasilewska went to Stalin to try to help her friends the poets. It took, however, quite some time.

After Nazi Germany attacked the Soviet Union, those not in prison fled still farther east, into the Soviet interior. A southern Russian city named Kuibyshev became a gathering point for the Polish communist intelligentsia: Janina Broniewska and Wanda Wasilewska went there, as did Adam Ważyk. Later they all moved to Moscow.

Jakub Berman, Aleksander Wat's Communist Party tutor from the days of the *Literary Monthly*, grew close to Wanda Wasilewska during the war, at a time when both of them were close to Stalin. Wanda Wasilewska and Jakub Berman were, perhaps, lovers, although—as Jakub Berman said in his last interview—this was not the point. Jakub Berman and Janina Broniewska were not lovers, but they did—together with Adam Ważyk—become postwar dictators of cultural policy during the harshest years of Stalinism in Poland.

In June 1941 Nazi Germany broke the Nazi-Soviet nonaggression treaty and attacked the Soviet Union. Now Stalin joined the Allies. That August the Polish government in exile and the Soviet Union concluded an agreement granting amnesty for Polish prisoners in the Soviet Union and permission for the creation of a Polish army. Aleksander Wat was released from prison. After his arrest at the restaurant in Lvov, Ola Watowa and her son had been among those deported from Lvov to a Soviet labor settlement in Central Asia. Eventually the three found one another in Kazakhstan.

When Władysław Broniewski was released from prison, he left for the Middle East with the newly formed Polish army. Soon Broniewski found himself in Jerusalem, surrounded by Polish-Jewish readers from Warsaw who adored him even more in Palestine.

On New Year's Eve of 1954 a friend presented Aleksander Wat with a complete collection of the short-lived *Literary Monthly* and the dedication *"In memory of the shared sins of our youth."*

In Paris, in the summer of 1967, Aleksander Wat swallowed some forty tablets of Nembutal. On the bed, by his feet, he'd left a note for Ola: *"DO NOT SAVE ME."* In the archive I found the small piece of paper, the letters written all in capitals. It was 2001. The bequeather had stipulated that the files be closed until the twentieth century had come to an end.

Children of the Revolution

I arrived in New York during the first week of September 2001.
A few days later, I was in my apartment on the Upper West Side
when the phone rang. A few minutes later I turned on the computer and found a message from my Russian friend Ksenia. She was
a world away in Moscow, watching CNN at her office, and knew
everything I knew at exactly the same moment.

"*It felt,*" Vlasta wrote from Prague, "*as if completely everything in
this world, life, that was valid before, became absurd all of a sudden, unbelievably.*"

Pan Sławek and Mikołaj and Dariusz all wrote to tell me that in
Warsaw, thousands of miles from New York, people were praying
for the victims, lighting candles in their windows, and bringing
flowers to the American embassy. The Polish government declared
three days of official mourning: Polish flags were lowered to half-
mast.

"*Neither America nor the whole world will ever be the same,*"
Mikołaj wrote the next day. "*Yesterday something ended and something began.*"

Pan Sławek wrote that when he saw on television sheets of
paper posted around New York City with pleas for information
about missing people, he was reminded of Warsaw: in 1939 when
the Germans attacked, in 1944 after the uprising. Then, too, people
desperately hoping for news of brothers and sisters, friends and

children, husbands and wives and lovers, hung those sheets of paper, wandered the streets with photographs, in despair . . .

■ ■ ■

AT COLUMBIA UNIVERSITY I spoke with a poetess, a Polish-Jewish émigré from March 1968, about Michał Głowiński's Holocaust memoir, *The Black Seasons*. She was somewhat resentful—not that Michał Głowiński *had* written the book but rather that he *had not* written it for so long.

"He was on 'Aryan papers' until 1996," she said to me. "Why did he take so long to come out of the closet?" "Aryan papers" were falsified identification documents that Jews who escaped from the ghetto during the war used in order to pass as non-Jews.

Later I went to her poetry reading at a Polish bookstore downtown. She read poems in Polish about her Jewish father and about her exile in America. The émigré audience was moved.

"We have you to thank for the fact that now, once again, we feel like Poles," one of the men in the audience told her gratefully.

These were the Polish Jews whom Władysław Gomułka had cast out: those who, over three decades later, above all still wanted to be—who still were—Poles.

■ ■ ■

THAT SPRING OF 2002 I returned to Toronto to give a lecture about the Berman brothers. It had been several years since I'd seen Stefan M., who had advised my master's thesis there and who had first sent me to the Jewish Historical Institute in Warsaw. Now we sat at a café at the university, and Stefan told me once again of how he had met Adam Ważyk's daughter while hiking in the mountains.

"I loved her dearly," he said.

Stefan M. had invited a friend to my lecture. Henry Dasko was a businessman in his fifties. The child of devoted communists, internationalists "of Jewish origin," he had once been Henryk Daszkiewicz—before he had left Poland in the wake of the "anti-Zionist" campaign. He had been a student in Warsaw in March 1968 when his father came home one day and said, *"I just heard Gomułka deliver a pogrom speech."* For Henryk it was unthinkable that his communist father would speak that way about the general secretary of the Party. His father lay down on the sofa, turned his face toward the wall, and barely moved for days.

Henryk Daszkiewicz took an active part in the protests against censorship. After he coauthored a student manifesto, he was expelled from the university and interrogated by the secret police. One night soon thereafter his father said to him and his mother, *"Let's go to the Majewskis'."*

The Majewskis were perhaps not friends but at least acquaintances; their son went to school with Henryk, and they lived nearby. When Henryk's father rang the doorbell, it was the father, an army colonel, who answered the door.

"We'd like to stay the night," Henryk's father said.

"Is it that bad?" asked the colonel.

"I'm afraid it might be," answered Henryk's father.

Henryk and his parents spent that night in the Majewskis' living room, on the hardwood floor, covered by a rug.

A few days later Colonel Majewski came to their apartment and asked Henryk's father for a loan. Henry never learned how his father responded, whether he loaned the colonel the money or not, but even many years—decades—later, in emigration, Henry Dasko never felt free of the shame of that night spent on the Majewskis' living room floor.

Soon afterward, Henryk's father lost his job, and more devastatingly, after having dedicated his entire life to building communism, he lost his Party card.

For his son, the decision to leave or not to leave Poland was the most tormenting of his life. In the end Henryk Daszkiewicz packed a war-vintage hard-shell green suitcase full of books by his favorite Polish writers and exchanged his Polish citizenship for an exit visa.

▪ ▪ ▪

BY SEPTEMBER 2001 Chaim Finkelstein was no longer alive, but in New York Stephanie arranged a meeting for me with his daughter. Awiwa was warm and open. I stood with Stephanie on the balcony of Awiwa's penthouse in Chelsea, and Awiwa showed us where she had watched the World Trade Center burn—and told us of how, fifty-eight years earlier, she had stood on a roof in Warsaw's "Aryan Side" and watched the Warsaw Ghetto burn.

I looked at the black-and-white photograph of Awiwa, her mother and her beautiful older sister—taken in the ghetto during the war, and sent to their father, who was already in America. Only Awiwa survived. She had been hiding in a Polish village. After the war she went to a Jewish committee and mentioned Adolf Berman's name . . . in this way she found her way to her father's old friends, who in turn sent the fourteen-year-old girl to her father in the United States. Awiwa still remembered her prewar Warsaw telephone number, but her Polish—the pure, proper Polish her parents had been so careful to speak to her—had faded.

I'd brought to the apartment copies of the letters her father had written to Adolf Berman during the decades following the war. I offered them to Awiwa hesitantly, guiltily—knowing there were things in them that would hurt her. Who was I to give them to her? And who was I to have them when she did not? I wanted to warn her, but I did not know how. I only asked if she wanted the letters, assured her that of course she need not . . . She did.

▪ ▪ ▪

ON THE FIRST of May 2002, the last remaining Bundists gathered in downtown Manhattan to celebrate the workers' holiday by singing "The Internationale." They wanted me to give a speech and were very disappointed to learn that I was only a friend of the klezmer musician who had come to accompany them on the accordion, that I was a historian and not a revolutionary. For so long they had been waiting for the younger generations to join them.

The klezmer musician introduced me to an elderly man from Warsaw, a Bundist who before the war had known Jakub Berman.

He spoke in Yiddish, but because my Yiddish was not very good I answered in Polish, so the Bundist switched to Polish as well. I began to ask him about the Berman brothers and the broad leftist alliance of the late 1930s that had brought together people like Adolf Berman, Michał Mirski, Wanda Wasilewska, and the Bundist leader Wiktor Alter, but before I could finish the question the elderly man interrupted, "Finally someone is speaking proper Polish!"

Then he lowered his voice: "Everyone here speaks Polish, of course, but badly, ungrammatically . . ."

And suddenly I felt the resilience of that Polish-Jewish snobbery, that phenomenon of the prewar years—nonsensically, absurdly, and yet somehow affectingly still present in twenty-first-century Manhattan.

■ ■ ■

I WANTED TO ask Adolf Berman's erstwhile student Aleksander Masiewiecki for permission to use his letters. I knew this was painful for him, that I was asking for something I had no right to, that my existence in his life was an intrusion. I took Stephanie with me to Brooklyn. I needed her; I sensed that somehow she would make everything better. And she did.

We were both taken with them, Olga and Aleksander Masiewicki, this couple married for sixty-five years who had shared their first kiss in Warsaw's Saxon Gardens, where in the spring I would take walks, pushing Rachel's little baby in a stroller. They had met in 1935, at a student communist gathering held at the home of a friend, a girl whose parents were Hasidim but who herself had chosen Marxism.

For several hours we talked, and Stephanie and I were absorbed by their extraordinarily complicated relationship to Polishness—and to Jewishness. Before the war Aleksander Masiewicki had been obsessed with the weakness, the vulnerability, of the Jews, the Jewish merchants so humiliatingly susceptible to anti-Semitically driven Polish boycotts. Above all, he had believed then, it was necessary for the Jews to become *productive*. It was reminiscent of an Enlightenment-era argument made by an eighteenth-century

Polish philosopher: the Jews could not continue to be parasites, making their living as middlemen, trading in goods created by others; they must engage in productive labor. The communists, too, believed this—as did the Zionists.

I remembered what Aleksander Masiewicki had written to Adolf Berman after arriving in Brooklyn:

> FOR MORE THAN THIRTY-FIVE YEARS, I followed a path that—as it turned out—was deceptive and ruinous. Nonetheless I don't approach my failed past ahistorically. At the time when ideologically, emotionally, and organizationally I joined a movement that foretold so much yet had so little . . . it was the only alternative, the only HOPE. Zionism didn't constitute any alternative. At present it's able to RESOLVE the problem of ten or several tens of thousands of Polish Jews, but at that time it was powerless with respect to Russia's three and a half million. It gave possibilities to individuals, but the fate of a whole nation had to be determined in that land which revealed itself to be inhospitable. And an awareness of that truth led us toward a movement that on its banners inscribed the noblest ideals of humanity—humanism, democracy, internationalism—but whose practice was already then the polar opposite of these ideals. Unfamiliarity or incomplete familiarity with the truth cannot constitute a justification for any of us. As in the great Greek tragedies, we stood before dilemmas, each of which portended disaster.

When after the war, Olga and Aleksander Masiewicki heard news of the pogrom in the Polish town of Kielce, they were unsurprised. They knew Polish anti-Semitism, yet they did not think of leaving Poland.

"We felt ourselves to be Poles," they told us.

It was Stephanie who, before we left, asked Aleksander Masiewiecki if he would agree to let me use his letters. By then he no longer resisted: it had all been so long ago, in another lifetime, in another world . . . the letters no longer mattered. I could use them.

The Taste of Caviar

I was preparing to finish my book about Aleksander Wat, Władysław Broniewski, and Adam Ważyk, about Janina Broniewska and Wanda Wasilewska and the Berman brothers. I had decided I would title it *Caviar and Ashes*. Over the course of a few years I had written several times to Jakub Berman's daughter, Pani Lucyna. There had never been a reply.

Then in February 2002, Jakub Berman's daughter answered me. She had read some of my work and had heard about my lecture at the Władysław Broniewski Museum—and had concluded that there would be little sense in our talking. My perspective, she believed, was ahistorical; I had not tried to grasp the motives for what her father and others had done in a specific time and place, given the alternatives that then existed. *"Especially,"* she added, *"for Jews."*

Something else, too, upset her:

> As far as the effective title of your book is concerned, I'm wondering where the caviar comes from . . . for I remember well what we ate in Moscow: black rationed bread that we stood in lines for hours for and kasha from the cafeteria. If, on the other hand, the caviar is an allusion to the receptions hosted by Stalin, there were two or three occasions, and to my father's taste that was very bitter caviar.

■ ■ ■

THAT SUMMER OF 2002 I went to the Russian archives. One Sunday when Ksenia and I were at the Moscow zoo, looking at the monkeys, Ksenia asked what I would title my book. I told her "Caviar and Ashes," and when she learned that I had never tasted caviar she insisted we buy some at once. At home in her Moscow apartment we unpacked the bag from the delicatessen and set the table. I took only a small bite of the caviar, those tiny eggs, a shimmering, translucent red—and I suddenly understood Sepp's description of flavor exploding inside your mouth; I nearly vomited. No taste had ever been so revolting.

It was not my first visit to Russia. I had first been in Moscow in the fall of 1993, when the capital of what Ronald Reagan had called the Evil Empire did not feel evil but did feel terrifying. Everything was larger than life, the streets grotesquely wide, the metro even deeper and more frightening than in Prague, with its violent turnstile that would assault anyone who did not correctly enter a ticket and its escalators racing down into the depths. The stations had been dug deeply to double as bomb shelters. The city had none of the beauty of Prague. It was dark and miserable. The faces were the mocking inverse of those in the photographs in all the communist-era newspapers: no one was happy. Faces habituated to brutality. I saw a man lying dead in the metro.

When I next returned, seven years later, the city felt less terrifying. Still, inside the vastness of Moscow remained a brutality absent even in Petersburg. Ksenia loved this harsh city, Ksenia who was the antithesis of harshness, who was so delicate. Moscow was her home; it was beautiful to her.

On Arbat Street I spoke to a woman selling puppies. I held one in my hands; he wanted to stay with me, and I wanted to keep him. I asked the woman how much he cost.

"Ty znaesh', chto nevozmozhno," Ksenia told me sadly, pleadingly.

She was right. I knew it was impossible to keep the puppy; I was only in Russia for a few days more. Before I left, Ksenia and I went together to see Lenin's body, a body without blood, so pale, reminiscent of a vampire. At the last moment Ksenia grabbed my hand. I, too, had not been prepared for something so macabre, so grotesque.

∎ ∎ ∎

IN 1940, NIKITA Khrushchev sent two men, Ukrainian communist apparatchiks, to apologize to Wanda Wasilewska for the murder of her husband Marian Bogatko. One of those two men, the playwright Oleksandr Korneichuk, became her third husband. In 2002 I went to Kiev because Wanda Wasilewska had decided to remain there with Oleksandr Korneichuk after the war. It was there that she died in 1964, before her sixtieth birthday.

Kiev was full of fountains and playgrounds, street musicians and churches with gold domes. Linguistically, it was a disorienting city: all of the street signs, the price lists, the advertisements were in Ukrainian—yet all around me I heard Russian. In the cafés the menus were in Ukrainian, while the waiters and waitresses spoke in Russian.

At Babi Yar I saw an enormous monument—and an enormous ditch. So this was where the dead bodies of some thirty thousand Kievan Jews had fallen, one on top of another. A massacre in a ravine. I had not realized that Babi Yar was in the city, in Kiev, not so far from the center, where on Khreshchatyk Boulevard a man had let me hold his pet monkey.

∎ ∎ ∎

AT THE ARCHIVE where her papers remained, I learned that Wanda Wasilewska and Oleksandr Korneichuk had shared not only an apartment in Kiev but also a dacha in the country, not more than an hour away by car. That afternoon I approached a young taxi driver outside a café and asked him to take me there. During the drive I told him I'd come to Kiev from New York, and he asked me if I had been there on September 11. How had I felt? He was the first person I'd met in the former Soviet Union who had asked me this question.

The dacha was now a museum, although since the fall of communism it was a museum that rarely had visitors. When we arrived, the student at the polytechnic university who moonlighted as a taxi driver suggested he wait for me in the car, but I asked him to come with me.

"It could be interesting," I said.

The older woman who let us inside believed we were together, and she was obviously pleased: a young couple interested in Ukrainian history, a young Ukrainian man teaching his American wife about Ukrainian culture. She showed us the bedroom, the bookshelves, Wanda Wasilewska's typewriter. The taxi driver listened attentively, he studied the photographs she showed us, he asked interested questions, and the woman who was the museum's caretaker told us the story of how Ukrainian nationalists had murdered Wanda Wasilewska's husband Marian Bogatko.

"It's not true," I said to the taxi driver during the ride back to Kiev. And I told him the story of Wanda Wasilewska, and how it had been the NKVD who murdered her husband in Lvov, and how Nikita Khrushchev had sent Oleksandr Korneichuk to tell her the truth and to ask for her "understanding." And how she had understood.

■ ■ ■

AT THE DACHA I'd asked the caretaker about Wanda Wasilewska's daughter, Ewa. She told me that yes, Ewa Wasilewska was still alive, and living in Moscow. And she gave me Ewa Wasilewska's phone number.

When I returned to Moscow from Kiev I visited Wanda Wasilewska's daughter. In my mind Ewa Wasilewska was a fourteen-year-old girl who had lied about her age during the war so as to join the Polish division of the Soviet army and do her part to fight the Germans. Now she was a tall, handsome woman with gray hair in her seventies. Even after sixty years of living in Russia, she still spoke beautiful Polish—the Polish of the interwar intelligentsia. She was composed, open, reflective.

Her Moscow apartment, modest and old, had a kind of elegance—as did her small dachshund named Liza, who reminded me of the dogs Warsaw's preeminent literary editor had once brought to Café Ziemiańska. Ewa Wasilewska affectionately described Liza as their *domashnii tyran*—their domestic tyrant.

I asked her about her mother's reaction in 1956, when Khrushchev gave his "secret speech," admitting to Stalin's "excesses."

"*Rozrachunki sama ze sobą,*" Ewa said of her mother's silence then. An interior settling of accounts.

Was her mother Stalin's lover?

Perhaps there had been something between them . . . Ewa herself did not know for certain, she remembered only being a young teenager and listening with hands cupped to the door, when her mother was shut inside a room, speaking on the telephone to the man who was so much more than a dictator.

About the tragic death of Ewa's stepfather in 1940 in Lvov, Ewa Wasilewska's mother never said a single word. To the very end that taboo remained in place between them. And it—the murder, Marian Bogatko's absence, the silence—remained painful: Ewa Wasilewska had loved him very much.

"He was my father," she told me.

Her biological father had died when she was not more than two or three years old; it was the handsome and charming Marian Bogatko who had raised her.

As for her mother's third and last husband, the Ukrainian playwright whom Khrushchev had sent to solicit Wanda Wasilewska's understanding concerning Marian Bogatko's murder—Ewa had not liked him very much at all. After the war, he'd had one affair after another—all of Kiev knew, his wife alone chose blindness to his infidelities. In the end Wanda Wasilewska lived her last years as a tragic figure—a betrayed wife, a foreigner who always spoke Russian with an inelegant accent, a woman without friends in her adopted country.

"I cried when Stalin died," Ewa Wasilewska said to me before I left, "although I quickly calmed down. Those traces of Sovietization, they'll be in us until the very end, making us different from people in the West."

Files

I n fall of 2002 Piotr Sommer, a Polish poet in his fifties who had translated poetry by Charles Reznikoff and Allen Ginsberg and Frank O'Hara, came to Bloomington, Indiana, to give a poetry reading. Piotr reminded me of Jan: his expressive hand gestures, his soft disposition, his gentle eloquence. In Indiana Piotr read a poem called "A Visit." It was a poem about Piotr's friends who had left Poland after March 1968. In the poem one friend played the violin, another friend played the cello.

"Oh, everyone played," Piotr read, *"until they went away."*

■　■　■

THAT SPRING OF 2003 my colleagues at Indiana, where I now taught, organized a roundtable about the politics of cultural expression after communism. I invited Paul Wilson, the Canadian who had been the lead singer of the Plastic People of the Universe and who since then had been Václav Havel's English translator. I'd last seen Paul seven years earlier, when he came to the Czech Living Room Seminar at Gordon Skilling's apartment. By now Gordon was no longer here. In January 2001 he'd written to me, telling me of how much the seminar had meant to him those past years. Six weeks later, he died in his Toronto apartment. He would have turned ninety on his next birthday.

Now it was spring of 2003, and I spent the evening at a bar in

Bloomington with Paul Wilson, listening to tales of the Plastic People of the Universe's legendary band manager Ivan Jirous. Paul was not at all pretentious; on the contrary, he was self-effacing—with respect to his singing, but also his understanding of the work he had translated for many years. Paul was not a philosopher; he had always struggled with Havel's Heideggerian allusions. There was a deep irony in Havel's literary career: only now—when communism was over, and Havel had become president—did Paul feel self-censorship in Havel's writing.

A singer and actor named Florian, who wore his pale gray hair tied in a ponytail, had come for the roundtable from Bucharest. He spoke of how, in Romania in the 1950s, he would go to see news clips about America's exploitation of blacks—news clips showing the Harlem Globetrotters and Bill Haley and Comets singing "Rock Around the Clock." Florian hated Creedence Clearwater Revival because their music was played on the official Romanian radio station—and they must be stupid if the communists were playing them.

Florian spoke, too, of literature: the novels that could not be written during the communist years—the novels Romanian writers had dreamt of writing—were not being written now either. The moment had passed: they were novels that had existed only in their impossibility.

After the roundtable we all went to dinner at an Italian restaurant on Fourth Street in Bloomington. As I talked to Florian, I remembered Vera from Bucharest, the folk rock band playing at the open-air jazz club on the roof of a tall building in the city center, the Romanian Bob Dylan with the most beautiful voice I'd ever heard.

"Oh my God," I said to Florian suddenly, "you're the man on the roof!"

And it was true: he was.

▪ ▪ ▪

I HAD NOT answered Jakub Berman's daughter's letter, telling me she saw little sense in a conversation between us. A year and a half later, though, when I returned to Warsaw, I wrote to her again. This time she left me a phone message: "I am ready to talk to you. Call me."

Now I sat in the living room while Pani Lucyna made tea. Most of her family, she told me, had died in the Holocaust, including her six-year-old cousin, a little girl named Lena. Until today, every time she passed Umschlagplatz, where sixty years earlier trains had gathered before setting off for Treblinka, she saw Lena's face.

In person Jakub Berman's daughter was condescending but not hostile. Her feelings about me had not changed: I was someone who understood nothing. She did not know how I had been taught history. In Poland, though, historians were trained to approach their sources critically—which I had obviously not done. I had not tried to understand the *motivations* of her father and his generation—she told me—their sensitivity to human suffering, their selflessness, their devotion to a greater cause. She did not believe I could ever appreciate the sincerity of her father's idealism, his faith, his nobility of purpose. Nor did she believe I could ever understand the torment, the schizophrenia, of being both a Pole and a Jew.

Nearly a half century earlier, Pani Lucyna had learned she was pregnant. It was just after the trial of Rudolf Slánský, when her father knew he could be next in line—Wanda Wasilewska had even traveled from Kiev to warn him. Jakub Berman wished then only that he would live long enough to see the birth of his grandchild.

Pani Lucyna was hurt by what I had written; it was—she told me—"ethically unfortunate." She had loved her father very much. I could feel, as she talked, that he must have been a very good father to her.

■ ■ ■

JAKUB BERMAN'S DAUGHTER told me that even after her father was cast out of the Party in 1957, Janina Broniewska still came to their apartment for dinner, that she was faithful to Pani Lucyna's father.

It was rare in Poland to find anyone who had a kind word to say about Janina Broniewska—or about Wanda Wasilewska.

"Wanda Wasilewska was a mean bitch," Kostek told me.

I had gone to visit him in his spacious apartment not far from the university; we were sitting in his study, surrounded by books. Kostek's mother had served in the second Polish division that had fought alongside the Red Army, the Polish division whose existence Wanda Wasilewska herself had brought about. Kostek's mother had lain in the trenches and shot at Germans.

"It was her division," Kostek told me, "who was present at the liberation of Majdanek. When she arrived, the ovens were still hot. For her the choice was clear: the gulag or the gas chambers. And people came back from the gulag . . ."

And I thought about what Aleksander Masiewicki had said to me in Brooklyn: yes, people were dying in the Soviet camps, *but not in the ovens.*

■ ■ ■

IN DECEMBER 2003 I received permission to see Jakub Berman's secret police file. It was only then, sitting in the reading room of the Institute of National Remembrance, where the communist-era Ministry of Interior files now were kept, that I appreciated for the first time the primitivism of the secret police, their reliance upon uneducated functionaries who could not write in correct Polish and who themselves did not understand what Trotskyism meant, what Zionism meant, what Marxist revisionism meant.

In Jakub Berman's file from 1968 I found a forged speech, attributed to Jakub Berman and dated April 1945. It was written with spelling mistakes, in miserably awkward Polish, a Polish that no one as educated as Jakub Berman ever would have used. In the forged speech Jakub Berman advised Jews on how to take power from behind the scenes:

Jws [sic] have the chance to take the whole of state life in Poland into their own hands and extend their control. Not to push themselves into representative positions. In the ministries and agencies to create a so-called second team. Take on Polish names. Hide their Jewish origins. Create and disseminate among Polish society the opinion—and confirm Polish society in the conviction, that it's the Poles thrust out front who are ruling, and Jews are playing no role. . . . Regard anti-Semitism as the primary betrayal and condemn it at each step. If it's claimed that some Pole is an anti-Semite, liquidate him immediately with the aid of the security organs.

An informer quoted a comment Jakub Berman allegedly made during the events of March 1968: *"After all, half of the room wanted heads to throw to the lions. Because that's how it is here."*

In November of 1968 Jakub Berman was followed to Powązki Cemetery, where he was seen laying flowers on Bolesław Bierut's grave.

"Berman gives the impression of a man depressed, lost in thought," the informer noted.

The agents' reports revealed their authors to be generally neither knowledgeable nor savvy. The seemingly omnipotent secret police, who terrorized so many for so long, seemed to rely not on acumen but rather on large numbers: everything appeared more or less indiscriminately to interest them. They conducted extensive surveillance of enormous numbers of people. They noted that even though an aging former futurist had one affair after another, his wife continued to love him. They kept lists of writers and artists suspected of homosexual proclivities. They noted what their "figures under observation" ate for breakfast, who sat with whom at the cafés, whether they looked happy or sad.

And very often it seemed to the agents that the "figures under observation" did look sad. In 1963 the poet Adam Ważyk, who in 1939 became the editor of a Stalinist newspaper in Lvov and later wrote the bitter "A Poem for Adults," gave a poetry reading in a small town. An informer wrote that Adam Ważyk's tone created a depressive mood among the listeners there. At the conclusion of the reading a local poet asked Adam Ważyk why, as a former avant-gardist, he avoided this topic, and also why all his work seemed to have a depressive character. Adam Ważyk, according to the report, *"provided no concrete answer, making it understood, however, that he'd become disillusioned with life."*

The same year an informer noted that one of Adam Ważyk's friends had encouraged him to write his memoirs but that Ważyk was disinclined. He felt *"disgust for all of that." "All of that"*—his own past.

Thirteen years later, a 1976 report repeated verbatim the words of a report from 1965: *"From Adam Ważyk's words it ensues that in his own work he's always aspired to pure art, to art of justice, to art without ideology, to the 'full freedom of the writer.'"*

Perhaps the functionary had simply run out of things to write, the life of this broken old man having ceased to provide new material.

In another 1976 report an informer wrote that, as ordered, he had made contact with one of Adam Ważyk's daughters and had succeeded in learning that because of her dislike for her father she had moved out of her parents' apartment. A few months later, a different informer submitted a report. This second informer had learned that Adam Ważyk's daughter on the contrary had very good relations with both of her parents. She had moved into a different apartment in order to have better working conditions but visited her parents two or three times a week for dinner.

A 1964 report stated that *"people who until recently had harbored many resentments toward one another are presently uniting."* An example: an informer had reported that Antoni Słonimski did not like Adam Ważyk, yet yesterday Słonimski and Ważyk had been seen sitting at the same café table.

Another memo contained the information that every year on the Jewish New Year Antoni Słonimski received oranges and lemons from the Israeli embassy. In March 1964 Słonimski received a package of matzo and wine. In August 1967 an informer reported that Słonimski, *"in a conversation with his close acquaintance, expressed by way of an allusion his solidarity with Israeli aggression against Arab countries. When the acquaintance noticed that*

Słonimski looked wonderful and was surely feeling well, Słonimski answered: 'I look and feel the way victors do.'"

The files were not as useful as I had hoped. Even excluding the issue of deliberately forged documents—like that of the speech Jakub Berman had allegedly given in 1945—there was the issue of the questionable judgment and competence of the reports' authors. Reading them, it was impossible to know how Jakub Berman had really reacted to the events of March 1968, what Antoni Słonimski had really said about the 1967 Six-Day War, how close Słonimski and Adam Ważyk had really been in the 1960s, or why Adam Ważyk's daughter had really moved out of her parents' apartment.

"Everything Was So *Unattractive*"

In the summer of 2004 I left Indiana to spend a year in Austria. When my friend Kasia came to visit from Poland, we went to the Vienna Museum on Karlsplatz, where there was an exhibit devoted to John F. Kennedy and Nikita Khrushchev's 1961 summit meeting. In the photographs Khrushchev's plump, dowdy wife was pictured alongside the glamorous Jackie Kennedy—and it was the aesthetic contrast that struck Kasia. Memories of the communist years came back to her: the absence of fashion, of variety, of color.

"Everything was so *unattractive*," she said to me.

In Kasia's memory communism was above all a visual ugliness. Now she was delighted by Vienna: the Ringstrasse architecture, the art nouveau of the Viennese Secession, the high ceilings and chandeliers in the coffeehouses. Vienna was everything that communist—and even postcommunist—Warsaw was not.

Yet even in Vienna I remained more drawn to Warsaw. The first time I returned there from Austria I ran into Kostek in a bookstore, and we went downstairs to the café on the first floor.

"Warsaw," Kostek said to me, "Europe's ugliest capital."

The poet Piotr Sommer once tried to describe Warsaw for an American audience: *"Even when you specify—in terms of space and chronology—your relation with the city, that is when you make it more intimate, Warsaw is a bit big and a bit intimidating: not instantly translatable into my small-scale categories. It is immediately historical in a multilayered way, and as a matter of course."*

"I love this city," I told Kostek.

And I knew that Kostek, who could live anywhere he chose, did too.

Tim, who by then was my fiancé, had come with me to Poland. We had met because of Poland; he'd sought me out because he too was interested in writing about the Berman family. Unlike myself, though, Tim already knew Jakub Berman's daughter, Pani Lucyna. The director of the Jewish Historical Institute in Warsaw was an admirer of Tim's first book—a biography of a nineteenth-century Polish socialist, a bright young intellectual who died in 1905, at the age of thirty-three, his hands clean. The director had offered to introduce Tim to his wife. When he did, Pani Lucyna trusted Tim—more than that, felt toward him something like affection. They had agreed to do a series of interviews. Now, though, Tim felt he had, in some sense, betrayed her, and felt compelled to write to her.

"Your father was our matchmaker," he told her.

Pani Lucyna telephoned him and said she understood. She declined his offer to burn the notes from their previous conversation. But they understood they would not see each other again.

▪ ▪ ▪

IN VIENNA TIM and I were fellows at the Institut für die Wissenschaften vom Menschen. The institute had been formally founded in 1982, but the more significant date in its origins was 1977: the death of the Czech philosopher Jan Patočka. The director, a Polish philosopher named Krzysztof Michalski, had been among Patočka's last students. When, after the appearance of Charter 77, Patočka died under interrogation, Krzysztof and some of his friends sought to smuggle the philosopher's papers out of Czechoslovakia. Austria was the closest neutral country, and Krzysztof created the institute both as a home for Jan Patočka's archive and as a meeting place for East European and West European intellectuals, otherwise divided by the Iron Curtain.

There at the institute in Vienna I met Pavel, a Czech political the-orist in his forties who had once been an underground bass player in the Moravian city of Brno. Then, when he was twenty-nine, the Vel-vet Revolution came and Pavel decided to return to the university. His parents, who were no longer alive, had both been communists.

"How can you not believe in anything?" Pavel's mother had asked him in the 1980s, when her son had made clear his rejec-tion of communism. She had joined the Party in 1947, at the age of twenty; in the Party she had seen a continuation of the Protes-tant values of equality, hard work, and care for the poor with which she'd been raised. The man she married was much older: Pavel's father was a prewar communist who had spent the war in Buchen-wald, who had escaped being gassed as a Jew only because he was imprisoned as a communist—together with German communist comrades. Pavel believed that the "soft repression" his father suf-fered during the postwar era of show trials had saved him from committing Stalinist crimes himself. Pavel's grandfather, the son of a rabbi from the small Moravian town of Třest', had also been a communist. In his memoirs Pavel's grandfather said nothing about his Orthodox childhood, though, noting only when and where he was born and how many years this was after the publication of *The Communist Manifesto*.

Pavel and I had long talks about Stalinism, about Nazism, about the Holocaust, about Hannah Arendt and Zygmunt Bauman and Daniel Goldhagen. As a public intellectual in Prague, Pavel wanted to explain to the Czechs the enthusiastic American reception of Daniel Goldhagen's *Hitler's Willing Executioners*. Germans, Gold-hagen argued, had been for generations infected with virulent anti-Semitism. They were bad people who enjoyed killing Jews. It was a straightforward explanation, a simple explanation—much sim-pler, for example, than Zygmunt Bauman's insistence that, on the contrary, the Holocaust involved the "neutralization"—that is, the subduing or overcoming—of ordinary Germans' attitudes toward Jews and that the Holocaust had to be understood as an event that exposed the "hidden possibilities of modern society."

It was understandable, too, that the public had found Daniel Goldhagen so much more appealing than Hannah Arendt, whose ideas were more complex and more disquieting, who pointed to the eradication of subjectivity on the part of both the persecutors and the persecuted, and who wrote of how, in a state of radical evil, all people became superfluous: there was no more death, no memory, no grief. The line between public and private, between truth and falsehood, even between victim and perpetrator blurred: *"Totalitarianism has discovered a means of dominating and terrorizing human beings from within. In this sense it eliminates the distance between the rulers and the ruled."*

Hannah Arendt rejected all theories pointing to the inherently murderous "German national character." Her explanation was a universalist one: the Holocaust was an exploitation of a potential latent in modern society—and in the human condition.

"For many years now," Hannah Arendt wrote after the war, *"we have met Germans who declare that they are ashamed of being Germans. I have often felt tempted to answer that I am ashamed of being human."*

Now in Vienna, I told Pavel that it was true what he had written: *"In as far as Goldhagen is right, we can sleep soundly."* This was the comforting part of Goldhagen's argument, for it implied that insofar as all the bad Germans were dead—or far away—there was nothing to fear. And after all, I asked Pavel, what was the alternative? That we will never be able to sleep soundly, because now we know what is possible, what humans are capable of. . . . The problem with the universalist Arendtian interpretation was that it was psychologically unbearable.

One evening Krzysztof, Jan Patočka's former student, invited me and Tim to dinner at the magnificent Viennese apartment where, now that his daughters were grown up, he lived alone.

We ate pierogies and herring in oil. After dinner we sat in the living room, drinking wine, Krzysztof pacing and fingering a beaded necklace as he spoke to us. He was a fascinating man—eccentric and yet irresistible. A Catholic whose philosophical passions were

Nietzsche and Heidegger. A friend of the famous philosopher-priest Józef Tischner, and of Karol Wojtyła, who was now Pope John Paul II.

Krzysztof spoke, too, about his long friendship with Alik Smolar, and I told him about the letter Alik's father, Grzegorz Smolar, had sent to Władysław Gomułka in 1968, pleading for the release of his imprisoned children. Krzysztof believed I was wrong to have sent Alik the letter.

"One cannot play God," he told me.

■ ■ ■

WHEN WE MET, Tim was writing of Ukrainian-Polish ethnic cleansing, of various ghastly episodes, among which Volhynia in 1943 was the bloodiest. It had happened in the midst of the Second World War, precisely in that space east of Warsaw that suffered one totalitarian occupation after another. While caught between Hitler and Stalin, Ukrainian nationalist extremists herded Poles into wooden churches and set them on fire. They murdered with both bullets and sickles. There were hangings and decapitations. Skin was torn from muscles, hearts were gouged from bodies. Poles responded with cruelties of their own.

This, too, was the context for the 1941 massacre of Jews by their Polish neighbors in Jedwabne: a time and place where throwing babies into fires on pitchforks was no longer unthinkable.

Tim's oldest friend in Poland, Andrzej, came from a Polish family that had been ethnically cleansed by Ukrainians. Andrzej told Tim this only after his book was published, for Andrzej was very principled: he did not want to compromise Tim's historical objectivity. It had happened in Lvov, in 1943: Andrzej's grandmother had watched as Ukrainian nationalists murdered her husband and her son before her eyes. Then she fled west with her daughter, to the small town of Opoczno in central Poland, at the time still under German occupation.

In her new home in Opoczno, Andrzej's now-widowed grandmother hid a Jewish family, whose youngest member was a little girl of perhaps five. She became Andrzej's mother's playmate—until one day the little girl could not bear the confinement and ran out onto the street. She was shot.

During the summer of 2003, just a few days after the ceremony commemorating the sixtieth anniversary of the Ukrainian ethnic cleansing of Poles in Volhynia, I'd been sitting at Warsaw's very fashionable Café Szpilka on Plac Trzech Krzyży with my friend Mikołaj, whose own grandfather had been killed in 1939 while defending Warsaw from the Germans. Mikołaj was resentful that the Ukrainian president had not said what the Poles wanted to hear: "We are sorry."

"We swallowed Jedwabne, they have to swallow Volhynia," Mikołaj told me.

Yet now, just over a year later, the Orange Revolution had come to Ukraine. It was represented by two striking faces: the once-handsome face of presidential candidate Viktor Yushchenko, now disfigured from dioxin poisoning, his skin full of craters; and the face of his glamorous ally, the businesswoman-turned-politician Yulia Tymoshenko, her long blond hair braided over her head in the style of the Ukrainian peasantry, the forty-something sex symbol of the Orange Revolution.

November 2004 saw thousands of Viktor Yushchenko's supporters camping in the center of Kiev, demanding, as they froze, democracy and free elections. And nowhere in Europe was there more support for the Ukrainian revolution than in Poland. The brutal history of mutual violence notwithstanding, it was the Poles who understood why democracy in Ukraine was so important. At that time a young Polish graduate student was spending a semester at the institute in Vienna—together with his young wife, who was several months pregnant. When he heard of the demonstrations, he left his wife in Vienna and caught an overcrowded train headed for Kiev. Sympathetic railway conductors let the Polish students travel for free. In Kiev the young Poles joined the Ukrainian crowd, shouting, *"Polska z wami!"* (Poland is with you!).

▪ ▪ ▪

BY THE TIME Tim and I arrived in Kiev just after our Krakowian wedding, the Orange Revolution was over. No longer was anyone camped out in the square.

Once again, the women in Ukraine impressed me with their fearlessness, their surety of sexuality's power. An article in the Russian-language Ukrainian *Cosmopolitan* was devoted to why Western men were so eager to marry Ukrainian women. There were good reasons: they were beautiful—and free of American-style feminism. They were more giving to their husbands; unlike American women, they embraced their own femininity. The article was both a tribute to Ukrainian women and a satire of Western feminism. *"While Western women work out their gender problems,"* the author wrote smugly, *"Ukrainian women get married."*

One evening we spent at an outdoor café with two of Tim's Ukrainian colleagues, talking about the Orange Revolution. It had to happen sooner or later, they believed. One of them explained: some decade and a half earlier, Ukrainian society had gotten the government it deserved. But now society had matured, and the gap between the corrupt elites and the maturing society had widened. Now Ukrainians deserved something better.

We talked, too, about the passionately contested city that had once been Austrian Lemberg before it became Polish Lwów and still later Soviet Lvov. Now it was Ukrainian Lviv, a poorly run city with a crumbling infrastructure where water and electricity were available irregularly. He would be perfectly willing, Tim's Ukrainian colleague said, to give Lviv back to Poland, if only the utilities were to work reliably again.

A few days later Tim and I took the overnight train from Kiev to Lviv, and I understood then what his colleague had meant. Lviv reminded me of Krakow—I could see that it had once been a beautiful provincial capital with winding cobblestone streets. Yet now it was long impoverished and neglected, a world apart even from

Kiev. Once-magnificent stone buildings were now decrepit, the *hralni avtomaty*—dark rooms full of smoke and vodka and slot machines—were ubiquitous. On the streets adults with horrific deformities begged passersby for coins, as they had in Warsaw eight years earlier.

And now I saw more clearly how much Poland had changed. I saw, too, the sad paradox: a century ago, Warsaw had belonged to Russia, kept under the yoke of the tsarist regime, while Lemberg had been the provincial capital of Austrian Galicia, not so distantly connected to Vienna. Now, a hundred years later, the situation was reversed: Warsaw was the capital of a European Union member, while Lviv was an indigent post-Soviet town.

In Lviv Tim and I stayed at the Hotel George. Once it had been the base of Oleksandr Korneichuk, the Ukrainian communist playwright who became Wanda Wasilewska's third husband. In autumn 1939, just after the Red Army occupied the city, Korneichuk had received Aleksander Wat and other refugee Polish writers in his room at the Hotel George. And the hotel room *was* beautiful, with its chandelier and high ceilings, its dark oak furniture and golden cover draped over a large bed.

As I walked through the town I tried to imagine the city of great fear, the Lvov of autumn of 1939, filled with Red Army soldiers and refugees. The streets Adam Ważyk and Aleksander Wat walked on the way to the editorial offices of the Stalinist newspaper, the restaurant where Aleksander Wat and Władysław Broniewski were arrested that January night in 1940, the villa where Wanda Wasilewska's husband was shot by the NKVD.

Unrequited Love

In Toronto in 2005 Stefan M.'s friend Henry Dasko, who had left Poland after March 1968, was writing his memoirs. It was a race against time, for Henry was dying of brain cancer. He was not well: his writing was awkward and inelegant in a way it had never been. Yet the content remained intact.

Henry's father was a Polish patriot who loved to recite Polish poetry to his son. He was also a communist, and Stalinism was the setting for Henry's childhood:

> *The Russian newspaper* Pravda *was delivered daily to my father. My mother made sure that the paper was unfolded and appeared well read before being put outside with the morning garbage.*
>
> *It was one morning when I was still very little, no more than four and barely able to reach the counter when my father entered our kitchen, where our housekeeper and my nanny, a country girl named Mirka, was pounding her feet on the newspapers which covered the floor. What are you doing? asked my Dad.*
>
> *We are stomping out Stalin, said Mirka and continued to put her feet down on the large photo of Joseph Stalin, printed in the newspaper, as it often was.*
>
> *In a rapid motion my father made for the phone and grabbed the receiver. Don't—said my mother sharply before he could dial the number. They'll kill her, you know that.*

Henry's first books were in Russian; to this day he remembered the cheery, colorful illustrations. All images were aggressively cheerful ones in those years: socialist realism was militantly joyful. This was true even as Henry, born just after the war, grew up in its shadow.

> Although ten years have passed since the end of the war, it never ended for us. It was an everyday subject of my parents' talk. The war was all we ever played with my friends and it wasn't just sticks we used to imitate weapons.
>
> The taupe-colored stucco of our building was pockmarked with bullets. The Warsaw Uprising had played itself out in our area and one day we discovered on the ceiling of the cellars down below an inscription written in the soot of a burning candle. It said that the bodies of four freedom fighters were buried behind the end wall of the cellar. It was as frightening as discovering the bodies themselves would have been. At the age of eight I wrote a letter to Marshal Zhukov suggesting that our building should be plated in armor and machine gun nests placed in its windows, so that we could defend ourselves when the fascists returned.

In September 2005 I went to Toronto to visit Henry.

"You won't recognize him," Stefan M. told me.

And it was true: Henry was unrecognizable, his head shaven and his feet swollen. He could concentrate only for a few moments at a time. Yet what he wanted to talk about was Jan Gross and Jedwabne—or rather, about Soviet-occupied eastern Poland between 1939 and 1941.

When on 17 September 1939, in accordance with the Nazi-Soviet nonaggression treaty, the Red Army invaded eastern Poland, most of them—of us, the Jews—were happy to see the Soviets, Henry insisted.

"For the Jews September seventeenth was nothing," he said.

It was a brief moment of lucidity, then he fell back asleep.

■ ■ ■

THAT WEEKEND IN Toronto I also visited Pani Hanka, who a decade earlier had taught me Polish. In the years that had passed she
had retired, and her health had deteriorated. A heavy woman with
short dark hair, she moved about with difficulty now, aided by a
walker. I went to visit her in the small apartment where she lived
with an unusually attractive gray cat.

It was only now, for the first time, that she spoke to me about her
family, about Poland, about why she had left. She spoke in Polish,
slipping into Russian when she described her time in the Soviet
Union. She'd been born in the early 1930s, in the town of Płock.
Those were the years of the depression, and Pani Hanka was born
into poverty—and into a family of devoted communists. Her father
sat in prison, as did her aunt—who shared a prison cell with local
criminals. One day, as Pani Hanka's mother was pushing her two-
year-old daughter in a carriage, she was suddenly approached by a
known prostitute, who right there on the street embraced her and
said, "Greetings from Rachela!"

Rachela was Pani Hanka's aunt. In her cell she had become friendly
with the prostitute, a fellow prisoner.

"My mother nearly died," Pani Hanka said with a smile. She
found it amusing now, all these years—and worlds—later.

When in September 1939 the war came, Pani Hanka's family
fled east to Białystok, an eastern Polish city soon occupied by the
Red Army and incorporated into Soviet Belarus. Then, like Bruno
Jasieński and so many other Polish communists in the Soviet
Union, her parents were falsely accused of anti-Soviet espionage
and arrested, and Hanka was taken to an orphanage in Komi, far
from Moscow in central Russia. After the German attack on the Soviet Union and the amnesty for Poles imprisoned there, her father
made his way to Moscow. There in the capital Wanda Wasilewska
arranged permission for him to travel to Komi and search for his
daughter. That he found her was rather a miracle. Upon seeing him
for the first time since his arrest, the eleven-year-old Hanka asked,

"Ty shpion ili net?" She had to know: Was he a spy or not? Had he betrayed the Soviet Union—or not?

It was a long war. By the time it ended and the family returned to Płock, Hanka no longer spoke Polish well. When he enrolled her in a Polish secondary school, her father said to her teacher, "She has to be humanized."

"The worst possible situation," Pani Hanka said, "the only Jewish girl, Russian-speaking, with poor Polish."

She decided then that she would overcome all of this: Polish would be her best subject, and she would be the best student in her class.

Later she went to study at the university in Moscow.

"I was in Moscow when Stalin died," Pani Hanka told me. We were sitting at her kitchen table, drinking tea. And she described those days, just after Stalin's death, as a time of surreal contrast between hysterical crowds and quiet emptiness. She went to a beauty salon where she was the only customer. When she returned to the dormitory, with her hair done, her nails painted, her eyelashes freshly dyed with henna, the other girls asked her, "How could you?"

The dormitory, like the salon, was largely empty. And so Pani Hanka lay in bed, reading, enjoying the quiet—while the other students stood in line for two days to see Stalin's corpse.

It was only there, as a university student in Moscow, that she became disillusioned with communism. She began work on a thesis about the Polish futurist–turned–Soviet writer Bruno Jasieński, the dandy executed during Stalin's terror, in whose NKVD file I'd found a dead fly. She never completed the thesis.

Pani Hanka had lived in Toronto for some thirty-five years, but she had never reconciled herself to the anti-Zionist campaign of March 1968. She had never fully accepted her exile. Yet it had been necessary.

"How long is unrequited love possible?" she asked me.

"I took my departure very hard," she said, "the country where your friends are, where a boy kissed you for the first time, where you went to bed with a boy for the first time . . ."

She was smiling, remembering Poland, her Poland.

Before I left I showed her photographs from my wedding in Krakow that summer, and Pani Hanka began to cry. And I knew that she was crying not for my wedding but for a Poland that could, at moments, be so beautiful.

▪ ▪ ▪

IN THE SPRING of 2006 Kostek and Irena Grudzińska, a literary scholar who once had been Jan Gross's wife and remained his friend, came to Indiana University for a conference on Solidarity. Kostek had been there for all of it—from Solidarity's beginning to its end.

Irena—like Jan and Henry Dasko and Pani Hanka—had been part of the "March emigration": she'd left after March 1968, when as a student—like Jan and Alik Smolar and Adam Michnik—she had been arrested and sent to prison. She and Jan were in New Haven in the 1980s when they organized the Committee for the Defense of Solidarity.

"It was like theater in a certain way," Irena said, "suspension of disbelief—you had to believe that impossible things could happen."

For Irena, Solidarity was romantic. For Kostek, it was positivist. Nineteenth-century Polish positivism was a philosophy ultimately aimed at national liberation. It had emphasized "work at the foundations," and in particular the role of journalism and education. And there were parallels. Unlike Václav Havel, who invoked the phenomenon "*as if*" to describe the greengrocer who lived a lie, pretending to admire the emperor's new clothes, Adam Michnik had arrived at a very different notion of "*as if*": "as if" as normative, as a moral imperative. One should live *as if* it were a free country, as if words mattered, as if civic education were possible, as if there were such a thing as moral responsibility—even under the communist regime. Kostek's passion for journalism remained intertwined with this positivist side of Solidarity.

"Democrats have an obligation to know underground printing," he told the audience, "the way a person has an obligation to know first aid."

Today, paradoxically, things were more complicated.

"I never really expected I would live to see the day . . ." Kostek said.

In Kostek's mind Solidarity's strength had been its singularity of purpose: "getting the Reds out." "Contradictions galore," he added, "—it didn't matter."

Then suddenly—"after we had the misfortune of winning"—the contradictions *did* matter. People were unhappy.

"You get steadily fed a diet of miracles," Kostek said, "you come to expect them, and then eventually when the miracles run out . . ."

He put this more bluntly: "If Solidarity is mine, then I'm responsible for your unfulfilled dreams . . . but if this price was too high, then the bottom line would be—the smart thing to have done was nothing. . . . In the long run, the guys who refused to take underground literature from me in the seventies were right, I was wrong . . ."

But I knew he didn't really believe this. He would do it all again.

Later, at a bar in Bloomington, we ordered vodka and Kostek told me a story he'd heard from Adam Michnik. It was a story that had taken place decades earlier, before March 1968 when they had all still lived in Warsaw.

Adam Michnik was having a party, and a friend of his arrived there looking sad. When Adam asked him why he looked so sad, the friend said he had spent a whole half hour at the Hotel Europejski café with Irena Grudzińska.

"Well and what? You should be happy!" Irena Grudzińska was the legendary beauty of their generation.

"No one saw us!"

Irena, all these years later, remembered that day; she remembered how, during the whole time they spent at that café, the young man never looked at her but rather kept glancing around. She'd been quite irritated.

"Everyone wanted to impress Irena Grudzińska—that's why the revolution happened," Kostek said.

Irena was embarrassed.

"It's annoying," she said, "how they always tell me: 'How beautiful you were!'"

In fact she was beautiful still. She still had the same long golden hair with gentle waves she'd had forty years earlier.

In retaliation Irena told me another story: Kostek's older sister, Irena's close friend, had once called her and said, "Kostek is doing it again, hassling our mother, but this time, it's even worse."

"Doing what?" Irena said.

"Saying he's Jewish!"

Irena Grudzińska, Adam Michnik, Kostek Gebert, and his sister all shared largely the same biography—yet only Kostek had embraced Jewishness—and Judaism. Once, Kostek said, he and Adam had drunk endless amounts of vodka, trying to discover what had gone wrong and with whom—and to little avail. For Adam the Warsaw Pact invasion of Czechoslovakia in 1968 was a defining moment: for he felt shame at Poland's participation in that Soviet-led invasion, and he believed that he must belong to the nation on whose behalf he could feel shame.

"My shame for the acts of others," Kostek said, "came after Sabra and Shatila."

Sabra and Shatila were refugee camps in Beirut. It was September 1982, during the Lebanese civil war. Israeli forces were occupying Beirut. They were surrounding Sabra and Shatila when Christian Lebanese Phalangists massacred Palestinian and Lebanese civilians in those camps.

The following day was Saturday—Shabbat—and Kostek and I talked more in my Bloomington apartment.

"Someone who has witnessed 1989," he told me, "does not have the moral right to be a pessimist."

And this remained true, despite any disappointments of post-communist Poland. At one point a former secret police informer came to him to ask for a letter of recommendation. The onetime informer justified his absurd request: after all, Kostek did not recognize him, even though he had once trailed Kostek for quite some time. And insofar as Kostek had never noticed him, he must have been good at his job. Were not such people needed under every government?

For Kostek what was most haunting about the postcommunist years was Bosnia, the center of the Yugoslav Wars, the site of massacres of whole villages and rapes of tens of thousands of women. Ten years earlier Kostek had stood in the Bosnian trenches, covering the war for *Gazeta Wyborcza*. When he returned to Warsaw he was the only person on the United Nations cargo jet flying from Sarajevo—which might have carried 350 people to safety. The United Nations, though, did not evacuate civilians. What Kostek had seen in Bosnia still haunted him: the people who died together, their corpses locked in an embrace, the bodies that decomposed, melted into one another.

It was growing dark when Kostek told me about Bosnia. Afterward we performed the Havdalah ceremony marking the end of Shabbat, with ground cloves and ersatz candles made of paper napkins and lit on the stove.

It was especially poignant to hear stories about Bosnia from Kostek, whose parents had believed more in the logic of History than in individual choice. On the contrary, Kostek's father, a Polish immigrant who had been a founding member of the Communist Party of the United States, had been convinced of the justness of History's iron laws. In 1947, he had returned to Poland from the United States to help build communism there. Those were the years when being the child of communists came with "the very pleasant feeling of being on the right side of History."

Kostek went on to devote many years to destroying the very system his parents had devoted their own lives to creating. His father, to his death, remained an unrepentant Stalinist. His parents, Kostek believed, "contributed to building something that became truly evil." They knew, at the end, that their lives had been wasted.

"They lived too long," Kostek said.

And yet he had loved them very much. He believed, too, that he was similar.

"Everything good in me I have from my parents," he told me. "If I spent a dozen or so years of my life trying to pull down the system they pulled up, it was because of values that they had taught me."

A Star of the Stage

W hen in the summer of 2006 I flew from Paris to Moscow, the contrast, so disquieting, reminded me of my Warsaw–Jerusalem trips of a decade earlier. Paris was so small, so intimate, so intimidatingly beautiful. Moscow was so enormous, everything—the buildings, the streets, the escalators—on a scale larger than life. And terribly ugly. Even the Russian spoken in Moscow was harsher than the Russian in Petersburg. There was formality without civility. Moscow had always felt to me like a city where anything could happen to anyone and no one would be accountable.

Now, in the Moscow State University dormitory where I lived, mice ran about in the corridor. A pack of stray dogs, too, lived on the vast university campus. I passed them every day when I went jogging. Sometimes they ran with me. It was difficult to love Moscow, one could only reconcile oneself to her.

■ ■ ■

IN MOSCOW THAT July of 2006 I saw two of my favorite colleagues from Indiana, Yiddishists who had been traveling through Ukraine, videotaping oral histories of the few remaining native Yiddish speakers. I joined them one afternoon for an interview with one of the last surviving members of the Moscow State Yiddish Theater. The theatrical troupe had been founded in 1919, just after the Bolshevik Revolution. A communist project to promote a secular Jewish culture, the theater flourished for three decades—before Stalin's anti-Semitic, "anticosmopolitan" campaign of 1949 brought about its demise.

The eighty-eight-year-old woman who greeted us when we arrived at her old Moscow apartment had been a star of the Yiddish stage in her youth. She welcomed us as if she had been waiting expectantly all these years, anticipating that paparazzi would appear at her door at any moment. Now elderly, she greeted us in high heels and earrings, in perfectly applied makeup. She was not only lucid but also energetic—she had the articulation of an actor and the presence of a performer.

What did she remember?

She remembered, she insisted, very much. She had been born in a shtetl, a small town where she had lived only among Jews. And in that Jewish shtetl where she grew up, in Soviet Ukraine, she remembered that the school was beautiful and the theater was built of wood. There was a market, too, all on the street where she lived.

It had been a very long time since she had lived her life in Yiddish. It was her native language, yet now she continually slipped into Russian, and my colleagues had to bring her back.

Her father had been a merchant. They had lived well, in a very nice house, a tall house. Then came Stalin, and the forced collectivization of agriculture, and in 1932 and 1933 the famine in Ukraine that saw millions of deaths by starvation. While Stalin forcibly requisitioned their grain and sold it abroad for hard currency to finance Soviet industrialization, desperate peasants resorted to cannibalism. I had seen unbearable photographs of children's emaciated bodies.

"*Uzhas*," she said, then translated into Yiddish, "*a shod*." *Uzhas* seemed much stronger to me—it was less "shame" and more "horror." And it had been horror—the horror of the hunger—that made her family flee. Some family members left sooner, some later. They headed to the city, to Moscow, together with so many other young Jews from the shtetl trying to escape the famine. That was when she had to learn Russian. She was young then and liked to sing and dance, and people said of her, "*Zi muz zayn a yidishe aktrise*" (She must become a Yiddish actress).

And in Moscow she did become a Yiddish actress. She not only acted, she also sang and danced. She remembered, she claimed, everything—all the plays, all the songs, all the characters.

"*Ikh hob geshpilt gute rolen,*" she wanted us to know. She was still proud of that, that she had played such good roles.

She belonged to an excellent theatrical troupe. In 1935, as Ukraine was recovering from famine and the Stalinist terror was accelerating, the Moscow State Yiddish Theater put on a fantastically successful production of *King Lear.*

After all these years, her love for the theater, for music and drama, was indefatigable. She was so expressive, so animated—her articulation, her gestures, her intonation.

"What was your favorite song?" I asked her.

And in response she began to perform it: there in her small, tattered living room she sang and danced. She still remembered the melody, the lyrics, even the choreography. It was something remarkable, as if all those years in between, the years without Yiddish theater, had been inessential.

▪ ▪ ▪

AT THE MAYAKOVSKY Museum in Moscow, I was struck again by Mayakovsky's beauty. His paintings with their sharp shapes and dark, vivid colors reminded me of Pani Ryszarda, Szymon Zachariasz's daughter, who remembered the Stalinist years as a time of the brightest colors.

Inside the Mayakovsky Museum in Moscow was the furnished room where the poet had ended his life.

I read Vladimir Mayakovsky's letters to his lover Lilia Brik. He signed them, "*Tvoi shchenok*" (Your puppy). Mayakovsky loved dogs.

In the archives of the State Literary Museum I found a telegram sent to Lilia Brik and her husband, Osip, during their trip abroad to

Berlin. The date was 14 April 1930, the text a single line: *"segodnia utrom wolodia pokontschil soboi"* (This morning Volodia took his own life).

▪ ▪ ▪

IN MOSCOW I telephoned Wanda Wasilewska's daughter. We had met only once, four years earlier, but Ewa Wasilewska immediately recognized my voice, or perhaps my accent in Russian, and replied in Polish.

I went to visit her at her apartment on Leningradskii prospekt. When the elevator reached the eighth floor, Liza, the diminutive dachshund, ran out of the apartment to greet me. I was very happy to see her, the "domestic tyrant," I'd feared she would be gone.

"She remembers you," Ewa Wasilewska said to me.

I wanted to think it was true. Liza the dachshund was, in any case, very demanding of attention. I spoke to Ewa in Polish, but when I turned to the dog Ewa told me that I would need to switch to Russian, for Liza had never learned Polish.

Wanda Wasilewska's daughter was nearing eighty, she yet looked considerably younger. She was easy to talk to, intelligent and thought-ful. She told me about how her mother had played such a large role in raising her son, and about how her daughter had died of leukemia some two decades earlier, at the age of only nineteen.

Ewa Wasilewska advised me about marriage: there would be many times when my husband and I would disagree—there would be many such occasions, because men and women were different—and I would know that I was right, and I *would* be right—but even so, it was better to concede. It had taken her years to learn this, she told me.

Later her husband returned home and joined us, and we began to speak Russian. Like his wife, he looked much younger than his age. They were both unusually warm and sympathetic—in contrast to the city that surrounded us, which was so harsh. We drank a bottle of white Crimean wine—dry and heavy and strong.

Lustration

In 2007 I gave a lecture at a small college town in the Midwest where I met a university press editor who had grown up in Poland. Once, she told me, when she was a child, she had met a certain woman who had been a close friend of Wanda Wasilewska and Janina Broniewska and Jakub Berman.

This woman, the editor told me, was a nice person, a warm person. The editor had pictures of her at her grandfather's funeral, or perhaps it was her grandmother's.

"How did your grandparents know her?" I asked her.

"Kuibyshev," the editor began.

Kuibyshev, a city in southern Russia, on the banks of the Volga River, had been a gathering place for Polish communists in the Soviet Union during the Second World War. Wanda Wasilewska had set up editorial offices there. Janina Broniewska and Adam Ważyk had been there, among others. Since the fall of communism, "Kuibyshev" no longer existed: in 1991 the city had returned to its pre-Soviet name, Samara.

Unconsciously I raised my eyebrows—or perhaps I did nothing, yet the editor seemed immediately to regret having spoken the name of that Russian city.

Suddenly she looked at me nervously, "Please don't tell anyone, I don't tell people."

"Don't worry," I said.

Her father had grown up in interwar Poland. When he was six years old, his mother was taken away from him: like Pani Ryszarda's father and Alik Smolar's father, like the parents of many other people I had come to know, she went to prison because she was a communist. The police offered to release her if she would cooperate . . . but she refused. She would not inform on her comrades, so the editor's grandmother remained in prison.

"Nineteen sixty-eight was the end for them," she said, "so you know what kind of communists they were."

▪ ▪ ▪

WHEN IN 2003 Poland, together with the Czech Republic, Slovakia, Hungary, Slovenia, Lithuania, Latvia, Estonia, Malta, and Cyprus, was invited to join the European Union, most Americans assumed that the Poles would be thrilled and grateful. In fact it was not a foregone conclusion that in Poland the referendum on joining the European Union would pass.

For many in postcommunist Poland, the European Union meant national self-negation: cosmopolitanism, contraception, abortion, homosexuality—in short, godless decadence.

In the end, the Poles in favor of joining "Europe" won the referendum—but thereafter, their opponents took their revenge. A national-populist government came to power. Warsaw's mayor banned a gay rights parade and Poland's harsh antiabortion laws remained in place.

Then there was Wildstein's List. What happened in Czechoslovakia in 1992, during the controversies over lustration, happened in Poland thirteen years later. It was late January 2005, a year after Poland had joined the European Union and three years after the Jedwabne debate. The journalist Bronisław Wildstein copied a list of names from the state's Institute of National Remembrance, a list of names that included people who had cooperated with the secret police—and people whom the secret police had hoped to induce to cooperate. Bronisław Wildstein posted his list on the internet.

I had learned about Wildstein's List in February 2005 from Kostek. He had been in Vienna for a few days; we'd been drinking espresso at the café Alt Wien, Kostek had been smoking a pipe. He was very unhappy: from the opening of other people's files he was learning things about his friends, about people he had long admired, that he would have preferred not to have known.

In some way it was a diabolical thing Bronisław Wildstein had done: many of the names on the list were names of former dissidents whom the secret police had hoped to coerce into informing on their friends. The only way to prove one's innocence, though, was to make public the contents of the file.

Kostek's name was on the list. Now he could either suffer his innocence in silence or expose to the media nearly two decades of his private life—and the private lives of many close to him. Was he willing now to find out which of his friends had betrayed him? He preferred not to know, he did not want his life unraveled. And that was not the only reason: Kostek had been married for many years; he and his wife had four grown children. Under communism he'd known his apartment had been bugged. But what could he do—never talk to his family at all? Perhaps more importantly, was he willing to risk humiliating his wife by making public a file that could expose what they said to each other in bed?

Kostek chose not to open his file. He did not want to see it.

Others made different choices. That fall of 2005 a visiting Polish scholar at Indiana stopped by my apartment for tea.

Although her own name was not there, Wildstein's List had been traumatic for her as well.

"One of our friends hanged himself," she said.

And the rise of the new, populist Right was only beginning.

The Władysław Broniewski Museum fell under the supervision of a new appointee at the Literary Museum, a nationalistically inclined historian, who now "reminded" Pan Sławek of his past in the Party. And so, after decades of having been the devoted curator of the Broniewski Museum and its archival collections, Pan Sławek was considering early retirement. The assistant curator, who had worked with Pan Sławek for many years, begged him to stay. She liked Pan Sławek very much.

The good side, they both told me, was that the new director would likely succeed in procuring Władysław Broniewski's secret police file from the Institute of National Remembrance. As an archivist, Pan Sławek was eager to see it—yet as a person sentimentally attached to the famous poet who had loved both Poland and socialism, he was fearful as well.

"Most likely someone from his family . . . ," the assistant curator explained.

I understood. I would not believe it of Janina Broniewska, though; she was too principled.

At Café Brama on Krucza Street, Mikołaj and I talked about lustration. In the dozen or so years that had passed between the publication of Cibulka's List in Czechoslovakia and the publication of Wildstein's List in Poland, a new generation had come of age—and into politics. As German chancellor Helmut Kohl had once said of the generation in Germany too young to have taken part in Nazi crimes, this generation in postcommunist Poland had been "graced by a late birth." Many of these people—too young to have been implicated themselves—were very eager for this kind of "national cleansing."

"They have the least right," Mikołaj said of this younger generation, his own.

▪ ▪ ▪

ONE DAY A friend loaned me the film *Trzech kumpli* (*Three Buddies*), a documentary about Bronisław Wildstein, the maverick journalist responsible for Wildstein's List. In the 1970s, Bronisław Wildstein had been part of a trio of young friends, opposition-minded university students in Krakow. One of the three, Stanisław Pyjas, was in all probability murdered in 1977 by the communist secret police. The other—Lesław Maleszka—was then a secret police informer, who quite possibly bore some responsibility for his friend's death.

The three friends belonged to a circle of students critical of the communist regime and interested in banned literature. Lesław Maleszka was "turned" after they were arrested. He was young and scared, and the secret police intimidated him—that was all.

The filmmakers interviewed Lesław Maleszka's secret police handler, an unexceptional man in late middle age who had obviously been quite attached to Lesław Maleszka, or at least to the idea that he had recruited an authentic intellectual. Their encounters, the handler insisted, were not—or not only—intimidation sessions. On the contrary: they were social occasions, and the handler had looked forward to them. Even now, it remained a point of pride that he, a working-class man, had become so friendly with a Jagiellonian University student. He was flattered by their rapport, by the congeniality of their meetings, by Lesław Maleszka's company.

Lesław Maleszka's double life lasted for a long time. After university, he had remained in dissident circles—and in the service of the secret police. The truth emerged only more than a decade after communism had ended, when the archives began to open. For twenty years Bronisław Wildstein had been obsessed with finding out who was responsible for Stanisław Pyjas's murder. Now it turned out to be their closest friend. This was the context for Wildstein's List—a demonic gesture motivated by a very real betrayal.

Before Stanisław Pyjas's murder, the wider circle of their friends had received anonymous letters accusing Pyjas of being a secret police informer. The secret police was playing a game with the students: someone was an informer. No one knew who. The letters contained personal information, intimate details that only someone very close to them would know. A quarter century later, Bronisław Wildstein was still overcome with revulsion at the ugliness of it all, letters written by someone who could see into their bedrooms . . .

Now I felt sorry for Wildstein.

"I would like for my life to have some weight," Bronisław Wildstein said.

Here was Milan Kundera's distinction between people for whom life was heavy and people for whom life was light: Perhaps for Lesław Maleszka life was light?

Again and again the filmmaker who interviewed Lesław Maleszka asked him, *"Why?"* Why had he betrayed his closest friends? Why had he kept silent for so many years?

And each time he responded, *"An excellent question."*

Lesław Maleszka had no answer.

"A truly Dostoevskian character," my friend who loaned me the film described him.

When in 1976 Lesław Maleszka had been "turned," he'd chosen "Ketman" for his pseudonym. It was a reference to Czesław Miłosz's famous book *The Captive Mind*, a story of Polish writers seduced into collaboration with the new communist regime in the postwar years. "Ketman" was a kind of splitting of the self.

In November 2001, after the opening of the archives had exposed him as an informer and a quarter century after he had made his decision to collaborate, Lesław Maleszka wrote a long essay for *Gazeta Wyborcza* titled "I Was Ketman . . ."

"I seek no justifications," Lesław Maleszka began. He only wanted to explain.

It was 1976; the room was dark and the interrogation was brutal: the light shining directly in his eyes, the three interrogators in rotation, the curses and threats, the promises of beatings to come.

For several hours he dissimulated, trying to fabricate a story, but the interrogators already seemed to know so much. And he knew that in other rooms, at the very same moment, his friends were being interrogated; he was convinced that the secret police must already know everything about them.

So he began to plead with his interrogators not to expel him from the university. And by pleading, he made them understand he was weak.

Nothing justified what he had done, Lesław Maleszka acknowledged, neither the fact that he had made the dean's list from his first year at university, nor the talk in the Polish philology department of his being awarded a teaching assistantship after graduation, nor his fascination with literary theory.

"Do you want to study?" the interrogators asked him. *"You don't get something for nothing."*

They gave him a sheet of paper and a pen, and they dictated his declaration of cooperation.

Then they ordered him to choose a pseudonym. That was when Lesław Maleszka remembered "Ketman" from Czesław Miłosz's *The Captive Mind.* *"A person of two religions, who conceals his true views, feigning loyalty to the oppressive power. It seemed to me that such a game would be possible. At the time it didn't enter my mind that Ketman had to plunge into an internal lie, which in the end would penetrate his entire essence."*

The secret police were interested in everything. That they regarded him as their own did not deter them from foraging for material in his private life. They always wanted to know who drank vodka with whom, and where. They wanted to know if the priest who sympathized with the students had a lover—or lovers. Sometimes they paid Lesław Maleszka.

Nineteen seventy-six was the beginning of the Workers' Defense Committee, the moment when intellectuals truly reached out to workers. It was the moment that in Czechoslovakia never came: to the very end, Charter 77 remained a ghetto of intellectuals. But in Poland, the Workers' Defense Committee was the beginning of a real solidarity.

Lesław Maleszka and his friends were involved in the Workers' Defense Committee from the beginning. While Lesław Maleszka distributed underground literature, collected money, and gathered signatures, "Ketman" reported these activities to the secret police.

"I lived thus for years," Lesław Maleszka now wrote, *"in a psychic and moral schizophrenia."*

On 7 May 1977 Stanisław Pyjas was murdered. To this day no one knew exactly why—or exactly by whom. Perhaps Stanisław Pyjas had discovered that Lesław Maleszka was an informer and had threatened to expose him. Perhaps the secret police had only meant to frighten Pyjas away from the opposition with beatings but had lost control. Perhaps they had killed him as a warning to others.

In any case, after Pyjas's murder Lesław Maleszka—alias Ketman—realized: Who was he to think he could trust his handlers? To them he was just a kid to be exploited, *"a small, blackmailed and brow-beaten pawn, who plays a meager role in a theater not his own."*

This is how his illusion about the possibilities of Ketman came to an end.

A quarter century had passed since he had succumbed. A dozen years had passed since communism had ended. But Lesław Maleszka knew that he would carry the burden of what he had done to the end of his life.

How could he have betrayed his closest friends? How could he have continued to work with the secret police after they had killed Staszek Pyjas? Even today, all those years later, he was unable to answer that question, unable to understand his own motivations. He'd been very afraid, he'd lived with a fear he was unable to overcome. But still, he knew, this failed to explain it all.

In 1962, when the poet Aleksander Wat was living in exile in France, Adam Ważyk came to Paris. There he and Wat sat in a café and spoke about Stalinism. How was it possible—Wat wanted to know—that after everything Ważyk had experienced in the Soviet Union, he had still returned to Poland after the war as a Stalinist?

"I suffered from a splitting of the self," Adam Ważyk answered him.

This was true of Lesław Maleszka as well: he had suffered from a splitting of the self. And it suggested another question: Once a self was split in two, was either half real? Did any authentic self remain?

"I have only one wish," Lesław Maleszka wrote in conclusion. *"I would like my personal file amassed by State Security to be the first—and the last—to be made public. By means of blackmail, fear, provocation, beatings, the political police in a communist state broke*

the moral backbones of many people. They didn't always manage to break everyone as easily as they did me, but the results must have been equally lamentable. For the past dozen years each of those people has tried to forget about the drama he lived through. About the fact that he did evil to those closest to him—at the same time living with the feeling that he himself had fallen victim to violence. Today each of those people awaits his judgment day—when the opening of his file will tear apart the circle of people he knows, perhaps his family, when it will render him a villain."

Now Lesław Maleszka posed the question: Were the devastating social costs of making public the secret police files truly worth the advantages that opening the files would bring?

I remembered the line that my historian friend Dariusz had once quoted me from Wisława Szymborska's poetry: *"Tyle wiemy o sobie, ile nas sprawdzono."*

We know ourselves only insofar as we have been tested.

▪ ▪ ▪

BY SPRING OF 2007 Poland's nationalist-populist government succeeded in passing a lustration law. It was to take effect in May of that year: all Polish citizens working in government, education, journalism, or similar professions had to sign a declaration stating that they had not cooperated with the secret police during the communist period. If they refused to sign, or were proven to have lied, they were subject to loss of their positions for a period of ten years. It was the Institute of National Remembrance that was vested with the authority to verify declarations. Those born after 1 August 1972 were exempted—and thus was a single day determined to be a mark of generational divide.

Lustration reflected a public demand for accounting with people like Lesław Maleszka. In what other way, after all, could horrors like the murder of Stanisław Pyjas be avenged?

More broadly, lustration reflected a public demand for accounting with those who had benefited under the communist regime at the expense of others who had suffered. Communism in Poland had lasted for over forty years. There were people prominent in postcommunist public life—people like Kostek Gebert and Adam Michnik—who, as the young children of communists, had enjoyed privileged childhoods. Once they had been called the "banana youth," bananas having been a rare luxury item under communism.

There was yet a further layer of complication. Often these same privileged children had later sat in prison. For the "banana youth" had engaged in a collective Oedipal revolt against their communist parents: the children of Stalinists—and even more particularly, the children of Jewish Stalinists—were disproportionately over-represented among Solidarity activists. In this sense lustration was directed, not so subtly, against former dissidents, many of whom were now opponents of the populists. After all, it was precisely the former dissidents who had files; it was they who had been of such intense interest to the secret police. There was an irony in this: for it was safer now—as it had been then—to have been one of Havel's greengrocers.

In an editorial for *Gazeta Wyborcza*, Kostek explained why he would not submit to lustration.

"I won't demonstrate that I'm not a camel," Kostek wrote.

This was a Russian phrase popular during Stalinist times: "Prove that you're not a camel." It was a way of expressing the absurd impossibility of ever proving one's innocence.

Kostek's friend Staszek Krajewski, the mathematician working to improve Jewish-Christian understanding, wrote an editorial too, also stating his refusal to sign on principle. And Kostek and Staszek were not alone.

That April, just a month after Kostek's and Staszek's editorials appeared, Adam Michnik came to Yale University, where I now taught, to give a paper on "the new populism" in Poland. Over lunch I asked him about Antoni Słonimski. From Słonimski's secret police file I knew that they had spent much time together in Słonimski's last years, when Adam Michnik was a young man and Słonimski, long recovered from his postwar communist sympathies, had become the grand old man of the opposition. Słonimski had been full of sentiment for him. The affection had been reciprocated: now at a French restaurant on Chapel Street in New Haven, Adam Michnik spoke of Słonimski as *"mój szef"* ("my boss").

"In 1987," Adam Michnik said during his seminar, "Poles had three requests of God: that communism end; that the Soviet army leave; and that the Soviet Union fall.

"Suddenly we woke up in a new world," he went on.

To this day he still feared that he would open his eyes in the morning and realize it was only a dream—and that Poland was still living under communism.

Communism had taken away freedom, he pointed out, but in exchange it had provided security. This was the classic Hobbesian trade-off. Liberty and security were in a zero-sum relationship: more of one meant less of the other.

Adam Michnik believed that the current populism arose through a nostalgia for security, a longing for the past. A Catholic radio station, Radio Maryja, had returned to the xenophobic language of the 1930s. New populist leaders understood people whom Adam and Kostek and their friends did not. It was the populists who understood the Poles who imagined the European Union as Babylon: pornography, homosexuality, abortion.

Adam Michnik spoke, too, about lustration. He thought it absurd to judge people on the basis of the material in the secret police files—a single source, and still worse, a source *"begot with the worst of intentions."* By agreeing to it, the former dissidents were letting themselves be judged by their enemies. Suddenly, fifteen years after the fall of the Iron Curtain, it was the communist secret police functionaries—so many of whom were opportunistic, uneducated, self-interested, or simply stupid—whose word counted most.

Then in May 2007, just a month after his visit to New Haven, Adam Michnik broke. In an essay titled *"Otwórzmy teczki" (Let's Open the Files),* he called for all the files to be made public at once.

He had not ceased to regard it as absurd that *"our biographies will be written by our mortal enemies."* He had not ceased to think it relevant that those secret police functionaries who had tracked and interrogated, blackmailed and imprisoned so many people—including himself and his friends—had not been after truth. Their goal had been precisely to compromise people, to taint them, to humiliate them.

And now it was continuing. The current regime at the Institute of National Remembrance, *"acting on the directives of their political sponsors, are capable in the course of a single night of finding a 'hook' on every one of us. And then the next day the media publicizes these 'hooks' urbi et orbi. Every one of us can be defamed at any given moment."*

Adam Michnik wanted the files opened because it was not the case that the files were currently closed—it was rather the case that the powers that be at the Institute of National Remembrance had privileged access to them and moreover used them as *"a baseball bat to strike down those who think differently."* He used a still more colorful analogy: at the moment the secret police archives were like repositories of narcotics, guarded by drug addicts.

> *It's necessary, finally, to curtail the omnipotence of this nightmarish police of memory and blackmail, for after all this is what the present leadership of the Institute of National Remembrance is.... For this reason, today the files should be publicly accessible to everyone, with all the terrible consequences that will bring. It will be better than the present situation. We have to make the files public in order—this sounds paradoxical—not to live under the control of the files, which are toyed with, whose contents "leak out," which are ostentatiously used in a political game.*

"I don't see another way out. Better an end to the horror than horror without an end," he concluded.

The lustration law was overturned by Poland's constitutional court at the eleventh hour.

■ ■ ■

IN JULY 2007, at Krakow's Jewish Cultural Festival, Tim and I saw my former professor Stefan M. amid the crowd on Szeroka Street. It was already dark, and the festival's finale—a huge klezmer concert in the open air—had just begun.

I asked him about Henry Dasko's death. Had he been in Toronto then?

"I was there," he said, "sitting by his bed. It was awful. A nightmare. I cannot talk about it. Someday we'll talk about it."

He looked into the crowd, and then again at me, and repeated, "Someday we'll talk about it."

For some time we watched the musicians; then we walked to Klezmer Hois, where two summers earlier Tim and I had been married. It was a warm evening; we sat down at a table outside and ordered vodka.

"I hate 'small talk,'" Stefan M. began, then added, "In Polish we don't have such an expression, because we don't have this phenomenon."

Henry Dasko had felt similarly about Americans and our lightness of being. *"Americans are a nation of a cheery and carefree psyche,"* Henry had once written. *"Not for them is the Slavic question 'how to live,' German Angst, French existentialism."*

And so instead of small talk Stefan M. told us a story: In 1980, when he was a young scholar still in his twenties, he participated in an academic exchange with Humboldt University in Berlin. The university assigned him a spacious, comfortable room all to himself. Then, after a short time, a roommate appeared, a Polish student from the University of Lublin. The two young men quickly became friendly.

"In the evenings," Stefan told us, "we would go out to pick up girls together. I was somewhat bolder, and we would go together."

After two months, it was time for the roommate from Lublin to return to Poland. Stefan went along to the train station and helped him with his luggage. Only when Stefan returned to the room they'd shared did he notice that his friend had forgotten his student identification card.

Stefan picked it up, and when he returned to Poland, he telephoned the University of Lublin and asked for his former roommate's address so that he could return the student identification card.

"My dear," the university secretary answered him, "there is no such student, nor has there ever been."

Stefan realized then that in this way—by leaving behind the card provided to him, no doubt, by the secret police—his friend was trying to tell him who he was.

■ ■ ■

THE TRAUMA OF encounters with the secret police lingered long after communism's fall. Following various difficulties, Todd James, who had once been Jarmila and who had once been a Catholic, succeeded in graduating from a small liberal arts college in Pennsylvania. Afterward he returned to Vermont. In January of 2001 he wrote to me,

> Life is better when you come home from school and someone is there. For four and a half years now I've had Siamese cats, and life with the cats is much better. I take them everywhere with me. The male cat is named Ray and the female Joy. . . . I have several friends in Burlington, where I go to synagogue. There is a small Hasidic community and the people are very nice.

Todd James moved then to Boston, where he registered as an external student at Harvard and began taking courses to prepare for medical school entrance exams. He was concerned about calculus—but also certain that he could learn anything if only he put his mind to it.

That first semester at Harvard went well. In June he wrote proudly that he had gotten As on his exams and was now preparing for the MCAT. He spent all his time in the library, studying—while at home he continued to have his cats for company. He attached their photographs.

That August of 2001 Todd James came to California to visit friends, and we met for lunch. By then it had been several years since we'd seen each other. It was a warm visit but an awkward one. He was a Jew now, and unambiguously a man, and I had always—despite all gender ambiguity—related to him as if he were a woman. I felt resistant to opening myself to this man the way I had to Jarmila.

In the years that followed I seldom heard from Todd James. I knew only that he was still taking courses at Harvard.

Then one day in January 2007, some six and a half years after September 11 and the inauguration of President Bush's war on terror, I got a phone call from a lawyer in Massachusetts. Todd James, the lawyer told me, had been arrested. She would not say exactly why; she only alluded to some "unfortunately misinterpreted comments about Al Qaeda" that Todd James had made at a mosque near Boston. She was certain the judge would dismiss these unfortunately misinterpreted comments, yet now there was another problem: years before, Todd James had applied for political asylum. The case had dragged on—or perhaps had been ignored, or forgotten. Now, though, the American government had remembered. Todd James was in detention, facing deportation to the Czech Republic. His attorney was collecting supporting documentation for the asylum case, and Todd James had given her my name.

"At a mosque?" I asked. "I thought that Todd James was an Orthodox Jew; he converted from Catholicism."

"He's a Muslim now," the lawyer answered.

I talked to her about Czechoslovakia. It was very possible, I explained, to document Jarmila's participation in the anticommunist opposition, her role in the Velvet Revolution, likely even her experience of police persecution during the 1980s. It would almost certainly, though, be impossible to prove that returning to the Czech Republic would pose any physical danger. It could be psychologically traumatic, of course, but no credible source in 2007 would be

willing to testify to the likelihood that the agents who had interrogated Jarmila in the 1980s would now be seeking revenge. On
the contrary: in all likelihood those former secret policemen would
themselves now very much like to forget those times.

"Prague is a beautiful city," I told the lawyer. "The communists
are absolutely no danger any longer. Please try to persuade Todd
James to go back."

The lawyer promised she would tell him what I'd said about
Prague. In the meantime, though, she would be grateful if I were to
write a letter supporting the claim of past persecution and send it
to her together with any relevant documents.

I agreed. I enclosed the two long letters Todd James had sent me
in 1996. One of them, I told the attorney, alluded to some kind of
recruitment, or at least close involvement, with American diplo-
macy and the American military, as well as the CIA and Radio Free
Europe. The letter expressed, too, Todd James's subsequent disillusionment with American dignitaries and military generals.

A few weeks later an Immigration and Naturalization Service
prosecutor called me at my office. She had received a copy of the
letter I'd written at the request of Todd James's lawyer. Could I
prove everything in it? Could I begin by proving that I was who I
claimed to be? Had I in fact met Todd James at a mental hospital?
Did I have a history of mental illness?

I tried to reason with her: she had called me at my office, on
a Yale University telephone number. She could look it up on the
university website to confirm that. She could look up my profile as
well: it was on the history department faculty page.

The prosecutor was uninterested in that. She was unable to lo-
cate the Yale University website at all, she told me. In any case, the
burden of proof was on me: Could I prove my own identity? The
existence of *samizdat*? Charter 77? The Helsinki Accords? Communist Czechoslovakia? How was she to know this was not all the
invention of a delusional personality?

I began to tell her about the origins of *samizdat* literature in
Russia and the development of underground publishing in the

communist era, the philosophy of "antipolitics," the dissidents' adoption—following the 1975 Helsinki Accords—of a discourse of human rights.

The prosecutor cut me off: she wasn't interested in an *explanation*, she was interested in *proof.*

I mentioned the documents I'd included with my letter, but she was uninterested in documents written in a language she was unable to read—and which in any case could have been forged. Could I prove I had not met Todd James in a mental hospital?

I was in tears when I hung up the phone. Unlike Jarmila, I never would have lasted under interrogation.

▪ ▪ ▪

DURING THE YEAR I'd spent in Vienna, Jan Gross had sent me a draft of his new manuscript titled *Fear.* It was, in some way, a sequel to *Neighbors*—a long, reflective essay on postwar anti-Semitic violence, assaults against Jewish survivors returning to Poland from the Soviet interior and from the Nazi camps. The central narrative drama was a pogrom that had taken place in 1946, in the small city of Kielce. It began with the false accusation that Jews had kidnapped a Christian child. So it emerged that in Poland in 1946 the premodern myth of blood libel—the belief that Jews used the blood of Christian children to make Passover matzoth—remained potent.

On 4 July 1946 forty-two people were killed in Kielce. One pregnant woman survived but lost the child she was carrying when her assaulters pierced her uterus. An elderly woman was stoned to death. One man, while being chased by his assailants, dropped his newborn. The baby was shot in the head at once. Some victims knew their murderers personally. After all, they were their neighbors.

It was not the first thing Jan had written in recent years that was part history, part moral reflection, part self-criticism. Why—Jan wanted to know—hadn't the Polish intelligentsia, then and since then, seen this? Why hadn't Polish intellectuals—the "conscience of the nation"—done something, said something? Why had it taken himself so many years to confront these questions?

For Jan the answer, at least in part, was that so many past and present Polish intellectuals—himself among them—had been "blinded by social distance."

It was a persuasive argument. I thought about Aleksander Wat, descended from rabbis, who had barely experienced anti-Semitism in either prewar or postwar Poland. I thought about people like Władysław Broniewski and Wanda Wasilewska, Polish intellectuals who, while not Jews themselves, belonged to a milieu that included so many assimilated Jews—they saw little anti-Semitism as well. Aleksander Wat could imagine his friends denouncing him to the NKVD but not accusing him of ritual murder.

When, at the end of the Second World War, the communist poet Władysław Broniewski found himself in Jerusalem, he was adopted by the Polish Jewish intelligentsia there. He seemed to take this as a matter of course—like the fact that he had something to read from at his own poetry readings because Polish Jewish emígrés to Palestine had brought his books with them to Jerusalem.

Władysław Broniewski's granddaughter, Pani Ewa, who now lived in Greece, had married a Polish Jew in the 1960s. She had been raised by the dogmatically principled Janina Broniewska and would never have thought to make a distinction between "real Poles" and "Poles of Jewish origin."

But these people belonged to very particular milieus. Jan, too—born into a Warsaw intelligentsia family, his father, a Pole of Jewish origin, a lawyer, and his non-Jewish mother a translator from French—had not seen anti-Semitism when he was growing up in postwar Poland. It had not been part of his world. Yet, as it turned out, his world had been narrowly circumscribed.

Now Jan, fighting his way through the "blindness of social distance," was confronting a darker side of Polish society. He hypothesized that the origins of postwar anti-Semitism were actually to be found in wartime behavior—in particular the "widespread collusion" of the Poles with the Nazis' extermination project. Many

Poles were not sorry to see the Jews leave, they were quick to appropriate their property . . .

But was it collusion—I asked him in a letter—or simply indifference, or passivity?

In any case, the point remained: postwar anti-Semitic violence occurred not *in spite of* the Holocaust, but rather *because of it.*

It was a poignant manuscript—both compelling and in some way unsuccessful. For what Jan really wanted to know was: Why was there evil in the world? And to that question there was no answer.

■ ■ ■

I VISITED KOSTEK. We talked about Jedwabne, and Kostek told me that he'd first been in that very small and very provincial town in 1975, when he was a young man, hitchhiking around the Polish countryside. In Jedwabne he'd asked a local man he passed where he could find the road to the nearby town of Łomża.

The man pointed, "Over there, where the barn is, where they burned the Jews."

Something in the man's tone made Kostek ask, "The Germans burned them?"

"What Germans? It was us!"

"I blocked it out," Kostek told me.

■ ■ ■

AT A COMMUNIST period–style restaurant at the Stalinist Palace of Culture, Dariusz and I talked about *Fear,* about Jan's quest for answers to the question of evil.

"We can piece together narratives from fragments and palimpsests," I said to Dariusz. "In the best case we can learn what did happen, perhaps how it happened—but can we ever know for certain why?"

Dariusz was relieved that the mystery of human motivation lay beyond our competence as historians.

"If it were possible to know that," he said, "then some regime would come and control us all completely."

▪ ▪ ▪

MY CZECH FRIEND Vlasta was unable to picture me at Yale, in that atmosphere, the New England patriarchy, the snobbery—she found it unimaginable. That summer of 2007 I had come to Prague for just a few days, and we began drinking at one pub and continued all day, sipping wine and Becherovka and eating Bohemia potato chips. We rented a rowboat and went out on the Vltava River.

Recently Vlasta, who years earlier had translated Erica Jong's *Fear of Fifty*, had herself celebrated her fiftieth birthday. It was a new stage in her life: she was now the caretaker for her mother, who was dying of Alzheimer's disease. Theirs had always been a difficult relationship: Vlasta had been closer to her father, a revisionist Marxist philosopher. He had died in 1989, just two weeks after the Velvet Revolution. In the years that followed Vlasta thought of how it was good, perhaps, that her father didn't live to see the times of anticommunist backlash.

By now that moment had passed. In the Czech Republic, as elsewhere in postcommunist Europe, a market was emerging for communist nostalgia. Prague now had a Museum of Communism, with statues of Karl Marx and socialist realist posters and an original noose from Pankrác Prison, where Milada Horáková had been hanged. It was a market emerging not only for communist horror but also for communist kitsch. In Poland a new travel company was advertising "Communism Tours" to Nowa Huta, a Stalinist-era industrial settlement just outside Krakow: *"Experience Stalin's gift to Krakow in a genuine Eastern Bloc Trabant automobile!" "The only private tour of Krakow's communist district!"* The company offered several varieties of tours: Communism, Communism Deluxe, Commie Tour, and Disco.

Now Vlasta showed me the wedding pictures of her punk anarchist daughter. Diana was wearing a deep crimson medieval dress, and she'd dyed her hair a flaming Renaissance red. She was radiant and ravishing. She and her husband had a baby boy for whom communism would mean nothing at all.

When I saw Diana's father, Honza, in the pictures, I did not rec-ognize him, he had changed so completely. By now he and Vlasta had been divorced for ten years, and Honza's long hair—his entire gaunt, bohemian look—was gone. Now he was bald; he'd gained weight and become an advertising executive. He looked much more serious.

Diana, her new husband, and their son were now living in Vlasta and Honza's old apartment, far from the center of Prague. The apartment had been transformed since I'd last seen it, so long ago: Diana had painted the rooms in bright lemons and oranges and limes.

We went out on the balcony. Vlasta and Diana smoked, and I looked out over the apartment complexes to the park where, in the fall of 1994, the three of us had once spent an afternoon with Honza, Amanda, and Oskar. Thirteen years had passed since then.

"There are always surprises," Vlasta said to me.

▪ ▪ ▪

THAT SUMMER, AT the end of July, Tim and I went to Lviv, where there was a beauty salon on Hnatiuk Street, which had once been Jagiellońska Street. This was the home of the restaurant where in January 1940 Aleksander Wat and Władysław Broniewski's seduc-tive scenographer friend had hosted the party that ended in his friends' arrests.

We stayed at a newly opened hotel, conspicuously run by the Mafia, where the waitresses seemed perpetually terrified. "Please make up the room" signs were bilingual in Ukrainian and Russian, and pictured a long-legged woman in a tank top, black miniskirt, and green stiletto heels pushing a strangely phallic-looking vacuum cleaner.

All signs in Lviv, Tim pointed out, directed drivers and pedes-trians alike to the Grand Hotel. It was a telltale sign of corruption. The city was otherwise full of electronics and cell phone stores—absurdly, disproportionately so—as well as the ubiquitous *hralni avtomaty* with their slot machines and smoke.

Throughout modern history, Lviv had been a city that everyone wanted: Poles, Ukrainians, Russians, Germans, Jews. Now it was neglected by all.

One afternoon, Tim and I passed a crowd gathered outside a drab block of apartments. When we came closer, we saw that a cat was stuck on a window ledge between perhaps the fourth and fifth floors. There was a woman standing in the window of the higher apartment, a man standing in the window of the apartment beneath her, and a cat suspended on the ledge between them. The man and woman were passing between them a long stick with a bag tied onto one end; they were trying to cajole the cat into the bag. After some time the man succeeded in coaxing the cat from the ledge, but the cat did not manage to jump either onto the stick or into the bag. Instead the cat fell toward the pavement—where four people were holding the corners of a sheet to cushion its fall. The cat hit the sheet, and—as if the sheet were a trampoline—rebounded onto the pavement, landed on its feet, and scampered off.

In a city where human life had often appeared to be worth very little, there was much concern for a cat. It was a fantastically successful rescue operation, one involving six rescuers and dozens of onlookers. Yet the crowd that had gathered was silent—no one applauded. The cat was saved, and all turned and went on their way.

God-Seeking

The year I lived in Vienna was the year that my Ukrainian friend Galina, my fellow teacher in Domažlice, left the Czech Republic to study in England. For years she had dreamed of returning to university, a desire interspersed with dreams of going to the Holy Land, or joining a convent, or both. Earlier she had written to me, in Russian, of her joyous discovery: her task in life was to *"unite with God's will."*

The sentiment was reminiscent of communist-era self-criticism: the consummation of one's own subjectivity by its liquidation, the individual's dissolution into a seamless unity with the objective laws of History.

But Galina did not see it this way. For her, Christianity was ultimately less about will than about love. Love was always painful—Galina insisted—this was the unavoidable price we had to pay for the love of a human being, as opposed to the love of God.

"The longer I live," she wrote, *"the better I understand that our only hope is God. He is the only one whom you could trust completely, who will never leave you, who loves you as no human being is able to love. Meeting people is like a chain of painful experiences. The best possible man or woman is just a weak creature."*

"The distance between people here is too big," Galina wrote after she had arrived in Leeds. *"And in Russia it is too small."*

Galina did not stay in Britain for very long. She soon left Leeds to join a convent in British Columbia. There she finally felt at peace.

▪ ▪ ▪

IN 2008, MY Czech political theorist friend Pavel and his wife came to Yale for several months. In New Haven that summer, I showed them Todd James's letters from 1996, telling me of his struggle against the communist regime, his struggle for truth and for his own self. It was a case of the Russian weakness *bogoiskatel'stvo*: a kind of spiritual seeking, a relentless, despairing God-searching.

The letters reminded Pavel of their friend Petr Cibulka from Brno. He, too, had been a dissident; he, too, had signed Charter 77. In prison, under interrogation, Petr Cibulka had been daring, courageous, and enduring. In 1992, it had been Petr Cibulka—despite the opposition of Václav Havel—who took it upon himself to publish the unconfirmed list of secret police agents, collaborators, and informers: he was the Bronisław Wildstein of Czechoslovakia. And it was only then, in the years that followed the Velvet Revolution, that Pavel and his wife slowly realized that Petr Cibulka's in fact was a certain kind of personality with an insatiable craving for Manichaean divisions. Of his heroism during the communist years they now wondered: Where was the line between moral clarity and madness?

▪ ▪ ▪

IN SEPTEMBER OF 2006, Dariusz had written from Warsaw, *"Dear Marci and Tim, You may be interested in an article that I published in Gazeta Wyborcza. A new act on the Institute of National Remembrance may make you criminals too. I will be delighted to share a cell with you."*

The Institute of National Remembrance had come into being as a result of a December 1998 statute. It was a state institution, charged with educating the Polish public; investigating Nazi and communist crimes against the Polish nation; and overseeing the archives of the communist security organs. It was now the caretaker of approximately fifty miles of archival files. Dariusz's editorial in *Gazeta Wyborcza* concerned the statute on the Institute of National Remembrance being debated in the Senate. The statute included the provision: *"Whoever publicly imputes to the Polish nation participation in, organization of, or responsibility for communist or Nazi crimes is liable to up to three years in prison."*

Dariusz warned the legislators who were so concerned with protecting Poland's reputation that this law would have the opposite effect.

> *The original project authored by the Senate Legislative Office was unambiguous: It enjoined the prosecutor to act in every "case of imputing to the Nation or the Polish State, or a group of Polish citizens and/or individual persons being Polish citizens." With this the authors claimed that no Polish citizen has ever taken part in any Nazi or communist crime. . . . As a history professor I hope that such an opinion results only from thoughtlessness and not from a complete lack of knowledge about Polish history in the twentieth century, or an equally harmful desire to deprive Poles of a fundamental aspect of human dignity: the capacity to choose good or evil. For if neither groups of nor individual Polish citizens had anything to do with these crimes, then why all the ado about the iniquities of the communist regime? After all, everything bad was done by some alien creatures, most likely Martians.*

By then the proponents of a hard-line "historical policy" in Poland were waiting for Jan's new book. *Fear* had been published in English in 2006. It was scheduled to appear in Polish the following year—but was delayed: the Polish publisher was afraid of releasing the book before the October 2007 parliamentary elections and thereby possibly swinging the election to the populists. It was a not unreasonable concern.

And so the Polish version of *Fear* appeared in print only in January 2008. Shortly thereafter, a Krakow district attorney initiated an inquiry into the book on the basis of the new law. Jan appeared unfazed.

"It's nice," he told the press, "that the district attorney is reading my book."

The president of the Institute of National Remembrance called Jan "the vampire of historiography."

"Man is a savage, evil beast," said Marek Edelman, the hero of the Warsaw Ghetto Uprising, who was now well into his eighties.

Moreover, for Marek Edelman the pathology of those who had lived through the Second World War—the ease with which the prospect of personal gain or revenge could inspire murder—was a particular one.

"In my opinion the problem will end only when the generation who witnessed the Holocaust has died," Marek Edelman added.

I thought of Arnošt Lustig, so much more jovial and less cynical than Marek Edelman, who nonetheless felt similarly.

"No one who survived the war is normal," Arnošt once said, "it's impossible."

Adam Michnik was sitting around the same table with Marek Edelman that day in a Jagiellonian University auditorium.

"I would like," Adam Michnik said, "to treat the discussion about Gross's book as a Polish-Polish discussion and not a Polish-Jewish one."

It was not a trivial distinction. In Jan's mind, the discussion had always been a Polish-Polish one. It was his Polishness that had shaped him.

"I wrote this book as a Pole," Jan said.

And despite what his critics—and many of his American friends—believed, this was the truth. For this book, like Neighbors, was all about his Polishness, about wanting the Polish intelligentsia to be what it ought to be, what he'd grown up believing it should be: the conscience of the nation.

The journalist Anna Bikont wrote a long article about Jan—not about Fear but about Jan himself. It was the most personal, and the best one I'd read.

"The first person I saw back in Poland from the March emigration was Janek's father, Zygmunt Gross," one of Jan's friends remembered. *"He'd come with the ashes of his wife, Hanna Szumańska, which he wanted to bury in Poland. Many years later Janek buried his father in Poland."*

Adam Michnik told Anna Bikont that in the apartment where Jan grew up, it was if there were no communism. Inside that apartment people talked about poetry.

It created a difference between Adam and Jan—for Jan, Adam believed, didn't understand "Judeo-Bolshevism," he didn't perceive it. It wasn't Jan's world. It was, though, Adam's world: Adam Michnik was a child of Polish Jewish communists.

"But I, when I read in Fear, *that the lives of Jews in Poland after the war were a nightmare,"* Adam Michnik said, *"I have in the back of my mind that the people my father knew, Jewish communists who had sat in prison before the war, were getting apartments on the Alley of Roses, while in the meantime the Home Army soldiers in detention and in prison were kept up to their ankles in shit."*

Adam and Jan had known each other for a very long time.

"When we founded the Club of the Seekers of Contradictions," Adam Michnik remembered, *"Janek was fourteen, I was fifteen . . . We knew that in Poland there was a dictatorship based on lies, only I was a rebellious communist, I was interested in Trotsky and the differences between the young Marx and the older Marx, while Jan didn't care about that. He was interested in Thomas Mann."*

At a Starbucks in midtown Manhattan, Anna Bikont told me that her friends from the 1968 "March emigration"—even now, after forty years in the United States—"still *live* Poland." She had come to New York to escape from Poland for a while—but there was no escape.

▪ ▪ ▪

IN 2007, ANDRZEJ Wajda, the same Polish director who had made the films *Ashes and Diamonds* and *Korczak*, completed a film about the 1940 Soviet massacre of thousands of Polish officers near the Katyń forest. Toward the film's end there was a scene involving two sisters. The war had just ended. The German occupation was over, and the communists were coming to power in Poland. One sister chose cooperation with the new communist regime; the other chose resistance. And just before the principled and rebellious sister was arrested, the one who had opted for accommodation said to her, *"There will be no free Poland—not in our lifetime, not in the lifetimes of our children."*

That was almost true.

For in the end, the revolution did come in the lifetimes of the children of those women who were young in 1945.

Nineteen years after the fall of communism, Adam Michnik published in *Gazeta Wyborcza* an interview with his old friend Václav Havel. Both men had been among the victors of 1989. They had won: Václav Havel had become president of postcommunist Czechoslovakia; Adam Michnik had become the founder and editor in chief of Poland's most important newspaper. Yet the imprisoned playwright who had gone to live in the castle was not enamored of this new, postcommunist world.

"With the evolution of this global, consumer civilization masses of people are advancing who are not creating any values," Havel said. *"I feel a need for some kind of existential revolution. Something has to change in people's consciousness."*

Adam Michnik and Václav Havel had known each other for thirty years: they had first met in the mountains, in 1978, at a secret, illegal gathering of Czechoslovak and Polish dissidents. Out of that meeting came Havel's essay "The Power of the Powerless," the tale of the greengrocer, who every morning put the sign in his shop window saying, "Workers of the world unite!" If a twenty-year-old today were to read "The Power of the Powerless"—Adam Michnik wanted to know—what could he take from it?

"The fundamental imperative," Havel answered, *"to live in truth."*

∎ ∎ ∎

GENERATION, AN UNUSUALLY important category in communist times, remained so in the postcommunist years.

Adrian, a Polish poet from Łódź, was my own age.

"Our generation won the lottery," he told me in the summer of 2008. Adrian's friends, by and large, were living much better than their parents had. In 1989 they had been just about to enter the university. And so they had a chance: a chance to make practical choices, to study economics and foreign languages, to find well-paying jobs at multinational firms.

Adrian told me of one friend in particular, a devout Catholic who would not allow a critical word to be said about the pope in his house. It was an impressive house, outside of Łódź, on a large property bought with the profits from his business: an "erotic network," which offered services by e-mail and text message.

"The biggest secret," Adrian told me, "only guys work there. Because guys know what guys want."

This was the generation Havel believed was creating no new values.

My Lithuanian graduate student Jolanta was born in 1977—fourteen years before the Soviet Union disintegrated in 1991. In her mind her own generation was a transitional one, with one foot in the Soviet world of her parents and the other in the new world of cell phones. It gave her, she believed, a unique perspective: for she understood both of those worlds, both the older generations formed by Soviet times and the younger ones formed by high-speed internet.

"Some of my friends, mostly those older than me by four or five years, did not come out of the changes as unscathed as I did," Jolanta wrote. *"They had already finished high school and were at university when the Soviet system collapsed. Some had just started new jobs that became redundant with the gusts of strong new winds. Even now, lots of them find it difficult to live in the Soviet-free Lithuania, and it's difficult for me to explain why. . . . Iskalechennye sud'boi, that's how my friends call them. Broken by fate."*

Another of my graduate students, Ania from Gdańsk, was also of Jolanta's generation, born in the mid-1970s. In the 1990s, Ania had studied in Gdańsk and in Geneva before beginning her doctoral work in the United States. Like Jolanta, Ania had been too young to take an active part in 1989, yet too old not to realize that something momentous was happening. She felt closer to the generation older than her own than she did to the generation only a few years younger.

"Those just several years younger already knew how to think about Europe without that absurd mixture of superiority and inferiority complexes," she wrote to me. *"I have the feeling that twenty-five-year-olds perceive Europe as part of their horizon, as something their own, as a self-evident element in their lives. For those in their thirties—Europe is still more a divertissement, an ornament in their lives, than it is a foregone conclusion."*

One day that summer of 2008, my Czech political theorist friend Pavel and I talked about "Eastern Europe." Pavel had never been among those offended by that description—he'd always presented himself as an East European. Now, though, "Eastern Europe" was a vanishing category, and Pavel was finding that he needed that label less and less. So, too, did he no longer conceal the Marxist-Leninist part of his philosophy degree: the nineties were over, some shame had passed. For Pavel this was a critical distinction: guilt versus shame. About communism—about having studied Marxism-Leninism at the university—he felt no guilt. But for a long time he had felt shame.

Pavel and I talked about Václav Havel, who told Adam Michnik that only when a new generation matured, a generation wholly untainted by communism, would there be a chance for real change, a chance to escape the influence of the opportunists, a chance to bring new values into public life. This was how Marek Edelman and Arnošt Lustig felt about the generation who had lived through the war. The twentieth century had not been a good one.

That summer Pavel's sister and her family came to visit New Haven. Pavel's nephew was born in 1991; his niece was born in 1993. They were of the new, untainted generation in which Havel placed his hopes. Multilingual, cosmopolitan teenagers from Prague, they had gone to school in England and Spain and traveled in the United States. The distinction between Eastern and Western Europe was not something they rejected: rather, they were not especially aware that such a distinction existed at all.

One day I asked Pavel's sixteen-year-old nephew what he thought about communism.

"Everything belonged to the state," he answered, "that's the main thing."

After a moment he added, "It sounds good, but it was proven not so good."

"Socialism with a human face"—the slogan encapsulating the hopes of 1968—brought no associations at all. Pavel's nephew and niece had an idea that tanks had arrived in Prague in 1968 but were not certain from where. And they knew that Jan Palach was someone who'd set himself on fire but were unsure why. They knew, too, that Charter 77 was something people had signed, but they had no idea what it said.

"Do you know who Stalin was?" Pavel's sister asked her son.

"A dictator?" he answered after some hesitation.

"And Stalinism?"

"Probably the rule of Stalin . . . I don't know."

Tragedy and Romance

I n the spring of 2009, Vlasta came to Boston. And there, for the first time in fourteen years, we talked about Oskar's suicide. It was a long time before Amanda had told Vlasta exactly how it had happened: Oskar had gassed himself with carbon monoxide.

Vlasta told me, too, that during that year at Stanford from 1993 to 1994—the year Amanda and I were studying Czech with her, the year we all met—she had tried to dissuade Oskar from thoughts of returning to Prague. Already then Vlasta saw that returning would not be what he imagined it would be. His friends had made compromises Oskar would never understand; they had suffered things Oskar could never share.

Nearly fifteen years had passed since then; now it was a cool spring day in New England, with just a little bit of rain. Walking through Boston Vlasta and I talked for the first time about Oskar's memorial service, that awful scene in the pub, the awfulness of which Vlasta did not believe Amanda had even been able to absorb. And Vlasta remembered in particular something Honza, then still her husband, had said to her there. Amanda was talking—trying to talk—to Oskar's friends, middle-aged Czech men who did not want to listen to her. And when, as Amanda talked, the first one stood up to leave, Honza said to Vlasta, "Go over and slap him." Vlasta was struck by this: it was somehow very sensitive and very insensitive at once, and so very uncharacteristic of the lighthearted Honza.

■ ■ ■

I WAS IN Warsaw for a week that spring of 2009 when Adam Michnik published an essay about Henry Dasko, my friend from Toronto who had died of brain cancer two and a half years before. Adam remembered Henry from the years before March 1968, when Henry Dasko was still Henryk Daszkiewicz: diabolically bright and wildly handsome, an artist and a dreamer, a playboy with literary passions.

"One had to be a bit of a wanderer and an exile, a survivor of one of the dead worlds, of which there were so many in our century," Henry wrote much later, *"in order to fully understand* Lolita, *in order to truly decipher Nabokov."*

Henry had been born in Warsaw in 1946. His parents had been active members of the Communist Party since their youth.

The same was true of Adam Michnik—and just for that reason it was not easy for him to write about his friend Henry Dasko. This was especially so because he could never forget that both of their parents were "Polish communists of Jewish origin."

"All of us," Adam continued, *"of that generation, from that background . . . despise the communist system; we reject the notion that at one time it was good but later it got spoiled. No: we believe that communism was a falsehood from the beginning. We try, though, to understand the people who were engaged in communism, their heterogeneous motivations and their biographies, sometimes heroic and tragic, always naïve and brought to naught. We do this, driven perhaps by a conviction hidden somewhere in our subconscious that it's necessary to distinguish the sin from the sinner: the sin we condemn—the sinner we try to listen to, to understand."*

"It is surely our lot," Adam wrote of himself and Henry Dasko, of Irena Grudzińska and Kostek Gebert and Staszek Krajewski and their many friends, the children of Polish-Jewish communists,*"—we,*

the plague-stricken sons—to live to the end and die with that 'Christian' blemish. We have been thus marked."

▪ ▪ ▪

IN PRAGUE IN autumn 2007 an eighty-six-year-old woman was put on trial as an accomplice to murder. Nearly six decades earlier she had been a young prosecutor in the show trial of Milada Horáková, who was sentenced to death for Trotskyite conspiracy on behalf of American imperialism, with the goals of destroying the Czechoslovak people's democracy, restoring capitalist exploitation, and plotting a third world war. Now this elderly woman was the last participant in that show trial who remained alive; there was no one else with whom to settle accounts. The defendant did not appear in court—her health was too poor and she could no longer see. Yet she did make a statement to the press: *"I was fighting for my country and for a social order where no one could be out of work."*

The eighty-six-year-old former prosecutor was sentenced to six years in prison.

Six months later Prague saw the premiere of an opera based on the trial of Milada Horáková. The trial that had been staged so theatrically in 1950 was now restaged as theater once again, and Milada Horáková's farewell letter was set to music.

In autumn 2008 a very young historian named Adam Hradilek was working as a researcher at the Prague-based Institute for the Study of Totalitarian Regimes, the Czech counterpart to Poland's Institute of National Remembrance. He was investigating the story of an aspiring fighter pilot. When the communists took power in Czechoslovakia in 1948, Miroslav Dvořáček was twenty years old. At that time he and nearly one hundred other young cadets had been expelled from the Airborne Military Academy for "lacking a positive attitude" toward the new people's democracy.

Miroslav Dvořáček was among a group of the expelled cadets who, after defecting from Czechoslovakia to the American-occupied zone in Germany, became couriers for the Western-sponsored, anticommunist Czechoslovak intelligence service. The Czech general who recruited the young men promised them that once they'd completed their assignments he would arrange for them to become military pilots in the West. These boys had been formed by the war. Above all they wanted to fly.

In the West, Miroslav Dvořáček was given some six weeks of training. He was taught how to communicate by Morse code and how to read a map. In December 1949 his instructors gave him a compass, false identification papers, and a bottle of whiskey and sent him across the border.

Miroslav Dvořáček was not experienced at intelligence work. Nor was he especially skilled at it. During his second trip back to Czechoslovakia, in March of 1950, he was riding a tram across the Vltava River in Prague when he spotted an old friend named Iva. Excited to see her again, he got off the tram and went along with Iva to her student dormitory. He left his suitcase in her room and went off to look for the man he'd been sent to contact.

In the meantime Iva told her boyfriend that he couldn't spend the night with her because Miroslav Dvořáček was visiting. Iva's boyfriend, who could not have been pleased, mentioned this to his friend Milan Kundera, who also lived in the dormitory.

Later in the day Miroslav Dvořáček returned to Iva's dormitory room. There the police arrested him.

Digging around in the secret police archives, the young historian Adam Hradilek found a police document naming Milan Kundera as the student who had reported Miroslav Dvořáček's presence in the dormitory.

In *The Art of the Novel,* Kundera described Prague as the *"city of the weak."*

Miroslav Dvořáček spent fourteen years in a communist prison camp.

Martin Šimečka, the author of the touching Slovak novel *The Year of the Frog,* was now the editor of the Czech weekly *Respekt.* It was Martin who first published the story about Miroslav Dvořáček and Milan Kundera's fateful denunciation—in a rather more sensationalist way than the inexperienced Adam Hradilek would have liked.

The story caused a scandal—although I did not entirely understand why. I was not surprised by what Adam Hradilek had found in the archives. The possibility—or probability—that Milan Kundera was the informant did not change how I thought about him: he was an unusually gifted writer who had been a Stalinist in his youth.

Martin Šimečka's colleague Samuel Abrahám—also from Bratislava, of the same generation, a political scientist, a writer and editor who shared many of Martin's liberal democratic commitments—wrote to Milan Kundera in Paris. Samuel was shocked by the *Respekt* article: a high-quality intellectual weekly had suddenly deteriorated, he believed, into tabloid journalism.

And Milan Kundera answered Samuel Abrahám: *"I did not think it was possible to start such an international persecution on the basis of a single lie."*

I wondered: Was Milan Kundera truly surprised? The legacy of totalitarianism is *"the spirit of the trial,"* he had written.

Samuel, though, was surprised. He was also angry and hurt. He published an essay that was in part an open letter to Martin Šimečka.

Respekt, *the magazine in which the article was published, reproduced a facsimile of a police document from 1950. To assure the public that neither the story nor the document was a matter of speculation by the authors, the editor in chief, Martin Šimečka, wrote in the editorial of the same issue of the journal: "We did not search for it, it was revealed to us for reasons that can only be of a metaphysical nature." Who cares about facts, logic, motivation, or what the accused has to say? The journalists do not doubt the "holy writ" of the communist police from the 1950s. Kundera can say whatever he likes, deny the accusations a thousand times, but it will not take away the stigma of guilt.*

In spring 2009, at a conference in Vilnius, I saw both Samuel Abrahám and Martin Šimečka, who now no longer spoke to each other. Late at night, in the hotel bar, Samuel, Tim, and I talked about the "Kundera affair." Samuel could not believe it was possible: Milan Kundera might have been a communist, but surely he had not denounced Miroslav Dvořáček. Milan Kundera, after all, was from a cultured family in Brno, his father was a classical pianist, he had been raised up among the bourgeois intelligentsia, amid Habsburg liberalism . . .

Samuel was a bright man, but he was misunderstanding something fundamental about Stalinism: a childhood spent listening to Mozart offered one no immunity against it. In 1950 Milan Kundera, like so many young Czechs whose political consciousness had been formed by the "betrayal at Munich" and the German occupation that followed, was an impassioned young Stalinist, deeply committed to building communism in Czechoslovakia. In accordance with the worldview that he himself entirely publicly at that time avowed, reporting the presence of a foreign agent in his dormitory would have been not a crime but, on the contrary, a moral imperative.

And unlike Milada Horáková and Rudolf Margolius and so many other victims of Stalinism, Miroslav Dvořáček *was* working for foreign intelligence.

Milan Kundera's sympathies in those years were not at all a secret: his poetry was published in the Stalinist-era literary newspapers. And after all, it was not only Kundera. This was the trajectory of a generation: those born in the 1920s who became the young Stalinists of the 1940s and 1950s, writing court poetry for the Party, and subsequently the revisionist Marxists of the 1960s, striving for "socialism with a human face," and finally the dissidents and émigrés of the 1970s and 1980s, articulating the most sophisticated critiques of totalitarianism.

"My own youth, my own 'lyrical age' and poetic activity coincide with the worst period of the Stalinist era," Kundera said in an interview in the mid-1960s. In Kundera's opinion, no one of his generation could really be satisfied with himself.

This is what I told Samuel Abrahám in Vilnius, in the bar of the neoclassical Hotel Conti, which extended the length of the block in two directions. When Tim and I had flown into Vilnius via Helsinki the day before, no one had checked our passports at the airport: Lithuania was now a member of the European Union. Yet in the hotel room, in the binder containing hotel information, included among the list of "services available for an additional charge," together with "dry cleaning," "fitness center," and "sauna," was the service "bodyguard." It was a reminder that Vilnius was still a post-Soviet city.

The next day I talked to Martin Šimečka, who unapologetically stood not only by his decision to publish the article but also by his conviction that Milan Kundera was guilty. For the files in the Czech archives, Martin insisted, were 99 percent trustworthy.

Martin, like Samuel, was a very bright man, but this, too, made little sense. No archive was 99 percent trustworthy: documents always concealed as well as revealed. The author of any given report could always prove to have been manipulative and self-interested, or simply stupid or sloppy or confused. There was no such thing as a perfectly objective source, produced outside time and place and human frailty.

In any case, it seemed to me that if there were to be a public discussion, the real questions should be these: Why did so many of the brightest minds of Milan Kundera's generation become Stalinists in their youth? Why in 1946 did the communists win 38 percent of the vote in genuinely free elections? How was Stalinism in Czechoslovakia able to happen?

"Kundera's past as a young Stalinist," Martin wrote to me later, *"was actually forgotten or pushed away from national memory."*

Martin's father had been of Kundera's generation. And during all the years of debates about communism between father and son, Martin had never once asked his father if, in the 1950s, he had ever done anything like this—if he had ever committed crimes, played a direct role in arrests, imprisonments, executions. Now it was too late.

Martin had loved his father very much, yet I did not doubt that had Milan Šimečka still been alive today, Martin would have asked him these questions, no matter how difficult. Despite his blindness about the archives, Martin was imbued with a self-critical spirit. He agreed with Václav Havel that his generation, too, was tainted.

"We are still not free," he told the audience at the Vilnius conference. "All of us who lived at least part of our adult lives under communism have been marked by the past to the extent that we may never be able to discuss it in the language of a natural, free world."

Martin said something else as well: in 1989 East Europeans had hoped that they would have something to teach, to give to Western Europe; they cherished the conviction that the experience of suffering had made them more sensitive, more inquisitive, more intellectual.

"Today," Martin said, "that hope looks pathetic."

▪ ▪ ▪

"SOMEDAY," HEDA MARGOLIUS had told me when I'd interviewed her in 1997 in Prague, "I'd like to see a public discussion come into being here about those people who truly to the depths of their souls believed that communism was a new opportunity for humanity, who were willing to renounce everything that was theirs alone for a better future for everyone. Today it's only with difficulty that we can conjure up such people in our minds."

Now was not yet the time, Heda acknowledged. But someday.

The "Kundera affair" might have been the beginning of such a discussion—but was not. The Czechs and Slovaks perhaps were not ready. In Poland, though, there were some who were ready.

That same spring of 2009 Poland's Institute of National Remembrance sent a letter to the city council of Klimontów, the hometown of Bruno Jasieński, the dandy and futurist who once wore a top hat and a monocle. It had come to the Institute of National Remembrance's attention that in the small Polish town of Klimontów there remained a street named after Bruno Jasieński—a street that was in effect *"a glorification ... of the politics of Josef Stalin, of the criminal ideology of communism."*

The letter continued:

*I wish to direct attention to the fact that maintaining a name
of this type in independent Poland should be considered an
act having a negative educational impact; a glorification of a
criminal ideology; and a betrayal of the Homeland; as well as
an objective encouragement to commit acts in violation of the
Constitution of the Polish Republic.*

The Institute of National Remembrance demanded that the
street's name be changed.

The street in question was a small street, on which stood a
school, a church, and the house where Bruno Jasieński was born.
Fans of the largely forgotten futurist poet signed a petition in protest. In the Institute of National Remembrance's letter, they wrote,
*"There is not a shadow of benevolence or even understanding for a
person caught in the gears of the totalitarian system."*

Bruno Jasieński's supporters continued:

*One can find weak points in the biography of virtually
everyone . . . In the opinion of the Institute of National Remembrance's historians, patrons of streets should be without flaws!
Bruno Jasieński with certainty does not fulfill such criteria.
With his complicated biography he is the perfect admonition
against Stalinist totalitarianism. For the errors of his youth he
paid the highest price. He spent more than a year in Soviet
prison. He was tortured. He lived through hell on earth. Death
for him was a long-awaited redemption. Yet even then, pushed
into the depth of despair, he maintained his humanity. He did
not drag innocent people with him to ruin . . .*

Bruno Jasieński was perhaps not quite so innocent as his twenty-
first-century fans made him appear—during the Stalinist years he
more than once played the role of accuser. Still, what the petition's
authors wrote was true: his biography revealed the tragedy of Stalinism. And for his youthful idealism he did pay the highest price.

"Fortunately," the letter written by Bruno Jasieński's fans went

on, *"his poems survived the Stalinist terror. If language is our spiritual Homeland and the testament of our ancestors, then as a poet Jasieński did much more for Poland than have those custodians of patriotism who are currently accusing him."*

Days later *Gazeta Wyborcza* published a letter of protest by an older Polish literary critic.

"Was Jasieński a communist?" he wrote.

> *He was an antifascist, a romantic of proletarian revolution, a victim of Soviet pathology, a deeply tragic figure. Painfully sensitive to injury and intolerance, he believed—naïvely?—in a utopia of humanity liberated from national and social conflicts, just as, in the early twentieth century, so many of the great thinkers and artists believed. Anyone unable to distinguish human dreams from brutal totalitarian politics does not understand the twentieth century.*

Gazeta Wyborcza published his letter on 23 April. The following day, the Institute of National Remembrance's president recoiled: he apologized to the Klimontów city council and withdrew the institute's demand.

▪   ▪   ▪

I WAS VISITING Poland that spring of 2009. A few months earlier, the Polish translation of *Caviar and Ashes* had appeared. Now a liberal Polish writer named Daniel Passent published a column about the book. It began with a satire of the Institute of National Remembrance: If the institute were to seek a new president, who would be a viable choice? Those on the right would have a reason to oppose all potential candidates: One was a renegade for having left when the current president appeared. Another had a father who had been a communist. Still another had a husband who was politically involved on the left.

"It seems," the columnist wrote, *"that no Pole can be seated upon the barrel of gunpowder that is the Institute of National Remembrance*

(unless it were to be a real Pole, in the style of Dr. Chodakiewicz), and that it will be necessary to entrust that position to someone un-burdened by studies at a totalitarian university, with professors who have not undergone lustration, someone uncompromised by collab-oration with Gazeta Wyborcza, someone who, in addition, needs to have been conceived in vitro, in order that his father be unknown (and his grandfather from the Wehrmacht as well)."

The "authentic Pole" Marek Chodakiewicz was the paradigmatic model of a "historian from the Institute of National Remembrance," determined to defend Poland's good name abroad. He had devoted a weirdly sexual diatribe to *Caviar and Ashes*, in which, by fusing "homosexual" and "Cominform," he coined the pejorative neolo-gism "Hominform."

"This is a work about the unhappy, the complex-laden, the lost and the alienated, about the neurotics, hysterics, and the frustrated ones, about drunks, suicides, homosexuals," Marek wrote.

"It's a pity," he commented further, *"that Shore chose to occupy herself with these pathological types, rather than writing a book about normal people."*

Daniel Passent's satire of the Institute of National Remembrance and historians like Marek Chodakiewicz was poignantly reminis-cent of Antoni Słonimski's sardonic columns of the 1930s. In 1937 Słonimski had asked his readers the rhetorical question: *"If such an enormous majority of the nation is Judaized and communized and the rest is composed of Masons, Germans and Ukrainians, then where are the real Poles?"* The subject of another column that year was how often one heard, *"Are you a Pole? A quarter Pole? Can you prove your Polishness?"*

As at Shabbat dinner at Bogna's apartment more than a decade earlier, the spirit of the 1930s—the return of the repressed—was palpable.

Daniel Passent proposed me to head the Institute of National Remembrance—precisely because I was not a Pole and had written a book that could not have been written by anyone in Poland, in a tone that could not have been taken by anyone in Poland.

I was unsure if this was true. It was the case, though, that listening to the Polish reception of *Caviar and Ashes* at moments felt like eavesdropping on a collective psychotherapy session. Those who loved the book were preoccupied with the same question as those who hated it: Why hadn't a Pole written this book?

One critic declared that the existence of *Caviar and Ashes* was the price of the Poles' own laziness: now an American woman had taken the opportunity to tell the Poles' story in her own way.

Another reviewer wanted to know: Why was it only from an American woman that Polish readers were finally learning what their country had really been like?

A reader wrote to the magazine that had published Daniel Passent's column, thanking the editors for introducing her to *Caviar and Ashes*, for finally someone without complexes had told this story.

"But it's a shame," the reader added, *"that it had to be an American woman who did this."*

A sympathetic radio interviewer asked me if I had been able to write this book, when no one in Poland had been, because they had complexes while I was free of complexes.

It was a strange notion. I assured him that I had many complexes as well, surely as many as he had. But just as we each had our own complexes, we each wrote our own books. After all, books were personal things.

Another journalist wanted to know: Had I not been afraid to write about people like Wanda Wasilewska and Janina Broniewska—people who were hated, whose names were anathema in Poland? Where had I found the courage?

This was a misunderstanding: it was not courage at all. As had been the case in Domažlice all those years before, when the stove was broken and I let the students put their winter boots back on, what appeared to be courage was only an absence of acculturation.

▪ ▪ ▪

DURING THAT VISIT to Poland in spring 2009 Pan Sławek invited me to give a talk about *Caviar and Ashes* at the Broniewski

Museum. Among the people from the audience who approached me afterward was a woman of around sixty. Her name was Alina, and she had a story to tell me about Janina Broniewska: she was that friend of Janina Broniewska's granddaughter, Pani Ewa, whom Janina Broniewska had taken in, together with her infant, in 1968. She and Ewa, both nineteen years old with newborn babies, had been afraid to tell Ewa's grandmother what had happened to Alina's young husband: that he had been among the students imprisoned. That was why Alina and her baby had been evicted from their apartment. Three months passed, and finally the two young women had to explain Alina's husband's absence.

"And do you know what *Babcia* said?" Pani Alina whispered in my ear. Like her friend, Pani Ewa, Pani Alina called Janina Broniewska *Babcia*—"Grandma."

"Fuck, they're locking up children now!"

"Grandma" made a phone call. Three days later, Alina's young husband returned from prison.

▪ ▪ ▪

AT THAT TIME Jan's friend, the literary editor Basia Toruńczyk, published an open letter to the young Poles of the "New Left." The letter was both warm and critical, supportive and condescending. Basia Toruńczyk, like Jan Gross and Irena Grudzińska, like Alik Smolar and Adam Michnik and Pani Alina's young husband, had been among the Warsaw students arrested for their participation in the March 1968 protests. She wrote about herself and her friends: their hunger for complete freedom and their distaste for school, for uniforms, for any kind of conformity, for petit bourgeois life— above all in its communist version. The students demonstrating in March 1968 had had no illusions of victory, only a belief in the value of a noble defeat. Some of them had been raised by influential parents, prewar communists, often of Jewish origin. They were young people who had been under the influence of Marxism since childhood, who, as they grew up, had watched reality confront ideology. They became fearful of the collectivist spirit and the desire for grand narratives. Their challenge, then, was to abandon grand narratives without abandoning ethical values, to extricate themselves from ideology without falling into nihilism.

Basia Toruńczyk dedicated this essay to a young man named Sławomir Sierakowski.

I met Sławomir Sierakowski in March of 2009. He was twenty-nine years old and already the spokesperson of Poland's "New Left." And in fact this was a *new* Left—not a postcommunist Left—whose core was composed of people now in their mid- to late twenties, too young to have been fully formed by communism. They were, on average, several years younger than the generation "graced by a late birth" and calling for lustration. Sławomir Sierakowski talked manically with his hands. He slept very little. Instead he chain-smoked and poured spoonfuls of sugar into endless cups of espresso.

Sławomir Sierakowski had invited me to give a talk about *Caviar and Ashes* at the salon he hosted. He was a neo-Marxist of a sort, a social democrat with revolutionary proclivities, and a student of postmodern philosophy who wanted not only to deconstruct but also to build something again. He had founded a society dedicated to reviving the legacy of a brilliant nineteenth-century Polish Marxist philosopher who had died of tuberculosis at the age of thirty-three.

About *Caviar and Ashes* Sławomir Sierakowski was fanatically enthusiastic. He understood the book as revolutionary—and prescriptive. He reminded me of the Plastic People of the Universe's band manager, Ivan Jirous: an *animateur,* a cultural figure without his own definable vocation per se but with an extraordinary ability to mobilize other people, to persuade them to do things. He was considering, Sławomir told me, whether he should found a new political party.

The room was crowded, there were not enough seats, people were standing. The audience greeted me as if I had come to deliver a secret message from another world. Sławomir was the host, and the audience asked me questions:

"So what can we do?"

"How can we today, as intellectuals, engage on behalf on the revolution and get it right?"

"How can we save the world?"

Excellent questions—to which I had no answers.

The lives of these angst-laden poets and their friends had not disclosed to me the secret of how to save the world. What I had learned from figures like Aleksander Wat, for whom life was unbearably heavy, was rather that pathological narcissism was not only something one reveled in but above all something one truly suffered from; that absolute subjectivity brought absolute anguish; that radical nihilism and radical contingency were psychically unbearable. I learned that the noblest of motives could lead to the basest of outcomes, that actions inevitably had consequences in excess of their intent. I learned that I could not write a book with a satisfying conclusion, for the lives of the intriguing protagonists were breathtaking catastrophes. I learned that the past could not be made okay.

■ ■ ■

IT WAS A Sunday afternoon, 18 December 2011, when Sławomir Sierakowski rang our doorbell in New Haven. He had spent the previous few months at Yale, where he had captivated my students with his manic energy and his insistence—following the ideal of the nineteenth-century Russian intelligentsia—that ideas were to be *lived*. Now he was about to return to Warsaw and wanted to say goodbye. I answered the door.

"Václav Havel is dead," he told me, still in the doorway.

"I know," I said. It had not been a fairy-tale ending. Havel had died that morning, at home in his cottage in the Bohemian countryside, after a long illness. He was seventy-five years old. Ivan Jirous had preceded him to the grave just a few weeks earlier.

Could we say something to the Polish New Left, Sławomir asked us, about what Havel had meant to us?

"There is no such thing as neutrality; there is only, as Havel grasped, inauthenticity," Tim replied.

"What I learned from Havel about the moral ambiguity of being both a victim and an oppressor was my entryway into postcommunist Europe," I told Sławomir. "It was the beginning of my fascination with those historical moments in which there are no innocent choices."

When he reached the other side of the Atlantic, Sławomir organized a series of public discussions about Havel. Havel remained timely today, Sławomir told his audience, as a voice that implicitly warned us against ignoring the commonalities between the old oppressive era of communism and the new free era of democracy—who warned us about the instrumental reason that leads to cynicism. Sławomir believed this should be our wake-up call. Postcommunist Poland, he lamented, was a part of a postcommunist world in which there was no common set of values that proved stronger than each person's private interest. And on a daily basis, everyone—like Havel's greengrocer who hung the "Workers of the world unite!" sign—accepted this. "We are all greengrocers from Havel's essay," he told his audience.

"In today's world we know more and more," Sławomir said, "but we don't use our knowledge to get together and change the world. We use it so that each of us, individually, can adapt to this imperfect world. That we can get together and change this imperfect world almost no one believes."

Sławomir wanted very much for his generation to be the one Havel had been waiting for: the one that, having escaped, by the "grace of late birth," being wholly formed by communism, would reject selfishness and opportunism and would bring rediscovered moral values into public life. It would involve a touch of romanticism, a revolutionary rejection of cynicism, and a desire to reenchant a disenchanted world.

I remembered, then, the day two and a half years earlier when I had first been introduced to the Polish "New Left." In the front row that evening had sat a bright young man who was thin and wore glasses with thick plastic frames. He had thanked me for the book. Finally someone had rehabilitated the Polish intellectuals engaged in Marxism, finally someone had presented him and his peers with a vision of history that could serve as a signpost for the young Polish Left.

"I'm very, very flattered," I had said to him—to all of them, "that you liked my book. And it's true that I tried to write with empathy. I wanted to understand these people—Aleksander Wat and Władysław Broniewski and Wanda Wasilewska, Jakub Berman and Janina Broniewska, Bruno Jasieński and Adam Ważyk and all of them—I wanted to understand why they came to make the choices they did.

"But," I added, "these people I wrote about—things turned out *really, really badly* for all of them. This book—their story—is a tragedy."

"But I didn't read it as a tragedy!" said the bright young man in the front row. "I read it as a romance."

ACKNOWLEDGMENTS

This is a deeply subjective book. During my first long stay in Warsaw over a dozen years ago, Piotr Wróbel encouraged me to write in the first person, owning the perspective of a young American woman who wanders into a completely different world and attempts to untangle the dark mysteries of Polish-Jewish relations. The notes I made then in some way form the core of what follows. Now I find myself unsure of how to write acknowledgments for a book among whose motifs is the guilt of writing. Writing is bearing witness, as Roger Cohen and others have said; yet I am also aware that bearing witness contains within itself an exposure of other people's lives.

I began this book in 1997, as a graduate student at Stanford University. The content was inspired by my European friends, colleagues, and acquaintances and by my European interlocutors from the dead, encountered in books and archives. The writing was inspired by the passionately American Gilbert Sorrentino, who insisted that aesthetic academization must be resisted, that writing must be kept fresh. Two of his seminars in the early 1990s, on William Carlos Williams and on the *Ouvroir de littérature potentielle*, introduced me to the power of form and radically altered how I thought about language. I owe to him, and to our dialogue over several years, a sense of the palpability of words.

I returned to this book when I was teaching first at Indiana University, and later at Yale University, institutions to which I'm indebted for providing the structural stability that allows me to indulge in an intellectual life. At Yale my students in a fall 2008 seminar devoted to European intellectuals' responses to totalitarianism read excerpts from an early version of this manuscript. I thank them for their goodwill, their enthusiasm, and their thoughts. I completed a draft of this book at the Institut für die Wissenschaften vom Menschen in Vienna, a very special place, and the only institution where I have ever felt "at home." I owe my having found my way there to the late Tony Judt, whose loss can never be made okay.

This is a book that is unusually beholden to (the perhaps dying art of) conversation. I am grateful to everyone who talked to me, including those who might prefer not to be named. A February 2010 seminar at the Institut für die Wissenschaften vom Menschen was unusually valuable. Comments there by Slavenka Drakulić, János Mátyás Kovács, Ivan Krastev, and Hiroaki Kuromiya were especially thought-provoking. Slavenka Drakulić was also a fellow participant in the panel discussion on totalitarianism's afterlife, organized by the Central European Forum in Bratislava, which inspired the subtitle of this book.

While most of the translations in the book are my own, I have drawn upon published English translations in several instances: Miron Białoszewski, *A Memoir of the Warsaw Uprising*, trans. Madeline Levine (Evanston: Northwestern University Press, 1991); Karel Čapek, *War with the Newts*, trans. M. and R. Weatherall (Evanston: Northwestern University Press, 1985); E. M. Cioran, *The Trouble with Being Born*, trans. Richard Howard (NY: Arcade Publishing, 2011); Michel Jakob, "Wakefulness and Obsession: An Interview with E. M. Cioran," *Salamagundi* 103 (Summer 1994): 122–45; Fyodor Dostoevsky, *The Brothers Karamazov*, trans. Andrew H. MacAndrew (NY: Bantam Books, 1970); Václav Havel, "The Power of the Powerless," trans. Paul Wilson, *The Power of the Powerless*, ed. John Keane (Armonk, NY: M.E. Sharpe, 1985): 24–96; Radu Ioanid, *The Sword of the Archangel*, trans. Peter Heinegg (Boulder: East European Monographs, 1990); Hanna Krall, *To Outwit God*, trans. Joanna Stasinska Weschler and Lawrence Weschler (Evanston: Northwestern University Press, 1992); Milan Kundera, *The Book of Laughter and Forgetting*, trans. Michael Henry Heim (NY: Penguin Books, 1981); Milan Kundera, *The Joke* (NY: HarperPerennial, 1992); Arnošt Lustig, *The Unloved* (NY: Arbor House, 1985); Pope John Paul II, "Pope John Paul II Speaks in

Victory Square," *From Stalinism to Pluralism,* ed. Gale Stokes (NY: Oxford University Press, 1991): 200–203; Antony Polonsky and Joanna Michlic, eds., *The Neighbors Respond* (Princeton: Princeton University Press, 2003); Martin Šimečka, *The Year of the Frog,* trans. Peter Petro (Baton Rouge: Louisiana State University Press, 1993); Vladimir Tismăneanu, "How was Ceauşescu Possible?," trans. Julie Dawson (NY: Romanian Cultural Institute, 2011); Leon Volovici, *Nationalist Ideology and Antisemitism: The Case of Romanian Intellectuals in the 1930s* (Oxford: Pergamon Press, 1991); Aleksander Wat, *My Century,* trans. Richard Lourie (NY: W. W. Norton, 1988); Yitzhak Zuckerman, *A Surplus of Memory,* trans. Barbara Harshav (Berkeley: University of California Press, 1993). The drawing by Szymon Zachariasz on page 174 (sygnatura 476/24) is reproduced with permission from Archiwum Akt Nowych in Warsaw.

Over a dozen trips to Eastern Europe were made possible by a variety of sources, beginning with a Stanford University Undergraduate Research Opportunities Grant in 1993. I want to acknowledge as well the American Council of Learned Societies, the University of Toronto Centre for Russian and East European Studies, IIE Fulbright, the Stanford University Center for Russian and East European Studies, the International Research and Exchanges Board, Fulbright-Hayes, the Mellon Foundation, the Taube Center for Jewish Studies at Stanford, the American Council for International Education, the Russian and East European Institute and the Borns Jewish Studies Program at Indiana University, and the Yale University Macmillan Center.

For years Kasia Chamera-Marquez, Agata Jagiełło, Kaśka Jesień, and Agnieszka and Andrzej Waśkiewicz have welcomed me to Warsaw, where much of this book is set. Norman Naimark and Sepp Gumbrecht were the best dissertation advisers in the world. Brad Abrams, Iwona Butz, Jan Gross, Jacek Leociak, Amir Weiner, Ksenia Zadorozhnaia, and Steven Zipperstein were ever-provocative dialogue partners, as were my graduate students Jolanta Mickute and Anna Muller. My friend Izabela Kalinowska appeared at my door one evening with a copy of the film *Trzech kumpli.* My irreplaceable colleagues from Indiana University, Dov Ber Kerler and Jeffrey Veidlinger, took me along on one of their expeditions into a past lived in Yiddish.

Marcin Szuster, the unusually talented and unusually patient translator of this book into Polish, offered wise advice at moments of vacillation. Paul Robinson inspired an appreciation for the continuing resonance of Freud—and of his "dark psychic closet." Eliza Shaw Valk and her architectural talents played an essential role in helping me to think visually. Pavel Barša, Andrea Baršová, Ian Bremmer, Jonathan Brent, Chris Calhoun, Lan Samantha Chang, Slavenka Drakulić, Paul Freedman, Konstanty Gebert, Amelia Glaser, Gail Glickman, Jan Tomasz Gross, Irena Grudzińska-Gross, Hans Ulrich Gumbrecht, the late Tony Judt, Eva Kalivodová, Andrew Koss, Nitzan Lebovic, Joanne Meyerowitz, Krzysztof Michalski, Norman Naimark, Ashley Noel, Meredeth Rouse, Jamie Sarfeh, Dan Shore, Aleksander Smolar, Mary Snyder, Timothy Snyder, Piotr Sommer, the late Gilbert Sorrentino, Stephanie Steiker, Dariusz Stola, Nancy Wingfield, Larry Wolff, Alexander Zeyliger, and Steven Zipperstein all read excerpts and in some cases full drafts of this manuscript. Sometimes they laughed, sometimes they cried, sometimes they cringed—I am indebted to all of their readings, and under no circumstances should they be burdened with any responsibility for what I have written.

Some final grateful thoughts: working with two people as sensitive, intelligent, and committed as my literary agent, Gillian MacKenzie, and my editor, Vanessa Mobley, has been a stroke of enormous good fortune in my life. I am thankful to Ian Bremmer for introducing me to Gillian, and to Gillian, in turn, for introducing me to Vanessa. This book has benefited more from their enthusiasm, insights, and literary sensibilities than I can express here.

Maria Andrade, Katherine Bednarczyk, Christine Plateroti, and Amelie Stummer took very good care of my baby, Kalev Tristan Snyder, while I made the final revisions to this manuscript. Kalev, unlike his American parents, is, by virtue of his multilingual, citizenshipless Viennese birth, an authentic Central European and rootless cosmopolitan. While his father has been an incomparably perceptive reader of multiple drafts, Kalev has yet to read any of my writing. I hope that someday (naturally once he's learned to read in one language or another) he'll find that these pages bring him closer to the place where he was born.

CAST OF HISTORICAL FIGURES

MORDECHAI (MORDEKHAI) ANIELEWICZ (c. 1920–1943) Zionist youth activist; leader of the Warsaw Ghetto Uprising; committed suicide when the Germans discovered his bunker.

ION ANTONESCU (1882–1946) Romanian marshal; in 1940 established the short-lived National-Legionary State with the fascist Iron Guard; eliminated the Iron Guard in 1941 to become dictator of the pro-German Romanian government; sentenced to death by a communist court after the war.

WŁADYSŁAW BARTOSZEWSKI (b. 1922) Polish historian and politician; during the Second World War active in the Polish Home Army, the anti-German resistance loyal to the Polish government in exile and in Żegota, the Council for Aid to the Jews; imprisoned in Auschwitz by the Germans; spent about seven years in prison in Stalinist Poland; active in Solidarity; after the fall of communism, served as ambassador to Austria, minister of foreign affairs, and senator.

EDVARD BENEŠ (1884–1948) Foreign minister under Czechoslovakia's founding president Tomáš Garrigue Masaryk (1850–1937) and later president of Czechoslovakia; chose not to resist Germany in September 1938; during the Second World War established a Czechoslovak national committee in exile; returned to Prague as the war ended and reestablished a government; capitulated when faced with the February 1948 communist coup.

ADOLF BERMAN (1906–1978) Younger brother of Jakub Berman; active in the Jewish resistance and in Żegota during the war; in postwar Poland, leader of the Marxist Zionist party Poalei Zion–Left; emigrated to Israel in 1950.

JAKUB BERMAN (1901–1984) Older brother of Adolf Berman; a liaison of the Communist Party of Poland with the intelligentsia during the interwar years; one of a triumvirate of Stalinist dictators in the postwar years, when he oversaw cultural affairs and the security apparatus; expelled from the Polish United Workers' Party in 1957.

BOLESŁAW BIERUT (1892–1956) Polish communist leader; general secretary of the Polish United Worker's Party during the interwar years; oversaw Sovietization in postwar Poland; died in Moscow in 1956 shortly following Khrushchev's "secret speech."

MARIAN BOGATKO (1906–1940) Bricklayer who became Wanda Wasilewska's second husband; active in the Polish Socialist Party during the interwar years; killed by the Soviet secret police in Lvov in 1940.

JANINA BRONIEWSKA (1904–1981) Author of children's literature; journalist in the Soviet Union during the war and a Party activist in the postwar years; the first wife of Władysław Broniewski and the closest friend of Wanda Wasilewska.

WŁADYSŁAW BRONIEWSKI (1897–1962) Polish poet who fought against the Red Army during the Polish-Soviet War; flirted with the Warsaw futurists; a revolutionary writer by the mid- to late 1920s; imprisoned in the Soviet Union, 1940–1941; spent the latter part of the war in Jerusalem after leaving the Soviet Union with the Anders army.

MARTIN BÚTORA (b. 1944) Slovak sociologist; founding member of Public Against Violence, which played a leading role in the Velvet Revolution of 1989; human rights adviser to Václav Havel, 1990–1992; Slovak ambassador to the United States, 1999–2003.

ZORA BÚTOROVÁ (b. 1949) Slovak sociologist; author of studies on attitudes toward minorities, transition to democracy, and gender issues in Slovakia.

NICOLAE CEAUŞESCU (1918–1989) General secretary of the Romanian Communist Party, 1965–1989, whose brutal rule was characterized by dynastic nationalism and a personality cult; executed together with his wife, Elena (1916–1989), in December 1989.

CORNELIU ZELEA CODREANU (1899–1938) Founder of the Romanian fascist movement known as the Iron Guard; imprisoned by King Carol II in 1938; shot to death shortly thereafter, allegedly while trying to escape.

DOINA CORNEA (b. 1939) Romanian French professor and human rights activist; dissident under communist leader Nicolae Ceauşescu's regime; persecuted by the Securitate (secret police); active in the democratic opposition after the fall of communism.

HENRY DASKO (HENRYK DASZKIEWICZ) (1947–2006) Polish student expelled from his university for taking part in protests against censorship in March

1968; emigrated to Canada, where he became a successful businessman active in Polish-Jewish dialogue and literary circles.

ALEXANDER DUBČEK (1921–1992) General secretary of the Communist Party of Czechoslovakia who led the Prague Spring of 1968; expelled from the Party in the aftermath of the Soviet-led invasion of Czechoslovakia in August 1968.

MAREK EDELMAN (C. 1919–2009) Bundist and leading figure in the Jewish Combat Organization; one of a handful of survivors of the 1943 Warsaw Ghetto Uprising; after the war became a cardiologist in Łódź; active in Solidarity.

KONSTANTY (KOSTEK) GEBERT (AKA DAWID WARSZAWSKI) (b. 1953) Polish Jewish journalist; active in Solidarity; key figure in Poland's "Jewish revival"; war correspondent in Bosnia during the Yugoslav Wars of the 1990s; founding editor of the Polish Jewish monthly *Midrasz*.

WŁADYSŁAW GOMUŁKA (1905–1982) Polish communist leader; accused of "nationalist deviation," expelled from the Polish United Workers' Party in 1949, and arrested in Stalinist Poland; rehabilitated in 1956 to lead a de-Stalinization campaign; as general secretary of the Polish United Workers' Party, directed the anti-Semitic "anti-Zionist" campaign of March 1968; forced to resign in 1970 following violent clashes between security forces and shipyard workers.

MIKHAIL SERGEEVICH GORBACHEV (b. 1931) General secretary of the Communist Party of the Soviet Union, 1985–1991; led policies of *glasnost* ("openness") and *perestroika* ("restructuring"); set in motion the end of the cold war.

JAN GROSS (b. 1947) Polish émigré sociologist and historian; imprisoned for his role as a student activist in the 1968 Warsaw University demonstrations; emigrated from Poland following his release from prison; active in supporting Solidarity from abroad.

IRENA GRUDZIŃSKA-GROSS (b. 1946) Polish émigré literary scholar; imprisoned for her role as a student activist in the 1968 Warsaw University demonstrations; emigrated from Poland following her release from prison; active in supporting Solidarity from abroad.

VÁCLAV HAVEL (1936–2011) Czech essayist and absurdist playwright; cofounder of the human rights dissident movement Charter 77; leader of the Velvet Revolution in 1989; first president of postcommunist Czechoslovakia.

MILADA HORÁKOVÁ (1901–1950) Democratic and feminist activist in interwar Czechoslovakia; arrested by the Germans in 1940 and interrogated by the Gestapo; liberated by the U.S. Army late in the war; show-tried by the Czechoslovak communist government on false charges of espionage and executed in 1950.

GUSTAV HUSÁK (1913–1991) Slovak communist imprisoned by Slovakia's German-allied fascist government during the Second World War; leader of communist Czechoslovakia, 1969–1989; succeeded by Václav Havel.

ION ILIESCU (b. 1930) Romanian politician; joined the Communist Party of Romania in 1953; fell out of favor with Ceaușescu in 1971; leader of the postcommunist Party of Social Democracy in Romania; president of Romania, 1990–1996 and 2000–2004.

BRUNO JASIEŃSKI (1901–1938) Polish futurist poet; emigrated to France in 1925, where he wrote the novel *I Burn Paris;* emigrated to the Soviet Union after being deported from France in 1929; executed in 1938 during the Great Terror.

IVAN (MAGOR) JIROUS (1944–2011) Czech poet and art historian; artistic director of the underground psychedelic band the Plastic People of the Universe; imprisoned for more than eight years between 1973 and 1989.

JAN KARSKI (1914–2000) Heroic courier of the Polish anti-German underground during the Second World War; arrested and tortured by the Gestapo in 1940; brought news of the Holocaust to the Western Allies; after the war became a professor at Georgetown University.

VÁCLAV KLAUS (b. 1941) Czech economist and politician; served as prime minister of postcommunist Czechoslovakia, and later as president of the Czech Republic; frequently in conflict with Václav Havel; prioritized and oversaw postcommunist economic privatization.

PAVEL KOHOUT (b. 1928) Czech poet, novelist, and playwright; enthusiast of Stalinism in his youth; reform communist in the 1960s; founding member of Charter 77; prevented from returning to Czechoslovakia from Austria during the last decade of communist rule.

JANUSZ KORCZAK (HENRYK GOLDSZMIT) (c. 1878–1942) Physician, author, and children's rights activist; orphanage director who refused any attempt to escape from the Warsaw Ghetto and was murdered together with the children in 1942 in Treblinka.

KAREL KOSÍK (1926–2003) Czech philosopher; member of a communist anti-Nazi resistance; young Stalinist in the postwar years; a revisionist Marxist during the 1960s; expelled from the Communist Party and his professorship at Charles University in 1970; returned to the university in 1990.

STANISŁAW (STASZEK) KRAJEWSKI (b. 1950) Polish mathematician, philosopher, and essayist; activist in Solidarity; cofounder of the Jewish Flying University in the late 1970s; leading figure in the Jewish revival and in interfaith dialogue.

MILAN KUNDERA (b. 1929) Stalinist poet in his youth, later a revisionist Marxist; Czech-turned-French essayist and novelist; emigrated to France in the 1970s.

VLADIMIR IL'ICH LENIN (1870–1924) Russian Marxist revolutionary; in 1902 published *What Is to Be Done?*, which argued for a professional vanguard of revolutionaries who could bring class consciousness to the workers; in 1917 returned to Russia from Swiss exile to lead the Bolshevik Revolution.

ARTUR LONDON (1915–1986) Czech communist; fought in the International Brigades in the Spanish Civil War and in the French resistance during the Second World War; co-defendant in the Slánský trial of 1952; sentenced to life imprisonment; released in 1956 and rehabilitated.

ARNOŠT LUSTIG (1926–2011) Czech Jewish novelist and survivor of Theresienstadt, Auschwitz, and Buchenwald; joined the Communist Party after the Second World War: reform communist in the 1960s; left Czechoslovakia following the August 1968 invasion and later became a professor at American University in Washington, D.C.

HEDA MARGOLIUS KOVÁLY (1919–2010) Czech literary translator and survivor of the Łódź Ghetto and Auschwitz; wife of Rudolf Margolius; fled Czechoslovakia after the 1968 invasion and worked as a librarian at Harvard University.

RUDOLF MARGOLIUS (1913–1952) Survivor of the Łódź ghetto, Auschwitz, and Dachau; deputy minister of foreign trade in the Czechoslovak communist government; co-defendant in the Slánský trial; sentenced to death in December 1952.

ALEKSANDER MASIEWICKI (1917–2011) Polish Jew who became a communist in his youth; student of Adolf Berman in the interwar years; deported to a Soviet labor settlement in 1940; returned to Poland in 1945; resigned from the Party during the March 1968 "anti-Zionist" campaign and subsequently emigrated.

VLADIMIR VLADIMIROVICH MAYAKOVSKY (1893–1930) Russian futurist poet and passionate enthusiast of the Bolshevik Revolution; committed suicide in Moscow in 1930.

VLADIMÍR MEČIAR (b. 1942) founder of the postcommunist nationalist party Movement for a Democratic Slovakia; three-time prime minister of Slovakia in the 1990s.

ADAM MICHNIK (b. 1946) Polish dissident and intellectual; leader of the 1968 student protests; activist in Solidarity who spent more than six years in prison; leading figure in the Round Table Talks; founder of the newspaper *Gazeta Wyborcza*.

STANISŁAW MIKOŁAJCZYK (1901–1966) Leader of the Polish Peasant Party; prime minister of the Polish government in exile in London, 1943–1944; returned to Poland at the end of the Second World War; fled postwar Poland with the onset of Stalinism.

CZESŁAW MIŁOSZ (1911–2004) Polish poet, essayist, and translator; defected in 1951 while serving in the Polish communist regime as cultural attaché in France; became a professor at University of California, Berkeley.

MICHAŁ MIRSKI (1905–1994) Member of the Communist Party of Poland in the 1920s and 1930s; active "on the Jewish street"; editor of both Polish and Yiddish postwar communist publications; left Poland in the wake of the "anti-Zionist" campaign of 1968.

IMRE NAGY (1896–1958) Hungarian communist prime minister during the 1956 Hungarian Revolution; appealed unsuccessfully to the West for help against the Soviet invasion; executed in communist Hungary in 1958; rehabilitated posthumously and reburied with honors in 1989.

JAN PALACH (1948–1969) Czech student who, in protest against the passivity of his country after the Soviet-led invasion of August 1968, set himself on fire on Prague's Wenceslas Square.

JAN PATOČKA (1907–1977) Czech philosopher who studied with Edmund Husserl and Martin Heidegger; one of the original three spokespeople for the human rights petition Charter 77; arrested in connection with Charter 77; died in March 1977 after long interrogations.

JÓZEF PIŁSUDSKI (1867–1935) Polish patriot and socialist revolutionary before the existence of a Polish state; organizer of the Polish Legions, which fought against the Russians in the First World War; imprisoned in Germany; arrived in Warsaw in November 1918 as a national hero; took power in a coup in 1926.

SŁAWOMIR SIERAKOWSKI (b. 1979) Public intellectual, essayist, and left-wing social and political activist; founder and editor in chief of the journal *Krytyka Polityczna* (Political critique); animating force behind the left-wing movement devoted to creating an *engagé* cultural intelligentsia.

MARTIN M. SIMEČKA (b. 1957) Slovak writer and editor; published in *samizdat* before 1989; son of the Czechoslovak philosopher communist-turned-dissident Milan Simečka (1930–1990).

ANDRÉ SIMONE (OTTO KATZ) (1895–1952) Foreign editor of the communist daily *Rudé Právo* in postwar Prague; co-defendant in the Slánský trial who was falsely accused of treason; sentenced to death in December 1952.

H. GORDON SKILLING (1912–2001) Canadian historian of Czechoslovakia; fellow traveler who was sympathetic to communism in his youth; supporter of the Czechoslovak dissidents.

RUDOLF SLÁNSKÝ (1901–1952) General secretary of the Communist Party in postwar Czechoslovakia; played a central role in the communist takeover of Czechoslovakia in February 1948; show-tried in 1952 and sentenced to death.

ANTONI SŁONIMSKI (1895–1976) Poet and author of a famous weekly column during the interwar years; spent the Second World War in England; returned to Warsaw in 1951 and lent his support to the new communist regime; leading anticommunist dissident in the last decade of his life.

ALEKSANDER (ALIK) SMOLAR (b. 1940) Son of Grzegorz Smolar; imprisoned in March 1968 for his role in student protests; subsequently emigrated from Poland; active in supporting Solidarity from abroad; political scientist at Le Centre national de la recherche scientifique in Paris and president of the Stefan Batory Foundation in Warsaw.

GRZEGORZ (HERSH) SMOLAR (1905–1993) Communist revolutionary, author, and editor; served six years in prison in interwar Poland; organized partisan detachments in Belarus during the Second World War; a key figure in the Central Committee of Jews in postwar Poland; emigrated from Poland following the "anti-Zionist" campaign of March 1968.

CORNELIU VADIM-TUDOR (b. 1949) Writer, journalist, and politician; court poet of Nicolae Ceaușescu; leader of the nationalist and xenophobic Greater Romania Party.

WANDA WASILEWSKA (1905–1964) Polish Socialist Party activist and novelist from Krakow; became the Polish Left's personal connection to Stalin during the war; remained in Kiev after the war with her third husband, the Ukrainian communist playwright Oleksandr Korneichuk (1905–1972).

ALEKSANDER WAT (1900–1967) Futurist poet in the early 1920s; editor of the legendary Marxist newspaper *Miesięcznik Literacki*, 1929–1931; imprisoned in the Soviet Union during the war and returned to Poland in 1946; spent the latter part of the 1950s and 1960s abroad in Western Europe; committed suicide in Paris in 1967.

OLA WATOWA (1904–1991) Aleksander Wat's wife from 1927 until his death in 1967; deported to Soviet Kazakhstan during the war; died in France in 1991.

ADAM WAŻYK (1905–1982) Avant-garde poet in his youth; one of the "terroreticians" of socialist realism in the Stalinist era; author of "A Poem for Adults," which in 1955 inaugurated de-Stalinization in the literary sphere.

KAROL WOJTYŁA (1920–2005) Polish priest and theologian influenced by phenomenology; in 1978 became Pope John Paul II, the first non-Italian pope to be elected by the Vatican since the sixteenth century; spiritual leader of Solidarity.

SZYMON (SHIMON) ZACHARIASZ (1900–1970) Communist active "on the Jewish street" since his youth; served some seven years in Polish prison between the world wars; leading figure in the Central Committee of Jews in postwar Poland.

YITZHAK (YITSHAK, ICCHAK) ZUCKERMAN (CUKIERMAN) (1915–1981) Polish Zionist youth leader; the Jewish Combat Organization's liaison with the Polish resistance during the Warsaw Ghetto Uprising; emigrated to Palestine in 1947 where he founded Kibbutz Lohame ha-Geta'ot.

SZMUEL (SHMUEL) ZYGIELBOJM (1895–1943) Prominent activist in the Bund, a Yiddishist diaspora nationalist Jewish socialist movement; served as representative to the Polish National Council in London during the Second World War; committed suicide in May 1943, when faced with the news of the suppression of the Warsaw Ghetto Uprising.